ALONE ON THE ICE

ALSO BY DAVID ROBERTS

ALONE ON THE ICE

The Greatest Survival Story in the History of Exploration

DAVID ROBERTS

W. W. Norton & Company

New York London

For information about permission to reproduce selections from this book,
write to Permissions, W. W. Norton & Company, Inc.,
500 Fifth Avenue, New York, NY 10110

For information about special discounts for bulk purchases, please contact
W. W. Norton Special Sales at specialsales@wwnorton.com or 800-233-4830

Manufacturing by Courier Westford
Book design by Helene Berinsky
Production manager: Julia Druskin

Library of Congress Cataloging-in-Publication Data

Roberts, David, 1943–
Alone on the ice : the greatest survival story in the
history of exploration / David Roberts.
p. cm.
Includes bibliographical references and index.
ISBN 978-0-393-24016-0 (hardcover)
1. Mawson, Douglas, Sir, 1882–1958—Travel.
2. Australasian Antarctic Expedition (1911–1914)
3. Antarctica—Discovery and exploration. I. Title.
G8501911 .R63 2013
919.8904—dc23
                                2012037677

W. W. Norton & Company, Inc.
500 Fifth Avenue, New York, N.Y. 10110
www.wwnorton.com

W. W. Norton & Company Ltd.
Castle House, 75/76 Wells Street, London W1T 3QT

1 2 3 4 5 6 7 8 9 0

For Sharon—
without whose love and support
I would not be a writer today

CONTENTS

Kathryn Sall

Track of *Aurora*
to and from Antarctica 1911–1912

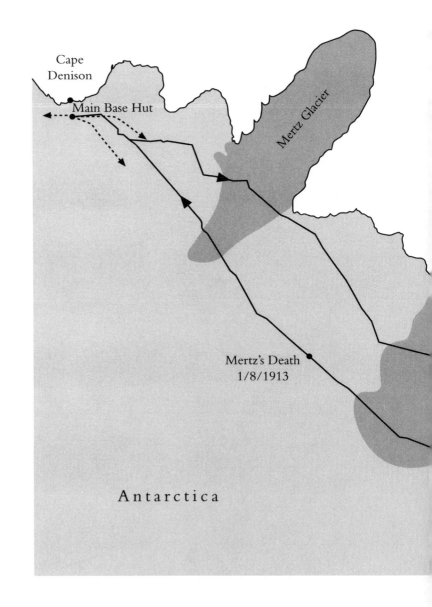

Cape Denison

Main Base Hut

Mertz Glacier

Mertz's Death
1/8/1913

Antarctica

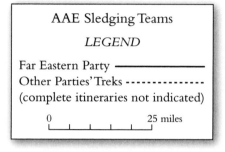

AAE Sledging Teams

LEGEND

Far Eastern Party ————————
Other Parties' Treks ----------------
(complete itineraries not indicated)

0   25 miles

Southern Ocean

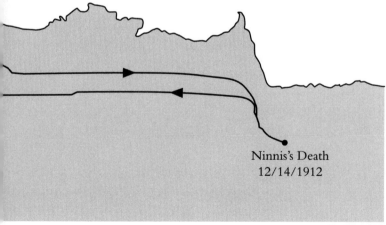

Ninnis's Death
12/14/1912

Kathryn Sall

ALONE ON THE ICE

1

FORGOTTEN BY GOD

It was a fitful start to the most ambitious venture ever launched in Antarctica. After eight days of arduous toil on the featureless plateau of snow and ice, the three men were camped only 20 miles from their base, the sturdy hut at Cape Denison in which the whole party had wintered over during the previous ten months. Those eight days had been plagued by backtracking trips to relay loads, by constant tinkering with balky gear, and by a two-day storm with gales so strong the men could not budge from their tent.

The date was November 17, 1912. Douglas Mawson, leader of the Australasian Antarctic Expedition (AAE), was a thirty-year-old lecturer in mineralogy and petrology at the University of Adelaide in South Australia. He was already the veteran of one expedition to the southernmost continent, during which he had served heroically from 1907 to 1909 under the command of Sir Ernest Shackleton.

Mawson's tentmates were Belgrave Ninnis and Xavier Mertz. Born in London, a twenty-five-year-old lieutenant in the Royal Fusiliers, Ninnis had Antarctica on the brain, having unsuccessfully applied for Captain Robert Falcon Scott's *Terra Nova* expedition shortly before Mawson snatched him up for his own team. Mertz was a twenty-nine-year-old lawyer from Basel, Switzerland, as well as a highly accomplished skier and mountaineer.

Among the eighteen hands who had spent the first year in the Cape Denison hut, which the men called Winter Quarters, both Ninnis and Mertz were exceptionally well-liked. Ninnis had been nicknamed Cherub by the crew, "partly on account of his complexion," recalled one teammate, "which was as pink and white as that of any girl. He was tall and rather ungainly in build, and had more boxes of beautiful clothes than seemed possible for one mere man."

In the best-known portrait of Ninnis, he sits in full uniform, hands clasped on the hilt of his sword, as he looks upward with a serene and innocent gaze. An eloquent diarist, Ninnis recorded in a breathless outburst his incredulity at finding himself in Antarctica only days after the ship made landfall at Cape Denison in January 1912:

From the creation the silence here has been unbroken by man, and now we, a very prosaic group of fellows, are here for an infinitely small space of time, for a short time we shall litter the land with tines, scrap timber, refuse and impedimenta, for a short time we shall be travelling over the great plateau, trying to draw the veil from a fractional part of this unknown land; then the ship will return for us and we shall leave the place to its eternal silence and loneliness, a silence that may never again be broken by a human voice.

Xavier Mertz was nicknamed X by his teammates, who teased him throughout the expedition on account of his uncertain command of English, German being his first language. He was much admired, however, for his skill on skis (one teammate hailed him as "a magnificent athlete"), for his sense of humor, and for his skill at making omelettes out of penguins' eggs, on which the whole team feasted on the eve of their departure from Winter Quarters.

In a studio portrait, Mertz sports the bushy mustache of an alpine montagnard, while his sidelong gaze seems to project both wariness and intelligence. His diary, written in German, is plainspoken, with occasional flights of reverie or passion. On November 17, 1912, despite the disheartening start of the journey across the plateau, Mertz recorded his dawning joy at the prospect of discovery in a brief passage akin to Ninnis's outpouring from the previous January: "from now our route goes farther on, into unexplored land, which no human eyes have yet seen."

Over the winter, Douglas Mawson had proven himself to be a firm leader who detested idleness and demanded the maximum of effort from his men. Yet he had also won unstinting loyalty from all but one or two, for he had worked harder than all of them, chipping in to help with the most onerous and dangerous of tasks. An innate tendency toward aloofness was tempered by his personal charm. Unlike Scott, who on his expeditions preserved the distinction between officers and men with a naval rigor that extended to separate messes on shipboard, Mawson fraternized constantly with his teammates, ate with them at a communal table, and both gave and sought advice at every hand.

Lean, six feet three inches tall, with piercing blue eyes, Mawson cut a striking figure at the age of thirty. In his own way he was as strong and athletic as Mertz, and his endurance and capacity to withstand pain would become legendary. The best-known studio portrait of Mawson, taken in 1911, reveals an impossibly handsome face, with just the hint of a receding hairline. In the photo Mawson holds a penetrating gaze that proclaims his calm composure and adamantine will.

A certain reserve also stamped the man's character. There is little or no evidence of any women in his life before the age of twenty-seven, when, at an outdoor dinner party in the Australian mining town of Broken Hill, he met a seventeen-year-old beauty named Paquita Delprat. She was the well-born daughter of Dutch parents, with an admixture of French and Swiss on her mother's side. It was love at first sight on both sides, although a year would pass before they met again. In December 1910, they became engaged, but their marriage would be postponed until after the completion of the AAE.

Throughout the expedition, Mawson wrote letters to Paquita, even though he knew it would be months before she would be able to read them. And from the Netherlands and Australia, Paquita wrote her own letters, even as her fears about her beloved's safety grew and darkened in what she called "this everlasting silence."

Just an hour before his departure on the great overland journey that would win Mawson his lasting fame, he wrote to Paquita from the hut on November 10:

> I have two good companions Dr Mertz and Lieut Ninnis. It is unlikely that any harm will happen to us but should I not return to you in Australia please know that I truly loved you from an admiration of *your spirit*. . . .
>
> Good Bye my Darling may God keep and Bless and Protect you.

Since the second decade of the twentieth century, Mawson has lurked in the shadow of his contemporaries Scott, Shackleton, and the great Norwegian polar explorer Roald Amundsen. In part this is because he was Australian. (Though born in England, Mawson emigrated to New South Wales with his family at the age of two.) But the greater reason for the neglect of Mawson and the AAE lies in the fact that, unlike nearly all the Antarctic explorers of what is called the heroic age (1897–1917), Mawson was completely uninterested in reaching the South Pole. What mattered to the man instead—and what drove the vast ambitions of the AAE—was the urge to explore land that had never before been seen by human eyes, and to bring back from the southern continent the best science that men in the field might be capable of.

The AAE, then, had set its focus on the stretch of Antarctica that lay directly south of Australia—a 2,000-mile-long swath of ice and land that was still terra incognita. After wintering over at Cape Denison, Mawson had divided his team into three-man sledging parties, each sent out to explore in different directions. His own Far Eastern Party, with Mertz and Ninnis, had taken on the most ambitious mission of all—to push at least 350 miles east and south, exploring and mapping a huge tract of land no one else had ever glimpsed. If the trio could cover that distance, it would link the vast unknown with land spotted the previous year from the Ross Sea by men aboard Scott's *Terra Nova*. A colossal blank on the map of Antarctica would be filled in for the first time.

Aboard the *Aurora*, the ship that took the men south from Australia, were thirty-eight Eskimo huskies from Greenland. Ninnis and Mertz, who alone among the team members had sailed from London to Hobart with the ship, had spent the long ocean voyage caring for the dogs and getting to know their individual characters. In the process, they had become very fond of the animals. They (and other team members) gave the huskies whimsical names, including Ginger Bitch, Gadget, Jappy, John Bull, and Blizzard. Shackleton and Franklin were named in honor of famous polar explorers. Pavlova was an homage to the great Russian ballerina Anna Pavlova, who, intrigued by the news of the upcoming expedition, had come on board the ship in London and presented Ninnis with a ballerina doll as a token of good luck.

Not all the dogs had survived the voyage south, and others perished during the first winter. On November 10, when Mawson, Ninnis, and Mertz set off from the hut, they took seventeen dogs to haul three sledges. The total weight of their impedimenta was 1,723 pounds. Of that, 475 pounds were food for the men, based on a calculation of nine weeks of travel, each man consuming a little less than two and a quarter pounds per day. The dog food—almost entirely seal meat, seal blubber, and pemmican—added up to 700 pounds, or two-fifths of the team's total supplies. Even so, it was taken for granted that if a dog could not keep up, it would be shot and fed to the other huskies.

The discouragements of the first week weighed heavily on all three men. To measure distance, the team used a "sledgemeter," a wheel tethered to one of the sledges that counted revolutions to add up to a daily total of miles traversed. But the very first day, as Mawson wrote in his diary, the sledgemeter "got badly damaged by dogs running away for a few minutes—these meters are much too flimsy for dog sledging on ice."

Each night the men crawled into sleeping bags made of reindeer hide with the fur still attached on the inside. Weighing ten pounds each, the bags were warm enough, but instead of resting atop some kind of mattress, they were laid directly on the ground cloth that served as a tent floor. Mertz complained, "In the morning I had backache, because I am still not accustomed to sleeping on hard ice and snow." Another nuisance derived from the fact that the reindeer fur was constantly molting, so that "in some mysterious way" reindeer hair regularly found its way into the mugs from which the men ate their dinners.

A 35 mph wind kept the men tent-bound on November 12. The next day, despite the wind blowing unabated, the trio pushed on to a camp 18½ miles from their base. There, during a spring foray, a party had laid a depot of supplies, but in conditions verging on whiteout, Mawson's team could not find it.

Now a two-day storm struck, confining the men to the tent on November 14 and 15. "Strong blizzard threatened to demolish tent," Mawson wrote in his diary. "Wind increased to about 80 mph during the night. I did not think the tent would stand, so took all most valuable things into my bag." The men got no sleep that night. On the 15th, "We are all feeling pretty rotten having no exercise. Ninnis quite faint at noon."

During the storms, the huskies simply curled up tail to head in the snow, their fur insulating them from the bitter cold and the drifting snowfall. Each morning Mertz had to dig some of them out of their lairs. Still, he insisted, "Our Eskimo dogs are always happy. They jump around when I give them food. They look like snowballs with the ice and the snow lumps which hang on their fur."

Yet all was not well with the dogs. On the 15th, Pavlova gave birth to a litter of pups. They were instantly devoured by the huskies, including their own mother. (Such an event, so shocking to the dog-loving armchair observer, was a norm in the grueling conditions of Antarctic travel.)

Gadget, too, was pregnant. "A rather miserable animal," in Mawson's view, since she seemed incapable of hauling, Gadget was carried in a box on top of a sledge through the day's march on November 16. When she failed to give birth, she sealed her fate. "We leave camp at 10 minutes to 12 (noon)," Mawson wrote dispassionately on November 17, "after killing and cutting up Gadget as she could not walk nor we carry her. She cut up into 24 rations counting 7 [unborn] pups." That evening, "Dogs did not like 'Gadget' tonight, dogs very quarrelsome today." By the next day, however, hunger trumped the huskies' reluctance. "They ate 'Gadget' meat voraciously," noted Mertz, "except 'Shackleton,' who turned his nose up."

On November 18, Mertz crowed in his diary, "Beautiful weather, a miracle!" The Swiss alpinist surged ahead in a rapture of discovery. "We move in an unknown and infinite world, which exerts a very special attraction on us. We never know how the land would be, therefore it's so interesting."

Yet at the same time, the barrenness of the vast plateau was intimidating. A few days earlier, Mertz had written, "This area seems to have been forgotten by God."

Trained since birth to pull sledges, the Greenland huskies, for the most part, performed their thankless task to perfection. Wrote Mawson later, "We found that they were glad to get their harnesses on and to be led away to the sledge. Indeed, it was often a case of the dog leading the man, for as soon as the harness was in place, the impatient animal strained to drag whatever might be attached to the other end of the rope."

The endless sastrugi—ridges of hard, windblown snow—around and over which the sledges had to be carefully maneuvered, formed a fiendish gauntlet slowing progress throughout the journey. The dogs' impetuosity caused many an overturned sledge. Even worse were downhill grades:

The sledges were now commencing to run more freely and improvised brakes were tried, all of which were ineffectual in restrain-
ing the dogs. The pace became so hot that a small obstacle would
capsize the sledge, causing it to roll over and over down the slope.
The dogs, frantically pulling in various directions to keep ahead
of the load, became hopelessly entangled in their traces and were
dragged along unresistingly until the sledge stopped of its own
accord or was arrested by one of us.

Accustomed to being in control even in the most ticklish of logistical operations, Mawson lost his temper in the face of the sledging
chaos. The depth of his irritation emerges not in the pages of his
own diary, but in a telltale entry in Mertz's. On November 19, on one
more downhill slope, Mertz wrote, "I stopped, because I felt that the
tempo was too fast for the sledges. This was correct: two sledges had
turned over, and Mawson complained, believing again that the whole
expedition was ruined."

Even during storms, the glare on the polar plateau was so bright
that the men had to wear goggles to ward off snow blindness. Yet
the goggles were constantly fogging up due to exhaled breath. On
November 19, Ninnis marched for too long without his goggles, and
that evening suffered from a bad case of snow blindness. The afflic-
tion, caused by ultraviolet rays burning the cornea, is excruciating,
for it feels as though grains of sand are being constantly rubbed across
one's pupils. A snow-blind explorer is also helpless to see where he is
going.

As he would throughout the expedition, Ninnis bore this mishap
stoically. Mawson ministered to his teammate with the treatment of
the day: as Ninnis lay on his back in his sleeping bag, Mawson pulled
open his eyelids and inserted tablets of zinc sulfate and cocaine
hydrochloride under them. These medicines dissolved in Ninnis's
tears and gave him instant relief. (It could take days, however, for
vision to return to normal.)

During the first week, the men had experimented with different configurations of dogs, sledges, and leaders. One man had to go

solo in front, for otherwise the dogs, with no leader to indicate the intended path, would head off every which way. At first all three men took turns in the pilot role. They had brought only a single pair of skis, for among all eighteen teammates at Cape Denison, only Mertz was an accomplished practitioner of travel on the flat boards.

By November 20, the men had adopted the system they would use throughout their journey. Mertz usually took the pilot role, skiing at times far ahead of the rest of the team as he sought the best route through the bafflingly uniform landscape. Two sledges were tied together in tandem, with a dog team pulling from the front, managed by one man—usually Mawson—who walked or rode along. Those two sledges bore only half the total load of supplies. The third sledge, in the rear, hauled by another dog team and regularly supervised by Ninnis, bore the other half of the weight. The plan was deliberately to overload the third sledge, wearing out its runners while saving the wear and tear on the other two sledges. When enough dog food and human rations had been consumed, the third sledge would be abandoned.

The huskies continued to perform unevenly. On November 19, one of them, Ginger, suddenly ran away. Mertz ran after her but gave up the chase. That night in camp, as Mertz was feeding the dogs, Ginger showed up. "The runaway knew quite well where she could find food!" Mertz wrote in his diary.

Another dog, named Jappy, had begun to lag. On November 20, Mawson shot the husky, replenishing the dogs' larder with fresh meat. "Jappy killed after dinner," Mawson recorded laconically.

So monotonous was the endless plateau of snow and ice that any feature that interrupted it commanded the men's attention and curiosity. One such cynosure was a genuine mountain sticking out of the undulating wasteland. Passing south of it on November 20, the men calculated its height as 1,700 feet above the surrounding terrain. They named it Aurora Peak after the plucky ship that had carried them to Antarctica.

By November 21, the men realized that they were approaching a massive glacier that sprawled across their path, flowing from some unknown headland to the south down to the ocean, where it pushed a terminal tongue into the sea many miles beyond the coastline that bordered it. The team would eventually name this ice flow the Mertz Glacier.

In a true mountain range such as the Himalaya or the Alps, a glacier stands out clearly from the surrounding faces, ridges, and stable snowfields that compose the peaks themselves. In Antarctica, the distinction is far less clear. A glacier blends in almost seamlessly with the vast plateau of snow and ice that fringes it. No explorer welcomes a glacier crossing, for the powerful and tortured movement of the ice downhill tears its surface into crevasses and seracs, or towers and blocks of ice that teeter unsteadily above one's path. The most jumbled and chaotic stretches of glacier, called icefalls, can be too dangerous for even expert alpinists to cross with light packs—let alone men and dogs hauling sledges laden with over 1,000 pounds of gear and food.

Crevasses, or deep cracks in the ice, are formed by the stress of the glacier's flow, as one massive chunk of frozen H_2O detaches from another. An "open" crevasse presents a relatively benign threat, for the explorer can see its outlines and scrupulously detour around it. It is the hidden crevasse that causes glacial travelers to lose sleep. As storms blow the surface snow into drifts and grotesque congealed shapes, an initially open crevasse can be covered with a snow bridge that completely hides its menace. The Australian explorers called these bridges "lids." They can be so fragile that the mere weight of one's body on the bridge causes it to collapse, or pokes a deadly hole in it, plunging the unwary traveler into the dark depths below.

No region on earth possesses deeper or more treacherous crevasses than Antarctica. And what wreaks havoc with every team of explorers that tries to traverse its unforgiving wastes is the fact that crevasses there are not confined to the glaciers. Even the relatively immobile shelves of the plateau itself are subject to the stress and fracturing that open huge cracks, and the drifting surface snows easily pave them over with bridges that are all but indistinguishable from the safe terrain on either side. In other words, crevasses can develop almost anywhere in Antarctica where there is snow, which is more than 99 percent of the continent.

Mawson had his first encounter with this fiendish peril on November 20, still several miles short of the edge of Mertz Glacier. In his expedition narrative, *The Home of the Blizzard*, Mawson left a dramatic account of the event. After "smooth travelling" all afternoon,

> Suddenly without any warning the leading dogs of my team dropped out of sight, swinging in their harness ropes in a crevasse. The next moment I realized that the sledges were on a bridge covering a crevasse, twenty-five feet wide, the dogs having broken through on one edge. We spent some anxious moments before they were all hauled to the daylight and the sledges rested on solid ground.

Not long after that debacle, two unharnessed dogs, Ginger Bitch and Blizzard, broke through other snow bridges and managed, by scrambling frantically with their forepaws, to crawl back to the surface. Undaunted, Ginger Bitch a few hours later "gave birth to the first of a large litter of pups"—fourteen in all by the following day.

On November 21, the men climbed onto the Mertz Glacier. Now the crevasses grew more numerous, but most of them seemed open and visible. Wending their way slowly through a maze of cracks, the men grew weary. They stopped for lunch, pitching the tent to gain a couple of hours' respite from the wind. Mertz cooked up tea while Ninnis and Mawson strolled off to photograph a "blue abyss" nearby. As Mawson later recounted:

> Returning, we diverged on reaching the back of the tent, he passing round one side and I on the other. The next instant I heard a bang on the ice and, swinging round, could see nothing of my companion but his head and arms. He had broken through the lid of a crevasse fifteen feet wide and was hanging on to its edge. . . . After hauling him out I investigated the fissure and found nought but black space below; a close shave for Ninnis.

To their horror, the men discovered that they had pitched the tent on top of the same crevasse. They packed up as quickly as they could and marched on.

By November 21, according to Mertz's calculation, the men had traveled 73 miles from Winter Quarters, not counting "detours." That was less than one-fourth of the total distance the men hoped for. Mawson had given all the teams a deadline of January 15 to return to the base camp hut, for the *Aurora* was due on that date to pick the men up at the end of the expedition.

During the first eleven days of sledging, the men had averaged a little under seven miles per day. Eight weeks remained before the January 15 deadline. At the pace they had been traveling, in another four weeks of outward journey, the men would reach a point only 260 miles from Cape Denison, almost a hundred miles short of their goal. Yet Mawson firmly believed that, with their routine down pat and the loads steadily lightening, the team could pick up speed and reach the western peaks of Victoria Land, linking the unknown terrain to the *Terra Nova* discoveries from 1911.

Sure enough, between November 22 and 30, the trio pushed eastward, covering as many as 14, 15, and 16 miles in single days. Though the sledgemeter was still unreliable, Mawson dutifully recorded its number of revolutions in his diary each evening. A total of 24,500 on November 27, with a factor thrown in for "sledgemeter slip," thus translated into a day's run of over 14 miles.

A scientist in his very bones, Mawson began each day's record in his diary with a notation of the hypsometer reading (a hypsometer was a device used to measure altitude above sea level, based on the boiling point of water), the temperature, the wind direction and velocity, the atmospheric and cloud conditions, and, when possible, his calculation of latitude and longitude. The day's incidents are given curt and obviously understated play: "Great difficulty in getting over broad crevasse in morning." Only rarely does emotion break to the surface. Mertz's diary, though not nearly so data-centered, tends also to be dry and laconic. For one thing, the men were usually exhausted by the time they crawled into their sleeping bags. Writing a diary entry could loom as a dreary chore.

It is only in *The Home of the Blizzard* that the drama of the last ten days of November gets full expression, and those pages make it clear that despite their increased pace, the men faced setbacks every day. Problems with the dog teams continued to bedevil their progress. "The dogs are in good shape," wrote Mertz on November 25, but the very next day, "We had to shoot 'Fusilier'."

On November 27, the men unharnessed the dogs to manhandle the sledges down a steep slope. When the animals were rounded up, a dog named Betli was missing. Mawson and his teammates expected the husky to show up later in the day, as Ginger had on November 19, but Betli never reappeared. The men concluded that the animal had either gotten irretrievably lost or had fallen into a crevasse.

The very next day, Mawson shot Blizzard, one of the AAE's favorite canines, born during the overwintering. Only two and a half weeks out of Winter Quarters, the huskies had been reduced from seventeen to twelve.

High winds every day made sledging miserable. But the true enemy of the expedition was the relentless succession of crevasses. On November 22, the day after Ninnis's "close shave" when he had caught himself by the arms as he started to plunge into a crevasse right next to the tent, the third and most heavily laden sledge went through a snow bridge, "but fortunately jammed itself just below the surface," Mawson wrote. "As it was, we had a long job getting it back up again, first having to unpack the sledge until it was light enough to be easily manipulated." It was a testimony to the men's skill in strapping each piece of cargo tight to the sledge that they lost not a single package as the sledge dangled inside the crevasse. The strenuous and dangerous work of lying prone on the edge of the fissure, reaching into the depths, unfastening each piece of gear, and hauling it to the surface must be imagined, since Mawson alludes to it so glancingly.

The next day, Ninnis's sledge again plunged into a crevasse. Though it dangled just below the surface, once more the men had to lie on the edge of the void, attach the cargo box by box to a rope, unstrap each one from the sledge, and haul it to the surface. "The freight consisted chiefly of large, soldered tins, packed tightly with dried seal meat," wrote Mawson. "Each of these weighed about ninety pounds."

On November 27, the men woke to bright sunshine and finally got a good look at the terrain ahead of them. As Mertz wrote in his diary, "In front of us there was a huge glacier with crevasses in the depths. In the distance there were broken ice blocks, and low hills, everything in white." The Ninnis Glacier, as the AAE would later name this previously unknown ice flow, was considerably larger than the Mertz Glacier, which the men had traversed the previous week. More than 30 miles wide where they crossed it, the new glacier would require intricate routefinding and desperately hard work. It also occasioned the most serious near-catastrophe so far encountered by the trio.

On November 29, as usual, Mertz was in the lead scouting on skis, while Mawson brought up the tandem pair of sledges roped together and pulled by six huskies, followed by Ninnis and the heaviest sledge in the rear. For once, in *The Home of the Blizzard*, Mawson gives the dramatic incident its due:

> Just before lunch my two sledges were nearly lost through the dogs swinging sharply to one side before the second sledge had cleared a rather rotten snow bridge. I was up with the dogs at the time, and the first intimation of an accident was observing the dogs and front sledge being dragged backwards; the rear sledge was hanging vertically in a crevasse. Exerting all my strength I held back the front sledge, and in a few moments was joined by Ninnis and Mertz, who soon drove a pick and ice-axe down between the runners and ran out an anchoring rope.
>
> It was a ticklish business recovering the sledge. It could not be lifted vertically as its bow was caught in a V-shaped offshoot from the main fissure. To add to our troubles the ground all about the place was precarious and unsafe.

After some unsuccessful efforts to salve it, Ninnis and Mertz lowered me [on a 70-foot alpine rope] down to where a rope could be attached to the tail end of the sledge. The bow-rope and tail-rope were then manipulated alternately, until the bow of the sledge was manoeuvred slowly through the gaping hole in the snow lid and finally its whole length was hoisted into safety.

On November 29, having added up the distance the three men had covered during their first twenty days of sledging, Mawson noted in his diary, "Not less than 220 m[iles] straight to do." However arbitrary the team's destination, somewhere on the edge of Victoria Land, Mawson was fiercely committed to it. And he could not hide his discouragement. In a rare outburst of emotion, he wrote in his diary that day, "We have had a most aggravating morning. . . . Dogs very done—things are looking serious for onward progress. This afternoon will mean much for our prospects. If only we could have a straight-out proposition instead of these endless snow hills and crevasses."

The men had sledged every day since they had waited out the two-day storm on November 14–15. But on the 30th, they awoke to "whirlies"—violent bursts of wind coming from all points of the compass, interspersed with weird lulls of dead calm. The worst gusts reached 75 mph. Instead of packing up, the men loitered in their tent through the morning and early afternoon. Mertz voiced his displeasure in the pages of his diary: "It's difficult to travel in this region. When there is sunshine, a gale blows with more or less drift. When it's windless, the clouds bring a bad diffused light." And, "We have stiff backs because we are sleeping on hard ground, and we have terrible dreams." What was more, "We are always hungry after a work day and also in the morning."

It is no mean feat to plan the rations for a nine-week sledge journey in the Antarctic. Many a team has verged on starvation by underestimating the food a party in the field would need, or the time it would take to reach a certain goal and return. To minimize the likelihood of running out of food, Mawson had imposed a Draconian regulation upon his companions. On "rest days," when storms confined the men to their tents, they would drastically reduce the amount of food they ate.

Unwilling to waste a whole day in the tent, the men got started after 4 p.m. on November 30, trudging a mere three miles before camping on a shelf surrounded by crevasses. The next day they left the Ninnis Glacier behind them. Looking forward to faster and safer sledging, the men were vexed by a new difficulty. With summer waxing, the temperatures rose, turning the snow soft and wet. On December 1, the thermometer registered a new high of 34 degrees Fahrenheit. "The snow became so sticky," Mawson wrote, "that it was as much as we and the dogs could do to move the sledges up the slopes." Despite a full day's arduous labor, the men gained only six miles.

On December 2, a new obstacle worked its mischief—hard ice contorted into a labyrinth of sharp sastrugi, ranging from two to three and a half feet tall. "The sledges flew round," wrote Mertz, "at times turned over, so we had to put them upright, push them, etc. I nearly broke my right forearm when the heaviest sledge did a forward roll over me. The dogs were doing the best they could, but often they didn't have enough strength." The team made nine miles that day, "a good performance as the surface at times drove us to despair."

During the next three days, the sledging improved, as the men made successive runs of 12¼, 15, and 11¼ miles. On the last of those days, one more husky faltered. "Ginger in last few hundred yards," Mawson noted in his diary, "has got worse and worse and now fell down—evidently done in, perhaps near pupping."

Between their starting date of November 10 and January 14, the day before the *Aurora*'s scheduled return, sixty-seven days intervened. The return journey, the men guessed, should be faster than the outward push, with lighter loads across known terrain. Yet the weakening of the dogs could undercut that assumption. If the men shaved the margin as thin as possible and allowed themselves forty days out and only twenty-seven back, that would dictate a turnaround date of December 19—only two weeks in the future.

On December 6, a blizzard with winds up to 60 mph confined the men to their tent. Peeking out the door, Mertz could not even see the nearby sledges through the driving snow. When the storm failed to let up through the 7th and 8th, the men's spirits plunged to a new low. "Taunted by vivid dreams in half dozing condition, Ninnis the same," wrote Mawson on the 7th. "I hear him calling 'Hike, Hike' vociferously in his sleep." ("Hike" was a dog command.) The next day, "This is an appalling state of affairs—when will it end?"

To make matters worse, Mawson was suffering from a "swollen and burst lip" and from "neuralgia on left side"—a painful and debilitating condition that afflicted his nerves—while Ninnis had developed excruciatingly painful infections on the tips of two of his fingers. Stoic as ever, Ninnis made no complaint. As Mawson recalled in *The Home of the Blizzard*, "He had continued to do his share of the work and bore up splendidly under the ordeal. On several occasions I had waked up at night to find him sitting up in his sleeping-bag, puffing away at a pipe or reading."

There was, however, not much to read, as Mawson, to save weight, had strictly limited the number of books the men could carry to one apiece. As he wrote in *The Home of the Blizzard*, "Ninnis was not so badly off with a volume of Thackeray, but already, long ago, Mertz had come to the end of his particular literary diversion, a small edition of 'Sherlock Holmes,' and he contented himself with reciting passages from memory for our mutual benefit."

Only on December 9 did the wind drop sufficiently to allow the men to pack up and move on. Despite sledging through soft, deep, new-fallen snow, they covered fifteen miles that day. Mertz could not resist twitting his leader in his diary, "The dogs and my comrades moved with difficulty, because they sank into the snow. Mawson gradually realizes how useful the skis can be in Antarctica."

During the next three days, still hindered by drifts of new snow, the men made excellent progress, logging 12, 12½, and 11½ miles on successive marches. By December 11, they had gained an altitude of 1,800 feet above sea level, and they were pleased to see the terrain sloping slightly downhill ahead of them. The worst of the crevasses, they were convinced, lay behind them. On the 11th, Mertz calculated that the team had traveled 270 miles since leaving the hut on November 10.

Thirty-three days out by December 12, Mawson's team had run a monotonous gauntlet of snow and ice. Yet the men had made major discoveries, including that of the two huge glaciers across which they had so gingerly woven their way. They had proven that some 300 miles of Antarctica east of Cape Denison was solid land, not islands interspersed with frozen sea channels, as some geographers had hypothesized. They had discovered and named peaks and rocky outcrops thrusting out of the ice cap. On December 10, Ninnis had been the first to spot "small ice-capped islets fringing the coast to the north." Although the men had been traveling steadily southeast, this new sighting proved that the continent itself cut away to the southeast. They could see headlands in the distance, the most prominent of which they named Cape Freshfield, after the great British mountaineer and explorer Douglas Freshfield, who was president of the Royal Geographical Society.

Mawson could still not be sure that the vague features ahead were the same as the westernmost hills spotted by Scott's crew aboard the *Terra Nova* in 1911, but he knew that he was close to linking up hitherto unknown country with Victoria Land.

On the 12th, the men once again entered a region crisscrossed with crevasses, dictating renewed vigilance and a less direct course. The next morning, the team finally carried out the logistical reduction Mawson had planned almost a month before. They abandoned the battered sledge that had traveled always in the rear and always with the heaviest load, repacking their supplies on the two sledges that had taken less of a beating. The dogs were so famished they chewed the leather straps off the discarded vehicle.

Under Mawson's direction, the men loaded one sledge with fifty pounds' more weight than the other. That craft would carry virtually all the dog food and human rations, as well as the most essential gear, including the tent. The six strongest dogs would pull it, with Ninnis in command. Guiding the lighter sledge, Mawson would come second, following Mertz's scout on skis. Ninnis would take up the rear. The thinking was that if any sledge broke through a crevasse, better that it be the less vital one. Mawson chose thereby to take on the most dangerous role for the rest of the expedition. (Because his skis more evenly distributed his weight, Mertz was the least likely to break through a snow bridge.)

The men did not start moving on December 13 until 2 p.m. Under overcast skies that gradually cleared, with the temperature rising to 29 degrees Fahrenheit, they accomplished a creditable run of 13¾ miles, camping only at midnight.

Mawson could well take satisfaction in his team's achievement. By the evening of the 13th, the men had crossed some 295 miles of terra incognita. If they could push on for another week, or even only four or five days, they ought easily to match the goal of 350 miles from Winter Quarters.

That day, however, the men received two hints of danger ahead. Gazing into the distance, Mawson discerned, "We are apparently coming to another great glacier with its attendant troubles." Even more ominously, the men were startled by sudden sharp noises that seemed to surround them. In his diary, Mawson dryly recorded, "Booming sound heard today." Neither he nor Ninnis had ever experienced the like. But Mertz, the Swiss alpinist, had. He wrote:

> Soon we reached a flat area, which we crossed until midnight. At 8 pm, it suddenly cracked a few times under us. The vault of the ice masses seemed to break. The sound was similar to far cannon shots. My comrades were a little afraid, as they never heard before the sound when huge ice masses broke off.

The booming sound was produced by the sudden settling of gigantic layers of unstable snow, some of them perhaps under the men's very feet. In the mountains, such reports are surefire warnings of avalanches about to break loose.

Ninnis's fingers were causing him more and more pain. That morning, Mawson lanced the worst of the two infected digits. "During the day he had much relief," Mawson noted. And that night, Ninnis got his first good sleep in three days.

"We were a happy party that morning," Mawson later wrote of the team's departure on December 14, "as we revelled in the sunshine and laid plans for a final dash eastwards before turning our faces homewards." The temperature at 9 a.m. was 15 degrees Fahrenheit, with a light breeze out of the east-southeast. In the lead, Mertz sang some of his favorite songs, whose notes wafted back to his companions. At noon, only a quarter mile out of camp, Mawson paused to take sun angles to calculate the team's latitude. Then the men headed on.

Shortly after noon, Mertz paused and held up his ski pole, the signal that he was crossing a crevasse. Mawson took note. By now, the procedure had become a daily routine. To compute his latitude equations, Mawson climbed onto his sledge to ride behind the pulling huskies. In *The Home of the Blizzard*, Mawson recounts what happened next:

> A moment later the faint indication of a crevasse passed beneath the sledge but it had no appearance of being in any degree specially dangerous. However, as had come to be the custom I called out a warning to Ninnis. The latter, who was close behind walking along by the side of his sledge, heard the warning, for in my backward glance I noticed that he immediately swung the leading dogs so as to cross the crevasse squarely instead of diagonally as my sledge had done. I then resumed my work and dismissed the matter from my thoughts.
>
> There was no sound from behind except a faint, plaintive whine from one of the dogs which I imagined was in reply to a touch from Ninnis's whip. I remember addressing myself to George, the laziest dog in my own team, saying, "You will be getting a little of that, too, George, if you are not careful."

When next I looked back, it was in response to the anxious gaze of Mertz who had turned round and halted in his tracks. Behind me nothing met the eye except my own sledge tracks running back in the distance. Where were Ninnis and his sledge?

At once Mawson jumped off his sledge and hurried back along his tracks. "I came to a gaping hole in the surface about eleven feet wide. The lid of the crevasse that had caused me so little thought had broken in; two sledge tracks led up to it on the far side—only one continued beyond." The 70-foot alpine rope was packed on Mawson's sledge. Frantically, he signaled to Mertz to bring the sledge back to the edge of the crevasse. Meanwhile,

I leaned over and shouted into the dark depths below. No sound came back but the moaning of a dog, caught on a shelf just visible one hundred and fifty feet below. The poor creature appeared to have a broken back, for it was attempting to sit up with the front part of its body, while the hinder portion lay limp. Another dog lay motionless by its side. Close by was what appeared in the gloom to be the remains of the tent and a canvas food-tank containing a fortnight's supply.

We broke back the edge of the hard snow lid and, secured by a rope, took turns leaning over, calling into the darkness in the hope that our companion might be still alive. For three hours we called unceasingly but no answering sound came back. The dog had ceased to moan and lay without a movement. A chill draught rose out of the abyss. We felt that there was no hope.

The team's whole modus operandi was predicated on the assumption that if a sledge broke through a snow bridge over a crevasse, it would be the first one, steered by Mawson, pulled by the weakest dogs, and carrying the least vital gear and supplies. By December 14, thanks to the consumption of food in the last few days, Ninnis's sledge weighed only 30 pounds more than Mawson's. Later the men would guess that the simple fact that Ninnis was walking

beside his sledge while Mawson rode his made all the difference—
a man's weight borne on the small surface of his boots could provide the punch necessary to break a hole in the snow, collapsing the
whole bridge. Still, it seemed unthinkable that everything—six dogs,
sledge, and Ninnis—could hurtle unchecked into the void of what
had seemed to Mertz and Mawson a quite ordinary crevasse.

Using a fishing line, the two survivors measured the depth of the
shelf that had caught the two dogs and some of the debris as 150 feet
below the surface. They tied their alpine rope to whatever bits of cord
they had that might hold a man's weight, but realized this improvised
safety line reached nowhere near the distant shelf. There was no possibility of descending into the crevasse to search for Ninnis.

Deeply shocked, Mertz and Mawson tried to figure out what to
do next. "In such moments," Mawson later wrote, "action is the only
tolerable thing." Driven by a desperation born of their long-cherished
exploratory goal, that afternoon the two men pushed on to try to
reach a height of land from which to make their last assessment of the
terrain to the east. Mawson took a final set of observations, calculat-
ing the distance from the hut at Cape Denison as 315¼ miles.

Then they returned to the fatal crevasse. Once more, they shouted
into the abyss "in case our companion might not have been killed
outright, and, in the meantime, have become unconscious. There
was no reply."

At 9 p.m., the men held a burial service beside the edge of the
crevasse. "Then Mertz shook me by the hand with a short 'Thank
you!' and we turned away to harness up the dogs."

In a stupor, the pair sledged through the night, regaining their
campsite of December 12 after an adrenaline-fueled march of 24
miles. Despite their exhaustion and horror, both men wrote about
the day's events in their diaries. So rigorously ingrained was Mawson's scientific bent that he began his entry for December 14 with
six lines dutifully recording temperature, wind, sky conditions, and
geographic coordinates, before confessing, "A terrible catastrophe
happened soon after taking latitude." Mertz, on the other hand, got

right to the point: "At 4 am, we were on the way back, but without our friend Ninnis. Our dear old Ninnis is dead."

The men had realized in an instant what the loss of the second sledge meant. With it were gone not only Ninnis and the six dogs in the best condition, but nearly all the men's food, all the dogs' food, the tent, their spade, their pick, and numerous other pieces of gear. They still had their sleeping bags and a stove and fuel, and they managed that night to jury-rig a tent out of a spare tent cover. But Mertz had lost his over-trousers and helmet, crucial clothing made of a heavy cotton called burberry, woven so tight that it was effectively wind- and waterproof. The men were five weeks out from Winter Quarters, with at most a week and a half's worth of rations. They realized that to have any hope of returning alive, they would have to kill and eat the remaining dogs one by one.

Of the burial service, Mertz wrote, "We could do nothing, really nothing. We were standing, helplessly, next to a friend's grave, my best friend of the whole expedition."

In his own diary, after detailing the accident, Mawson added a single line: "May God Help us."

2

PROF DOGGO

Mawson's family cherished a vignette of the two-year-old's behavior aboard the clipper ship *Ellora*, as he sailed with his father, mother, and older brother from London to Sydney in 1884. According to the oft-told tale, one day in mid-voyage Douglas climbed off the cot affixed to his mother's bunk, escaped the cabin through a door left open, roamed the deck as the ship pitched and rolled, and climbed the rope ladders strung to manage the sails, heading for the top of the main mast, before a sailor followed him and seized the child in his hands.

> Kicking and protesting loudly he was brought down by the grinning sailor.
> "Plucky little cuss! What will he do next?"

Douglas Mawson was born on May 5, 1882, in the Wharfe valley of Yorkshire, England. His father had gone bankrupt in a clothing business he had started, and was reluctant to recoup his losses on the family farm he had inherited. Instead, he decided to emigrate to Australia.

In the village of Rooty Hill west of Sydney, Robert Mawson set himself up as a grower of fruit trees and vineyards and a purveyor of wines and jams. These businesses likewise faltered. Only when he took a job as an accountant to one of Australia's leading timber merchants was the father finally able to provide comfortably for his family. Douglas and his brother, William, attended a series of suburban schools, the most formative of which was the Fort Street Public School in Glebe Point, close to the center of Sydney.

From Fort Street emerged a prophecy that, however apocryphal it sounds, may well have occurred, for the congenitally modest Mawson swore to it the rest of his life. Upon Mawson's graduation at the age of sixteen, the headmaster of the school purportedly remarked, "What shall we say of our Douglas as an acknowledged leader and organizer? This I will say—that if there be a corner of this planet of ours still unexplored, Douglas Mawson will be the organizer and leader of an expedition to unveil its secrets."

Both William and Douglas entered the University of Sydney in 1899, even though Douglas was eighteen months younger than his brother. William turned to medicine (he eventually became a doctor), while Douglas gravitated toward engineering. In only three years, he graduated from the best university in Australia, earning his bachelor's degree in mining. By 1901, at the age of nineteen, Mawson had decided that he wanted to be a geologist.

The pivotal mentor in Mawson's life was a professor at the university named T. W. Edgeworth David, who, "in his forties, with high cheekbones and a weathered and wizened face, gentle by disposition, always courteous, was an inspiring teacher much loved by his students." David had participated in expeditions to various remote parts of Australia, and he organized, in 1897, an inquiry into coral atolls on the remote Pacific island of Funafuti that would win him worldwide acclaim within his field.

David also had a keen fascination with Antarctica, and it was this passion that would transform not only his own career but that of his star protégé. In 1896, David had published a paper analyzing the rock specimens brought back from the southern continent by the

Norwegian whaling expedition that had made the first landing on the mainland. Seaman Carsten Borchgrevink not only claimed to be the first man actually to set foot on Antarctic terra firma, but he had been in charge of gathering rocks to be studied by professional geologists. (Though Norwegian-born, Borchgrevink had emigrated to Australia in 1888.)

In 1901, David exhorted his first-year geology class to write a letter tendering best wishes to Robert Falcon Scott as he set out on his *Discovery* expedition, the first concerted effort to reach the South Pole. And when Ernest Shackleton came through Australia on the eve of his own *Nimrod* expedition in late 1907 (the second attempt to sledge to the pole), David managed to raise five thousand pounds from the Australian government to help bankroll the privately funded venture.

Several months earlier, David had written to Shackleton to ask whether he might join the expedition on the *Nimrod* to sail down to Antarctica to drop off the polar party, then return with the ship to Australia. If he did so, he would miss only the long summer vacation at the University of Sydney. Although he had studied ancient glaciation in Australia in the form of the marks it had left in the bedrock, David had never seen an actual glacier. Shackleton granted the request.

In Sydney in December, Shackleton met with David, who, according to Mawson's biographer Philip Ayres, "sang his old student's praises." Shortly thereafter, Mawson received a telegram from Shackleton that would change his life.

After earning his bachelor's degree in engineering in 1902, Mawson applied for the post of Junior Demonstrator in chemistry at the University of Sydney. The salary was a not-quite-princely one hundred pounds per year, but the teaching job would allow Mawson to pursue both a second degree and the field studies that were dear to his heart.

David wrote the glowing letter of recommendation that clinched the appointment.

In 1903, with David's encouragement, Mawson joined a six-month expedition to the New Hebrides, the island chain in the Pacific that lies a thousand miles east of northern Australia. It would provide by far the greatest adventure so far in the twenty-one-year-old's life.

Though under the command of Royal Navy officers, the expedition had as its aim to study the geology and biology of the island chain. The natives of the New Hebrides had the reputation among the few Europeans who had penetrated their homeland not only of being intensely hostile to foreigners, but of eating them after they killed them. By 1903, virtually all the reports of cannibalism in the New Hebrides had come from missionaries, and thus might be taken with a grain of salt; but anthropologists have since confirmed the practice as continuing well into the twentieth century. Mawson himself believed that the islands swarmed with cannibals, especially in their hinterlands, but the threat dissuaded him not at all.

The boldest exploit during the expedition was an attempt by Mawson and botanist W. T. Quaife to climb Losumbuno, the highest peak on the island of Santo. They hired three native guides who were mistakenly thought to have been to the summit before on a hunt for flying foxes, the indigenous bats that were one of the locals' favorite foods. On Mawson and Quaife's second attempt, the party reached a point only 1,200 feet and a mile and a half short of the top, but there their guides quailed. As Mawson dryly reported:

Stopped at 11 O'Clock as natives would go no further. Reasons

1. Seemed to be as far as ever
2. Ravine in front
3. Mist came up so we could not see
4. Very cold wind

Collected a few species coming back.

On the New Hebrides expedition, Mawson also suffered an apparently trivial accident that came close to ending his career as an explorer. On a remote part of one of the islands, Mawson, wearing shorts, was geologizing with his rock hammer. Years later, his wife would record Mawson's own account of the incident and its aftermath:

> While he hammered away to procure a typical specimen of rock a sharp piece of it struck him on the knee. He did not take much notice of this at the time; he felt only a sharp little blow. But when he began to use his leg it became evident that the injury was serious. A small sliver of rock had pierced the skin and lodged under his knee-cap. . . . The only medical help available was on board the naval vessel many miles away. For thirty-six hours they rowed back in the small boat, two men rowing while one rested. . . . For Douglas each movement was agony, especially when he was rowing and had to bend his injured knee. His leg became puffed, red and then blackish up to the groin. . . . By the time they reached the ship he was practically unconscious. The naval doctor told him frankly that amputation was the only way of saving his life. However, he began by opening up the knee, and releasing about a pint and a quarter of dark fluid. For some weeks Douglas lay on a cot in the ship's hospital, dangerously ill. Then continued expert care and his own remarkable constitution saved him and his leg.

Mawson's expedition was celebrated later that year at the university's Commemoration Day. A fellow student later recalled "Douglas dressed as a New Hebridean cannibal and H. J. Jensen, as a cowering missionary, on the opposite side of a big pot, being driven in a lorry from the University to the Town Hall."

Mawson's own interest in glaciation was aroused by reading the breakthrough papers of geologist Walter Howchin, who taught at the University of Adelaide. Howchin's great discovery was of evidence in the stratigraphy of massive glaciation in South Australia during the Precambrian era (570 million years ago)—the oldest proof of an ancient ice age yet detected anywhere on earth.

In 1904, Mawson learned of an opening in the geology department at the University of Adelaide. Though tempted to stay at the University of Sydney under the wing of Edgeworth David, Mawson applied for the Adelaide job and got it. On March 1, 1905, Mawson began as a lecturer on mineralogy and petrology. His salary was three hundred pounds a year—three times what he had been making in Sydney. Mawson would spend the rest of his career at the University of Adelaide.

During 1906 and 1907, Mawson set off into the field to study the geology of the Australian outback in the vicinity of the mining settlement of Broken Hill. Guided by Howchin's example, Mawson found abundant evidence on his own of ancient glaciation. It was this fieldwork that would earn him his doctorate of science in 1909.

Yet like his mentor, Edgeworth David, Mawson, at the age of twenty-five, had never seen a glacier. In December 1907, when Ernest Shackleton made a brief stop in Adelaide on his way to Sydney, Mawson offered his services at no cost, just as David had, on the ship to Antarctica and back. "My idea," Mawson later told a Shackleton biographer, "was to see a continental ice-cap. . . . I desired to see an ice age in being."

Shackleton rather brusquely told the eager geologist that he would think over his offer and get back to him in a few days. In Sydney, he was apparently won over by David's lavish encomiums of his star student. To his astonishment, one day in December Mawson received a telegram from Shackleton, offering him not simply passage aboard the *Nimrod* to Antarctica and back, but appointing him the official physicist "for the duration of the expedition." Even though he was not a physicist, Mawson realized the offer was too good to pass up. He quickly found a substitute to teach his classes and negotiated a year's absence from the University of Adelaide.

In late December 1907, Mawson sailed with David to New Zealand to catch up with Shackleton. The leader's quirky, impulsive decision had fixed the compass of Mawson's exploratory career for good.

As it turned out, Shackleton had also signed up Edgeworth David "for the duration of the expedition." On January 1, 1908, hailed by brass bands and cheering crowds, the *Nimrod* set sail from Lyttelton, New Zealand, bound for the southern continent. Aboard the ship, mentor and protégé keenly anticipated the great adventure.

The ship's quarters, however, were squalid in the extreme. Raymond Priestley, the team's official geologist, later described the aft hold, where the men slept and where most of the scientific equipment was stored, as "a place that under ordinary circumstances I wouldn't put ten dogs in, much less 15 of the shore party. It . . . is more like my idea of Hell than anything I have ever imagined."

During the *Nimrod*'s passage through the roaring forties and the furious fifties, most of the men were seasick, none more wretchedly so than Mawson. Eric Marshall, the chief surgeon of the British Antarctic Expedition (BAE), formed an early impression of the tall, lanky Australian that could hardly have been more contemptuous. "Mawson is useless & objectionable," he wrote in his diary, "lacking in guts & manners." Felled by seasickness, Mawson, according to Marshall, simply lay "in a sleeping bag . . . vomiting when he rolled to starboard, whilst the cook handed up food from the galley beneath him."

The first mate of the *Nimrod* was John King Davis, with whom Mawson would form a bond lasting for decades, despite periods of intense friction. Fifty-four years later, Davis would recall his own first impression of the seasick scientist:

> As daylight came, I noticed a man lying prostrate in one of the lifeboats. . . . "What are you doing there, why don't you get below?" I shouted. All I could get from him in response to my queries was "Can't you stop this b[loody] boat rocking?" He had been lying there sea-sick and wet through without food or drink since the gale began.

Davis persuaded the invalid to eat some canned pears, which Mawson managed to digest. But hours later, the mate found him still lying in the lifeboat. He pleaded for more canned pears. At last Davis talked Mawson into going below, where he heated a cup of cocoa for him. Thus began the lifelong friendship.

Shackleton hoped to make his base at Hut Point, on the southern tip of Ross Island, where Scott had built his *Discovery* expedition hut in 1901. In that refuge, as the third officer on Scott's first expedition, Shackleton had wintered over through 1902. But on learning of Shackleton's BAE expedition in 1907, Scott had written to his former teammate not only forbidding him the use of the hut, but in effect ordering him not to establish his base anywhere in McMurdo Sound. By the first decade of the twentieth century, claiming a piece of Antarctica for one's country had become a normal practice, but Scott's preemptive thrust amounted to claiming the whole of the western Ross Sea for his own future expeditions.

The bitter blood between the two great British explorers stemmed from the *Discovery* expedition of 1901–04. According to Scott's early biographer, George Seaver, the two men were jinxed from the start by a "temperamental incompatibility." Scott recognized in Shackleton a dangerous rival in his quest for the South Pole, and he seems to have resented his former officer's ambition and popularity among his fellow teammates.

In 1902, however, recognizing Shackleton's drive and talent, Scott had chosen him to be one of the team of three who would establish a new Farthest South of 82° 17' on December 30. The third, Edward Wilson, turned out to be the peacemaker trying to keep his two strong-willed partners from each other's throats. All three men developed serious cases of scurvy and were lucky to make it back to their base camp hut alive.

It was during that grim trudge south, with their sledge dogs giving out daily, that the antagonism between the two men reached its peak. Roland Huntford, Shackleton's magisterial biographer, illuminates the conflict. One evening early in the trek, Shackleton accidentally knocked over the Primus stove, spilling the precious dinner of "hoosh" and burning a hole in the groundsheet. Scott exploded. According to Huntford, "the burning of the groundsheet was the trigger that exposed a profound dislike of Shackleton."

Meanwhile, Shackleton developed a persistent cough that troubled his teammates. Unwilling to submit to his weakness, "Shackleton in his traces [sledge harness] seemed demonic. . . . It was as if he were *willing* them all on to the Pole. There was urgency and passion in his every, jerking step."

Shortly thereafter, the following exchange, recorded in a note by a teammate to whom it was recounted weeks later, occurred:

> Wilson and Shackleton were packing up after breakfast when Scott called out, "Come here you bloody fools."
>
> They went over, and Wilson quietly asked Scott whether he was speaking to him.
>
> "No, Billy," was the answer.
>
> "Then," said Shackleton, "It must have been me."
>
> There was silence.
>
> "Right," Shackleton continued. "You are the worst bloody fool of the lot, and every time you dare to speak to me like that you will get it back."

Throughout the desperate return to base camp, Shackleton was constantly coughing and short of breath. During the worst stretch, he rode the sledge while the other two man-hauled it, as he coughed up blood and gasped for air. According to Huntford, Scott "now regarded the 'sick man' as a burden stopping useful work like sketching and surveying,"

Back at Hut Point, the men found that the *Discovery*, the ship that had brought them south and on which they had overwintered, was still stuck fast in sea ice. The team would have to spend a second winter in Antarctica. But when a relief vessel arrived and anchored in open water four miles to the north, this fortuitous event offered

Scott a chance to send home eight "undesirables." Seven volunteered for the escape, but Scott ordered Shackleton to join them, "invalided home," to his lasting mortification and wrath. Despite his ailments, Shackleton was determined to winter over, but he could not defy the command of the expedition's leader.

"Of course all the officers wish to remain," Scott wrote patronizingly, "but here, with much reluctance, I have had to pick out the name of one who, in my opinion, is not fitted to do so. It has been a great blow to poor Shackleton."

Being sent home against his will was an insult Shackleton never forgave. For the rest of their short lives, Britain's two greatest Antarctic explorers hated each other passionately. The impetus for Shackleton's *Nimrod* expedition at the end of 1907, as much as a quest for new discovery, was revenge against the commander who had treated him so severely. In Huntford's phrase, "Shackleton's enterprise was born out of an obsession with *Discovery* and its captain. Anything Scott had done, Shackleton would do better."

Even as he was scrambling to organize the British Antarctic Expedition, Shackleton was aware that Scott was planning his own second attempt to reach the South Pole—an effort that would result in the *Terra Nova* expedition of 1910–13. In this competition, Scott had all the advantages. Shackleton was Anglo-Irish, the son of a farmer; Scott was a well-born Englishman from a family steeped in naval service. Despite its nationalistic-sounding title, Shackleton's British Antarctic Expedition was a privately funded venture, whereas Scott had the official backing not only of the British navy but of the equally powerful Royal Geographical Society.

In the view of Roland Huntford (whose bias against Scott is relentless), "Scott's assumption of prescriptive right [to McMurdo Sound] was certainly preposterous, arguably pathological. The barren lands were surely anybody's game." But the politics of British exploring were byzantine. Growing increasingly stressed as his departure neared, Shackleton caved in to Scott's imperious demand. He even put his promise in writing:

> I am leaving the McMurdo sound base to you, and will land either at the place known as Barrier Inlet or at King Edward VII Land whichever is the most suitable, if I land at either of these places I will not work to the westward of the 170 meridian W.

King Edward VII Land, 500 miles east of McMurdo Sound, had been discovered and named by Scott on his *Discovery* expedition in 1902. Whether or not it offered a launching pad for a trek to the pole, however, remained a complete mystery. By 1907, the only known corridor leading south over landfast ice was the one pioneered by Scott, Shackleton, and Wilson in late 1902. For all Shackleton knew, a sledging route southward from King Edward VII Land might run into sea ice that surrounded isolated islands, or into uncrossable mountain ranges. His pledge to Scott thus represented a considerable sacrifice.

The *Nimrod* first sighted the Ross Ice Shelf, which stretches 600 miles from King Edward VII Land west to Victoria Land, on January 23, 1908. For the next several days, the ship zigzagged along the coast, prevented by floating sea ice from reaching the towering shelf itself, let alone discovering the hypothesized "Barrier Inlet" or making landfall on King Edward VII Land. Shackleton named the easternmost corner of the troublesome Ross Sea the Bay of Whales. Meanwhile, his mood grew dark as he imagined having to scuttle the whole expedition. A great irony would unfold three years later, when Amundsen successfully established his Framheim base in the Bay of Whales, from which he launched his race against Scott to the South Pole.

At last Shackleton decided that, rather than give up, he would break his promise. Even after embarking on what he privately acknowledged was a betrayal of Scott, Shackleton was thwarted in his effort to reach Hut Point in McMurdo Sound, where the team might have installed itself in the well-preserved storage hut built by the *Discovery* expedition seven years earlier. Sea ice blocked the sound 16 miles north of that southernmost promontory of Ross Island. In the end, Shackleton chose to debark 25 miles farther north, at Cape Royds, where his teammates would build their own base camp hut from the materials carried on board the *Nimrod*. Unloading began on February 3. The essential structure was completed within ten days of the men's coming ashore, but it would take more than a month to improve the hut, in Shackleton's words, from "an empty shell" to its "fully appointed appearance." Then fifteen men settled in to spend the winter at 77½ degrees south.

Of Douglas Mawson's doings and thoughts during this initial phase of the expedition, we know virtually nothing. He had not yet started to keep a regular diary, and his biographers all gloss over the *Nimrod*'s wayward course along the coast and the frantic establishment of a base in a paragraph or two. Shackleton himself recorded a one-sentence vignette of Mawson's exhaustion at the end of the hardest day of ferrying supplies from ship to shore, just before the *Nimrod* sailed north:

Mawson, whose lair was a little store-room in the engine-room, was asleep on the floor. His long legs, protruding through the doorway, had found a resting-place on the cross-head of the engine, and his dreams were mingled with a curious rhythmical motion which was fully accounted for when he woke up, for the ship having got under way, the up-and-down motion of the pistons had moved his limbs with every stroke.

Once ensconced in the hut, the men had little to do but while away the time until the far-distant spring season. Shackleton was anxious to lay a depot of supplies somewhere along the route of next summer's attempt on the pole, but the steepness of the coastal slopes and a sheet of open water lying between Cape Royds and the ice packed against Hut Point made such a venture impossible.

The first exploratory deed performed by the BAE, instead, was the ascent of Mount Erebus. The only active volcano on the continent, the peak stands in the center of Ross Island, its summit only 14 miles from the newly built hut. Yet in that short distance, Erebus rises from sea level to the remarkable altitude of 12,448 feet. In 1904, three members of Scott's party had reached 3,000 feet above sea level on the mountain's lower skirts, but had made no real dent in its defenses.

By the standards of mountaineering even in the first decade of the twentieth century, however, those defenses were trivial. Climbing Erebus amounts to little more than a tedious, fatiguing, and bitterly cold slog up snow-covered slopes at relatively low angles. But none of the fifteen members of the BAE was an accomplished mountaineer, nor did the team have proper climbing equipment. The men had ice axes and a modicum of alpine rope, but lacked mountain boots, crampons, and backpacks of any kind.

The idea, apparently, was Edgeworth David's. In *The Heart of the Antarctic*, Shackleton's narrative of the BAE, the leader—among the principal Antarctic explorers of his day, the least interested in science—went to some pains to justify the climb as a contribution to meteorology and geology. Yet he added, "apart from scientific considerations, the ascent of a mountain over 13,000 ft. in height [the team's measurement of Erebus's altitude], situated so far south, would be a matter of pleasurable excitement both to those who were selected as climbers and to the rest of us who wished for our companions' success."

For the ascent team, the Boss (as his men called him) chose David, Mawson, and Alistair Mackay, a twenty-nine-year-old Scot who had served as a surgeon in the Royal Navy, with three other members to act as a support party. Mawson would prove to be a leading force in the exploit.

Given the men's lack of mountaineering experience, the gear they had to improvise, and the daunting weather they endured, the climb would turn into an adventure and even an ordeal. For crampons, some of the men poked nails through strips of leather attached to the soles of their finnesko—soft boots made of reindeer hide with the fur still attached on the outside. Instead of finnesko, others donned "ski boots," equally soft and pliable, made of cowhide rather than deer-skin. The wisdom of the day erroneously decreed that only soft boots could prevent frostbite.

Lacking rucksacks, on the upper part of Erebus the men had to carry their reindeer-hide sleeping bags on their backs, held in place with cumbersome tangles of cords and straps. The team set out with eleven days' food for the summit party, six for the support trio. At first they hauled their gear and food—600 pounds of it—on a sledge. The assault began in the early morning hours of March 5, with the brief Antarctic summer already a thing of the past.

Mawson never wrote about the ascent of Erebus. The fullest account of the adventure is a thirty-four-page narrative that Edge-worth David contributed to the expedition's in-house publication, *Aurora Australis*. David's account of Erebus has a jaunty tone, full of comic self-deprecation and inside jokes. Yet he was a felicitous writer, and in his pages both the magic and the misery of the climb emerge.

By the end of the first day, the team of six had wrestled the sledge to an altitude they recorded as 2,750 feet, traversing seven miles eastward from their base. The labor verged on backbreaking. To cross a rocky moraine, some of the men had to slip their ice axes under the cargo and "portage" it with brute force while others slid the sledge across the obstacle. On blue ice covered with a thin skin of snow, they were reduced to crawling on their hands and knees lest the sledge's weight wrench it from their grasp. Sastrugi, the raised ridges of wind-carved snow, further blocked their progress. Not all the men had crafted homemade crampons. Wrote David, tongue in cheek:

> Occasionally we came to blows, but these were dealt acciden-tally by a long armed finneskoe-shod cramponless sledger, who whirled his arms like a windmill in his desperate efforts to keep his balance after slipping. On such occasions the silence of our march was broken by a few words, more crisp than courteous, from the smitten one.

That evening, snug in their green tents supported with bamboo poles, the men dined on hoosh—a porridge mingling pemmican, biscuit, and melted snow. According to David, it was the first time any of the six had eaten that staple of polar cuisine. "We had all developed a sledging appetite," he reported, "and found the 'hoosh' delicious."

The next day, the men covered only three miles, but gained another 2,800 feet of altitude. As the slopes of Erebus steepened, sastrugi regularly capsized the sledge, sometimes forcing them to repack the cargo from scratch. That night the thermometer dropped to 28 degrees below zero Fahrenheit. As the climbers crawled into their three-man sleeping bags, "Some of us . . . found our socks firmly frozen to our ski-boots, and sock and boot had to be taken off in one piece."

From this second camp, the support party had planned to return. But Lieutenant Jameson Adams, second in command of the whole BAE but relegated to the trio of supporters on Erebus, abruptly decided that all six men should push on toward the summit. The team cached the sledge, marking its location with a bamboo pole topped with a black flag, and headed out with loads of about 40 pounds apiece. David described this "procession" as "more bizarre than beautiful."

> Some of us with our sleeping bags hanging straight down our backs, with the foot of the bag curled upwards and outwards, resembled the scorpion men of the Assyrian sculptures: others marched with their household gods [sic] done up in the form of huge sausages; yet another presented Sinbad, with the place of the "Old Man of the Sea" taken by a huge brown bag, stuffed with all our cooking utensils; this bag had a knack of suddenly slipping off his shoulders, and bow-stringing him around his neck.

Alistair Mackay, who had a reputation for impetuousness, took the lead, chopping steps in the hard snow with his ice ax, only to slip and fall a hundred feet, fetching up without serious damage on a projecting snow ledge. That evening, the team set up camp at 8,750 feet. The sun set in a clear sky, but by 10 p.m. a blizzard had moved in. For thirty hours the men lay in their bags, unable to cook hoosh or even melt snow for water; they had left the tent poles behind with the sledge, forcing them to drape the tents over their recumbent bodies like ill-designed bivouac sacks, leaving no room to set up a Primus stove. At the peak of its fury, the wind roared so loud and slung such blasts of snow that, ten feet apart, the occupants of one tent could neither see nor hear the occupants of the other.

In the middle of the storm, as he went out to relieve himself, Philip Brocklehurst, one of the supporting trio, dropped a mitten. Making a dash to grab it, he slipped and fell. When he did not return in a few minutes, Jameson Adams went out to look for him and also slipped down the slope. After a considerable time, both men separately regained their tent, crawling on hands and knees. "It was a close call," wrote David later. Brocklehurst "was all but completely gone, so biting was the cold."

The blizzard finally blew itself out on the morning of March 9, the team's fifth on the mountain. Battered by their grim bivouac but still ambitious, the men resumed their ascent. The slope of the volcano grew steeper. By now, the men were also suffering from the effects of thin air at altitude.

That day, with a dogged effort, the team reached the crater rim. None of the six men had ever before peered into an active volcano. According to David, they expected to see "an even plain of névé, or glacier ice, filling the extinct crater to the brim, and sloping up gradually to the active cone at its southern end." But the scene that greeted them on the rim was Dantesque:

> Beyond the wall and trench was an extensive snowfield, with the active cone and crater at its south end, the latter emitting great volumes of steam; but what surprised us most were the extraordinary structures which rose every here and there above the surface of this snowfield. These were in the form of mounds and pinnacles of the most varied and fantastic appearance. Some

resembled bee-hives, others were like huge ventilating cowls, others like isolated turrets, or bits of battlemented walls; others again in shape resembled various animals. We were wholly unable at first sight, to divine the origin of these remarkable objects.

What the men were seeing were gargoyle-like ice formations created as scalding steam, blown furiously out of the volcano's core, froze almost instantly in the patterns in which it splashed back onto the surrounding plain of snow.

The team was still well short of the summit. The men hurried along the rim until they found a shelf flat enough to pitch their fourth camp. During dinner, Eric Marshall, the surgeon, examined Brocklehurst's feet. "We were all surprised and shocked," wrote David, ". . . to see that both his big toes were black, and had evidently been 'gone' for several hours, and that four more toes, though less severely affected, were also frost-bitten." His condition meant that Brocklehurst would have to lie in his sleeping bag, hoping to recover circulation in his toes, while the other five went for the summit.

The next day, rather than head straight for the top, the men descended into the crater itself. Leery of crevasses, they roped together, apparently all five on a single rope. Examining the "extraordinary structures" up close, David the geologist declared them to be "the outward and visible signs of fumaroles." (A fumarole is the vent hole in the earth's crust through which an active volcano spews both steam and lava.) It seems that the team was oblivious to the extreme danger of trudging across newly formed volcanic crust. Both Mackay and Marshall fell up to their thighs in "concealed conduits," but arrested their plunges with their ice axes. Back in camp at 6 p.m., the men brewed up tea and took in the "glorious view" that lay before them.

Brocklehurst seemed no worse off after his day in a sleeping bag, so on March 10 the other five men climbed along the crater rim to the summit. "Our progress was now painfully slow," David wrote, "as the altitude and cold combined to make respiration difficult." So far in his account, Mawson goes unmentioned, but on summit day the young geologist took charge of the photographic documentation of everything the team discovered. He also measured the depth of the crater at 900 feet, and its width at about half a mile. In four hours, the men climbed 2,000 feet, to a high point they calculated at 13,370 feet above sea level.

The descent verged on chaos. Anxious to get back to the hut as fast as they could, the men began "glissading," sliding not on their feet with ice axes as brakes, as experienced alpinists would, but on their rear ends, throwing caution to the winds. They also simply flung their lumpy loads down the slopes, then gathered them up where they came to rest. In this slapdash matter, the men descended 5,000 feet and regained their cached sledge. Since another storm seemed on the verge of arriving, they were tempted to push on through the night to regain the hut, but exhaustion trumped impatience.

On March 11, the men packed all their remaining gear—some of it had been lost when the bundles rolling down the slopes had come apart—and pushed on to their first night's camp. By now, the gathering storm was almost upon the worn-out team, so they abandoned the sledge and much of the gear and stumbled on toward the hut at Cape Royds. (Another party later retrieved the valuable equipment.) "Many were the hand-shakings, and warm the welcome," wrote David of their arrival. "How cosy and luxurious were our winter quarters after the wind-swept slopes of Erebus! And how delightful it was to pour out our travellers' tales into the ears of willing listeners!"

David fully believed that the probe of Erebus would bear scientific fruit. In a pair of appendices to Shackleton's *The Heart of the Antarctic*, he argued that observations on the volcano were a crucial key to understanding the larger pattern of Antarctic climate and weather. Modern scientists endorse his views as sound.

Shackleton himself embraced the climb as a bold deed. In his expedition narrative, he detailed the celebratory dinner the famished climbers devoured back at the hut:

In a few minutes Roberts had produced a great saucepan of Quaker oats and milk, the contents of which disappeared in a moment, to be followed by the greater part of a fresh-cut ham and home-made bread, with New Zealand fresh butter. The six had evidently found on the slopes of Erebus six fully developed, polar sledging appetites. The meal at last ended, came more talk, smokes and then bed for the weary travellers.

One would like to know what Mawson thought about the climb of Erebus, but both he and his biographers are silent on the subject. Reading between the lines of David's account and of Shackleton's *The Heart of the Antarctic*, however, it seems clear that the wretchedly seasick sailor on the voyage south, whom the hypercritical Marshall had dismissed as "useless & objectionable," had quickly developed on land into one of the strongest and most trusted members of the expedition. On the ascent, he had suffered none of the close calls experienced by Mackay, Adams, and Brocklehurst. He had carried out even more of the scientific program ancillary to the climb than had his mentor, Edgeworth David, taking the trouble on the descent to pause to gather specimens of feldspar, pumice, and sulfur.

There was nothing to do now but settle into the hut and wait out the dark, dreary months of winter. By the first decade of the twentieth century, wintering over in an Antarctic hut had taken on a predictable pattern, one closely adhered to by the BAE. The greatest enemies of the cooped-up men were boredom and getting on each other's nerves. Thus all kinds of entertainments were concocted to leaven the tedium: special dinners on occasions ranging from the teammates' birthdays to holidays celebrated at home. Midwinter day (June 21) was a cardinal event, marking the initially imperceptible return of the sun to the men's lives. Shackleton's men put on theatricals (with the more flamboyant members in drag), read books aloud, played records on a Victrola, and filled their idle hours with "cags"—endless arguments about unresolvable theoretical questions, such as what caused the wind to blow in particular directions.

By the end of October, Shackleton was ready to start his trek toward the South Pole. He had chosen the three teammates who would join him on the final push, which he was confident would attain 90 degrees south: Frank Wild, Eric Marshall, and Jameson Adams. The other members would lay depots in support of the polar party or carry out geologizing forays secondary to the main purpose of the expedition—except that three men, the stalwarts of Erebus, would set out in a completely different direction to discover a different, equally inaccessible Antarctic locus, the South Magnetic Pole, which lay somewhere far to the northwest of Cape Royds. By the middle of the winter, Shackleton had designated Mawson, David, and Mackay to carry out that mission.

The ultimate success of Amundsen's expedition in reaching the South Pole in December 1911 would depend on two crucial logistical choices: the decision to use skis and the reliance on dog teams to haul the sledges. It was the tried-and-true Norwegian style of polar travel, but one that British explorers never fully embraced. Instead of dogs and skis, Shackleton chose to assault the South Pole with ponies and a motorcar. On board the *Nimrod*, he had shipped ten Manchurian ponies that he had obtained through connections in China. And he also brought along what he proudly described as "a 12–15 horsepower New Arrol-Johnston car, fitted with a specially designed air-cooled four-cylinder engine and Simms Bosch magneto ignition."

The ponies proved almost useless. One died on the voyage south, while another had to be shot on arrival. Four more died during the first month in winter quarters, when they ate quantities of sand in a desperate search for salt. As for the automobile, it too proved useless. For its first trial, the machine was unloaded on the ice only days after the team's arrival at Cape Royds. As one member recounted the fiasco:

It . . . went a few feet and stopped dead, pulsating violently, until [Bernard] Day, moved no doubt by a feeling of pity, soothed it by a series of hammerings and screwings. After a brief rest, the

machinery was started again, and the after wheels in duty bound
turned violently round in the snow, burying themselves to such
an extent that the car moved not an inch.

On October 29, Shackleton set out with his three teammates and
the remaining four ponies. Worn down by lameness and overwork,
all four died during the subsequent weeks, after which the team had
to resort to man-hauling.

For Mawson, David, and Mackay, man-hauling was built into the
program from the start. Shackleton put David, as the senior member
of the trio, in charge of the party. As they set out from Cape Royds,
David was fifty years old, Mawson twenty-six, and Mackay thirty.
As it would turn out, David would be by far the weakest of the three
men, and would be the main cause of so many problems that all three
men nearly lost their lives.

For both Mawson and David, as professional geologists, the magnetic pole was a far more interesting goal than 90 degrees south.
Rather than an arbitrary point determined by latitude, the magnetic
pole was a real thing, one of the twin foci of the earth's magnetic
field. The compass, invented in China in the third century AD and
used for marine navigation from the eleventh century on, depended
on the magnetic poles to attract the quivering needle of its simple but
elegant apparatus. For almost a millennium, all terrestrial discovery
had been governed by the compass.

In pursuit of the elusive Northwest Passage, the finest British
Arctic explorer of his day, James Clark Ross, had discovered the
North Magnetic Pole on June 1, 1831, on the west coast of the Boothia Peninsula in Arctic Canada. Ross recorded its position as 70°
05.3' N, 96° 46' W. The second observation of the pole was made
seventy-one years later, by Roald Amundsen, in the course of the
first continuous traverse of the Northwest Passage. To Amundsen's
surprise, the pole in 1904 was located some 40 miles northeast of
where Ross had found it.

Since 1831, the North Magnetic Pole has drifted almost 700
miles, generally in a westerly direction. It is currently migrating at

a pace of about 25 miles per year. Why the magnetic poles move at all remains a deep scientific mystery, itself a corollary to a larger unsolved question: why do some planets, including Earth and Jupiter, have magnetic fields (Jupiter's being more than 19,000 times stronger than Earth's), while others, such as Venus and Mars, have none at all?

To ascertain whether one has reached 90 degrees north or south requires a series of relatively straightforward observations with a theodolite or sextant. Determining if one is at the North or South Magnetic Pole is much trickier and more uncertain. The closer one gets to those poles, the more erratic a conventional compass becomes. Within 50 miles, it is virtually useless. Instead, the explorer must use a device called a dip circle or inclinometer—a kind of compass in which a vertically oscillating needle indicates the angle between the horizon and the invisible lines of the magnetic field. At the true pole, those lines in theory should point straight down into the earth. There, the dip ought to read exactly 90°. In 1831, on the shore of the Boothia Peninsula, Ross got a dip circle reading of 89° 59'.

Ten years later, Ross tried to reach the South Magnetic Pole, but was thwarted when he ran into the edge of the continent itself. (The Ross Sea is named for the great explorer.) By 1908, no one had come anywhere near the South Magnetic Pole.

The written instructions Shackleton placed in David's hands, however, were confusing. On the one hand, the three men were charged with making magnetic observations as they trekked northwest toward the magnetic pole. Along the way, they were supposed to make a geological survey of the coast of Victoria Land, the huge, complex shore that borders the Ross Sea on the west. But Shackleton added a third injunction that seemed to preclude the other two: a thorough investigation of the so-called Dry Valley (an anomalous pair of ice- and snow-free troughs that begin some 10 miles inland from the southern ramparts of Victoria Land), in order to see if those regions could ultimately be exploited for mineral wealth.

The ambiguity of Shackleton's directions may be attributed in part to the Boss's fickle interest in true science. But the arrangement he proposed for the men's return was so casual and risky as to seem almost callous. The *Nimrod* was due to return by January 15, 1909, to pick up the expedition members. Ideally, David's trio would have arrived at the hut at Cape Royds by that date. But as it would turn out, there was no way the three men could get anywhere near the magnetic pole and return in time to catch the ship.

In that eventuality, as Shackleton off-handedly directed, "If you are not returned by 1 February, *Nimrod* will proceed N along coast and look out for your signal. She will not go N of Cape Washington." Shackleton surely knew that such a search would be like hunting for a needle in a haystack. And if the *Nimrod* failed to find the overdue men, they would be condemned to a slow death.

For the official expedition narrative, *The Heart of the Antarctic*, David contributed several chapters about the journey toward the South Magnetic Pole. They essentially whitewash the story in a bland, understated narrative. Fortunately, however, all three men kept diaries during the trip. What convinced Mawson to start writing his own diary cannot be determined today. It would, however, become his unfailing practice on all his future journeys. And though the writing in *The Home of the Blizzard*, Mawson's book about the AAE, hews to the tradition of keeping an expedition's dirty laundry mostly out of sight, the diary he kept from October 5, 1908, through February 10, 1909, is as rich, candid, and unblinking as the most voyeuristic reader could wish.

Mawson, David, and Mackay set out from Cape Royds on October 5, more than three weeks before Shackleton launched his polar party southward. The best estimate of the distance to the South Magnetic Pole was 420 miles, compared to some 800 miles from the hut to the South Pole. What no one could have foreseen was the extreme difficulty of the terrain that thwarted the northwest-bound trio at every step.

The first obstacle was crossing the frozen sea ice of McMurdo

Sound, which separated Ross Island from the mainland. With neither ponies nor dogs to aid them, the men hauled their pair of sledges by themselves, yoked into harnesses with ropes attached to the frames of the low-slung craft. The crossing of the sound went relatively smoothly, taking a week, as the men were able to hoist makeshift sails to reinforce manpower in the hauling of the sledges.

Once the men reached the coast of Victoria Land, both difficulty and danger multiplied several-fold. Here the men found themselves "in the strange half-world between land and sea; crawling along the fragile frontier strip of ice that formed a precarious coastal path. At any moment it might break away and sweep them in a current out to sea."

It soon became obvious that along the coast, the men had too much weight to move in a single effort. Thus for weeks, they had to resort to double-hauling—all three men pulling one sledge ahead a certain distance, leaving it there, hiking back, then hauling the second sledge. For every mile gained, three had to be traversed. There is no more soul-destroying toil in polar travel.

The wintering over in adjacent bunks must have sparked in Mawson a growing irritation with his mentor. From the very start of the journey toward the magnetic pole, Mawson's diary voices that irritation. On October 5, the first day of the journey, Mawson wrote, "The Professor dog tired all day as he had not slept the night before." The next two days: "Professor doggo again," and "Prof doggo."

It would take only four days of travel for Mawson's vexation to erupt in a diary outburst:

> Prof broke attachment of sledgemeter this evening in rage when camping. Prof finds it necessary to change his socks in morning before breakfast, also has to wear 2 [pairs] per day. And comes in late for bag and sits on everybody. God only knows what he does.

For the BAE, Shackleton had chosen to use three-man sleeping bags made of reindeer hide. Three-man bags were warmer and more efficient in terms of weight than three single bags, but the hardships they wreaked would virtually negate those advantages. Every time one man turned over, he disturbed his companions. And by crawling into the bag last each evening, David invaded the cocoons of comfort Mackay and Mawson had hollowed out for themselves.

The warmest position, of course, was the middle. It would have seemed only fair for the three men to have rotated places every few days; but from the start, without a word said, David seems to have arrogated for himself the central sleeping space. In the same October 8 entry, Mawson rails on:

> He is so covered in clothes that he can hardly walk and hardly get into bag—that is to say, hardly leaves any room for us as he very nicely made us take side places. He wears at least 1 singlet and 1 shirt, Jaeger wool waistcoat, waistlet sweater, blue coat and burberry, drawers, blue pants, double sealed burberry pants, fleece balaclava and fleece lined helmet, burberry helmet.

Except in unusually damp conditions, one normally stays warmer in a sleeping bag on cold nights by removing a good deal of one's clothing: the warmth radiated by the torso thus heats one's extremities. David's over-bundled body, however, was guaranteed comfort by the warmth given off by his bedmates on either side. Yet he seems to have been oblivious to the annoyance it caused his companions.

At the first promontory they reached on the mainland, named Butter Point, the men cached some of their load, hoping to reduce their weight and improve their speed. Still, they could gain only an average of four miles per day, while sledging and hiking twelve.

Mackay had not yet begun keeping a diary. He would first lay pen to paper only on November 30. David's own diary confined itself chiefly to practical matters of navigation and meteorology. So, during the week from October 9 to 15, did that of Mawson, whose entries are curt and short.

But tempers were fraying. The complaints in Mawson's diary about the Prof's behavior resume on October 16. He is vexed again about David's late crawling into the sleeping bag, and the space he monopolizes; by the older man's physical state ("doggo"); by his slowness on the trail; and by his slovenliness inside the tent. A long, exasperated entry on October 20 makes another inventory of the excess clothing David wears inside the sleeping bag, adding:

> His pockets are full of food scraps, specimens, books, Bonza set [a toolkit] etc. so that there is little room left in the bag for us. He is so warm that he likes to leave his toggles undone while we shiver. The weight of these clothes makes him ill on the march but he cannot see it. There is no getting him to hurry up and partial rows are frequent at meal times.

On October 22, the three men had their first major argument. Dubious of the three-pronged expedition objective from the start, Mawson now urged giving up the magnetic pole in favor of surveying the coast and thoroughly examining the Dry Valley. But David and Mackay overruled him, and, as leader, David had the last say. The argument was not resolved until the 23rd, when "this morning culminated in the Prof offering up no alternative but Magnetic Pole, which must, he says, be done on ½ rations, pulling one sledge only." Such a desperate expedient, besides driving the men to their physical limits, would, Mawson recognized, almost certainly preclude their return to Cape Royds by January 15.

On October 30, after twenty-five days on the trail, the trio crossed the hard ice of what they named Granite Harbour. They guessed that they had completed one-third of the journey to the magnetic pole, though the daily runs on the sledgemeter added up to a paltry 109 miles—barely four miles a day. (In actuality, of course, thanks to their double-hauling, the men had covered nearly three times that distance.) Reconciled to a late return to Cape Royds, David had the team build a large stone cairn in which they deposited letters. One, addressed to Shackleton, promised to try to return to the Drygalski Ice Tongue, a point on the coast more than 100 miles north, by January 25. There they would wait for the *Nimrod* to pick them up.

As October slid into November, the tension between Mawson

and David escalated. The two younger men, physically larger than their leader, could not abide the idea of reducing their intake to half rations. Instead, they recommended killing seals to supplement their diet. On October 31, the men dined for the first time on seal meat. At Mawson's insistence, they continued double-hauling.

The interchanges between mentor and protégé began to take on a ritualized formula. David would retreat into an over-polite, indirect way of asking questions, while Mawson forced him to be more blunt. The issues over which they wrangled seem absurd, except that the men were entering a life-or-death predicament in which every detail could be consequential. David, for instance, had put Mawson in charge of the team's chronometer. But then, on the trail, "On all occasions he has asked for the time, especially 3 or 4 times in the early hours of the morning, by saying until I am sick of it 'Would you mind kindly letting me know the time presently, there is no hurry, if it would not be troubling you too much, please.' "

More serious was David's pokiness. As Mawson described it:

> He is full of great words and deadly slow action—the more we bustle to get a move on the more he dawdles, especially tying strings to one another and all over the sledges, which all have to come off again in unpacking.
>
> He dodges packing sledges every morning, then, when we are waiting to press on, having packed up, he comes along with a lot of wants and things to be put into the already packed bags. Finally, when all ready to go, he must have a rear [i. e., defecate].

As the men trudged north along the coast of Victoria Land, they kept looking for a passage by which they could head inland, for they knew that the magnetic pole lay well to the west of the shore of the Ross Sea. The trekking was not only dangerous; sastrugi regularly capsized their sledges, and a two-day blizzard reduced visibility almost to zero. As the days warmed with the approach of summer, the men decided to travel at night, on firmer snow. By now they were supplementing their diet daily with seal meat and blubber, as well as penguin meat. Whether or not they knew it, those additions to their staple food sufficed to ward off any threat of scurvy. (The link between vitamin C deficiency and scurvy was not demonstrated until 1932.)

The brutal labor was steadily wearing all three men down, but David, nearly twice the age of his erstwhile star pupil, was suffering the most. In his diary on November 24, he wrote, "up at 10 p.m. very sleepy, very hard to keep awake after 2 hours sleep, and only 4 or 5 for 2 nights preceding. Keep awake during day by nibbling . . . chocolate."

On November 23, Mawson and Mackay began to suspect a dereliction of duty on the leader's part that was truly unforgivable. As Mawson wrote:

> The Prof is certainly a fine example of a man for his age . . . but he is a great drag on our progress. He certainly and admittedly does not pull as much as a younger man. . . . Seeing that he travels with his thumbs tucked in his braces . . . one concludes he lays his weight on harness rather than pulling. Several times when we have been struggling with hauling he has continued to recite poetry or tell yarns.

In other words, David was apparently faking his contribution to pulling the sledge, just putting his weight on the harness, leaving the other two to do all the actual hauling.

The trio's immediate goal was the Drygalski Ice Tongue, the snout of a gigantic glacier that thrust far into the Ross Sea at about 75½ degrees south. It had been named from shipboard by Scott in 1902, in homage to his German rival, the Antarctic explorer Erich von Drygalski. Not only was it one of the most prominent landmarks along the whole coast of Victoria Land, it was the place from which the three men were determined to head inland.

By November 30, they could see the ice tongue looming ahead of them. David described it as looking like "a great billowy sea of pale green ice." The glacier was guarded, however, by ridges of ice up to

20 feet high lying perpendicular to the men's path, and the surface was riddled with crevasses. Here the men faced by far the most hazardous terrain of their now nearly two-month-long journey. It would take them a full thirteen days to solve the chaotic maze and gain access to the relatively smooth plateau inland.

On November 30, for whatever reason, Mackay began his diary. The first entries reveal the leaden discouragement of those days spent trying to solve the Drygalski Tongue. December 1: "Country continued to grow worse. We decided it was impassable and resolved to return to the southern shore." December 2: "I spent a sleepless night thinking the others were inclined to give up, but this morning they both declared themselves keen."

On top of their other problems, the men were running out of seal meat, which they had counted on to help provision their push inland. On December 4, David made an extraordinary request of Mackay, who faithfully carried out the thankless job. That was to backtrack six miles by himself, kill seals, and carry forward the meat. The effort took Mackay "twelve hours of continuous walking." He added laconically, "I got lots of seal meat, and one Adelie penguin."

During these days of wandering in search of a route to the inland plateau, the men sometimes separated to reconnoiter. All three fell into crevasses, but managed to stop themselves at about waist level. But on December 11, just when the men thought they were clear of danger, David suffered a genuine close call, as he left the tent briefly to sketch the distant hills. He did not bother to take his ice ax. As David later wrote in *The Heart of the Antarctic*:

> I had scarcely gone more than six yards from the tent, when the lid of a crevasse suddenly collapsed under me at a point where there was absolutely no outward or visible sign of its existence, and let me down suddenly nearly up to my shoulders. I only saved myself from going right down by throwing my arms out and staying myself on the snow lid on either side. The lid was

so rotten that I dare not make any move to extricate myself, or I might have been precipitated into the abyss.

Hearing David's cry for help, Mawson emerged from the tent and reached out with the haft of his own ice ax. David seized it and pulled himself free.

On December 12, despairing of finding an easy "road" to the inland plateau, David urged his teammates to build a giant ice mound on the northern edge of the Drygalski Ice Tongue to leave as a cairn. In it they left extra clothes, geological specimens, and a letter explaining their plans to anyone who might come looking for the men. And they decided at last to leave behind one of their two sledges. After laying over for three days, waiting out a blizzard and sorting their belongings and food, the men set out on December 16. For the first time in more than a month, they would not have to relay loads, but their parsimony meant reducing their rations. The single sledge and load, Mawson noted, still weighed "not less than 660 lbs," and pulling it uphill through deep snow was agonizingly hard.

Initially smooth going on a uniform snow slope gave way, by December 18, to a broken glacier riddled with crevasses. On the 19th, it was Mawson's turn to break through a snow bridge and fall into a hidden fissure. "I fell into one but hauled out with aid of alpine rope," he deadpanned the mishap in his diary. "It was a job to get him up," Mackay noted in his own diary; "looks bad for the pole," he added gloomily that evening.

Despite the exhaustion that was overtaking the men, Mawson diligently recorded each day's geological finds. Whether or not those entries would ever prove useful to science, they testify to the young man's ceaseless curiosity about the natural world. A sample, from December 21:

Very coarse pegmatites crossing some granite . . . in eskers near camp. Tiny ruby-like crystals of rutile (?) and larger crystals of ferriferous rutile noted in these. One of these eskers (further out)

was found formed of granite at shore end and passing suddenly
into quartz porphyry at outer end.

Every stratum and intrusion the men came across, of course, had
never before been seen by humans. But Mackay's and David's diaries
exhibit very little of Mawson's geological zeal.

There was no ignoring the fact that the men, with too little to
eat, were wearing down. And David was by far the weakest. Mawson recorded his concern about the deterioration he saw in the trio's
leader. On December 21, "The Prof was doggo this afternoon. I had
him well under observation and showed him to be in nothing like
the condition we are in." Three days later: "Prof getting flatfooted."
And on December 25: "Prof very doggo and day easy. He has of late
appeared to have lost all interest in the journey."

There was no feast to celebrate Christmas, just another day of
sledging. Mawson noted merely, "Had lunch, saving cheese by using
excess meat." Meanwhile, Mackay, an inveterate pipe smoker, had
run out of tobacco. As a kind of joke Christmas present, David gave
him some sennegrass—the dry, grass-like sedge that explorers used
to insulate their finnesko—to smoke instead.

On December 27, to lighten their loads even further, the men
made a second depot, leaving behind their ice axes, the alpine rope,
ski boots (which were less effective in the cold than finnesko), some
kerosene, and even a little food. They had reached an altitude that
Mawson, using the hypsometer, estimated at 4,050 feet above sea
level.

Along with geologizing and recording the temperature and altitude each day, Mawson had been taking dip readings with the inclinometer to determine how close the men were to the magnetic pole.
The results dismayed him. On the last day of the year, he wrote, "Dip
reading very little less than previous and very discouraging—regard
it as erratic." On December 28, Mawson told his companions that
the pole was at the very least still 170 miles away, 230 at the most.

By now it was obvious that the team had no hope of returning to
Cape Royds by January 15. Mackay, in particular, was beginning to

doubt whether the three men could even reach the coast by February 1, when the *Nimrod*, according to Shackleton's instructions, would begin to search for them. Yet to have come so far only to admit defeat and turn around was intolerable. The men marched on, making surprisingly good runs of 10 or more miles per day.

David, though keen to push on, was starting to break down. Mackay's diary was reticent on the matter, but Mawson's was not. On December 31, he unleashed another outburst:

> The Prof is dreadfully slow now, he does nothing. Mac mends tent, I mess [cook], he is always sitting down when we are packed and pushing our way out of tent. This morning I told him he was keeping us waiting as he was not attempting to get ready. . . . He looked very angry at my saying this. . . . He never, or seldom, helps pack a sledge. . . . Something has gone very wrong with him of late as he [always] morose, never refers to our work, shirks questions regarding it, never offers a suggestion.

Despite the strong marches on relatively easy snow, the men's reduced rations were taking their toll. On January 6, Mawson wrote:

> We are now almost mad on discussing foods, all varieties having a great attraction for us. We dote on what sprees we shall have on return—mostly run to sweet foods and farinaceous compounds.
>
> We don't intend to let a meal pass in after life without more fully appreciating it than formerly.

On the 12th, the men "planned menus for dinner to be given by Prof to us on arrival in Sydney." Mawson recorded those menus in the back pages of his diary. The delicacies included "Jugged Hare with mashed potatoes, black currant jelly and champignons," "Omelet au Rhaum," and "Fried trout (Loch Leven preferred) in oatmeal and butter."

Despite such fanciful flights, Mackay and Mawson had begun to worry about David's state of mind, as well as his physical collapse.

"The Professor is very nearly crocked now," wrote Mackay on the 13th. Ten days earlier, Mawson had observed, "The Professor seems most affected by the altitude, and is quite prostrated between hauls. . . . Also his memory seems fainter. He is certainly doing his best— how much better though we would get along had we [as] a third [a] younger man."

Since heading inland, the men had been steadily climbing uphill. By January 5, they were camped at 8,000 feet. They were counting on the downhill slope of their backward track to speed their return to the shore. But Mackay had grave doubts. On January 13, he confided to his diary, "I think now, that we have not more than a 50 percent chance of getting back to the coast in time for the *Nimrod* to take us home."

In their undernourished state, the men suffered severely from the cold. In a blizzard, Mawson suffered superficial frostbite on one cheek, as well as a touch of snow blindness caused by taking off his goggles. "Biscuit now always tinged with blood from lips as I eat," he recorded on January 10. "Mac's lips are bad also." David had lost his burberry helmet, so Mackay gave him his, further exposing his own head to the wind and cold. The night temperatures were regularly below zero Fahrenheit.

Mawson continued to be deeply troubled by the conflicting results of the inclinometer. The men, he had at first calculated, should by now be very close to the magnetic pole. But on January 12 he carefully went over his readings before announcing the result to his teammates. They were stunned by the new calculation. "Last night," Mackay wrote on January 13, "Mawson made the astounding announcement that the pole is prob. 40 miles farther off than we had ever thought."

The men had a strenuous debate about what to do. Mawson came up with a plan—to go ahead for three more days, trying to push each day's trek up to 13 miles, then to return to the coast, still averaging 13 miles per day. By his calculation, that schedule would exactly "pan out provisions on already reduced scale." In other words, by the time the men reached the coast, they would be out of food, with no guarantee the *Nimrod* would be waiting to pick them up. On the coast, however, there was always the hope of subsisting on seals and penguins.

It was a desperate proposal. David somewhat passively agreed to it, though by now his thinking had turned almost dreamy. To the further alarm of his comrades, he had virtually stopped eating. Mackay, however, thought Mawson's plan was folly. "Mac then protests strongly against going on," Mawson wrote, "says if we go on past the 15th we cannot get back as head winds and bad weather will retard us, and 13 m per day impossible."

In the end, out of loyalty to his teammates, Mackay acquiesced. During the next three days, which were graced by almost perfect weather and by the leveling off of the plateau, making small depots of supplies each morning to be picked up on the way back, the trio carried out Mawson's plan to perfection. On January 15, Mawson got a dip reading of 89° 45', indicating that the men had to be very close to the magnetic pole.

The next day, they hauled their sledge two miles, left it behind with supplies, recalculated their position, and walked at a very fast rate five more miles to what Mawson determined to be "the mean position" of the magnetic pole. Even as early as 1909, Mawson, along with other scientists, knew that the magnetic poles shifted position slightly on a daily basis. An "exact" magnetic pole could not be determined.

It was good enough for the played-out trio. At 4:15 p.m., they hoisted a Union Jack they had fabricated in the hut over the winter. David uttered an official proclamation: "I hereby take possession of this area now containing the Magnetic Pole for the British Empire." Mawson set up the expedition camera with a string attached to the shutter for a group portrait. With the Union Jack on a pole planted in the snow, all three men took off their helmets and stared into the camera. David, in the middle, pulled the string.

The photograph remains one of the most famous images ever exposed in Antarctica. In it, exhaustion radiates from the haggard faces of all three men.

They had 260 miles to cover in order to reach the coast near the Drygalski Ice Tongue. Ahead of them lay the fight of their lives.

Mawson's diary entries from January 17 through 29 are clipped and terse, as though after each day's march he barely had the energy left to record the day's details. For a man normally unwilling to complain about hardship, these passages resonate with anguish and suffering:

My feet and legs pain a little. Mouth no better.

Dreadful day, very cold.

Eyes bad as have gone several days without goggles.

Tent torn again, drift this morning, in agony.

My leg gave excruciating pain for large part of day and have hardly ever had a worse time in my life. Agony all day.

Likewise Mackay, who for four days after January 27 found it too much trouble to write in his diary at all.

I don't feel so horribly exhausted and inclined to vomit up my food, as I have done for the last two or three days.

The strain of the whole thing, the exhaustion and actual muscular pain, the cold, the want of food and sleep, the monotony, and the anxiety as to what is to happen at the end, make me think that this must be the most awful existence possible.

Both men were deeply worried about David's state. The leader still showed little interest in food. One day he found it impossible to put on his crampons, so he clumped along behind his comrades, fitting his feet into the shallow steps their spikes gouged in the "marble" snow. Wrote Mawson on the 29th, "Prof crampy about left calf and very much done. One can see he is much worn out but sticks it well."

Indeed, despite the trio's debilitation, they were making remarkable progress, several times covering 16 miles in a day. From January 16 to 27, when he stopped writing, Mackay closed each diary entry with the men's estimate of the mileage left ahead of them to reach the coast. Steadily the numbers declined, until he could write "43 miles" on January 27.

Now the morale that had bound the team together fractured. The always short-tempered Mackay exploded, directing all his wrath against David. Curiously, this debacle is recorded neither in Mackay's nor David's diaries, but only in Mawson's. January 31 was "an awful day of despair, disappointment, hard travelling, agonising walking—for ever falling down crevasses, etc. Mac called prof a bloody fool once on falling into crevasse, and all sorts of other names."

Mawson's own assessment of David's state was grim: "Prof's burberry pants are now so much torn as to be falling off. He is apparently half demented [judging] by his actions—the strain has been too great." That day, Mackay delivered his ultimatum:

> Mac, it seems got on to the Prof properly at one halt in the afternoon whilst I was reconnoitring. He told Prof also that he would have to give me written authority [to take over] as commander or he would, as a medical man, pronounce him insane.

Stunned and perplexed, David did not respond. The next day, according to Mawson, "Prof's boots were frozen on and foot gone. . . . During most of the day the Prof has been walking on his ankles. He was no doubt doing his best in this way, and Mac appears to have kicked him several times when in the harness."

In camp on February 2, Mackay renewed his ultimatum. "The

Prof was now certainly partially demented," wrote Mawson, and David finally gave in to Mackay's demand. On February 3, having taken up his diary again, Mackay recorded his own version of the momentous event:

> I have deposed the Professor. I simply told him that he was no longer fit to lead the party, that the situation was now critical, and that he must officially appoint Mawson leader, or I would declare him, the Professor, physically and mentally unfit. He acted on my proposal at once.

Mawson, however, was not comfortable usurping the leadership of his mentor. Even as David wrote out the formal transfer, Mawson twice demurred. "I said I did not like it and would think on it," he noted in his diary. But Mackay's will prevailed.

In *The Heart of the Antarctic*, the only version of the journey to the South Magnetic Pole readily available before the publication of Mawson's diaries in 1988, David glossed over this humiliating denouement. He wrote that on February 3, as Mawson sought a campsite,

> I joined him a few minutes later and as I was feeling much exhausted after the continuous forced marches back from the Magnetic Pole, asked him to take over the leadership of the expedition. . . . I thought it best for Mawson, who was less physically exhausted than me, to be in charge. He had, throughout the whole journey, shown excellent capacity of leadership.

In David's account, there is no hint of any threat from Mackay, nor any indication of his own mental breakdown.

At last the men reached the coast near the Drygalski Ice Tongue, where they had left their cairn with its substantial depot of cached supplies, including some penguin and seal meat. They pitched their tent and crawled into the three-man sleeping bag.

There was no sign of the *Nimrod*.

The relief ship, under the command of Captain Frederick Pryce Evans, with John King Davis as first officer, had sailed into the Ross Sea in early January, only to find the last twenty miles north of Cape Royds blocked by fast ice. Two days later, a fresh wind broke loose the pack. The *Nimrod* came into view of the hut on January 5. But the reception the crew got there alarmed them.

There was no news of Shackleton's four-man party that had set out for the South Pole at the end of October, and no news of David's three-man team that had started man-hauling north and west even earlier. According to Davis, the instructions Shackleton had left behind were so vague that he and Evans could not even be sure what objective David, Mackay, and Mawson's journey had been intended to pursue. Shackleton had specified simply that if David's Northern Party (as the team was dubbed) "had not returned by a certain date," the *Nimrod* should search for the men along the western coast of the Ross Sea, starting at Butter Point in Victoria Land.

During the next several weeks, the crew of the *Nimrod* were kept busy with a series of harrowing efforts. Two men who had set out overland from the ship when it was still blocked by ice were missing and feared dead. And a third team, the Western Party, sent out to explore inland from the southernmost corner of Victoria Land, needed to be picked up. In the end, the two who had left the icebound ship, having survived crevasse falls and out-of-control glissades, stumbled into the hut after a nine-day ordeal that should have taken less than two. The *Nimrod,* searching for the Western Party, became icebound for a week. Only on January 26 was the ship able to find the three-man team at Butter Point. That trio had suffered its own share of extremely close calls.

The *Nimrod* carried the Western Party back to Cape Royds, only to learn that there was still no news of Shackleton. Thus it was not until the very end of January that Captain Evans recrossed McMurdo Sound and, starting at Butter Point, steered north to look for David's party. It was an arduous assignment, covering some 200 miles of coastline. As Davis later wrote:

In order to carry out [the search] effectively the ship had to be kept as close inshore as the ice would permit. Slowly we steamed northward at a distance off shore of from two cables [about one-fifth of a mile] to three quarters of a mile, keeping a close look-out for anything that could be a tent or human figures. Needless to say, we strained our eyes to the utmost and after a while each distant penguin, basking seal or small outcrop of dark rock seemed to take on human shape.

Captain Evans was extremely agitated about the ship's diminishing supply of coal. He declared that the *Nimrod* would push the search only as far as Cape Washington, a major promontory at about 74½ degrees south. If there was no sign of the overdue trio by then, he told Davis, "we would have to leave them to their fate and return to Cape Royds."

At 4 a.m. on February 3, the ship drifted past the Drygalski Ice Tongue. On watch, Davis peered through a light falling snow. "There was nothing noteworthy in sight except a group of tabular bergs close inshore and faintly visible," he later wrote. He climbed to a lookout post atop the main mast and peered again. "I . . . had a good look round but saw nothing that in my opinion warranted further investigation."

The *Nimrod* had steamed past the stranded men's camp without seeing it.

In their green, conical tent on that very day, the three played-out explorers were discussing what to do if the *Nimrod* never appeared. Mackay recommended waiting until February 10, then starting to trek south along the shore, killing penguins and seals for food along the way. Mawson and David urged setting out only on the 20th. But Cape Royds was more than 200 miles away, and all three men knew that that desperate march would probably prove fatal. "The Professor could not have lived many weeks," wrote Mackay in his diary, "and his weakness would have delayed us to such an extent as to finish us."

On board the *Nimrod*, Davis was having nagging doubts. Could those dimly glimpsed icebergs near the Drygalski Tongue have blocked a hidden inlet? At last he voiced his uncertainty to Captain Evans, who badgered him mercilessly for hours to make up his mind. Evans demanded, "Are you sufficiently uncertain of what you saw to make it worth my while to return to those bergs?" Without hesitation, Davis answered, "Yes!"

The ship pushed on to Cape Washington, some 50 miles north, to complete its search mission, then turned back south.

In the middle of the day on February 4, Mawson, Mackay, and David were squatting in the tent as they finished "a meal of penguin livers, etc. and an exceedingly thin and bulky pem[mican hoosh] as a drink." Suddenly a shot rang out.

Davis's hunch had been dead on. On the 4th the sky was far clearer than it had been the previous day. Weaving its way among the icebergs, the *Nimrod* found the hidden inlet Davis had intuited. All at once, the crew spotted the tent pitched on a small but conspicuous knoll of ice. As Davis described that discovery fifty-three years later:

> Immediately on sighting this we fired a rocket distress signal from the bridge and as the echoes rolled back from the shore the tent seemed to be shaken by an internal upheaval. First one tall figure appeared, Mawson, beyond a doubt. He was closely followed by a second who seemed to trample on a third who had apparently been lying next the entrance of the tent. They were *all* safe! And as the two leading figures ran like excited schoolboys towards the ship, all hands on the forecastle-head cheered them wildly. Professor David followed more slowly, limping as he came. It was a wonderful moment. But suddenly and as if by magic the tallest and nearest of the two runners vanished from sight. The *Nimrod* was at that moment being brought alongside the ice foot and we could hear Mackay shouting, "Mawson has

fallen down a crevasse! Bring a rope!" and, almost in the same breath, "We got to the Magnetic Pole!"

Mawson's fall into the crevasse was the expedition's last straw. It might have been a comic denouement except that he had plunged 20 feet before fetching up on a narrow snow bridge, in the most serious crevasse accident of the whole journey. His partners were too weak to get Mawson out. In the end, Davis had himself lowered into the crevasse, tied a rope around Mawson, and supervised the ship's crew as they pulled him to the surface.

On board the *Nimrod*, the three men gorged on food for two hours as they regaled the crew with their adventures. As Captain Evans later described them, they looked "abnormally lean . . . the colour of mahogany with hands that resembled the talons of a bird of prey." In the soiled, tattered clothes they had worn for four months, they smelled so bad that Evans demanded they "adjourn to the engine room for ablution and fresh raiment."

The three survivors wanted nothing but to head north toward home. But the BAE was not over. Almost at once, Captain Evans turned the *Nimrod* south again, toward Cape Royds, to find out what had happened to Shackleton's four-man polar party.

In Shackleton's absence, his written orders placed Evans in command of the expedition. Now Evans decided that, no matter how close Douglas Mawson had come to death on the journey to the magnetic pole, no matter how weakened the man was physically and mentally by the ordeal, he would be in charge of any subsequent search for Shackleton and his three companions. If that search came up empty by the time encroaching autumn and diminishing coal forced the *Nimrod* to leave McMurdo Sound, Mawson would be placed in charge of a smaller contingent of men who must spend a second winter in Antarctica, if only to discover the fate of the polar party during the following spring.

3

CAPE DENISON

On the day the *Nimrod* picked up Mawson and his two companions near the Drygalski Ice Tongue, Shackleton, with his three teammates—Frank Wild, Eric Marshall, and Jameson Adams—was still almost 300 miles south of Cape Royds. Thanks to dysentery and near starvation, they were verging on collapse. A month before, Shackleton's diary entries had been rich and expansive. Now they were reduced to telegraphic jottings: "February 4.—Cannot write more. All down with acute dysentery; terrible day. No march possible; outlook serious."

The four ponies pulling the sledges, with which the polar party had set out in October, had proved to be of little use. By December 1, three of them had had to be shot, their carcasses butchered and cached in depots for emergency food for the return journey. On December 7 the men reluctantly decided to shoot the last remaining pony, a stalwart but gimpy animal named Socks. But before the men could make camp, Socks broke through a snow bridge and plunged to his death in a hidden crevasse. The pony would have taken the vital sledge he was hauling along with him, had a swingle-tree—a wooden cross brace rigged between sledge and horse to facilitate changes of direction—not snapped in two. Wild had been pulled halfway into the crevasse, but saved himself by flinging his arms out to catch the far edge of the chasm.

Obsessed with reaching the pole, Shackleton drove his team on and on, as they man-hauled a 1,000-pound load through soft snow and mazes of crevasses. The terrain rose steadily in altitude to over 10,000 feet. By early January, Shackleton recognized that the men could not attain the pole and hope to return alive, but he forced them onward for nine more days, determined to get within 100 miles of 90 degrees south. On January 9, he confessed defeat in his diary: "We have shot our bolt, and the tale is latitude 88° 23' South, longitude 162° East. . . . Whatever regrets may be, we have done our best."

That reckoning placed the men 97 miles short of the pole. Experts have wondered ever since how accurate the reading was, for Marshall, the team's navigator, had not been able to get a sun sight with his theodolite and had to rely on dead reckoning. Given that Marshall's private diary records the growing fear that Shackleton's fanaticism might cost the men their lives, it is possible that he certified the latitude just to fulfill his leader's arbitrary hopes.

Shackleton turned homeward tasting only bitter defeat. Eight decades later, however, his biographer Roland Huntford saluted the polar party's accomplishment:

> Shackleton had set a marvellous record. He had beaten Scott's Furthest South by 360 miles. He had made the greatest leap forward to either Pole that anyone had ever achieved. Of that, he could never be deprived. He had shown the way to the heart of the last continent. Whoever finally reached the Pole would have to follow in his wake.

During the return journey, the men grew steadily weaker. Only the recovery of the cached pony meat and of food in depots laid by supporting parties allowed them to keep sledging. But they were running out of time. Shackleton had left orders that if his team had not reached Cape Royds by March 1, the *Nimrod* should sail for home without them. This was no deed of heroic bravado, but a pragmatic decision, for the Boss knew that by March the relief ship ran a serious risk of getting frozen into the pack ice of McMurdo Sound, as Scott's *Discovery* had in 1902. In Shackleton's mind, being left behind by the *Nimrod* would not inevitably spell a death sentence. During the return journey, he proposed to his comrades the outlandish last resort of rowing and sailing the open whale boat the team would have left behind all the way to New Zealand.

As it turned out, in 1909 the foursome cut it exceedingly close. By February 25, Marshall was suffering from what Shackleton called "paralysis of the stomach and renewed dysentery." Two days later, he was incapable of hauling at all. Shackleton left him in a tent with Adams to care for him, stripped the sledge down to two sleeping bags, one day's food, and a compass, and pushed on with Wild. On the last day of February, the two men set out at 4:30 a.m. and marched nonstop for sixteen and a half hours. Shackleton tried several times to send a signal with a sun mirror, but no answering flash came from the hill above the hut.

In the end, Shackleton and Wild abandoned the sledge and dashed for the hut. There they found a note stating that all the other men had been picked up, and that the *Nimrod* would linger under nearby Glacier Tongue only until February 26—already two days in the past. Inside the hut, Shackleton and Wild scrounged a meal, then spent a sleepless night wrapped in a piece of roofing felt. As Shackleton later wrote, "If the ship was gone, our plight, and that of the two men left out on the Barrier, was a very serious one."

The next day, however, the two men climbed the hill behind the hut and spotted the ship in the distance. A signal from the sun mirror roused an answering flash. By 11 a.m. on March 1, Shackleton and Wild were aboard the *Nimrod*.

All that remained was to trudge back south and bring in Adams and Marshall. Wild was too done in for the task, but Shackleton insisted on heading the relief party. As companions, he took the ship's stoker (a virile athlete) and two of the survivors of the equally desperate return from the magnetic pole—Alistair Mackay and Douglas

Mawson. By March 4, all the men of the BAE were aboard ship and headed home.

What this last ordeal meant to Mawson we can only conjecture, for he never wrote about it. According to Wild, upon the relief party's return to the ship, "Mackay fell into the wardroom crying out to the ship's doctor, 'Into thy hands, O Doc, I deliver my body and my spirit.' " He and Mawson were confined to their bunks for the next two days, the stoker for five. Shackleton, more sleep-deprived than any of them, stayed awake to supervise the ship's departure from Cape Royds as it wove a circuitous path through the ice pack that was forming up steadily. In a few days' time, the ice would have trapped the ship fast, condemning the whole party to another winter in Antarctica.

Shackleton may have felt that the BAE ended in failure, 97 miles short of its goal, but upon his return to England in June, he was feted as a national hero. "Edwardian England knew how to honour success," writes Roland Huntford, "and its ultimate reward was the exclusive, scintillating and exacting summer social round called the London Season. . . . He could hardly have done better if he had actually reached the Pole." The king himself, vacationing in the south of France, declared the BAE's achievement "the greatest geographical event of his reign." In November, Shackleton was knighted by Edward VII—an honor that Scott would never receive.

In Australia, David and Mawson were likewise greeted by cheering crowds and wild adulation. Met at the railway station in Adelaide, Mawson was carried on his students' shoulders along North Terrace.

Despite the intense friction between the men that had burst to the surface at the end of the return from the magnetic pole, David and Mawson patched up their differences almost instantly. David was magnanimous in the extreme. At a reception at the University of Sydney, he lavished praise on his former student: "I say that Mawson was the real leader and the soul of our expedition to the magnetic pole.

We really have in him an Australian Nansen, of infinite resource, splendid physique, astonishing indifference to frost." (Fourteen years after his own greatest exploit, reaching a new Farthest North of 86° 13.6', the Norwegian Fridtjof Nansen was still considered the greatest polar explorer of the day.) Mawson and David would remain loyal friends for the rest of their lives.

It would take decades for the magnitude of the feat undertaken by Mawson, David, and Mackay to be put in proper perspective. During 122 days, the trio had pulled their heavy sledges a total of 1,260 miles, 740 of those miles in soul-taxing relay trips. Theirs would remain the longest unsupported man-hauling sledge journey ever accomplished until the mid-1980s.

As for the scientific results of the trio's gutsy push to the South Magnetic Pole, Mawson was destined to be sadly disappointed. On a visit to England in 1911, Edgeworth David consulted with the leading experts on terrestrial magnetism. He had his own doubts as to the accuracy of the inclinometer readings Mawson had obtained. The records brought back in 1909 were eventually scrutinized by other experts, and the conclusion, which David himself accepted, was that on January 16, 1909, the three men had unfurled their Union Jack on a spot as far as thirty miles from the true magnetic pole. According to Mawson's biographer Philip Ayres, knowing how distressing the revised result would be for Mawson, David withheld the glum discovery from his protégé until 1925. After 1930, Mawson rephrased his entry in *Who's Who in Australia* from "one of the discoverers of the South Magnetic Pole" to the more modest "magnetic pole journey 1908."

Subsequent expeditions would strive to reach the elusive magnetic pole, which Sir James Clark Ross had first tried to find in 1841. It seems likely that the true discovery took place only in December 2000, when Australian geologist Charles Barton reached a point, by his own estimate, within nine-tenths of a mile of the pole. He did so not via an overland trek on Antarctica, but on board a ship—for by 2000, the pole, which oscillates daily and has been moving steadily northwest for at least 170 years, lay at 64° S 138° E in the South

Pacific, well offshore from the continent. Barton's even gloomier assessment of Mawson's quest was that the three men in 1909 had reached a point a full eighty miles short of the magnetic pole.

None of this detracts from the courage and tenacity of Mawson's first Antarctic journey. As one of the experts who examined the data in 1911 wrote to David, "Everyone, I am sure, appreciates the truly heroic quest made by you and Dr Mawson. It showed that the true spirit of the crusaders still exists." The south magnetic pole may have been harder to find than the geographic pole, but it remains a place of scientific importance, anchoring the profoundly mysterious phenomenon of the earth's magnetic field. Today's best astronomers still struggle to understand that wandering pole, which they know may ultimately provide a key to the very nature and origin of our planet.

Upon regaining the *Nimrod* at the end of his ordeal with David and Mackay, Mawson vowed that he would never again go to Antarctica. It would take him only two and a half years to break that pledge.

Between 1909 and 1911, other duties and projects claimed Mawson's attention. In Adelaide, he plunged back into teaching at the university. With the conferral of his PhD at the end of 1909, he became Dr. Mawson, a bona fide professor. Meanwhile, he dipped his toe into several get-rich-quick schemes that promised commercial cornucopias harvested in far-flung locations. One, suggested by Mawson's father, was the establishment of a rubber plantation in New Guinea. Another, Shackleton's brainchild, was to speculate in gold mines in Hungary. (Mawson took this boondoggle seriously enough to travel to Hungary, where he and Shackleton tried to evaluate the potential of the diggings.) A third was Mawson's own idea: during a visit to the Flinders Ranges in central South Australia, he identified a mineral vein rich in uranium, and with a partner promptly founded the Radium Extraction Company.

Fortunately for polar history, none of these enterprises panned out. In August 1909, the chance meeting occurred that would change the course of Mawson's life as profoundly as any expedition.

Broken Hill, the remote mining town near the western border of New South Wales, was the scene of the fieldwork that produced Mawson's doctoral dissertation. He had made many visits to the outpost, and that August, on his way to deliver a guest lecture at the local technical college, he was the dinner guest of Adam Boyd, the underground manager of BHP, or the Broken Hill Proprietary Company. Also present at the dinner was BHP's general manager, the Dutch-born magnate Guillaume Daniel Delprat, and two of his daughters. The younger was named Francesca, known to her friends and family as Paquita. She was seventeen that Australian winter; Mawson was twenty-seven.

Tall, lithe, and strikingly handsome, Mawson had become a darling of Australian social circles since his ballyhooed return from the Shackleton expedition. Yet for all his forcefulness in the wilderness, he was shy and reticent in his private life. If he had been romantically involved with any woman before 1909, no vestige of the attachment has survived in the biographical record.

Paquita had actually caught sight of Mawson at a sporting event in Adelaide some weeks before. As she recalled fifty-five years later:

> He had turned and smiled warmly at some friends who spoke to him. That grin did something to me. Throughout the years that passed, whenever he returned from his many absences, that grin greeted me and took me back to the fateful moment: the misty day, the men in their sports clothes, the wet grass and the tall slim figure smiling at his friend.

In contemporary photos, Paquita looks full-figured, her oval face beaming with serene contentment. One Mawson biographer describes her as "dark-haired, ivory-skinned, patrician-looking." Almost six feet tall, she had a regal bearing. Born in England, she was, at seventeen, already a sophisticated woman and traveler, fluent in Dutch, Spanish, and English.

Claiming to base her insight on interviews with family members, Nancy Robinson Flannery, the editor of the letters written during the AAE between Douglas and Paquita, embellishes the love-at-first-sight drama with perhaps a touch of fictional license. At the sporting event, according to Flannery, Paquita whispered to her friend Hester, "Who's that?"

"Oh, 'Quita, don't you know?" Flannery has Hester reply. "It's Douglas Mawson. You remember—he came back from the Antarctic a few weeks ago. Went with Shackleton. Quite a hero, apparently."

And at the dinner party in Broken Hill:

Her flashing black eyes met his mischievous blue ones. She blushed; and he surprised himself by being fascinated. Always an easy conversationalist, with an innate ability to put people at their ease, Paquita chatted with Douglas about his university work and his Antarctic experiences.

The hostess, Mrs. Boyd, observed the conversation with interest and pleasure. She had long held a soft spot for the youngest of the Delprat girls, and was heartened to see her coping so maturely as a vibrant dinner guest. While Douglas responded keenly to Paquita's charm, her father sat back to enjoy the interplay.

Thanks to an international tour that Mawson launched shortly thereafter, nearly a year would pass before he and Paquita saw each other again.

The ostensible purpose of the tour was to meet the world's leading geologists. Once again taking a leave of absence from the University of Adelaide, Mawson sailed for England in December. On January 14, 1910, his ship entered the harbor at Plymouth, and Mawson stepped onto his native land for the first time since the age of two, when his family had embarked for Australia and a new life.

During the next six months, Mawson not only crisscrossed England, but traveled through Europe as far as Hungary and across the United States as far as Omaha, Nebraska. He did indeed meet prominent geologists, but already the idea of another Antarctic expedition was percolating in his mind. Robert Falcon Scott was immersed in preparations for his second quest for the South Pole, which he would launch in June 1910. Shackleton was in continental Europe on a grueling lecture tour, seeking to raise the funds to cover the massive debt that the BAE had incurred. Yet when he heard that Mawson had arrived in England, he urgently cabled him, "On no account see Scott till I return."

The feud between Scott and Shackleton had only intensified since the end of the BAE. On learning that Shackleton had broken his promise not to establish a base in McMurdo Sound, Scott called his rival "a professed liar" and "a plausible rogue." In Roland Huntford's pithy judgment, "[Scott] refused to associate with him ever again." Supported by his patrons at the Royal Geographical Society, Scott even publicly called into question Shackleton's claim to have reached a point only 97 miles from the pole.

Scott was sure that his upcoming *Terra Nova* expedition would succeed in getting to the South Pole, and Shackleton, despite the exhaustion of his recent ordeal, found the prospect of having his life-long goal stolen from him by his enemy insupportable. Even as he chased the will-o'-the-wisp of Hungarian gold mines, he planned another Antarctic expedition.

Mawson ignored his former leader's injunction not to visit Scott. "I have no connection with Shackleton in any way," he wrote indignantly to Edgeworth David, "and he is foolish to write me so." Mawson had also learned that David had warmly recommended him to Scott for inclusion on the *Terra Nova* expedition. Yet at the same time, Mawson was bound to Shackleton, in part because the Boss still owed him 400 pounds of his salary for the BAE. During the first half of 1910, he would follow Shackleton all the way to Hungary, and then all the way to Nebraska, as the two men tried to concoct another Antarctic expedition.

The meeting with Scott in early 1910 did not go well. Mawson had already made up his mind as to what he wanted to attempt on the southern continent, and it had nothing to do with marching toward the South Pole. He had become fascinated by the huge swath of terra incognita that lay directly south of Australia. Except for several fugitive sightings of land by the captains of ships that had sailed those waters seventy years before, that expanse of terrain at 65° south remained completely unexplored.

Scott had assumed that Mawson was visiting him to ask for a place on the *Terra Nova* expedition. Swayed by David's hearty recommendation, Scott badly wanted the Australian as a member of the team. "He offered me not less than £800 for the two years," Mawson wrote in an "abbreviated log" of his doings in England, "and that I should be one of the 3 to form the final pole party provided nothing unforeseen happened before the final dash." Scott seemed nonplussed when Mawson turned down the offer.

Instead, Mawson proposed that he go along on Scott's expedition to be dropped off at Cape Adare, at the northwestern corner of the Ross Sea, with three companions, who would then, with *Terra Nova*'s support, conduct their own exploration westward along the coast. Scott promised to think the idea over.

A second meeting went even more poorly. This time Edward Wilson, the naturalist and artist who had played peacemaker between Scott and Shackleton in 1902, was in the office with Scott. "I did not like Dr. Wilson," Mawson recorded bluntly, without elaborating. Scott explained that while he was greatly interested in the "north coast" Mawson wanted to explore, he could not divert manpower and ship support from his all-out bid to get to the South Pole. Mawson ended the awkward encounter with a stiff withdrawal: "I said finally that as I could not be landed on the north coast I would go in no other capacity than as Chief Scientist and that as Wilson had been appointed to that position I would not dream of making the suggestion."

Now Mawson turned to Shackleton, who had returned to England. At once the Boss appropriated the whole concept of Mawson's expedition as if he had thought of it himself. "I have decided to go to the coast west of Cape Adare," he told Mawson imperiously, "and you are to be the Chief Scientist. I hope you will agree to this. I can get the money." Taken aback, Mawson dared not repudiate Shackleton's proposal, for the Boss was indeed a genius at fundraising, and could count on his recent knighthood to garner the support of patrons in high places.

So ensued a cat-and-mouse game stretching over four months and from Hungary to Nebraska. Shackleton could not make up his mind what he wanted to do. He was torn between the Hungarian gold mines and another stab at Antarctica. The two men never really fell out, but by the time he left Omaha in mid-May, Mawson was convinced that "there was little hope of [Shackleton's] going." The Boss magnanimously pledged that even if he did not lead the expedition himself, he would exert all his powers to raise money for it. He had already secured a contribution of ten thousand pounds from Gerald Lysaght, a steel baron who had supported the BAE.

By the time he returned to Australia, Mawson was convinced that he would have to organize and lead the ambitious exploration of the "north coast" by himself. The last straw came when the Lysaght contribution simply disappeared, a casualty, Mawson thought at first, of a rupture between the Boss and his patron . In desperation, he wrote directly to Lysaght, pleading for only one-tenth of the promised donation. As the magnate was hospitalized at the time, his wife replied, in effect scolding Mawson for asking for more money.

In this roundabout way, Mawson discovered that Shackleton had already squandered the ten thousand pounds, perhaps on his goldmine scheme. As he later reported, Mawson felt "double-crossed" by his former leader. In 1922, six months after Shackleton's untimely death of a heart attack at age forty-seven, Mawson would write to the Boss's first biographer, "When it comes to the moral side of things, S. and I part brass rags, as they say in the navy; that is why I have not rushed into print to heap eulogies on him."

Back in Australia, Mawson faced the overwhelming challenge of raising money and enlisting a crew for his grand exploration. But there was a great reward in his return home: the chance to see Paquita Delprat again. Using his friendship with Paquita's father as a pretext, Mawson visited the family several times in Broken Hill. At last he got up the nerve to ask her out on a date. As Paquita later wrote, "One day he telephoned me and asked if I would care to go to the theatre with him and bring one of my sisters. That did rather put ideas into my head. It was a musical comedy but I don't think I remembered a word of it next morning."

According to Paquita's great-granddaughter, "All of Paquita's siblings were very much in awe of Douglas." Gradually they realized, however, that his attentive interest in their doings served mainly as an excuse to spend time with their sister, who that winter was still only nineteen years old. Mawson visited the Delprats not only in Broken Hill, but at their seaside summer house near Adelaide. He and Paquita played tennis together. In December, Mawson finally proposed. Paquita's memory of that enchanted evening gleams through a veil of Edwardian gauze:

> While the family were making music inside, Douglas and I were out on the verandah, looking at the sea—and the sound of waves will always be associated with the moment that I knew my feelings for him were reciprocated. . . . It all seemed like a dream, He so tall, so good-looking and so much in demand—Adelaide's hero.

Equally Edwardian was Mawson's decorum as he asked Paquita's father for her hand in marriage. His plea took the form of a seven-page letter, handwritten on University of Adelaide stationery. Mawson addressed Guillaume Daniel Delprat first as "My Dear Dr Delprat," then added, "and I hope with your consent, *My Dear Father*." He went on, "Love has run out to meet love with open arms—it is the ideal story. I hope you will approve for the persons referred to are your much beloved daughter and myselfallunworthy [*sic*]."

Mindful of the mining tycoon's lofty social status, Mawson laid out his modest financial situation—a salary from the university of "but £400 per year," the money owed him by Shackleton, the dribs and drabs he expected from his own commercial ventures. But he boasted, "Personally, I have never yet failed in anything I have undertaken and look forward to a bright future."

It was not money that Delprat *père* was worried about. Replying by mail the very next day, he reassured Mawson: "I fully approve of you as a son-in-law. Let me tell you that I don't know a better man than yourself in Adelaide to whom I would trust the future happiness of Paquita with greater confidence." His qualms arose instead from Mawson's upcoming Antarctic expedition.

> Do you think it is a wise thing to run these risks and expose your wife to the terrible anxiety and all its consequences when you go away for 15 months on a dangerous trip where you may meet with accidents or where your health may be be permanently injured through hardships and exposure[?]
>
> Do you think it is a fair thing to make a woman go through? Do you think it helps you to build up the home you want to provide her with? You have made a great name for yourself there already—what good can a second trip do you?

Delprat went as far as to ask Mawson to give up his expedition in order to marry Paquita. He invited the eager suitor to "think it over" and to visit in person to discuss the proposition further.

The father's doubts were certainly reasonable ones. Yet somehow Mawson overcame the objections. In the end, he could have his expedition and Paquita too. They were formally engaged in January 1911. Almost at once, Mawson set off on another long trip to England and Europe to raise money, crew, and a ship for what would become the Australasian Antarctic Expedition.

Mawson's motivations for the AAE can be divided into three categories: commercial, nationalistic, and scientific. As a geologist, he believed that the icebound continent might hide vast reserves of precious minerals, oil, and gas, and in 1910 he could see no reason why mines and wells might not someday tap those resources.

As for the nationalistic: in the second decade of the twentieth century, Antarctica still loomed as the last great tract of land on earth that no nation had yet convincingly claimed. The swath from 90° to 160° east of the Greenwich meridian lay unexplored. In a tradition dating back into the Renaissance, the first discoverer of a new land (whether or not it was inhabited by natives) promptly claimed it for the country under whose flag he sailed.

Mawson, then, fully intended to stake a lasting claim to that unknown land, not simply for the British Commonwealth, but for Australia.

Yet the scientific motivation for the AAE was by far the most important. On his journey to the South Pole, Amundsen made no pretense of doing science. Shackleton offered only a token nod to that goddess. Scott's *Terra Nova* expedition had had genuine, if secondary, scientific aims.

But Mawson was serious about science. The AAE, he believed, would be little more than a capricious exercise if it did not issue in scores of voluminous scholarly reports. Indeed, he would spend the rest of his life coaxing those reports into print.

In 1910, field science meant above all the gathering of specimens and data. Yet quite aside from the taxonomic minutiae of species and strata, for explorers such as Mawson science meant above all the discovery of unknown lands. To go where no one else had ever been, to see vistas that no human eye had previously beheld—those were the deeds not merely of romantic adventurers, but of men serving Science with a capital S by extending the realms of human inquiry. Knowledge for its own sake was a credo that Mawson and his peers lived by.

It would seem, with Shackleton's thrust to within 97 miles of the South Pole, that the general outlines of the Antarctic continent were becoming known. Nothing could have been further from the truth. All that Shackleton and, before him, Scott had proved was that there was a corridor of ice-covered land stretching south on either side of longitude 160° east. By 1910, no one could say with any authority whether Antarctica really *was* a continent, as opposed to a scattering of polar islands separated by huge frozen seas.

In his official account of the AAE, *The Home of the Blizzard*, Mawson published a map that astounds the modern reader. Titled "Antarctic Land-Discoveries Preceding 1910," it renders the "continent" as a virtual blank, except for a swath of gray hatching along the Scott–Shackleton corridor. Otherwise, only the most fugitive dots interrupt the blankness within the Antarctic Circle at 66° 33' south. These dots, based on the unreliable sightings of earlier explorers, bear names such as Balleny Islands and Enderby Land. Most of them would eventually be proven not to exist.

Thus the ultimate goal for Mawson in devising the AAE, embodying its most devout homage to Science, was to find out what was there, in the almost limitless blank that lay south of Australia. In 1911, the only way to find out what was there was to go there, and to march for weeks and months into the unknown, mapping as you went.

The nearly six months abroad that Mawson spent in 1911 organizing the AAE passed in a frenzy of anxiety and dashed hopes. Almost at once, however, he secured the services of John King Davis, the chief officer on board the *Nimrod* who had effectively saved Mawson's life by finding him and his two companions near the Drygalski Ice Tongue in February 1909. Davis's first task was to get a ship. After endless machinations and haggling over prices, Davis and Mawson managed to buy a vessel that had been built in 1876 to serve the Newfoundland sealing industry. She was named the *Aurora*, and though thirty-five years old when pressed into service for the AAE, the ship was so stoutly built and so seaworthy that a substantial part of the expedition's eventual success could be credited to her—and to Davis's cautious but canny navigating.

Back in Adelaide in July, Mawson soldiered on with his fundraising. Slowly the money came in, much of it donated by the various Australian states and territories. Meanwhile, Mawson recruited no fewer than thirty members of his team, not counting the twenty-four who would serve as the *Aurora*'s crew. Three of the team were British, one Swiss, and four were New Zealanders. (It was in deference to the Kiwis that the expedition chose "Australasian" rather than "Australian" for its title.) Besides Mawson, only one man had previous Antarctic experience—the redoubtable Frank Wild, who had played pivotal roles in both Scott's *Discovery* expedition from 1901–04 and the BAE from 1908–09. Some of the Aussies were mere students, whom Mawson had cultivated at the university. The youngest team member was nineteen, the oldest forty-three. Most were in their twenties, and however reliable Mawson considered them as scientists and workers, only a handful had much wilderness experience. As the expedition left Hobart on December 2, 1911, Mawson himself was only twenty-nine years old.

Those months of fundraising, buying equipment and food, buying and refitting the *Aurora*, and recruiting his team took a heavy toll on Mawson. Ever loyal, Paquita could not help noticing that her fiancé "looked thinner and thinner as the months went by." At a farewell dinner in his honor in Adelaide, Mawson confessed to the gathering, "I think we shall all be glad to get away. Personally I feel I would never have the energy to get up another expedition. I am prepared to go on exploring for the rest of time, but it is the organization from which one shrinks."

With Davis at the helm, the *Aurora* sailed from London on July 29. Aboard were forty-eight Greenland huskies, intended for sledge-hauling on the southern continent. In charge of their care and training were two members of the team, Belgrave Ninnis and Xavier Mertz. Ninnis, the young lieutenant in the Royal Fusiliers, had been heartbroken when he was rejected by Scott for the *Terra Nova* expedition, but had promptly applied for a position with Shackleton. Finding the eager youth entirely likable, the Boss signed him up, then passed Ninnis on to Mawson when he realized he would not be going to Antarctica himself.

Mertz, a lawyer from Basel and a champion skier, had applied for a position on the AAE by mail from Switzerland. In his letter to

Mawson, the twenty-eight-year-old had waxed enthusiastic about the potential usefulness of "skys" (as he spelled them in his uncertain English) in Antarctica. Mawson appointed Mertz to the expedition sight unseen.

After the first winter on the southern continent, Mawson would be so pleased with Ninnis's and Mertz's talents and verve that he chose them as his teammates for the Far Eastern journey. But on board the *Aurora*, John King Davis was at first less than favorably impressed. "The only two idlers in the ship [are] the two passengers," he wrote in his diary, distinguishing the dog-handlers from the crew. They "are too fond of their bunks in bad weather." Ninnis in particular, Davis thought, was "lazy and ignorant." As for Mertz, the Swiss athlete would "probably turn out to be a decent sort when he gets used to roughing it which is part of your life on this sort of job."

Taking care of the dogs, which were housed in makeshift shelters on the deck of the *Aurora*, turned into a nightmare. The proximity of males and females led to numerous pregnancies. On August 16, no fewer than thirteen puppies were born, but in the squalid conditions of heat and heaving seas, most of them died within days, either washed overboard or eaten by the adults. The huskies' constant howling kept sailors awake, and their excrement fouled the deck. Then several of the dogs came down with fits, foaming at the mouth; the men attributed the condition to distemper or epilepsy. When these huskies did not soon recover, Ninnis had to take on the doleful job of shooting them.

One scholar later speculated that the strange malady affecting the dogs was piblokto—"a mysterious hysterical disease affecting the seemingly unrelated triad of Greenland dogs, Arctic foxes, and Inuit women." In any event, by the time the *Aurora* left Australia, only thirty-eight of the original forty-eight huskies were still alive.

In choosing dogs as the animals to propel his sledges, Mawson emulated the logistical gambit that would win success for Amundsen in his quest for the South Pole only months in the future. But another locomotive innovation for the AAE was a bit too far ahead of its time. Mawson had decided to use an airplane in Antarctica. In

England, he hired the Vickers manufacturing firm to custom-build a light monoplane, and enlisted Vickers pilot Hugh Watkins to fly it.

The monoplane was carried from England to Australia on board a commercial steamer. But then, in a test flight-cum-fundraising show at a racecourse in Adelaide, disaster struck. With Watkins as pilot and Frank Wild as passenger, the plane took off, hit an air pocket, and plummeted to the ground. Wild, in his characteristically droll way, later wrote:

> I remember feeling my head strike earth & getting a mouthful of it, & in the same fraction of a second felt as though a thousand mules had kicked me all over at once, & saw the whole blessed machine coming over on top of me. When to my surprise I found I was still alive, lying on my back, my legs mixed up in the body of the machine & a fearful weight on my chest, unable to move. I could not see Watkins, but in a few seconds . . . I heard him say, "Poor old bus, she's done."

Mawson, who had paid nearly a thousand pounds for the plane, was furious. The wings were irreparable, and Watkins was removed from the expedition roster, but in an effort to salvage what he could of the machine, Mawson had the plane's body shipped aboard the *Aurora*. In Antarctica, he hoped to convert the crippled plane into an "air-tractor," a motorized sledge-pulling device. Despite being coddled and tinkered with through the first winter in Antarctica, the air-tractor proved almost as worthless as Shackleton's motorcar in 1908.

Because of its multipronged program, the AAE was by far the most ambitious expedition yet launched in Antarctica. To explore as much land as possible, Mawson originally intended to subdivide his thirty-one-man team into four autonomous parties. The Main Base, run by Mawson himself, would be placed as close to Cape Adare on the west as the *Aurora* could land. Once having dropped off the men who would staff that headquarters, the ship would sail farther west, eventually landing two more parties, each to build its

Douglas Mawson at 28

Near the South Magnetic Pole, January 16, 1909. From left, Mackay, David, Mawson

*Belgrave Ninnis in uniform
of the Royal Fusiliers*

*Xavier Mertz, Swiss lawyer
and ski champion*

Penguins near the remains of a wrecked ship, Macquarie Island

Enraged elephant seal, Macquarie Island

Ice mushroom near Cape Denison

Chopping ice off the Aurora *after a storm*

The Aurora *anchored off Cape Denison*

The Main Base hut covered in deep snow

Mertz emerging from trap door in the roof of the hut

Mertz ice climbing on a coastal serac

own hut, placed far enough apart so that their sledging journeys would not overlap.

The fourth sub-party would not be based on Antarctica at all, but rather on Macquarie Island, a skinny upthrust of tussock grass and rocky hills at 54°30' south, roughly halfway between Tasmania and Antarctica. Discovered accidentally in 1810 by a British expedition, the island so teemed with seals that during the century that followed, the animals that flocked to its shores were hunted to the edge of local extinction. It was Mawson's forward-looking plan to drop off five men on Macquarie to erect towering radio masts that in theory ought to be capable of relaying messages from Australia. Another set of radio masts and equipment would go with the *Aurora* to Antarctica, to be erected near the Main Base hut. If all went well, using Macquarie Island as a relay station, the AAE could become the first Antarctic expedition ever to have live communication with the outside world.

On the afternoon of December 2, 1911, the *Aurora* glided slowly out of the Hobart dock, as thousands of spectators cheered from shore. The ship was so overloaded that Davis found her exceedingly difficult to manage. Besides the thirty-eight huskies, the decks were strewn with radio masts, timbers and boards to be assembled into two huts, the air-tractor, a number of sledges, food for both men and dogs (the precious tins of butter being placed out of the reach of the leashed dogs), thousands of gallons of fuel, and all kinds of miscellaneous equipment. "The piles of loose gear presented an indescribable scene of chaos," wrote Mawson later. "The deck was so encumbered that only at rare intervals was it visible."

Realizing that even an overloaded *Aurora* would not suffice to carry everything the expedition needed, Mawson had chartered a second vessel, the steamship *Toroa*, to depart five days after the *Aurora*, carrying sixteen members of the team, more cargo, tons of coal, and fifty-five sheep. Its captain, Tom Holyman, was no match for Davis as a pilot. As Charles Laseron, one of the team aboard the *Toroa*, wryly recalled decades later, "If the skipper had a proper name we never heard it, as he was known, not only on board, but in shipping circles generally, as Roaring Tom. A rather burly personage with a black beard and a habit of shouting at the least provocation, his ways were, to say the least, very casual." The second in command was no better. According to Laseron, "The mate was deaf and a Christian Scientist. His hobby was to argue on every conceivable subject, even if he had never heard of it before, and as he never heard any replies he won all the arguments to his own satisfaction."

On the first day out of Hobart, the *Aurora* ran into a fresh gale, and waves breaking over the deck threatened to tear loose the cargo. The plug of one of the water tanks popped out, a calamity that severely restricted the team's drinking water all the way to Macquarie Island. Wrote Davis:

> Such boisterous weather so soon after our departure was a severe test, but the heavily-laden *Aurora* came through it very well. Living conditions aboard were hardly less crowded than in the old *Nimrod* but everyone co-operated and settled down to a ship routine, in spite of sea-sickness and discomfort. Mawson once having acquired his sea legs presumably never lost them again, for on this occasion his diet was not confined to tinned pears.

Despite Davis's recollection of shipboard tranquility, tensions broke out almost at once on both vessels. They tended to pit the ship's crew against the explorers. According to Laseron, on the *Toroa*, "The crew are about the worst lot I have ever met. All day there is nothing but a constant stream of grumbling. They are never satisified, and though they get exactly the same food as we do, good tucker too, they are never satisfied." As so often is true on expeditions, discontent focused on food. According to Percy Gray, second officer on the *Aurora*, "The cook we have signed on is apparently a fraud, as he has made no effort to cook anything since the ship has been rolling. We had no breakfast, and there is no sign of dinner."

An exception to the mutual disdain between crew and explorers was Gray's esteem for Belgrave Ninnis, which had blossomed during the long journey from England to Australia. "I shall be very sorry when he leaves the ship to go on shore, as we are great friends," Gray recorded on December 18. "In all this six months that I have been in daily contact with him I don't think we have had a single difference."

Laseron's dim view of Roaring Tom's capabilities as a captain took another comic turn as the *Toroa* approached Macquarie Island:

> The mate could navigate, but the skipper never believed his results, and the skipper himself, from day to day, forgot on which side the variation of his compass lay. The course he set tended naturally to wobble a bit. One day he took Hoadley and Dovers [two of Mawson's team members] into his confidence. He had just determined his position, but was puzzled at the result. According to his figures, the *Taroa* [*sic*] was in the centre of India.

When he did ultimately blunder upon Macquarie Island, Roaring Tom boasted, "I have found this bloody island without a chart & I will enter the bay without one."

During the eight days it took the *Aurora* to reach Macquarie, the ship was constantly buffeted by waves crashing over the decks. On December 9, the worst of those storm-lashed days, a single "mountain of water" smashed in the rear end of the motor launch (the vital craft needed to ferry goods from ship to shore), and also broke open the box containing the air-tractor, leaving the unwieldy contraption protruding four feet out of its casing. On deck feeding the dogs at the time, Ninnis and another man were nearly swept overboard.

In the early morning hours of December 11, the ship came in sight of Macquarie. Having visited the island in 1909 on his way home from the BAE, Davis opted for a preliminary anchorage in Caroline Cove, a protected bay on the southeast shore. Twelve members of Mawson's team jumped aboard the launch and motored toward the beach. Historian Beau Riffenburgh captures their rapturous excitement:

> They were staggered by its beauty: a steep hillside matted with thick tussock-grass, streams rushing down rocky cliffs, and stunning patches of moss and lichens—green, yellow, grey, and

orange—running over the darkness of the rock. The wildlife was equally amazing—crested penguins in their thousands on the cliffs and leaping from the water around the boat, while elephant seals warmed themselves on the shingle beach and sea birds screamed overhead.

One of those twelve was twenty-six-year-old Frank Hurley, the expedition's official photographer, for whom this was the first expedition of any kind. As he would write fourteen years later about that first landing, "I felt that had I sufficient plates and films, I could live here for the rest of my life. How helpless I felt to portray even a glimpse of it all in a few hours. I must have more time: I must return. But how was this to be done?" Hurley knew that in all likelihood, Mawson would choose a site on the opposite, northern end of the island for the Macquarie party's base, some twenty miles away. So, on the spur of the moment, he concocted a ruse that would ensure his second chance to film and photograph Caroline Cove. "I took one of my indispensable lenses from its case," wrote Hurley, "wrapped it in waterproof, and hid it beneath a rock."

Meanwhile, on board the *Aurora*, Mawson and Davis were taking the soundings that proved that Caroline Cove was too shallow and treacherous to serve as an anchorage. Indeed, as the captain sailed across what looked like "a fine clear bay," the ship struck a submerged rock. "Fortunately we were not moving much at the time so no damage was done," wrote Davis in his diary. "It was however a very nasty shock and the first time I have been on the bottom."

The next day, as the *Aurora* lay offshore in Hasselborough Bay, at the northern end of Macquarie, Hurley "simulated dismay" and told Mawson about the accidental loss of his camera lens. "I received a verbal trouncing for my apparent carelessness," Hurley later remembered, but he was immediately ordered—just as he had hoped—to take two companions and march the length of the island to retrieve the irreplaceable lens.

As the AAE would prove time and again, such chicanery was characteristic of Frank Hurley, who early on seized the role of the expedition's practical joker. Eventually Hurley would build a career that justifies the common judgment of him as the finest photographer in Australian history, but at twenty-six he had only begun to show his talent, and his inclusion on the AAE was far from a done deal.

Hurley had grown up in the Sydney suburb of Glebe, not far from Mawson's Fort Street School. His indulgent father was a prominent typesetter and printer who had high hopes for his son, but at thirteen, Hurley ran away from both school and home. The precipitating event was a practical joke played on "a cantakerous tubby little man" who was Hurley's tutor. The joke escalated into expulsion after the lad threw a pair of inkwells at the enraged teacher.

Or so Hurley later claimed. His biographer, Alasdair McGregor, casts doubt on this Dickensian anecdote, as he does on many of Hurley's stories, for entwined with the practical joker was an inveterate embellisher of tall tales. In any event, the runaway hopped a freight train west into the Blue Mountains, where he landed a grueling job as a handyman at an ironworks. A series of equally drudgerous jobs filled his adolescence, until he drifted back to Sydney. There, one day, "I found a new toy. A fellow worker induced me to purchase his camera and to take up the study of photography. Soon I became so deeply absorbed in 'this new fad' as my friends called it, that everything else fell into neglect."

By 1911, Hurley was recognized as one of Sydney's leading professional photographers, but he was also saddled with huge debts as the co-owner of a postcard-producing firm that was on the verge of going under. His forte with the camera was taking dangerous pictures of events never before seen on the page. One of his favorite tricks was to plant his tripod on the tracks in front of a fast-moving train, shoot the chugging behemoth at the last possible instant, then dive off the tracks as the locomotive thundered by.

When Mawson announced that he was accepting applications for official photographer for the AAE, Hurley jumped at the chance—as did quite a few of the country's other leading cameramen. Hurley was by no means the leading candidate, but he wangled an "accidental" meeting with Mawson on a 75-mile train ride, during which he used every minute to plead his case and trot out his virtues.

Or so, again, Hurley later claimed; Mawson never reported the meeting on the train. In any event, the AAE leader was all set to appoint Hurley to the job when a warning came to him in the strange form of a confidential letter from Hurley's mother. Worried about her son's safety if he set off for Antarctica, she told Mawson, "I am certain that he is not strong enough for the position. He has never roughed it in any way during his life. He has lung trouble so bad that if he started I do not think he would come back."

Mawson was sufficiently alarmed by the letter to grill Hurley during the weeks before the departure from Hobart about the state of his health, though he heeded Mrs. Hurley's plea not to divulge the source of the warning. Hurley was utterly perplexed, for he knew that he had roughed it since childhood, and he felt in perfect health. He agreed to submit to a medical exam, which he apparently passed. Even so, Mawson came very close to dropping Hurley from the team. Had he done so, it would have been history's (and photography's) eternal loss.

Given the century-long legacy of seal-hunting on Macquarie Island, Mawson and Davis were not surprised to find the place inhabited. But on December 12, as the *Aurora* neared the island's northern tip, the crew on board spotted a shipwreck on the beach—"evidently a recent victim," as Mawson put it. Next, the men spotted a pair of rude huts, "but no sign of human life."

As the crew members discussed the meaning of these talismans, suddenly "a human figure appeared in front of one of the huts. After surveying us for a moment, he disappeared within to reappear shortly afterwards, followed by a stream of others rushing hither and thither; just as if he had disturbed a hornet's nest." These castaways were the crew of a New Zealand merchant ship employed to render valuable oil from seals and penguins. The *Clyde* had run aground in a gale about a month earlier, though no lives had been lost. Another dozen sealing men were also spending the summer on Macquarie Island, but had no plans to head home until the end of summer. On learning that the *Toroa* would soon arrive and could take them directly home, the refugees from the *Clyde* were overjoyed.

After several aborted efforts to approach the *Aurora* with their rowboat, the sealers signaled to Davis to circumnavigate the narrow northern promontory of the island and come into a sheltered cove from the west. Hasselborough Bay, named after the 1810 discoverer of the island, offered the only safe anchorage on any of Macquarie's shores. By late on December 12, the men had started unloading the cargo and food for the five-man party delegated to establish the radio link between Australia and Antarctica. The next day, the *Toroa* arrived, carrying the remainder of the team and yet more cargo— including the fifty-five sheep that would graze the tussock grass on Macquarie Island before becoming, as mutton, part of the larder for the Antarctic overwinterers.

In charge of the Macquarie party was George Ainsworth, a thirty-three-year-old meteorologist who had impressed Mawson with his physical strength and a knack for leadership. On the journey south, however, Captain Davis had formed a distinctly less favorable impression of the man. In Hasselborough Bay, the two disagreed vehemently over where to build the hut. Davis wanted to consult the sealers, while Ainsworth had already made up his mind. "Well I am glad I shall not be with Ainsworth," Davis confided to his diary, "he is an ass."

With the arrival of the *Toroa*, a frenzy of unloading and hut- and radio-mast-building began. Time was of the essence, for the *Aurora* still needed to land three parties on the unknown shores of Antarctica, where the AAE would carry out its wildly ambitious program. Meanwhile, Frank Hurley set off southward, hiking inland to retrieve the precious lens he had "misplaced" in Caroline Cove. His two companions were the expedition biologist Charles Harrisson and one of the Macquarie sealers, a man named Hutchinson, who volunteered to scout the way.

The journey of 20 miles out and back turned out to be far rougher than Hurley had bargained for. And Hutchinson proved to be not only a vivid local historian, but a gloomy pessimist who painted Macquarie Island as a kind of subantarctic hell. As Hurley recreated the man's monologues fourteen years later, Hutchinson inveighed against the wanton depredations of a hundred years of sealers: "They slaughtered every flipper that showed itself, not even sparing new-born 'pups.' It was a wicked business. One vessel, by the way, the same name as yours, the *Aurora*, carried back 35,000 pelts in one season."

When Hurley ventured to ask about ships wrecked on Macquarie shores, Hutchinson spat, "Wrecked! Why the reefs are ships' grave-yards and the rocks tombstones!" The man went on to tell the "sad-dest story of the lot," about a ship named the *Eagle*:

> Went to pieces during a gale on the West Coast. Nine men and a woman saved themselves after a hell of a struggle. They lost everything and the ten of them all lived together in a cave for two years. . . .
>
> The cave is littered with bones and, inside you can see all round the mouldy grass that they slept on for beds. There's a cross too, to the woman, poor soul. She died the very day relief came.

Hurley wondered why Hutchinson had chosen such a dismal pro-fession, and the doomsayer proclaimed, "Sealing is not all the big adventure it's cracked up to be—darned rotten grub, cranky little cockleshells of boats, seas swarming with icebergs and reefs and cold Davy Jones always waiting to tuck you up in his locker below."

The first night, the trio bivouacked in an abandoned sealers' hut. Hurley found it impossible to sleep, especially after "swarms of rats" crawled over the men's blankets. Hutchinson claimed the rats had arrived on board ships that, once wrecked, disgorged the stowaway rodents in such numbers that they now "infested the whole island."

On the second day, the men found the coastline impassable and had to climb inland, scaling short cliffs and wallowing through peat bogs. A steady rain began to fall, and all too soon night overtook the trio. Returning to the beach, they searched in vain for a decent open bivouac site, but the sea shingle was too rocky. Noticing that the abundant elephant seals slept on beds of kelp, the men drove the animals away by "pelting them with pebbles," then settled in. "We found their beds very wet and slimy," wrote Hurley, "yet preferable to the cold knobby pebbles of the beach."

Despite the hardships of the trip, Hurley was in a state of photographic ecstasy, even in the midst of chaos, including a penguin rookery that the men strode through with the animals "peck[ing] viciously at our legs." Hurley added, "The scene was one never to be forgotten, a writhing congestion of birds that maintained a raucous din. The drizzling rain which falls almost incessantly converts the rookeries into vast slushy areas of filth."

It was not until the third afternoon that the men reached Caroline Cove. Hurley had no trouble finding the lens he had hidden, but when he pleaded for time to shoot more landscapes, Hutchinson, fed up with the whole fool's errand, demanded an immediate turnaround. The return journey was even more arduous than the outward jaunt. In darkness the first evening, Hurley jammed his right foot between two boulders and badly sprained his ankle. The next morning, it had swollen so much that he couldn't get his boot on. Hutchinson swaddled the foot in canvas, "and this enabled me to limp along."

Harrisson had been gathering biological specimens the whole time. Between the enormous burden of his pack and Hurley's bad leg, it became a true ordeal for the men to hobble back north across the inhospitable terrain. When the *Aurora* at last came into view, the men gave hearty thanks. But in retrospect, Hurley's self-inflicted traverse of Macquarie Island seemed almost a lark. "We had been exploring," he wrote in 1925, "and had shaken hands with adventure in an unknown land."

During Hurley's absence, the rest of the men had chosen a nearby hill, rising more than 300 feet above the sea, for the site of the radio masts and telegraph center. Getting tons of gear up Wireless Hill, as the men named the promontory, was no trivial task. Here Frank Wild, the veteran of two previous Antarctic expeditions, came into his element. He improvised a "flying fox," a kind of aerial tramway supported by a tripod at the upper end and strung with a pair of steel cables that spanned the 800-foot carry. A bag filled with rocks or sand at the upper end acted as a counterweight to the load to be hauled from the foot of the hill.

For loads too heavy to be hoisted by the flying fox, the men strung out in a line and hauled their burdens by brute force along the ground. To invigorate the labor, they sang such chanties as "A'Roving" and "Ho, Boys, Pull Her Along." On top of Wireless Hill, five-foot-deep holes were dug in the stubborn ground, to be filled with heavy "dead men" to anchor the stays that supported the radio masts.

Eager to leave for the southern continent, Mawson prepared a departure for the day before Christmas, leaving Ainsworth's crew of five to build their hut from the prefabricated boards and timbers carried on shipboard from Australia. The last chore was to load the huskies, who had been given their liberty on shore, back onto the *Aurora*, and to round up and slaughter the sheep. According to one team member, "The sheep allowed themselves to be killed without trouble, but they strenuously objected to being caught, and a stern chase among the tussocky grass involved a great deal of language." Not all the sheep were slaughtered on Macquarie; others were carried aboard the *Aurora* to be turned into fresher cuts of meat during the coming weeks.

No one worked harder during the layover on Macquarie than Mawson himself. On December 15, he wrote a letter to Paquita, to be carried back on the *Toroa*, in which he reported:

The last few days have been very strenuous ones but I like it—I am in my element. Hard physical work agrees with me. I have only had one rinse of my face since leaving Hobart and there is very little skin on my hands now. Have brushed my hair twice. You would scarcely recognize your Dougelly.

The emotional parting between the Macquarie quintet and the rest of the AAE team took place on the morning of December 24 on the beach—"their cheers echoing to ours"—as the motor launch carried the southern-bound crew back to the *Aurora*.

One final Macquarie Island chore remained—to replenish the drinking water supply for the long haul to Antarctica. Despite his harrowing escape earlier in the month, when the *Aurora* had struck a submerged rock, Davis agreed to return to Caroline Cove, where freshwater lakes just inland promised a good supply of potable water. On Christmas Eve, anchored inside the cove, Mawson sent a bucket brigade on shore to fill two big barrels resting on the beach. It was a nasty job:

> It was difficult at first to find good water, for the main stream flowing from the head of the bay was contaminated by the penguins which made it their highway to a rookery. After a search, an almost dry gully was found to yield soakage water when a pit was dug in its bed. This spot was some eighty yards from the beach, and to reach it one traversed an area of tussock-grass where sea-elephants wallowed in soft mire.

That night, while Davis tried to catch a little sleep, the *Aurora* drifted loose, this time colliding with a sizable reef. It was a far more dangerous predicament than the one of December 11. As Davis wrote in his diary:

> I jumped up on deck found that the ship had dragged her bower anchor, and that the stern was bumping on the rocks (rather an unpleasant Xmas Box). I jumped on the bridge and rang up slow ahead, but the engines did not move. Meanwhile, all hands who were to be found were pulling on the kedge, and I think that this

really started her out, as to my relief the engines began to revolve and we soon straightened up.

By midday on Christmas, the *Aurora* was at last clear of Macquarie Island, steaming through open ocean, bound for Antarctica.

Mawson and Davis's intention was to head straight south from Macquarie, roughly along longitude 157° east, striking the continent a bit to the west of Cape Adare. Just the previous year, the crew of Scott's *Terra Nova*, returning from dropping off the team on Ross Island, had sighted land inland from Cape Adare, but had been unable to penetrate pack ice to reach the shore. Because the ship had reached New Zealand in early 1911, Mawson knew all about this discovery. But between Oates Land, as the crew named this remote plateau, and Gaussberg, an extinct volcano discovered by Erich D. von Drygalski's German expedition in 1902, at about 89° east, a sweep of possible coastline no less than 2,200 miles in extent (roughly one-fifth of Antarctica's gigantic circumference) was virtually unknown. Drygalski's ship, the *Gauss*, named after the great mathematician, had frozen fast in the pack ice, and barely escaped the next summer.

Only two expeditions had previously penetrated that swath of terra and aqua incognita. Both had coasted alongside floating bergs and possibly landfast ice in the summer of 1839–40. One was American, under the irascible naval officer Charles Wilkes; the other French, led by the flamboyant mariner Jules S.-C. Dumont d'Urville.

In January 1840, Wilkes thought he had sighted land at longitude 154° 30' E, 66° 20' S, very close to the destination toward which the *Aurora* was heading seventy-two years later. The next month, Wilkes landed some men on an iceberg that he gauged to be eight miles offshore. Finding stones and gravel embedded in the berg, he deduced a genuine continent to the south.

At almost the same time in early 1840, Dumont d'Urville spied an inland plateau whose height he estimated at 3,000 feet above sea level, some 23 degrees of longitude west of Wilkes's sighting. Later, the French team made a landing on a small isle only a third of a mile offshore from what the leader was convinced was mainland Antarctica. The team raised the tricolor and uncorked a celebratory bottle. "Never was Bordeaux wine called on to play a more worthy part," wrote an expedition officer; "never was a bottle emptied more fitly." Dumont d'Urville named the whole region Terre Adélie, after his wife. Thanks to Mawson, as Adélie Land, the name would stick.

Astonishingly, on January 29, 1840, d'Urville's ships passed so close to Wilkes's brig that the men could plainly see each other's crews on board. Yet thanks to a misunderstanding of signals, neither team chose to stop and compare notes. Almost three quarters of a century would pass before the next ship entered these virtually unknown waters.

Five days after leaving Macquarie Island, on December 29, 1911, the watchman aboard the *Aurora* suddenly cried, "Ice on the starboard bow!" The men, nearly all of whom had never seen anything remotely resembling an iceberg before, flocked onto the deck to stare. All their preconceptions vanished as they gazed in awe at the glittering phenomenon. During the following days, the ship was surrounded by floating masses of glacial ice. Even Mawson, who had seen plenty of icebergs on the BAE, was moved to poetic rapture:

> The tranquility of the water heightened the superb effects of this glacial world. Majestic tabular bergs whose crevices exhaled a vaporous azure; lofty spires, radiant turrets and splendid castles; honeycombed masses illumined by pale green light within whose fairy labyrinths the water washed and gurgled. Seals and penguins on magic gondolas were the silent denizens of this dreamy Venice.

Far less poetically minded, Captain Davis—nicknamed Gloomy by his men, in homage to his stern temperament—was concerned only with practical matters. The icebergs soon gave way to pack ice, still with no hint of a mainland in the distance. Wary of getting the ship trapped in the ice—as both the *Gauss* and Scott's *Discovery* had been in 1902—he kept darting among leads between ice floes, then steaming back north to escape the enclosing pressure. When it became clear that there was no hope of reaching any sort of mainland near the 157th meridian, he headed west.

Both Mawson and Davis constantly searched the sky to the south. Their previous voyages had taught them to distinguish "ice blink" from "water sky." The former was a bright white cast to the air, sometimes reflected off the undersides of clouds; it signified only ice beyond the visible horizon. The latter, which both men craved, took the form of dark streaks on the same clouds, the reflected image of open water to the south. For centuries the Inuit in the north had used ice blink and water sky to navigate.

Day after day, the men saw only ice blink. And as the *Aurora* pushed farther west, the broken pack through which Davis had been weaving a careful track gave way to a massive barrier of ice. Whether it was a huge iceberg or the edge of landfast ice, neither man could say. It would take another year for Mawson and Davis to realize that one such mass, whose ice cliffs towered as high as 150 feet, was nothing more than a colossal iceberg, fully 40 miles in length.

New Year's Day, Davis recorded, "passed uneventfully." Now the captain began to wonder about another matter—the supply of coal the ship had left. If too much fuel was expended searching for a place to land, the *Aurora* might lack the coal needed to return all the way to Hobart. This possibility nagged at the hypervigilant pilot.

On January 3, the ship's mate called Davis's attention to a large tongue of ice protruding into the sea. It looked for all the world like a glacier, which would signify mainland. Best of all, for the first time Davis could see water sky beyond the barrier. Yet this happy discovery only perplexed Davis further. "We were all very much puzzled to account for this huge tongue of ice as Wilke's [*sic*] track on the chart is shown 30 miles further south," he wrote in his diary. "Either the tongue did not exist in those days or his observations were at fault." (As Mawson would subsequently prove, most of Wilkes's purported sightings were fugitive at best, imaginary at worst.)

The extreme cold, at a latitude far to the north of McMurdo Sound, where the *Nimrod* had sailed in 1908, and the consistently hazy, misty weather confounded Davis. On January 6, he wrote in exasperation, "What an extraordinary thing the Antarctic is, every-thing seems to be different from the Ross Sea Zone. Probably we do not understand as much about this area."

Mawson had his own doubts and tribulations, which he did not readily confide in his men. One of the chief objectives he had set for the AAE was to launch an overland party to approach the south magnetic pole from the north—closing full circle, as it were, on the marathon discovery trek to the pole that he, David, and Mackay had performed in 1908–09 from exactly the opposite direction. But the farther west *Aurora* drifted, the longer and more difficult that jour-ney promised to be.

Even more troublesome was the knowledge that the farther west the main base for the AAE might have to be established, the more difficult and uncertain radio communications with Macquarie would become. Finally, Mawson himself could not ignore the coal prob-lem. Unless the ship could discover a viable harbor for the main base soon, Mawson's whole program was in jeopardy. Davis's anxiety on this matter leaked into his journal: "I feel that we must take chances if we are ever to land anyone here. . . . We must hope that after some bad luck, we shall get some better. Who knows what we might find if the weather would only clear up."

Mawson had begun to realize that his plan to establish three sep-arate bases scattered along the coast of Adélie Land would strain the coal supply beyond breaking point. Privately, he began to reconfig-ure the scheme. He would attempt only two bases—a main one that he would superintend himself, and a smaller contingent farther west under the charge of Frank Wild. Before he could explain the change to his team, rumors began to circulate. Some of the men, fearing the worst, suspected that Mawson intended to jettison his third party altogether, asking them to return to Australia with the ship. For sev-eral days, those "empties," as they thought of themselves, chafed under the premonition that all their Antarctic dreams might go for naught.

It was only on January 6 that Mawson explained his new plan to the whole team. Wild's western base would be staffed by eight men, the main base by the other eighteen. The prefabricated hut intended for the third base would serve as an annex to the main base hut.

Even this whittled-down agenda was predicated, of course, on finding a harbor anywhere to land the main party. Morale by now was reaching a nadir. On January 5, five of the huskies suddenly died. As Alexander Kennedy, a twenty-two-year-old engineering graduate whom Mawson had recruited from his own university, wrote the next day:

> The coroners verdict [that of the two expedition doctors] was gastritis and appendicitis probably induced by exposure. . . . Ninnis went about with a long face yesterday as the four above-mentioned dogs were having fits. "Four dead dogs," he said, and so it turned out. . . . The black dogs are the best, the white not so good & the piebald are the sick looking ones.

At noon on January 8, Wild burst into the ship's chart room to report that a substantial rock exposure could be seen about 15 miles ahead on the port side. Davis redirected the *Aurora* to get a better look at it. Soon the ship was coasting through a scattering of small offshore islets. Mawson and Davis grew more and more excited. As Mawson later wrote:

> Advancing towards the mainland, we observed a small inlet in the rocky coast, and towards it the [whale] boat was directed. We were soon inside a beautiful, miniature harbour completely land-locked. The sun shone gloriously in a blue sky as we stepped ashore on a charming ice-quay—the first to set foot on the Antarctic continent between Cape Adare and Gaussberg, a distance of about two thousand miles.

Seven men, led by Mawson and including Wild and Hurley, were the first to step ashore. "We had come to a fairyland of ethereal blue and silver," recalled Hurley more than a decade later. "High exaltation swelled our hearts as we inspected the site. . . . Doctor Mawson decided to establish his Winter Quarters upon it."

Mawson would name the perfect harbor Cape Denison, after an Australian patron of the expedition, and the enclosing cove Commonwealth Bay. Soon the rest of the team and much of the ship's crew had come on shore. While Mawson and Wild set out to explore the surroundings, the men broke out into a spontaneous snowball fight. "Accidentally hit Bickerton in the eye, splosh!" wrote Kennedy gleefully. "Madigan also hit 'Gloomy'."

The joyous lark was perfectly comprehensible—after all, some of those men had never seen snow before the present expedition. But it would not take long for the true character of Cape Denison to show itself—and to test every fiber of the team's patience and endurance.

4

THE HOME OF THE BLIZZARD

In the newly discovered Boat Harbour, as Mawson named it, the glorious sunshine under the blue sky soon faded. As soon as the seven reconnoiterers had rowed the whale boat back to the anchored *Aurora*, a breeze sprang up. Wanting to waste no time, Mawson had the motor launch lowered and prepared to take a first load of cargo ashore.

> By the time we had reached the head of the harbour, [Archibald] Hoadley had several fingers frost-bitten and all were feeling the cold, for we were wearing light garments in anticipation of fine weather. The wind strengthened every minute, and showers of fine snow were soon whistling down the ice-slopes. No time was lost in landing the cargo, and, with a rising blizzard at our backs we drove out to meet the *Aurora*.

It would take nine more days to complete the unloading and ferrying ashore of the tons of equipment and food for the Main Base party. During much of that time, Davis had all he could handle just to keep the ship from running aground against the surrounding ice cliffs.

On one windy day, the motor launch broke adrift from the *Aurora* and was driven out to sea before a 45 mph wind. The three men on board desperately tried to start the engine, which had been doused by waves breaking over the shallow gunwales. The rest of the team watched with growing apprehension as the boat drifted half a mile toward a small island onto which the sea was violently crashing. At the last minute, the engine caught fire, and the launch avoided a wreck.

Still the wind increased, until a steady gale of 70 mph turned Commonwealth Bay into a frothing maelstrom. For two days, no one dared leave the ship. Davis became distraught about the possibility of the ship's anchor failing to hold, after the strain on the cable completely flattened a steel hook two inches in diameter. When the officer on watch failed to realize the seriousness of the situation, the captain unleashed a diatribe in his diary:

> I feel that I have not an officer in the ship that can be trusted to do anything. The boatswain is the only one that has the ordinary knowledge of a sailor, and he cannot be on deck all the time. . . . It is too much to find that the officers are too lazy to take the ordinary precautions of seeing that [the strain on the cable] is eased as much as possible. . . .
> Anchor still holding but it may go at anytime.

Among the *Aurora*'s crew, the tension and resentment were reciprocal. In his own diary, second officer Percy Gray—as sanguine a man as Davis was choleric—complained about the captain, "It is his one hobby in life to find fault with anybody and anything."

Still, morale among the Main Base team remained high, as the men could not help marveling over the novelty of their surroundings. When the weather improved and cargo ferries could be resumed, some of the party indulged in hijinks of the same sort as their initial snowball fight. On January 14, four men took a stroll through a nearby penguin rookery.

They are beautiful birds . . . with their silvery white breasts and dark plumage. They are clumsy and foolish on land and in their element at sea. We amuse ourselves catching them suddenly from behind by the flippers before they have time to peck, and throwing them head first into the water. . . . Bickerton and Wild seized a few from a rookery full of furry chicks, and glissaded them down a snow slope.

Apparently the hijinks carried over to late-night carousal aboard the ship, for Percy Gray grumbled, "I shall be glad now once we land the first party and get some of the people off the ship, as the awful crowd and noise which is continually going on is apt to get on the nerves of a person who has a good deal of work to do. They very often keep me awake at night."

The unloading proceeded apace. Each load in the motor launch brought another five or six tons of gear and supplies. Had the shore consisted of ice or snow, the cargo would have been unloaded directly onto sledges, then hauled to the hut site, already chosen by Mawson, some 60 yards inland. But since the shore was solid rock, both the unloading and hauling were far more onerous. The ever-resourceful Frank Wild improvised a derrick, not unlike the flying fox he had constructed on Macquarie Island, to swing the heaviest burdens from boat to land.

The gales continued almost without interruption, further hampering the men's work. On the 17th, the impatient Davis wrote in his diary, "We have been quite long enough here, half the time doing nothing on account of the weather. It certainly seems to be a windy spot." By the next day, however, Mawson could boast:

a great assortment of material was at length safely got ashore. Comprised among them was the following: twenty-three tons of coal briquettes, two complete living-huts, a magnetic observatory, the whole of a wireless equipment, including masts, and more than two thousand packages of general supplies containing sufficient food for two years, utensils, instru-

ments, benzine, kerosene, lubricating oils, an air-tractor and
sledges.

On January 19, the *Aurora* prepared to sail west to deposit the
second party somewhere along the unknown shore. The parting
between the eighteen men staffing the Main Base and the eight who
would establish the Western Base was both celebratory and sad.
For just such an occasion, back in London, Davis had been offered
the handsome gift of some bottles of madeira that had been carried
aboard the *Challenger* during its pioneering oceanographic expedition of 1872–74—the first crossing of the Antarctic Circle by a
steam-powered ship. Mawson spoke briefly, and the bottles were
uncorked for the first time in thirty-eight years. The men drank
toasts all around. Frank Wild made a surprise appearance dressed as
Sir Francis Drake, in "long purple stockings, scarlet cap with white
feather, and tinselled coat."

The men sang "Auld Lang Syne" and exchanged three cheers. Then
the Main Base party climbed into the whale boat. Last to leave was
Mawson, whose "unwavering eyes" fixed Davis's as he said, "Good-bye,
and do your best." The parting was "rather a pull at our heartstrings,"
wrote Charles Laseron. On board the ship, Wild later admitted, "we
steamed away feeling more than a little melancholy. I for one could not
help thinking that our goodbyes were to some of them forever."

Second officer Percy Gray wrote, "Well, at last we have got rid of
the first party." But he added:

The whole thing impressed me very much, those 18 men on their
little boat pulling away to their icy home. I only hope they all
return safely, which I am sure they will. I was very sad at saying
goodbye to old Ninnis, he is one of the nicest chaps I know, and
we have been very thick, all through this rather trying voyage.
. . . I was sorry to see the last of old Mertz too.

Ninnis mirrored the feeling. In his diary, he wrote, "I could have
wept with the greatest ease. All the second party, the ships officers,

and many of the crew, were my friends, and they were leaving us and vanishing . . . into the unknown land to the west."

"They are a fine party of men," wrote Davis upon parting, with a vague sense of premonition, "but the country is a terrible one to spend a year in."

From the very start of the expedition, there was little doubt that Frank Wild would be in command of the Western Base. Born in England, at age thirty-eight he was the third oldest member of the AAE. Not only was Wild the only one in the team besides Mawson to have visited the southern continent before, but he was at the time the most experienced Antarctic explorer in the world. He had been a member of Scott's *Discovery* expedition in 1901–04, as well as of Shackleton's BAE in 1907–09. On the latter journey, he had proved the equal of Shackleton in drive and endurance during the grueling push to the new Farthest South and the ordeal by near-starvation and scurvy on the return march to Cape Royds. Before 1912, Wild had already overwintered in Antarctica three times—one more time than either Scott or Shackleton. After the AAE, still in love with the frozen continent, Wild would become second in command on Shackleton's disastrous *Endurance* expedition from 1914–17. The Boss would leave Wild in charge of the twenty-one refugees on Elephant Island as he set out on his open boat journey to South Georgia in an effort to save the whole expedition.

As the *Aurora* steamed away from Cape Denison on January 19, Wild and Davis carried with them Mawson's orders not to establish the Western Base closer than 400 miles to the west, so that none of Wild's sledging parties starting out the next summer would overlap in their explorations with Mawson's own parties. Yet day after day passed without a hint of mainland appearing on the port side of the ship. Once again Davis fumed over the purported sightings claimed by Wilkes in 1840. The captain's mood, already anxious, grew dark. "I only wish that our observations would fix the position of something more solid than this interminable pack," he griped to his diary on January 22. And the next day, "It is very disappointing to find the pack off the land. I had hoped here to have pushed between the pack and the land, but this is impossible so we must resume our journey round the edge of it again. I think that this is about the dreariest coast in the world."

The escalating dilemma of the dwindling fuel supply nagged at the captain. "We have still about 200 tons of coal left so I am not going to go past anything without seeing it, if possible," he wrote on January 25; "but the pack is a terrible obstacle and seems to hang on the coast here, unlike Adelie Land." By January 28, "Coal is getting less all the time and nothing can be done." February 1: "Nothing to be seen but the endless pack." February 3: "The position is becoming serious. We have now 150 tons of coal left, and this means that if we get caught in the pack, we shall have no chance of landing the party at all."

By January 28, the *Aurora* had steamed past a point 400 miles west of Cape Denison. The men kept a constant watch, day and night, for any black streak of outcrop that might signify solid land, but there were only ice and snow and, in the sky near the horizon, ice blink. Percy Gray grew exasperated with the captain. On February 5, after beginning his diary entry with the lament, "Still no land," he fulminated:

At 8. o'clock last night, the pack looked fairly thin to the southward so the "old man" decided to have another try. So in we went and made our way slowly south, until at 5 a. m. this morning the "old man" decided that it was getting a bit too thick and stopped, and we have been stopped ever since, goodness only knows why, as we don't do any good by stopping. For goodness sake, I say, let him push ahead into the pack, and if necessary get frozen in, or turn around and come out of it.

Like "Gloomy," "the old man" was a derisive epithet based on Davis's stern demeanor and cautious piloting: when Gray wrote his diary entry, the captain was only twenty-seven years old.

Davis knew what he was doing. As impatient as anyone on the ship to land the Western Base party, he knew that to get the *Aurora* frozen into pack ice would spell unmitigated disaster. Other Antarctic ventures, such as Scott's *Discovery* expedition, had had backup rescue plans built in. But as of February 1912, no one in Australia had a clear idea where Mawson's party had disembarked on the coast of Adélie Land. That knowledge—not to mention the fate of Wild's eight-man team and of the full ship's crew—depended on the *Aurora*'s returning safely to Australia in the early months of 1912. There was no plan in place for a rescue mission in case the *Aurora* failed to show up, and even if one could be mobilized, trying to find Mawson's men at Cape Denison and a ship locked in ice somewhere far to the west would amount to the proverbial search for a needle in a haystack.

As the days passed and nothing but ice appeared ahead, everyone on board began to face the possibility of utter failure. "We have just got enough coal to do about another week's searching, and then take us back again," Gray wrote on February 5. In other words, should the search for a harbor prove fruitless, Wild's whole team faced the prospect of returning to Hobart with the ship, having accomplished no part of the AAE's ambitious agenda of discovery. Wild and Davis discussed the alternative of returning the Western Base party to Cape Denison, "but there is such a crowd there already that it is of little use."

Davis's spirits plunged with each day's fruitless search for land. On February 7, he wrote, "I am feeling very low indeed about things, and now success seems further off than ever. Well, we will have a good buck at it before giving in, and we have done our best. We cannot fight nature any longer."

On February 8, however, the watch reported an "ice barrier" ahead. It was not land, but it might be the tongue of a huge glacier like the one that had presaged the discovery of the good harbor at Cape Denison. "I do not know that I have ever felt more relieved than I did to see this barrier," claimed Davis. During the following days, he was able to round the edge of the barrier and head south, with no pack ice to impede his way. But what was the barrier? Was it a huge shelf attached to land, like the Ross Ice Shelf near McMurdo Sound? Or was it a gigantic detached tabular iceberg?

The barrier's edge ended in sheer ice cliffs at least sixty feet high. Even if it were possible to anchor under its lee, the possibility of Wild and other men climbing onto the shelf to explore it seemed dubious. Day after day, Davis's hopes dwindled again. On February 13, he wrote, "I had hoped that a landing on the barrier would have been possible but even this does not appear to be so." And the next day, "I feel very miserable about the whole business, but we have done all we can and are now about at the end of our tether."

By February 14, it had been twenty-six days since the *Aurora* had left Cape Denison. The ship lay not 400 miles west of the Main Base, but 1,500. Yet the day before, Wild and Alexander Kennedy had managed to clamber through a weakness in the ice cliffs and reach the top of the barrier. They returned that evening from a quick reconnaissance with discouraging news. "Wild . . . reported that the land was at least 28 miles off, the ice floe was much older further in, and that the barrier appeared to terminate before reaching the land." Still unresolved was the question of whether this huge ice mass was attached to mainland Antarctica or floating free in the ocean, but Wild's observations appeared to favor the latter possibility.

Now the veteran explorer made a bold decision. Without ascertaining the true nature of the barrier shelf, he committed himself to establishing a Western Base upon it. Whether or not the shelf was attached to the mainland, it was unmistakable that its seaward edge calved regularly, dumping tons of ice into the ocean. To erect a hut on top of the shelf and establish a camp there for the long winter ran the very real risk that the mass, whether or not it was a glacier or a colossal iceberg, in its slow but ceaseless gravity-driven slippage toward the north would eventually pitch men, hut, and everything they owned into the sea, spelling quick and certain death for all.

Such a dangerous gambit had been attempted only once before— by Amundsen's party in the Bay of Whales in 1911. Living in tents while the men ferried supplies south across the Ross Ice Shelf, Amundsen's team eventually erected their base, which they named Framheim, a full two miles from the ocean's edge. It was still a calculated risk, but a much less dicey one than Wild proposed.

The day after Wild made his decision happened to be Sir Ernest Shackleton's birthday, so, at Davis's suggestion, the team named the vast plateau the Shackleton Ice Shelf. "The whole sheet was undoubtedly moving," Wild later wrote, "but I was confident that only a few yards broke away yearly."

Knowing, however, that this desperate stab at a Western Base could mean a life-or-death decision for his men, Wild told each of the seven that he was free to decline the proposition and sail back to Hobart with the *Aurora*. Yet "each said in almost the same words 'If it is good enough for you, it is good enough for me.' "

There followed a frenzy of unloading gear, food, and nine huskies. In four days, the men transferred forty tons of gear from the ship to the surface of the shelf, aided once more by a flying fox Wild contrived at the top of the ice cliff.

Davis's reaction was a blend of relief and deep concern for the men he was leaving behind. Yet no matter how hard they worked during those four days, the effort struck the always judgmental Davis as sometimes verging on the indolent. On February 20, he complained to his diary:

> The party themselves do not seem to be in any hurry to shift stores further in. . . . I do not like to be critical but I should not care to work with some of them. Today all hands started at 9:30 [a.m.] and I knocked our men off at 4 p.m. as we go to sea at daylight. The party also knocked off and although it is a beautiful evening, they are some of the[m] playing football on the floe, instead of getting their hut up to the site or doing something useful. . . . Wild is a first class man and so is [Charles] Harrisson. The rest are an indifferent lot and will not do anything very startling, I think.

Nonetheless, the parting on February 21 was a warm and congenial one. At Davis's request, Wild handed him a letter explaining his choice of the Western Base site. It read, in part:

> I am a very poor hand at making pretty speeches as you know, and I feel that I have not thanked you half enough for the way in which you have worked for us.
>
> No doubt some authorities will consider we are taking unjustifiable risks, and were this a *barrier* I should be of the same opinion. However, I am convinced that it is a *glacier* and with practically no movement. It is quite possible that during the twelve months of our stay here that small portions will break away from the edge, but at the distance back at which I intend to build the hut I consider we are certainly as safe as Amundsen on the Ross Barrier.

Whether or not out of over-confidence, Wild ultimately directed the building of the Western Base hut only 600 yards from the edge of the calving ice cliff—a mere one-sixth as far from the lethal sea as Amundsen's Framheim.

As he steamed north, Davis was keenly cognizant not only of the peril of the Western Base party but of how crucial the safe return of the *Aurora* to Hobart was to the survival of those eight explorers. As he would recall decades later, "In the event of the *Aurora* being lost with all hands on her voyage back to Hobart, a searching vessel would not have known where to search and the little party, left behind to explore the new land we had discovered, might well have had to remain there until they died."

After an uneventful journey, the *Aurora* arrived in Hobart on March 12. Upon disembarking, however, one of the ship's crew members told an Australian journalist, "Wild's party is camped on moving ice and there is little probability that they will ever be seen again."

Back at Cape Denison, the seventeen men supervised by Mawson, working sixteen-hour days, had immediately started to erect their hut. Before it was finished, the men slept in a makeshift shelter constructed out of benzine cases stacked in double rows to serve as walls, with boards from the crate that had housed the air-tractor as a roof. Their reindeer-skin sleeping bags kept them warm during the short hours of semi-darkness. "My first experience of a sleeping bag," John Hunter, a twenty-three-year-old biology graduate from the University of Sydney, marveled in his diary.

During those first weeks on shore, Charles Laseron, the expedition's taxidermist, witnessed a striking demonstration of Mawson's hardihood as a leader. The men had discovered that a crucial part of the hut stove was missing, and they remembered that one box had accidentally been dropped overboard during the unloading at Boat Harbour. Mawson was convinced the missing part would be found in the box. "Come on, Joe," he urged, "let us see if we can get it." ("Joe" was the nickname by which Laseron was known to his cronies.)

> Getting into the whaleboat, we pushed out from the shore. The case was clearly visible in about 6 feet of water. For some time we angled with a boathook, but without success. Presently Mawson remarked, "There is only one thing for it," and straightaway stripped off and dived over. His first effort was unsuccessful, but at a second attempt he was just able to lift it up, and I got it on board. The temperature of the sea was at the time about 30° F.— that is below the freezing point of fresh water—and the air was much colder. Ice was already forming on his body as he raced for the hut to dry himself and get into his clothes again.

Alas, the case turned out to be filled only with tins of jam. (The missing stove part was later found hidden beneath a pile of miscellaneous gear.)

The prefabricated hut had been manufactured by an Australian firm that specialized in making kits out of which wooden cottages could be assembled. The basic design was Mawson's idea, but team member Alfred Hodgeman, a twenty-six-year-old architect by trade, took charge of the finer details. Mawson's previous experience wintering over at Cape Royds dictated several of the choices for the hut plan. The building was a simple square, 24 feet to a side, with internal subdivisions to create separate cubicles or rooms. ("Not a very big room," Laseron observed of the whole hut, "when it is remembered that it had to serve as bedroom, kitchen, dining-room, and living-room for eighteen men.") Since Mawson expected snow to cover the hut through most of the winter, the only windows he called for were in the roof. Finally, the pyramid-shaped roof would extend down to only five feet off the ground, creating verandas on all four sides in which supplies could be stored, which would serve the additional purpose of helping to insulate the hut.

Since the *Aurora* had brought south another hut kit for the third base that Mawson had intended to make somewhere along the Adélie coast, he ordered that it be erected as an adjunct to the Main Base hut, sharing a common wall. That extra space would eventually serve as a multifaceted workroom. Inside the larger hut, bunks were laid out along the three walls not adjoining the workroom. A separate cubicle served as Mawson's private quarters. The dining table stretched across the center of the hut, in the least cold place. (See diagram, page 126.)

Some of the men were surprised when Mawson demanded that foundations for the hut be dynamited into the bedrock, then filled with tons of boulders. As Frank Hurley put it, "We, who were inexperienced, thought the precautions excessive." But Mawson's constant motto was "Be prepared for every contingency in Antarctica. If the worst does not come so much the better; if it does, then you are prepared." During the coming winter, the team would be deeply grateful for Mawson's foresight.

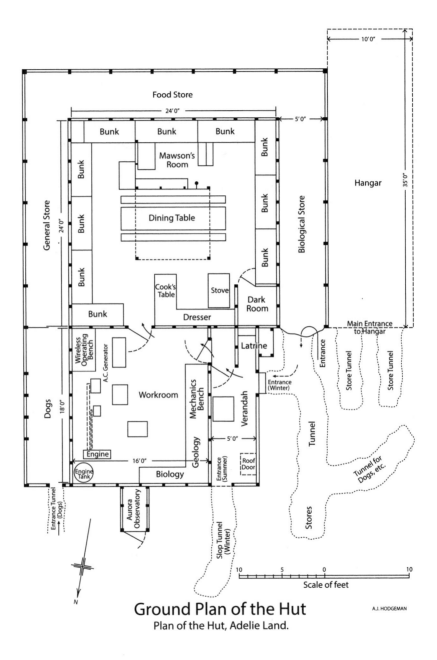

Food Store

Bunk

Bunk

Bunk

Mawson's Room

Bunk

Hangar

Bunk

Bunk

General Store

Bunk

Dining Table

Bunk

Biological Store

Bunk

Bunk

Bunk

Cook's Table

Stove

Dark Room

Bunk

Dresser

Wireless Operating Bench

Latrine

Main Entrance to Hangar

Entrance

A.C. Generator

Dogs

Workroom

Mechanics Bench

Entrance (Winter)

Store Tunnel

Store Tunnel

Geology

Verandah

Tunnel

Engine

Biology

Entrance (Summer)

Roof Door

Tunnel for Dogs, etc.

Engine Tank

Entrance Tunnel (Dogs)

Aurora Observatory

Slop Tunnel (Winter)

Stores

N

10   5   0   10
Scale of feet

Ground Plan of the Hut
Plan of the Hut, Adelie Land.

A.J. HODGEMAN

The construction of the hut produced its share of semicomic episodes. Hurley recalled one:

> Doctor Mertz was sitting astride the outer ridge cap [of the roof], nailing it down, and the learned bacteriologist, Doctor McLean, was "tacking" on the thin ceiling lining with four-inch nails directly beneath.
>
> Suddenly Mertz sprang into the air with a wild yell, lost his balance,—slid down the sloping splintery roof, clutched a stay that held the kitchen stove pipe and took the chimney with him in a headlong dive into a snow dump. . . .
>
> Investigation displayed two inches of bristling nail which had been driven through the ridge cap by the scientist below, and had caused the puncture which the aggrieved Mertz was rubbing.

On January 30, for the first time, all the men slept inside the nearly completed hut. As in the BAE hut during 1908, the various clusters of bunkmates and working quarters earned ironic nicknames. Frank Bickerton, the twenty-two-year-old Englishman whose main job was to care for the air-tractor, slept under the bunk of the Swiss ski expert Xavier Mertz; in recognition of the European flavor of that sector, Ninnis nicknamed it Hyde Park Corner. The doctor, Archibald McLean, commanded a lab table dubbed St. George's Hospital. Frank Hurley had his own darkroom, where, in his words, "By the light of the ruby lamp not only was the latent photographic image rocked into reality but latent wit was cradled into song." Already emerging as the team's practical joker, Hurley lent the darkroom to others bent on playful mischief. "It served as a lair," he later wrote, "in whose concealment surprises might be prepared. From its shuttered precincts the chef would emerge ceremoniously holding aloft some culinary triumph, or the grotesquely garbed actors of 'The Its Society for the Prevention of the Blues' would step forth dramatically into the acetylene glare to perform their latest farce amidst uproarious applause." As this passage indicates, amateur theatricals inside the hut sporadically enlivened the gloom.

Not all the bunk pairings were congenial ones. About Walter Hannam, the portly radio operator, one teammate wrote, "Hannam is our 'Ring Snorer.' Baby Bliss as we call him snores practically all night; in fact one night he was so bad that [Herbert Dyce] Murphy who sleeps next to him shifted his bunk to the little hut." Two of the men regularly talked in their sleep. Bickerton, in fact, was capable of keeping up his unconscious chatter "all night almost continuously."

In keeping with the egalitarian ethos that prevailed among the team, each member took his turn cooking, washing up, cleaning the hut, and gathering ice and snow for drinking water. Mawson himself put in his hand as cook, though, characteristically, he was unwilling to acknowledge his occasional blunders. As Laseron recalled:

> The first day that the stove was in commission he said to me, "Joe, come here and I will show you how to make blancmange."
>
> I looked on for a while and the Doctor explained the process, until, happening to look at a packet, I remarked: "Why, here are the directions on the packet."
>
> "Oh, yes," remarked the Doctor airily, "those are what I am following, but what is most important is the technique of the thing."
>
> Later, when the blancmange wouldn't set, the Doctor discovered that instead of boiling it for ten minutes, as the directions stated, he had simply brought the stuff to boil. Hannam came to the rescue with some cornflour and made a good job of it.

As the months wore on, four of the men, including Hannam and Laseron, who considered their culinary efforts as rising to a higher standard than the others', formed the Secret Society of Unconventional Cooks. The others were "class[ed] under the plebeian stigma of 'crook cooks.' " If one of these unfortunates managed to produce a "worthy dish," he was elevated to the Secret Society. "But even to the end there were a few who still ranked as 'crook cooks,' and even gloried in the title."

Nearly a century's legacy of overwinterings, first in the Arctic, then in the Antarctic, had taught explorers the essential value of keeping men busy and entertained during their long confinement through the darker months. On the AAE, reading out loud became a regular evening diversion, with Mawson usually taking the rostrum. His favorite poet, Robert Service, filled many a stirring recital. After hearing Mawson declaim "The Cremation of Sam McGee," McLean wrote in his diary, "The rest [of the poems] were realistic, virile, full of strong, manly life, like Mawson himself." Another of Mawson's favorite works was Robert Louis Stevenson's "Virginibus Puerisque," his tongue-in-cheek essay about the rewards and hazards of marriage.

The small library Mawson brought with him on the expedition included not only several volumes of Service, but Kipling's *Barrack-Room Ballads* and *Departmental Ditties* as well as *The Oxford Book of Verse*. Inspirational reading ranged from Marcus Aurelius's *Meditations* to such now-forgotten tomes as *Daily Light* and *Bible Talks*. The collection also comprised a generous store of Arctic and Antarctic narratives, including those by Shackleton, Fridtjof Nansen, and Otto Nordenskjöld. As evidence of Mawson's eagerness to connect with his men, the library contained a volume titled *German Self Taught*—perhaps a token of the leader's effort to go halfway linguistically with Xavier Mertz.

Like other Antarctic expeditions, the AAE had brought along a gramophone and a hefty supply of recordings. Of an evening, music could be even more soothing than Mawson's poetry readings. Wrote John Hunter on January 30:

I have always thought the gramophone an awful instrument, only fit for the rubbish heap, but to night it seemed quite different. As the gramophone played old familiar tunes, old memories were revived & every one seemed happy & contented. When we turned in at 11:45 we thought that after all the life of a polar explorer is not such a bad one.

Another source of entertainment for the hut-bound explorers was the coining of nicknames for one another. Some were mere shorthand, such as Madi for Cecil Madigan. Archibald McLean was called Dad for the simple reason that he tended to address everyone else as Dad. Other nicknames for the physician were Gee Whiz and Crusty. Eric Webb, the meteorologist from New Zealand, went by Azi, after the azimuth he wielded to measure celestial angles. Hurley became Hoyle, because of his penchant for interjecting the qualifier "according to Hoyle" in his utterances. The architect Alfred Hodgeman was addressed as Uncle Alfy and Bouncing Bertie. Bob Bage, a twenty-three-year-old engineering graduate—"the most popular man of the party," according to one teammate—earned the sobriquets of the Gadget King and Baldy Bob. Though generally affectionate, the nicknames could verge on the cruel. The overweight Walter Hannam was not only Baby Bliss but the Fat Boy. The twenty-nine-year-old medical student Leslie Whetter, clumsy and inclined to indolence, was sometimes called Error. As mentioned in the first chapter, Belgrave Ninnis became Cherub, because of his youthful looks, and Mertz was reduced to X because his teammates found "Xavier" all but unpronounceable.

The manufacture of nicknames could take on a baroque intricacy. In reference to the forty-year-old ex-military officer John Close, Laseron explicated:

> Close was a great reader of Nansen, and quoted him repeatedly. Nansen, under extreme conditions, had acquired a taste for raw seal blubber, so Close perforce had to try it, and pronounced it excellent, though we all noticed he did not tackle it again. From this grew the legend that he had an inordinate appetite, and was capable of devouring seals and penguins alive. As a result he was variously known as "Hollow-leg" or "Terror."

Of the thirty-eight huskies that had been shipped aboard the *Aurora* in Australia, only twenty-eight had survived the voyage to Cape Denison. Mawson kept nineteen for the Main Base, sending the other nine along with Frank Wild's crew to establish the Western Base. While the men were building their hut in Boat Harbour, the dogs were kept chained to rocks near the construction site. As they had ever since boarding the *Aurora* in London, Ninnis and Mertz cared for the animals they had come to love. Fed on fresh seal meat, the animals began to recover from the tribulations of their voyage south. They had, wrote Mawson, "an odd assemblage of names, which seemed to grow into them until nothing else was so suitable." Those names included Caruso, Pavlova, Grandmother, Gadget, and Ginger Bitch (not to be confused with Ginger). The lead dog was Basilisk; his second, Shackleton.

Charles Laseron left a memorable vignette of the dominant husky:

Basilisk was the king of the pack. He was a fine, dignified old chap, and carried himself with a certain air of responsibility. Yet he loved to romp, and would play like a puppy with any of the chaps. He was not the largest dog by any means, but quick as lightning when it came to a scrap. He ruled very strictly, and never allowed promiscuous fighting among the others.

By early autumn, besides the two conjoined huts, Mawson's team had built several other structures. On top of small rocky promontories about 300 yards northeast of the huts, the men put together what they called a magnetograph house and an absolute magnetic hut. Both were designed to measure the shape and fluctuations of the Earth's magnetic field, the province of Eric Webb's researches. The distance from the main buildings was required by the fact that nearly all nearby metal objects could distort the readings; for the construction of these stations, only copper nails could be used.

On Anemometer Hill, another promontory about 150 yards due east of the huts, the team put up sunshine and wind-speed gauges. Much closer to the huts, the men struggled to erect the wireless masts that would be essential to radio communication with Macquarie Island, 1,100 miles away. The masts were each made of four separate poles to be fixed end to end. Walter Hannam was to be in charge of this vital operation; in the end, no aspect of the AAE's fieldwork would prove more vexing than this endeavor.

During the first months at Cape Denison, Mawson had high hopes not only for a good start on the party's scientific programs but for sledging reconnaissances up the steady snow-packed incline leading to the polar plateau that stretched to the south. The setbacks of February and March, however, drove him beyond frustration, to an edge as close to despair as a man of his willful optimism could tolerate.

The problem was wind.

The glorious, sunny calm of the day the men discovered Boat Harbour was only a cruel climatic tease. During the rest of January, the norm was strong winds, blowing usually from the south or southeast off the high, invisible ice cap. No matter how well-built the hut, engineered so cleverly to withstand both snow and wind, the gales took their toll. During the days when the men had constructed the shelter, at least no snow fell, but, as Laseron recalled:

> On the very first night we slept in the hut it snowed hard, and Murphy, whose bunk was nearest the door, woke to find himself covered with a mantle of white. . . . In the high winds it was indeed hard to keep the snow out. Though the walls of the hut were double, with a layer of malthoid [felt] between, the wind found almost imperceptible cracks and forced the fine drift through. Much of our leisure was spent at this time in pasting newspaper, nailing slats or otherwise repairing the weak places above our bunks.

The stove inside the hut burned continuously, consuming 100 pounds of coal per day. Even so, until nearly all the chinks in the walls had been plugged, it was hard to keep the inside temperature as high as 40 degrees Fahrenheit; one morning, Mawson recorded 19 degrees.

February, if possible, was even windier. Steady gales were some-times punctuated by furious blasts. As Mawson later wrote:

One evening, when we were all at dinner, there was a sudden noise which drowned the rush of the blizzard. It was found that several sledges had been blown away from their comparatively secure positions to the south of the hut, striking the building as they passed. They were all rescued except one, which had already reached the sea and was travelling rapidly toward Australia.

Basing his experience on the winter of 1908, which he had spent at Cape Royds, Mawson was convinced that the February weather was abnormal. He told his men that conditions would soon improve. As Walter Hannam wrote in his diary, "The Doctor says that the snow or wind are not so bad in the winter. So things wont be so bad."

In high winds, erecting the radio masts was impossible, and work of any kind outside the hut could be perilous. In his diary, Mawson recorded a solo jaunt to the meteorological screen, located only forty yards from the hut, in the teeth of an 80 mph wind. "I had to go on all fours to read the screen. In getting a slab of blubber for the fire I was knocked over eight times and quite exhausted on arrival at the Hut door."

For Hurley, photographing in such conditions was trying in the extreme, but he was determined to capture the blizzards not only in his camera but on motion-picture film. He later recalled the ordeal:

To illustrate the pace and force of the wind I built a shelter from blocks of ice, and under its lee photographed the meteorologists as they fought their way to and from the recording instruments. . . . Frequently my fingers, which I had to withdraw from the mitt to turn the handle of the cinema camera, were frostbitten, and often, in moving from point to point, I was swept away by fierce gusts. On one occasion, when the wind attained a velocity of 120 miles an hour, I was lifted bodily, carried some fifteen yards with my camera and tripod which together weighed 80 pounds and dumped on the rocks.

According to Laseron, the men initially found it impossible to walk in a wind as strong as 60 mph; instead, they crawled on all fours.

Then with practice we learned the knack of wind-walking, leaning always at an angle and bracing our feet against every projecting piece of rock and ice. In this way we could walk against a 70-miler, and could stand against 80, but when 90 and 100 miles were reached we gave up, and were content to wriggle about like snakes.

Several of Hurley's photos illustrate the arcane art of wind-walking (see photo insert 2, plate 11). They are images the likes of which had never before been captured in the Antarctic. Because of the wind, the men began to wear crampons—sets of sharp metal spikes strapped to the sole of the boot—whenever they ventured very far from the hut.

All the men trusted Mawson's promise that the weather would improve with the coming of winter. "Day by day throughout March," wrote Laseron, "we looked forward to the calmer days that were to come, and it was well, perhaps, that we were spared the knowledge that this was but a foretaste of what was ahead." By the end of March, the anemometer readings proved that the average velocity of the wind throughout the month, hour by hour, day and night, was 49 mph—a measurement that "for a sustained velocity, was almost inconceivable, and far exceeded all world records." During several consecutive days, the wind never dropped below 70 mph.

In such wind, with the cold increasing at the end of summer, the dogs could no longer be kept leashed to rocks. Set loose, they gravitated toward the shelter of the verandas surrounding the hut. Sometimes, as the huskies ventured abroad, they would take momentary refuge in the lee of any large object they could find. "In such a position," wrote Mawson, "they were soon completely buried and oblivious to the outside elements. Thus one would sometimes tread on a dog, hidden beneath the snow; and the dog often showed less surprise than the offending man." Oblivious, perhaps—but occasionally the hair of a hunkered-down dog froze to the ice, and the poor beast had to be chipped loose with an ice ax.

The men also observed another husky ploy for staying warm. If a string of dogs was out walking with an explorer, then "No sooner would one halt for some purpose or another than all the dogs would squat down in a line, each in the lee of the other. As soon as number one realized he was being made a screen he got up and trotted around to the back. A moment later number two would follow him, and so on."

During the first month and a half at Cape Denison, the vital whale boat was kept moored to an ice cliff in the harbor. Fearful for its safety, Mawson decided to haul the boat out of the water and store it on land for the winter. On March 12, he dispatched Cecil Madigan to perform this errand, but the man returned to the hut to report that the boat had disappeared. "It was no fault of the rope-attachments," commented Mawson, "for they were securely made, and so we were left to conclude that a great mass of ice had broken away from the overhanging shelf and carried everything before it."

The loss of the whale boat and, before that, of one of the sledges instilled in the men the fear that any object that was not tied or weighted down could be carried off by a gale. Despite the men's precautions, Mawson wrote:

> Articles of value were occasionally missed. They were usually recovered, caught in crevices of rock or amongst the broken ice. Northward from the Hut there was a trail of miscellaneous objects scattered among the hummocks and pressure-ridges . . . tins of all kinds and sizes, timber in small scraps, cases and boards, paper, ashes, dirt, worn-out finnesko, ragged mitts and all the other details of a rubbish heap.

Even more disconcerting than the raging gales were the whirlies— "whirlwinds of a few yards to a hundred yards or more in diameter."

These freakish tempests would alternate with local lulls, over which the continuous roar of distant wind sounded like a ground bass. About the whirlies, Mawson wrote, "woe betide any light object that came in their path. The velocity of the wind in the rotating column being very great, a corresponding lifting power was imparted to it." One whirly lifted the lid of the air-tractor case, which weighed 330 pounds, into the air, then deposited it 50 yards away. An hour later, a second whirly returned the massive plank to its original position, shattering it in the process.

The winds were so constant that the rare, brief episodes of dead calm had a hallucinatory effect on the men.

> On such occasions the auditory sense was strangely affected. The contrast was so severe when the racking gusts of an abating wind suddenly gave way to intense, eerie silence that the habitual droning of many weeks would still reverberate in the ears. At night one would involuntarily wake up if the wind died away and be loth to sleep "for the hunger of a sound."

Mawson had hoped to make substantial sledging reconnaissances inland in the months of February and March, to scout the terrain upon which the next summer's journeys would unfold, but the weather severely limited his ambitions. On February 29, he took five men and hauled a sledge up the snow ramp that backed the hut. They traveled only a mile, gaining 500 feet of altitude, before the wind forced them to leave the sledge and head back to the hut. The next day, Mawson and two of the men returned, harnessed themselves to the sledge, and pushed on to a point five and a half miles from the hut, at 1,500 feet of altitude, where they planted a marker flag and installed a thermograph to measure temperatures during the coming months.

They camped there, at the spot that would come to be called 5-mile Depot, before returning to the hut the next day. Mawson's diary laconically noted the vicissitudes of the trip: "Heavy pulling, drift, could not eat our fill of hoosh. . . . Madigan almost fell down a nasty crevasse on the way back. We are more wary now." But that evening, according to Eric Webb, Mawson shared his pessimism with the whole team. "I have never met such conditions of wind & temperature before," he said at dinner. "You chaps know as much about it as I do so just get on with it!" Webb later recalled that Mawson's speech "both shook & stimulated us."

Indeed, life in the near vicinity of the hut could be hazardous enough. Frank Hurley had a very close call when, in a brief lull of relatively good weather, he ventured alone out onto sea ice that had recently formed to take pictures of otherwise inaccessible sea cliffs.

> I had just erected my camera, when, without warning, the ice gave way beneath me. In an instant I was floundering in the sea. I threw my arms out, and saved myself from being swept beneath the ice, but the thin sheet, once fractured, would no more than barely support me, and broke every time I tried to climb out.
>
> My predicament was desperate. I was two miles away from Winter Quarters and there was no help. The suck of the current was dragging me beneath the ice. . . . My muscles were contracting and my limbs growing numb. Fortunately I espied a heavy piece of ice that had fallen from the cliffs and was frozen in some fifteen yards ahead. Pushing my camera along on the ice, I broke my way towards it. By good fortune I found a hand-grip, and laboriously I drew myself out—a half frozen, but a wholly wiser, man.

Hurley was still not out of trouble. While he was floundering in the water, the wind had intensified, and the sea ice was breaking up and being pushed away from shore. "I went for dear life across the thin ice as fast as my stiffly frozen garments would permit," he later wrote. Just as he reached the rocky shore, the ice broke completely and flowed fast out to the open sea. As he hurried back to the hut, "My clothes were like armour; my trousers like stovepipes. But if I expected condolences, I got none. I was received with ironical cheers and much persiflage from my comrades who had little sympathy for my recklessness."

On another occasion, Alfred Hodgeman and Cecil Madigan left the hut in a blizzard for a routine visit to read the anemometer, a mere 150 yards away. As Mawson later recounted the event:

> Leaving the door of the Hut, they lost sight of each other at once, but anticipated meeting at the instrument. Madigan reached his destination, changed the records, waited for a while and then returned, expecting to see his companion at the Hut. He did not appear, so, after a reasonable interval, search-parties set off in different directions.
>
> The wind was blowing at eighty miles per hour, making it tedious work groping about and hallooing in the drift. The sea was close at hand and we realized that, as the wind was directly off shore, a man without crampons was in a dangerous situation. Two men, therefore, roped together and carefully searched round the head of Boat Harbour; one anchoring himself with an ice-axe, whilst the other, at the end of the rope, worked along the edge of the sea. Meanwhile Hodgeman returned to the Hut, unaided, having spent a very unpleasant two hours struggling from one landmark to another, his outer garments filled with snow.

Like Hurley upon his return from his dunking in the sea, Hodgeman was greeted by his teammates with more jeering than sympathy. Laseron wrote in his diary, "Poor Hodgeman will never hear the end of it, though it might well have been serious."

By the end of March, most of the penguins, so numerous in January, had fled north to their winter breeding grounds on sea ice. Likewise the seals, "no doubt disgusted with the continuous winds," Mawson fancied. "Every one that came near was shot for food."

By the beginning of April, Mawson realized that his prediction of better weather in the coming winter was not likely to be fulfilled. For some unfathomable reason, the climate of Cape Denison and Commonwealth Bay was utterly different from that of McMurdo Sound.

In the most famous passage in his narrative of the AAE, he voiced his glum verdict:

> We dwelt on the fringe of an unspanned continent, where the chill breath of a vast, polar wilderness, quickening to the rushing might of eternal blizzards, surged to the northern seas. We had discovered an accursed country. We had found the Home of the Blizzard.

Mawson and his teammates were convinced that, through sheer bad luck, they had established their Main Base in the windiest place on earth. Eighty-five years later, an international team of geophysicists would validate that hunch. The area around Cape Denison, they proved, was indeed the windiest place on earth, at least at sea level. (There are no year-round meteorological stations in places such as the summits of Mount Everest and K2.)

As winter crept over the continent, there was little for the men to do but while away the time. Mawson insisted on hard and steady work, which included hiking out to the various recording stations every day, no matter what the conditions, to record the data. Inside the hut, despite the egalitarian rotation of jobs, a quasi-military regimen obtained. Every morning precisely at 7:45, a "rise and shine" call would wake the men. Fifteen minutes later, with the ringing of a bell, breakfast was served, as the men all sat along the long, narrow table in the center of the hut. Lunch was served at 1 p.m., dinner at 6:30.

The duties of the cook, the messman (who assisted and cleaned up after the cook), and the night watchman were not simply passed on by word of mouth; typed instructions adorned the hut walls. The fussiness of these formulas testifies to Mawson's penchant for order in the tiniest of details. The night watchman, who served from 8 p.m. to 8 a.m., had as his main job keeping the fire going in the stove. But he was also charged as follows:

The nightwatchman is to sift the ashes accumulated during the day and burn them in conjunction with the blubber during the night. Coal should be used only after the cinders have been burnt. . . .

Any mess which the nightwatchman may have made is to be cleared away before 7 a.m.

The least pleasant of the messman's chores was spelled out in another typed notice: "A final duty is that of emptying the round-house box which will be effected into the sea until freezing of the bay waters renders it no longer possible." The "round-house box," of course, was the communal toilet.

As always with men confined under uncomfortable circumstances, life revolved around food. A "Cook's Notice" posted on the wall struck a note of mock formality, as if it were the bill of fare of a posh restaurant:

The "pièce de résistance" of dinner shall be as follows:—
Monday—Penguin,
Tuesday—Seal,
Wednesday—Canned meats,
Thursday—Penguin,
Friday—Seal,
Saturday—Variable,
Sunday—Mutton.

With eighteen men taking their places at the long table, meals took on the air of a festive ritual. As Mawson wrote:

No unnecessary refinements were indulged in, for example, should one desire some comestible, jam for instance, out of arm's reach it was quite *de rigueur* to call out, "Give the jam a fair wind," upon which it would commence travelling down the table in the right direction, often, however, very haltingly as it was fair game for anybody along its track who would exclaim, "on the way!"

On those occasions when a bit of wine or liquor was served with dinner, toasts echoed around the table. The most frequently uttered was "To our sweethearts and wives—may they never meet."

Decades later, Laseron could remember some of the midwinter dinners in the hut in exquisite detail. As he wrote in 1947:

> Dinner is ready, and the cook has done himself justice. No "crook cook" this, but one of the elite. The soup has not come from tins, but a ham bone, saved for the occasion, and with dried vegetables, a little emergency ration and other trimmings, it is tasty and hot. The soup finished, the cook gives the order, "Pass bowls and lick spoons." This is necessary, as spoons are short, and must serve for the pudding course. Fried breasts of penguins come next, in appearance not unlike very dark beef and, if carefully cleaned of all blubber, quite palatable. Next is the prize piece, baked jam roly-poly, nicely browned, light as a feather, and sizzling from the oven. There are loud cheers, for the cook has excelled himself. Dessert, figs or sweets, and coffee follow, pipes and cigarettes are lit, and a haze of smoke fills the hut.

The two most precious rations for the members of the AAE were tobacco and chocolate. The monthly issue for each man was two tins of loose tobacco and one tin of cigarettes. Mawson was one of the very few members who did not smoke. Every Saturday night, each man was also issued thirty squares of chocolate. These became the men's betting and bargaining chips, as well as their favorite sweet. The most spirited wagers came in a "calcutta sweep" on the first of each month, when the average wind velocity for the previous month would be calculated. On May 1, for instance, papers with numbers ranging from 40 to 55 were put on the table, as each man laid down two squares of chocolate for each number he bet on. When the average velocity for April turned out to be 52 mph, Bob Bage won a fortune consisting of 150 chocolate squares.

Bathing was a rare luxury. "No one washes, except in dire necessity," remembered Laseron, "the cook guards his supply of water too zealously for that; there is no shaving, so the morning toilet is only a matter of a few minutes." This was not strictly true. Every few weeks or months, a man might take a sponge bath in a folding canvas tub deployed within the hut. On March 15, after bathing for the first time since leaving Hobart, John Hunter confessed almost guiltily to his diary, "Three months without a bath seems quite a long time & if one did this in civilization he would be shunned by his friends." In the same vein, the portly radio operator, Walter Hannam: "Tonight I have had a ripping hot bath which is the first since I left Hobart ten weeks ago. I feel clean and a bit sleepy."

It was inevitable that confinement together would drive the men to buffoonery and elaborate pranks. Sometimes the AAE hijinks conjured up the Edwardian equivalent of a modern-day fraternity house. John Hunter recorded the pitched battles fought between the west end of the hut and the east end, with weapons ranging from sleeping bags and blankets to pots of water. Frank Hurley was "the life and soul of the party," according to Laseron. "He acts the giddy goat better than anyone I know." On March 18, "Hurley caused some amusement by putting a dead penguin in Archie McLean's bed." Hurley's jests could take on elaborate dimensions. Early on, after the forty-year-old ex-military officer John Close (who would become the butt of many of his teammates' jokes) killed a Weddell seal but recounted the battle in rather too heroic tones, his deed provoked a full-blown Hurley charade.

> On February 17, after dinner, the Doctor introduced Hurley to the gathering, and said that Hurley had an announcement to make. Hurley, for the occasion, had donned an old football jersey and a pair of pants over his Antarctic clothes, and with an old straw hat he looked a typical bottle-oh! In a rather rambling speech, with much studied and picturesque metaphor, he presented a medal, made of aluminum in the form of a cross and suitably inscribed. On the obverse it bore the words "For Valour" . . . and on the reverse, "*Bravado Killus Terror Weddelli Sealus Pro Bono Publichouso.*"

Hurley also had the gift of a raconteur. Wrote John Hunter on March 10, "At dinner Hurley . . . amused us by telling us stories of all his love affairs,—or how he has been jilted 26 times."

Hurley, however, was not the master raconteur among the team. That honor fell to Herbert Dyce Murphy, who had the most varied and bizarre background of all the members Mawson chose for his party. Thirty-two years old, from an affluent Australian sheep-raising family, with a year at Oxford on his résumé, Murphy claimed on his application that he had "been three times in the Arctic," had "done some dog driving in Northern Siberia and am accustomed to boat handling of all sorts at sea and in ice."

Taking Murphy at his word, Mawson initially planned for the man to lead the third base party on the Adélie coast, but after that part of the program had to be scrapped, Murphy, to his great disappointment, was relegated to a subsidiary role on the AAE. What Mawson probably did not know about Murphy was that he had dressed as a woman for years and acted in plays in drag, one of which prompted British intelligence to enlist him as a cross-dressing spy in western Europe during the years before World War I. By now, two biographies have filled out the flamboyant and eccentric career and life of Murphy, but in a man so gifted at telling stories about himself, separating fact from fiction is no easy matter.

His teammates in Winter Quarters valued Murphy chiefly as a spinner of tales. Laseron left a memorable encomium on the man. After dinner, as the cook clears the dishes, someone says, "What about a yarn, Herbert?"

Herbert fidgets, looks nervously at the speaker, and deprecates his ability to tell anything that had not already been told. There is a general chorus: "Go on, Herbert, tell us about Siberia, or Melbourne, or a visit to an English country house, or Cambridge, or anything you like." So Herbert, importuned from every side, and with a diffident little cough, begins rather haltingly. A small boy or a dog comes into the tale, a sure sign of inspiration, and he brightens. He tells of social life in Melbourne, of one of his friends who proposed to two girls in one evening, and of how both accepted him, and of the complications that followed. From this he wanders to scandals in high places, hair-raising scandals with lurid details. . . . His stories have a curious suggestion of truth; they are convincing and at the same time too impossible to be true. For Herbert is a genius, who from an ounce of fact can manufacture a mountain of entertainment. For an hour we rock with laughter.

Along with the gramophone, for music the team had an impromptu "Adélie band" exhibiting the talents of several members. The instruments were "piccolo, drum, fistagophone (Hurley's invention), and mouth organ, etc." Each man's birthday was celebrated with pomp and gifts. On March 27, Archibald McLean wrote in his log, "Today is best described in other people's diaries, being my Birthday. Many and various were the presents, and the worst ordeals were after-breakfast and after-dinner speeches." The men also celebrated the king's birthday on June 3, and made a grand occasion of Midwinter's Day, for June 21 marked the beginning of the imperceptible return of the sun, as each day grew longer by a few minutes. In his diary, Mawson recorded the special breakfast and lunch served up, each an hour later than normal:

Breakfast, 9 am   Cocoa
Bacon and eggs
Real bread
Honey, marmalade, butter.

Lunch, 2 pm   Tea
Veget-cheeze & Soda biscuits
Cherry cake
Bacon ration
Real bread
Honey, jam, marmalade, butter.

Though he did not record the dinner menu, Mawson later fondly recalled that the meal "was a marvel of gorgeous delicacies. After the toasts and speeches came a musical and dramatic programme, punctuated by choice choruses." Outside the hut, the wind blew at a steady 95 mph.

Seizing the flimsiest excuse to celebrate, as well as greeting unusual incidents with raucous ribaldry, did much to alleviate the grueling monotony of winter at Cape Denison. Whenever a team-mate committed a gaffe or a blunder, the hut reverberated with the cry, "Championship!" As Mawson explicated:

> "Championship" was a term evolved from the local dialect, apply-ing to a slight mishap, careless accident or unintentional disaster in any department of hut life. The fall of a dozen plates from the shelf to the floor, the fracture of a table-knife in frozen honey, the burning of the porridge or the explosion of a tin thawing in the oven brought down on the unfortunate cook a storm of derisive applause and shouts of "Championship! Championship!"

Yet for all the morale-boosting the men effected with their pranks and rituals, there was no ignoring the fact that wind was the central fact of their existence. The men's diaries often lapsed into entries veering between incredulity and despair. "I don't know what we should do if we have a year of it," wrote John Hunter early on, "for our scientific work is at a standstill." "How the infernal wind rages! Will it ever stop," Laseron inveighed after months of enduring it. Walter Hannam opened his diary entry many times with a three-word summation: "Another rotten day." Mawson himself began his diary jotting on three successive days in late April thus: "Blizzard, blowing hard." "Strong blizzard." "Strong blizzard."

During a rare lull in February, Xavier Mertz demonstrated the art of skiing, as he tried to teach the men, all of whom were novices, the art of which he was a master. The results were predictably ludi-crous. His teammates preferred to use the sledges for impromptu toboggan runs on a slope just above the hut—"an exhilarating if somewhat dangerous pastime," Laseron admitted.

> On the hard ice it was practically impossible to steer, and just as difficult to pull up. We generally picked a spot where a mound of hard snow made a terminus, arriving at which we all fell off, though sometimes we would lose a passenger or two en route. One day the sledge bolted with us completely, and charged a heap of benzine cases that formed a breakwind for a shaft in the ice. It was a terrific crash, and the corner runner went completely through two of the cases.

Fortunately, none of the four men was injured. For obvious reasons—the chance of damaging a vital sledge or of seriously injuring an equally vital teammate—Mawson tried to discourage tobogganing, to no avail.

Because of the wind, chores that would normally have been routine turned into mini-ordeals. The visits to the Magnetograph House, the Absolute Hut, and Anemometer Hill were the most arduous of the daily tasks. Often the men taking the readings would return to the hut with the burberry hoods of their jackets frozen into what the men called an "ice mask."

> This adhered firmly to the helmet and to the beard and face; though not particularly comfortable, it was actually a protection against the wind. The mask became so complete that one had continually to break it away in order to breathe and to clear away obstructions from the eyes. . . . An experienced man, once inside the Hut, would first see that the ice was broken away from the helmet; otherwise, when it came to be hastily dragged off, the hairs of the beard would follow as well.

Hurley captured some memorable portraits of teammates "wearing" their ice masks (see photo insert 3, plate 1). Despite the best precautions, the men sometimes suffered superficial frostbite of the face during their brief excursions to the scientific stations. Cecil Madigan "was once observed by an amused audience toying with a lifeless cheek endeavouring to remove it under the impression that it was ice."

Of all the crucial tasks facing the AAE during the autumn and winter of 2012, by far the most frustrating was the effort to erect the pair of radio masts, the key to communicating with Macquarie Island and thus, via relay, with Australia. The masts had been shipped aboard the *Aurora* in sections that on land needed to be fitted end-to-end to make a composite tower a full 120 feet in height. But the wind played havoc with the men's best efforts to plant anchors, attach guy wires, and get the masts up. By the end of April, two sections of each mast had been fixed in place. Walter Hannam, whose principal reason for being chosen for the expedition had been to operate the radio, was initially optimistic. In early April, he wrote in his diary, "Given a few days of weather like today (delightful) the first message ought to be through by the end of the week."

In the wind, the construction project proved so dangerous that Mawson decided not to attempt to affix the topmost section of each tower. It was not until late July that a third pole was affixed on top of the northern mast. Even this was a risky undertaking, requiring a man to be hoisted aloft to work like a telephone repairman. Because of his weight—by early July, he admitted to his diary that he weighed "something over 17 stone at present" (at least 240 pounds)—Hannam could not perform the aerial work. Instead it fell to the mechanically gifted Frank Bickerton (the man in charge of tinkering with the air-tractor), who spent three and a half hours on a bitterly cold July 26, in a 30 mph wind, wrestling the third section of the northern mast into place.

Hannam's diary entries, laconic and brief to begin with, grew more and more dispirited. He recorded his sporadic bouts of overeating ("Had a very bad turn of billiousness [sic] with good deal of vomiting caused through eating sardines"), and admitted to feeling sleepy all the time, a condition he attributed to the Antarctic air. His most oft-repeated one-line entry, besides "Another rotten day," was "Asleep most of day." On May 15, Mawson told Hannam that he doubted that the radio masts would be up and working before October.

Meanwhile, on Macquarie Island, the five-man team under George Ainsworth had been having their own troubles with their radio masts, being forced to repair them frequently after winds threatened to break their supports or snap them in half. But on February 14, they established radio contact with Sydney. The linkage worked so well that the men on the lonely island were furnished with news from home such as the victory of a horse named Piastre in the Melbourne Cup—"but as this was the first we had heard of the animal," Ainsworth wryly noted, "nobody seemed much interested."

From Antarctica, however, the Macquarie men heard nothing but silence, and they grew increasingly anxious about the fate of Mawson's team. It was not until September 12 that a single faint message arrived from Adélie Land. The Macquarie operator could make out only the cryptic words, "Please inform Pennant Hills." The man tried for hours to radio back, but got no answer. "Every effort was made to get in touch with them from this time forward," Ainsworth later wrote, "[Arthur] Sawyer remaining at the instrument until daylight every morning."

On October 13, dubbed "Black Sunday" by Hannam, a particularly ferocious gust completely leveled the north radio mast. The collapse made such a crashing sound that the men inside the hut at first thought that part of the roof had been torn away. On inspecting the wreckage, the men discovered the taller mast smashed to pieces, with the southern, half-completed mast looking as if it might topple at any minute. "With all the timbers broken up thus has gone our last hope of wireless communication," concluded Mawson. "It has been a long and steady job all the winter, the operation being conducted under the most adverse circumstances—and to end like this!"

The wind record kept so faithfully throughout 1912 by the men at Cape Denison stands as a stunning monument to their year-long ordeal by blizzard. Perhaps its cruelest aspect was that the winds only got stronger during the winter. Between March and October, no month recorded an average of less than 49 mph, while May—one of the darkest and coldest months of the Antarctic year—gauged the worst. In May 1912, for thirty-one straight days, through twenty-four hours each day, the wind averaged 60.7 mph.

It is a tribute to the men's hardiness (and perhaps to their good luck) that for all the tribulations of that winter, none of the team suffered a serious injury, not even a bad case of frostbite. The hut they had built was so sturdy that it withstood every gale and whirly the climate could assault it with. The long, dark days of confinement could seem tedious in the extreme, but companionship forged a morale that trumped boredom and depression. In retrospect, that vigil in the "home of the blizzard" could take on for some of its participants the aura of a domestic idyll. Thus Laseron, thirty-five years later:

> The day's tasks are ended, and all amuse themselves in various ways. At one end of the table Bickerton, Hannam, Hunter and I are engaged in a game of bridge, while Madigan, Murphy and the doctor look idly on. Farther down the table sits Mertz, choosing a record for the gramophone, while Bage, with his favourite old pipe, its stem mended with adhesive tape, offers his advice. Stillwell is reading a book, and Close is writing something in his diary. Lying on his bunk, Whetter has his nose in a medical treatise, and on the other side of the hut Hurley, with facetious remarks, is cutting Correll's hair, and doing a job that would cause any self-respecting barber to have a fit.

Or Mawson, at the remove of only a year after the expedition:

> The whole world is asleep, except the night-watchman, and he, having made the bread, washed a tubful of clothes, kept the fire going, observed and made notes on the aurora every fifteen minutes and the weather every half-hour, and, finally, having had a bath, indulges in buttered toast and a cup of coffee.

The Hut is dark, and a shaded burner hangs by a canvas chair in the kitchen. The wind is booming in gusts, the dogs howl occasionally in the veranda, but the night-watchman and his pipe are at peace with all men. He has discarded a heavy folio for a light romance, while the hours scud by, broken only by the observations. The romance is closed, and he steals to his bunk with a hurricane lamp and finds a bundle of letters. He knows them well, but he reads them—again!

The last touch was in a real sense autobiographical. For all his enthusiasm for the expedition, Mawson badly missed his beloved Paquita. He had with him the last letters she had written before his departure, and from Cape Denison he wrote longingly to her. One note, scribbled in haste on January 19 so that it could be carried back to Australia on the *Aurora*, promised, "We have made a successful landing and I don't anticipate anything in the nature of disaster. Your wandering Dougelly will return with the Olive Branch to his haven of rest in little over a year's time." And the letter closed:

Know O'Darling that in this frozen South I can always wring happiness from my heart by thinking of your splendid self.
There is an ocean of love between us dear.
Your loving Douglas

Mawson wrote to Paquita from Winter Quarters, even while he knew that the letter was not likely to reach her before he himself did: "I have concluded, once again, that it is nice to be in love, even here in Antarctica with the focus of the heartstrings far far away. . . . Good Bye my Darling may God keep and Bless and Protect you."

The Home of the Blizzard hews strictly to the convention of the day in expedition chronicles, of keeping conflict and criticism among the members of the AAE out of sight. The practical jokes the men played on one another, the buffoonery and the jesting, supply the good-natured anecdotes that only hint at the tensions of hut life. The men, Mawson seems to imply, may have had foibles and quirks, but not real faults.

The men's diaries, however, tell a different and truer story. Among other things, they record the antagonisms that various team members sometimes felt toward their leader, but dared not voice. On September 30, for instance, John Hunter wrote, "It is one of the Doc's worst traits to speak dogmatically of subjects of which he has only a surface knowledge." Or Laseron, on February 18, "We now like [Mawson] much better than at first. This is of course all in spite of his faults, of which he undoubtedly has a good many. One of his worst is a nasty sneery way he has of saying things at times, though perhaps he doesn't mean all he says and evidently forgets it soon after."

Among all the teammates, the one most critical of Mawson was undoubtedly Cecil Madigan, but the exact nature of his complaints, and the events that provoked them, are difficult to unearth. Madigan's decision to accept the invitation to join the AAE was an understandably ambivalent one. Only twenty-three years old when he sailed on the *Aurora*, he had been Mawson's student at the University of Adelaide, where he performed so well that he was selected as the Rhodes scholar for 1911 from South Australia. Madigan had actually arrived at Oxford to begin his graduate study when he learned that Mawson had pulled strings to persuade the Rhodes trustees to defer Madigan's scholarship by a year. When one official in Oxford encouraged Madigan to join the expedition, he sailed back to Australia after only two weeks in England.

What part these machinations played in Madigan's growing resentment of his leader at Winter Quarters is hard to judge. It was Madigan who coined the taunting nickname Dux Ipse (or "The Leader Himself") for Mawson, with its overtones of self-importance and authoritarian rule. That the other men adopted it as "D. I." (though never to Mawson's face) suggests that the sentiment was widely shared.

Madigan kept a detailed diary, but during recent decades it has not been available to scholars. Its contents emerge only in paraphrase in a very curious, privately printed book called *Vixere Fortes: A Family Archive*, published in 2000 by Madigan's son, David Madigan.

(Cecil Madigan died in 1947.) If *Vixere Fortes* accurately reflects Madigan's private feelings on the AAE, the annoyance with his leader began early, while the men were still on board the *Aurora*. "Cecil had been 'Maddy' to his university friends," writes the son, "and Mawson now began addressing him by this nickname, a familiarity that he resented." At first, in Winter Quarters, Madigan's attitude toward the leader seems to have been tempered, but as the winter wore on, his disdain built. One day, according to *Vixere Fortes*, Mawson attempted to install what he called a "puffometer"—a homemade device to measure peak gusts of wind—but "with his usual clumsiness at such jobs, of which, being the leader, he could not be relieved," the machine fell apart in the wind.

Such casual aspersions seam the text of *Vixere Fortes*. Mawson's toast on the king's birthday, Madigan may have thought, was insincere, for the Dux Ipse "was as loyal as a depressed Irish tenant" to the monarchy of the United Kingdom. In general, Mawson not only demanded ceaseless hard work from the men, but "treated them like children, and if he saw anyone apparently idle for a moment he began grumbling and dropping hints, though he did scarcely anything himself." Madigan may have felt singled out by Mawson's harsh treatment:

> His temperament was naturally equable but he sometimes became very irritable and peevish and in those moods of polar depression, as they were called, he could be most unfair, scolding everybody and reproving individuals for laziness. Cecil was sometimes the victim of this treatment, which annoyed him excessively, but he endured it philosophically and in silence. Mawson accused him of neglecting the meteorology, although he scarcely had a minute free all day.

Hand in hand with resentment on Madigan's part goes contempt—at least according to the son. Mawson's character is "irremediably prosaic"; he is always "fussing about and dropping hints"; only after it was obvious to everyone else did it "dawn on Mawson that he was driving his men too hard." With the coming of spring and the first sledging journeys, Madigan's irritation with his leader only intensified.

All this must be taken with a generous dose of salt. Short of being able to read Madigan's original diary, the historian is ill-equipped to judge the veracity of *Vixere Fortes*, whose tone of escalating contempt hints at some unspoken agenda. Years after the AAE, Madigan worked for several decades as a lecturer in geology at the University of Adelaide. He was thus a junior faculty member in the department that came to be chaired by Mawson. Who knows what long-simmering academic tensions may have underlain the relationship between mentor and protégé? Or what revenge a petulant son may have tried to enact in print fifty-three years after his father's death, and forty-two after Mawson's? A possible corrective to *Vixere Fortes* is the fact that in both *The Home of the Blizzard* and in Mawson's AAE diary, he has scarcely a harsh word to say about Madigan.

Mawson's diary, not published until 1988, or thirty years after his death, is far more candid about interpersonal tensions than is *The Home of the Blizzard*. During the four months from the arrival of the *Aurora* in Hobart until the firm establishment of the team in Winter Quarters, the diary is cursory in the extreme—one-line entries spaced widely apart. During those hectic times, the leader was evidently too busy to write. Only on February 28 does he begin to record longer observations, but even these are impersonal and telegraphic. ("Hurricane gusty"; "Blizzard as usual"; "Great numbers of seals up around bay.") Logistics command all of Mawson's attention.

Then, suddenly, on May 3, Mawson writes an extended treatise on the various characters of men on Antarctic expeditions, in by far the longest passage yet consigned to the diary. Virtually no names are named, but it is clear that the Dux Ipse has been carefully observing his men and sorting out their performances. The immediate provocation is Mawson's worry that the guy ropes supporting the radio masts are chafing in the wind and are likely to sever. Hannam,

Mertz, and Ninnis immediately rush to the site to survey the damage, "but I was sorry to see that others, who were not engaged on
special work, excused themselves and one even refused to go."

Mawson's disappointment in those "others" triggers a taxonomic
analysis of the makeup of polar explorers.

> First are the accomplished and painstaking stickers who are the
> backbone of things. Give them a piece of work to do and you may
> be sure that it will be done as well as can be. . . .
>
> Then there are the mediocre people—those who are not
> really good at anything but can assist under supervision. . . .
>
> Finally there are the men who don't fit in—who can't consci-
> entiously say they are good at anything. Fortunately such a one
> is a "rara avis." It is a curious thing that men who are clumsy at
> doing things show no desire to learn.

The awkward formality of this entry suggests that Mawson still
felt the presence of some future reader looking over his shoulder. He
complains about shirkers and misfits without betraying the code of
keeping an expedition's dirty laundry under wraps. It is not until
June 4 that his vexation drives him to name "the men who don't fit
in." In Mawson's view, two of them are the worst—the forty-year-old
ex-military officer John Close and the twenty-nine-year-old medical
student Leslie Whetter. (Whetter, with Eric Webb, was one of only
two New Zealanders in the Main Base party.)

Predictably, the initial charge against Whetter was laziness:

> At breakfast Whetter asks when the winter routine is to begin.
> When I ask him what that is, he says "Oh, you said we would
> then only work half a day." This is rot. What I said was that all
> should hold themselves ready for ½ day's general work. He has
> never had more than 2 hours per day.

The next day, Mawson observed sarcastically, Whetter "bucked
up." Charged with going outside the hut to chop ice for drinking

water, he "did not stick to it long," barely collecting a day's supply for the team. "I do not think he has been overworked nor do I think he is likely to accomplish his FRCS [Fellowship of the Royal College of Surgeons]," Mawson wrote. An evening exchange provoked the leader to further ire. "He told me last night that the scientific work of the others was a pastime with them. I told him that he was the most lucky man on earth to have such a job as he had, for it kept him in good health."

During the following days, the tension between the two men grew worse. By June 11, Mawson felt outright disgust.

> Whetter was sick last night, diarrhoea. He sleeps all day today though stating that he would get up and get ice this afternoon. Whetter is not fit for a polar expedition. I wish I had minded his mother's cablegram warning me. When unloading cargo he got dizzy and had to lie up. Of late he has complained of overwork, and he only does an honest 2 hours work per day.

On June 18, matters came to a head, after Whetter refused Mawson's request to go out and retrieve frozen penguin carcasses from the veranda, claiming that he had not finished gathering ice for the men's drinking water. Mawson ordered Whetter to his private room inside the hut.

> We then had a long talk in which I showed him that he was entirely unfit for an expedition, chiefly through lack of determination in character and failing to do his level best towards the interests of the expedition. As usual he attempted to make light of all the charges and seemed to think my opinion of little value.

For a few days after this dressing-down, Whetter's performance seemed to improve, but by July, according to Mawson, he was back to his indolent ways.

What was wrong with Whetter? There are hints that he had a drinking problem, for on July 3, Mawson noted, "Whetter has apparently drunk the Port wine." Alcoholism among overwinterers in Antarctica has always been a source of dangerous friction, for on an expedition such as the AAE, wine and liquor were strictly reserved for ceremonial occasions. A man sneaking drinks from a communal supply meant to last for months was guilty of one of the more serious offenses an expedition member could commit.

Whetter's long hours of sleep and disinclination to work hard, however, hint at a deep depression. "Polar depression" was indeed a real and recurrent phenomenon during Arctic and Antarctic over-winterings. In some cases, it could threaten to wreck an expedition. On the *Belgica* expedition from 1897–99, the first to winter over in Antarctica, the leaders, Adrien de Gerlache and Georges Lecointe, grew mysteriously ill, took to their beds (on the frozen-in ship, not in a hut), and essentially gave up on life, writing their final wills. Two team members—Dr. Frederick A. Cook, later to become infamous for faking both the discovery of the North Pole and the first ascent of Mount McKinley, and Roald Amundsen, on his first polar expedition—took charge and saved the whole enterprise. The men of the AAE knew all about this Antarctic horror story, for Cook's vivid account of the expedition, *Through the First Antarctic Night*, was in the library at Winter Quarters and was read by many of Mawson's team.

Mawson was not the only one in the AAE to complain about Whetter's feckless performance. On March 22, John Hunter wrote, "Whetter of course still pursuing his usual occupation of sitting down." Three months later, Hunter elaborated, "Whetter is a conundrum; he is a big fairly strong fellow, yet is lazy; chronically so I think & there is no one the Doctor dislikes more than Whetter." And Cecil Madigan (as filtered through his son's *Vixere Fortes*) pronounced, "Whetter was incurably lazy and fearfully careless."

Mawson racked his brains trying to figure out what was going on with Whetter. On a loose sheet of paper preserved in the Mawson Collection at the South Australia Museum, he made notes to himself about the New Zealander:

He appears to have changed since joining exped—appeared willing when he arrived at first. . . .

Why did he not mention to me at lunch time that he was not well enough to get the ice in during the afternoon as arranged[?] . . .

Whetter made no bread when cook Friday June 14th. . . .

The soup so badly burnt that not-fit-to-eat. No bread—the tapioca pudding a damned disgrace. . . .

According to his own words he came on the expedition so as to have a quiet time to study—I believe he came also for his health.

This is a *criminal* matter.

On October 3, Mawson lost his patience altogether and exploded at Whetter in the most intense outburst of rage recorded by any of the eighteen men in Winter Quarters. As he summarized the confrontation in his diary,

At something to 4 pm Whetter came in, took his clothes off and intended to read a book. Before lunch I had asked him to dig out the hangar in front after getting in the ice.

I heard at 4 pm that he had not done this, and his appearance in the Hut to read a book was in direct disobedience to my orders. I was very wroth about this and asked him why he was coming in under the circumstances. He said he had done enough. I asked him what he had come on the expedition for. He said "not to do such kind of work." I said he was a "bloody fool to come on the expedition if that was the case." He said "Bloody fool yourself" and "I won't be caught on another one." I instantly told him to come into my room. I was wild but immediately calmed and talked things over with him at length in the most lenient and persuasive terms possible to try and let him see his error.

It was of little use.

By now, with the spring and summer's sledging campaign growing near, Mawson sensed a wholesale crisis looming. Having read the riot act to Whetter in his private room, that evening at dinner he felt the need to exhort the entire team with a pep talk. "I gave quite a long address," Mawson wrote in his diary, "ended by saying that the united efforts of all are required to make the expedition successful, and a successful expedition meant success to them all." Afterward, several of the men came up to the leader and pledged their support in the hard work to come.

If Whetter kept his own diary during the AAE, it has either been lost or remains in private hands. According to historian Beau Riffenburgh, little is known of Whetter's career after the AAE. He returned to a medical practice in New Zealand, and died in 1955.

The problem with John Close was not so much "polar depression" as general incompetence exacerbated by anxiety. Mawson's first diary complaint about the forty-year-old, on June 14, has to do with a botched culinary effort for which Whetter and Close shared the blame:

> Whetter cooks but makes a hopeless failure of it. At 10 to 6 pm he is asleep and the messman also. The latter, Close, has however done almost everything that had been done in the afternoon—afternoon tea, etc. They got kerosene in the water tanks, soup hopelessly burned. No water and Hut cold.

Mawson's next comment about Close, on July 3, hints at a long-simmering disapproval: "Close has been laid up with a severe gum boil. He should never have thought of coming to the Antarctic with such remnants of teeth."

Mawson also taxes Close with being lazy and ineffectual. On July 20, "Close has put in much time at [mending] his clothes, but gets tired before the day is out and has a nap at intervals. After 4 pm he is prone to read a book and does the same when he is not asleep till after midnight."

The incompetence and anxiety that must have made the overwintering a terrible psychological ordeal for Close are revealed most clearly in the comments of other teammates. On April 7, John Hunter records his disgust that it takes Close half an hour to hike the 150 yards to the anemometer and another half hour to take a reading. "He cannot yet read the barometer," writes Hunter, "although nearly everyone has showed him the way. Poor old John Close." On May 3, Hunter remarks that Close avoided his chores, instead performing "his deep breathing exercises"—a suggestion of constant anxiety. "The Doctor was very annoyed with him," Hunter adds. "Close is certainly the jest of our party."

The hurricane winds that shook the hut seem to have frightened Close more than they did his comrades. Hunter again: "Poor old John Close is terribly afraid that the wind will lift the whole hut & dump it in the sea." The lighting and electrical system of the hut was based on acetylene, a colorless gas that can be highly explosive if mixed with oxygen. This too caused Close severe anxiety. Instead of reassuring him, however, his teammates taunted Close by setting off "little acetylene bombs near him."

Predictably, Close's cruelest tormentor was the practical joker Frank Hurley. Decades later, without naming the teammate, Laseron recalled the elaborate prank the photographer played on the addled man:

There was one member of the party who was very nervous of fire, as indeed we all were, for a fire would have been disastrous. But he voiced his anxiety too often. Moreover, he had a deep-rooted distrust of the acetylene generator, which he was sure was always on the point of blowing up. One night this member was the nightwatchman, so Frank took the long length of rubber tubing that always seemed to play a part in his schemes, and immersing one end in the water for the generator, carried the other to his bunk. Here at intervals through the night, and at the expense of his own rest, he blew hard, creating a most satisfactory bubbling. It was too much for the nightwatchman. After climbing up several times to investigate and finding nothing to reveal the cause, he at last woke the Doctor. D. I., annoyed at being disturbed, at once spotted the trouble, but did not give the show away. He merely remarked that it certainly was dangerous, but even if it did blow up, nothing could be done before morning, and calmly went back to his bunk again. The nightwatchman spent the rest of the night in anxious misery, and it was not until some days later that he came to understand the hilarity that greeted any discussion on the nature and habits of acetylene generators.

As with Whetter, no diary from the hand of John Close has come down to us, to give us his side of the story of that fraught overwintering. Close "rather vanished from sight after the AAE," writes Beau Riffenburgh. "Little is known of him before his death in Sydney in 1949."

Despite the growing resentment of at least one member, Cecil Madigan; despite the communal scapegoating of the two most hapless teammates, Whetter and Close; despite, above all, an ordeal by wind and cold the likes of which no party in the Arctic or Antarctic had previously endured, the AAE got through the winter of 1912 at Cape Denison with its morale intact. The ultimate credit for that feat of perseverance must go to Mawson himself. Yes, the D. I. could be stern and demanding. His fanaticism for hard work must have seemed at times tyrannical. He may well have been a leader unwilling to own up to his mistakes, while delivering "I told you so"s to his men. But he was not, as some of his critics have claimed, humorless. Most importantly, he led by example, not by command. No matter how tough or dangerous a job he asked his men to perform, there was no task that he himself ever shirked.

The proof that Mawson was, in the end, not only a great explorer but an inspired leader would emerge in the loyalty of every single member during the marathon sledging journeys of 1912–13, and in the trials that ensued beyond that summer of unprecedented discovery.

As he planned to send out his parties of three men each in every direction from Cape Denison, Mawson knew that he would have to assign three men to stay and guard the hut. This would be the most thankless and discouraging job of all; after ten months in Antarctica simply surviving its tempests, three men would have to accept the fiat that they would house-sit, playing no real part in the discoveries that were the raison d'être of the expedition.

One would think that Mawson would have chosen that hut-bound trio from the men who had most disappointed him through the winter: Whetter and Close, of course, and perhaps Madigan, if Mawson had become aware of his former student's mounting antagonism. But it was not to be so. Although Mawson would never publicly explain how he chose his trios, in the spring of 1912, Whetter would set out with the Western Party, hoping to use the air-tractor as a slingshot boost to their progress, and Close would be assigned to the Near Eastern Party, mapping the coastline east of Commonwealth Bay. As for Madigan, he would not only join the Eastern Coastal Party, charged with exploring the coastline even farther east than the Near Eastern trio might venture, he would be chosen as leader of that vital mission.

Whether Mawson made those appointments to test the men he doubted most with an ultimate challenge, or whether by October he had come round to finding in them the virtues for which he had originally signed them up, we cannot know. What we do know is that all five of the subsidiary teams, including Madigan, Whetter, and Close, pulled off their journeys with splendid fortitude and pluck. And when the most ambitious trio of all, Mawson's Far Eastern Party with Ninnis and Mertz, ran headlong into disaster, it was the fidelity of the other fifteen members of the Main Base party that turned tragedy into triumph.

5

THE PAINFUL SILENCE

Of all the expeditions launched during the heroic age of Antarctic exploration, the AAE was the most ambitious. The three autonomous bases—Macquarie Island, Main Base, and Western Base—formed a geographic triangle whose sides stretched 1,100, 1,500, and 2,100 miles in length. To use a rough North American analogy, if Mawson's Main Base were situated in Miami, Wild's Western Base would be in Boston, and Macquarie Island would lie somewhere in the Virgin Islands.

On the Antarctic continent itself, during the summer of 1912–13, seven separate teams of three men each would sledge across unknown terrain to distances as far as 650 miles round trip from their winter huts. In addition, four supporting parties, also of three men each, would lay depots to assist their comrades, on shorter sledging treks along the same or similar routes. And the whole time, almost every man would be charged with making scientific observations or gathering various kinds of specimens.

On the Shackleton Ice Shelf, as soon as the *Aurora* had steamed away on February 21, Frank Wild and the seven teammates who made up the Western Base party set about building their own hut, only 600 yards from the cliff that threatened daily to calve into the sea. The prefabricated building was similar in design to the one erected at Cape Denison, although smaller in size (20 feet square), with the pyramidal roof overhanging the walls to create verandas for storage on the sides. Bunks laid out inside for the men were in single tiers, unlike the Main Base's double-deckers. Wild, like Mawson, had his own private cubicle in one corner of the hut.

Among the eight men, the thirty-eight-year-old Wild was the only one with previous polar experience, and he was the only Englishman. His teammates, all Aussies, ranged in age from twenty-one to twenty-five, with the exception of the forty-three-year-old biologist and artist Charles Harrisson. The men were in awe of their leader, who had journeyed south with Scott and Shackleton—so much so that throughout the expedition they addressed him only as "Mr. Wild." Yet Wild was a far more relaxed and democratic commander than Mawson. Riffenburgh pinpoints the differences in the two men's leadership styles:

> Mawson not only was driven to work all the time but enjoyed it; so it was natural for him to push his men as he did himself. . . .
>
> Conversely, Wild, despite his position, was effectively a hired hand. He did not have a great investment in the science; his manner of dealing with it was to ask those around him what they wanted to accomplish, and then to give them assistance. . . . Rather than issuing orders, he tended towards management by discussion, and he regularly sat with the men around the table debating plans, with Wild having the final say, but everyone giving input.

Wild had grown up middle-class in Yorkshire, one of thirteen children of a religiously devout schoolteacher and his wife. His father wanted the young man to follow in his footsteps as a teacher, but as Wild would write in 1934, in the first sentence of his memoirs (not published until 2011), "As far back as I can remember, at the age of four, I wished to be a sailor and when eight years old read a book on Arctic adventure, and ever since have had a keen desire for Polar travel."

At the age of sixteen, Wild landed the first of several postings as a merchant navy man. These led eventually to his selection by Scott for the *Discovery* expedition of 1901–04 and by Shackleton for the *Nimrod* expedition in 1907–09. Upon joining the AAE at age thirty-eight, Wild was still single (he would not marry until 1921, after turning forty-eight)—a man with an unquenchable thirst for adventure and a seemingly limitless tolerance for hardship. He stood only five feet four and a half inches tall, with a muscular physique and, according to his biographer, "piercing china-blue eyes." Like many another navy man, he bore a number of tattoos on his arms (snake, eagle, ship, and anchor). In a well-known midlife portrait, Wild stares serenely into the camera, head propped on his right fist, a pipe clenched in the left corner of his mouth. His handsome face looks all the more rugged for the horizontal wrinkles on his brow, a receding hairline, and a neatly trimmed mustache and beard.

In *South with Mawson*, Charles Laseron left a memorable testament to the impact of Wild's leadership on his men:

> It was more than affection, it was almost worship. . . . Not a conspicuous figure at any time, yet there was something in his presence that inspired confidence. Like Kipling's sailor, he was a "man of infinite resource and sagacity," to which might be added the word "experience". . . . Moreover, his quiet cheerfulness, forethought and kindly consideration for those with him never slackened for a moment.

During the winter of 1912, the Western Base team suffered through ordeals and close calls nearly the equal of those borne by the eighteen men at Cape Denison, although the winds on the Shackleton Shelf were not quite as strong or as constant as those that raked Commonwealth Bay. The story of Wild's party from 1911 to 1913 deserves a book-length narrative of its own; but given that it served within the AAE as an adjunct to the even more ambitious program launched from the Main Base, it must be succinctly summarized here.

The nine dogs that Wild brought with him from Cape Denison had been so depleted by their months of shipboard misery on the *Aurora* that they were incapable at first of helping pull the sledges at all, even on short hauls from the landing cove to the base site. By May 1, only four of the huskies were still alive. Two had died, one had disappeared, and, as Wild wrote, two "bitches" had "refused to do any work so had to be shot, as food for the dogs was scarce." To try to rehabilitate the ailing huskies, the men had hunted seals for dog food from the moment they had come ashore. But on March 13, just as a prolonged blizzard petered out, a huge section of the ice cliff broke loose and crashed into the sea with a tremendous roar. The unfortunate result was that the comparatively gentle snow ramp that led down to the ocean's edge, by which the men had hauled their loads to the hut site, had disappeared, leaving a vertical face of fresh blue ice a hundred feet tall. For weeks, until the snows formed a new ramp, the men found it impossible to gain the sea edge to hunt for seals and penguins.

As the men settled into their new home, a certain snugness gave them comfort. It did not take long for the winds to pile snowdrifts so high on the hut walls that the men had to dig a tunnel forty feet long to reach the door. "This bad weather had its compensations," wrote the ever-sanguine Wild, "the temperature always rose during a blow and instead of being well below zero remained somewhere about 30° Fahrenheit." The drifts provided such effective insulation that inside the hut, "even with gusts of over one hundred mph there was not much more than a slight tremor to be felt."

The one serious oversight among the supplies carried 1,500 miles from Cape Denison to the Shackleton Shelf had to do with the vital business of sewing clothing and gear. The party had brought a sewing machine, but had inadvertently left behind shuttles, spools, and needles. So all the sewing had to be done by hand—an art that Wild painstakingly taught his protégés. The leader was particularly vigilant in supervising the sewing of each man's sledging harness. "If we were to fall down a crevasse," recalled twenty-five-year-old Morton Moyes, "our lives could depend on a strong harness. . . . Frank came over one day and said, 'Now then, no homeward bound stitching'. . . . So we had little stitches, and not long ones."

Instead of Mawson's day-long program of chores and observations, the laid-back Wild decreed that work would normally end with lunch, at 1 p.m. The afternoon would be reserved for "sport and recreation." Although the scholarly Harrisson carved a cunning set of chessmen, the most popular game was bridge. The men played every day, and kept a running score. "Two medals were struck," reported Wild, "a neat little thing for the highest scorer, and a huge affair as large as a plate . . . with Jonah inscribed on it, to be worn by the player at the foot of the list."

For exercise, the men practiced "slope running"—skiing on gentle slopes, sliding on one's rear end on steeper ones: "though diverting," one of the men wrote of the latter activity, "this is rough on clothes." The men also attempted to play hockey (apparently the gear carried to Antarctica included real hockey sticks), but with four men on a side, the sport was too exhausting. Instead, Wild devised golf balls made of string and rawhide and laid out a twelve-hole course on the ice. For "gokey," as the men called their invention, the balls were chipped with the hockey sticks. The same participant wryly commented, "This game is probably a good deal more exciting than ordinary golf as several of our greens are on crevasses and it is not rare to see some one break through a lid."

Crevasses were indeed an omnipresent hazard, even within a few yards of the hut. According to twenty-two-year-old Alexander Kennedy, the men developed the skill of deciphering when they were crossing a bridged crevasse by the sound of their boots in the snow alone: a sequence of "crunch crunch crunch crunch tang tang tang tang crunch crunch" signaled the successful traverse of a four-step snow bridge (the results verified by probing with an ice ax).

Eager to make the best use of the dwindling days of early autumn, Wild chose five teammates to man-haul sledges with him in a concerted effort to lay a depot of supplies inland for the next summer's journeys. With each man pulling a load of 200 pounds, the party set out on March 13. Until now, during their first three weeks on the ice, the men had yet to feel solid land beneath their feet. Gazing south, they had discerned the edge of the continent to be seventeen miles away from their hut.

This twenty-five-day mini-expedition turned into as grueling and dangerous a mission as even Wild himself in his most pessimistic mood might have envisaged. The crevasses were everywhere, "and we all had falls, [Archibald] Hoadley dropping with his head below the surface into one five feet wide." Some of the crevasses were so broad that the men had to lengthen their harnesses to avoid stranding two men on the same snow bridge at the same time. "We crossed one at least 60 feet wide," Wild remembered decades later, "with a badly broken bridge and a black bottomless pit showing through all the holes. This one looked so dangerous that we went over one by one on an alpine rope and hauled the sledges over after crossing ourselves."

The weather was so fiendish that the men were able to travel on only twelve of their twenty-five days away from base. Forced to lie in their sleeping bags while the storm raged outside, they had to deal with snow driven through the tent ventilators that was thawed by the men's body heat and that soaked their reindeer-skin bags. "When it is understood that for no purpose whatever is it possible to leave the tent during a blizzard and that a section of the floor snow must be used for drinking and cooking," Wild wrote in disgust, "it may be partially realised how irksome these storms are."

On the move again, Archibald Hoadley made a small error that nearly had major consequences. Feeling his fingers starting to freeze as he took meteorological observations, he tucked the record book under a strap on his sledge rather than replacing it inside the instrument box. Two hours later, he realized the book was missing. Judging the "track very easy to follow," with "no sign of wind," Wild sent Hoadley back alone to find the book. Three hours passed, with no sign of him. Just as Wild was preparing a rescue effort, Hoadley reappeared. "He had found the book two miles back," Wild recalled.

"That had not worried him, but the utter loneliness of that three hours had quite unnerved him."

On March 21, a seven-day storm began. For a full week, the men could not move. More than a year later, Wild's team would learn that during that same seven-day storm, some 1,700 miles away in another part of Antarctica, Robert Scott, Edward Wilson, and Birdie Bowers had perished one by one in their tent, as their hopes of returning alive from the South Pole slowly flickered out.

In the end, Wild's team succeeded in caching a depot containing food and paraffin for the stove for three men for six weeks on a forlorn snow ridge some sixty miles south of the hut. The return trip, if anything, was more trying than the journey out. In hideous soft snow, on what the usually understated Wild called "one of the hardest days I have ever experienced," the six men dragged their sledges only a mile and a quarter.

> We were pulling in pairs, Hoadley and I leading, sinking thigh to waist deep, and at one time tried going on our hands and knees, but found our faces went under. After one of our 40 yard struggles, I thought I might be halting too frequently and asked Hoadley if he thought so. He replied, "My God sir, if you go another yard I'll die!"

During those twenty-five days, the two teammates left to caretake the hut had their own desperate times. On a simple errand to go out and feed the dogs during a blizzard, Alexander Kennedy got lost a mere ten yards from the hut. As he wrote that evening:

> Unable to stand, or see, with a face covered with ice, and buffeted from all sides by a wind of force about 12 or more [greater than 70 mph], I crawled around and about in search of some object, anything would be acceptable. . . . [I] found the SE corner of the hut. After being blown headfirst from there to the [coal] brick pile, I crawled into the hut dazed & numb. Never again unless absolutely necessary.

As the days darkened and grew colder in late April, the men settled in for the winter. During the coming months, like their counter-
parts at Cape Denison, the residents of Western Base saw tensions
flare up among them. The most persistent source of conflict came
from Harrisson's dismay over the slovenly housekeeping his comrades practiced in the kitchen and at the dining table. As not only the
oldest man in the party but the only one who was married, Harrisson
recorded his vexation day after day in his diary.

The men survived one near-catastrophe. On August 11, trying
to fill the acetylene generator in the middle of a blizzard, one of the
men nearly set fire not only to himself, but to the hut. Two teammates
managed, after strenuous efforts, to put the fire out with water, snow,
and blankets. "Wondering when the buckets of kerosene inside & the
gas would go up & take us with it," speculated Morton Moyes about
this close call. "It also meant the ruin of hut & probably a death by
freezing to the rest."

Yet thanks in large part to Wild's inspired leadership, the men
at Western Base got through the winter without a wholesale plunge
in morale. As spring began to dawn on their remote outpost, like
their teammates 1,500 miles away at Main Base, Wild's crew looked
forward to the summer's journeys with keen, unalloyed enthusiasm.

The AAE presents a narrative conundrum. Unlike Scott's and
Shackleton's and Amundsen's quests for the South Pole—in which
the combined effort of a large team culminated in the final polar
party's thrust toward 90 degrees south, thus providing a dramatic
arc to the whole story—Mawson's expedition fielded no fewer than
eight three-man teams in the summer of 1912–13, operating for the
most part autonomously, in a kind of well-coordinated frenzy of discovery pursued in every possible direction. Since the dramas within
each team took shape simultaneously, there is no simple way to tell
their stories.

Mawson himself, in *The Home of the Blizzard*, succumbs to the awkwardness of the AAE's ungainly plot structure. He jumps, chapter after chapter, from one trio's doings to the next. His innate modesty leads him to downplay the climactic tragedy of the whole expedition— the fate of his own Far Eastern Party with Ninnis and Mertz—while giving generous play to what a century later seem to be only ancillary matters. The book, for instance, devotes three long chapters, written by George Ainsworth, to the accomplishments of the five men confined to the relay station on Macquarie Island. Subsequent historians have adopted the same clumsy narrative formula. (Indeed, it is a structure that proves hard to avoid.)

At the Main Base, Mawson chose three men—Herbert Dyce Murphy, John Hunter, and Walter Hannam—to stay and tend the hut. What further complicates the story, however, is that Murphy and Hunter also took part in the supporting teams that helped launch the Southern Party and the Near Eastern Party through the month of November. The shifting duties of these teammates and their companions during the late spring campaign take on the whirlwind quality of a game of musical chairs.

Those three house-sitters played an invaluable role in the AAE, and each was an interesting man in his own right. (As noted in chapter four, two full biographies of the enigmatic Murphy have been written.) But here, their contributions must go unsung, as must the work of the two supporting parties, whose numbers included not only the three hut-minders but, briefly, John Close, Alfred Hodgeman, and Charles Laseron as well.

After all kinds of preparations and reconnaissances in August, September, and October, the five main exploratory trios set out from Cape Denison in early November. The Western Party, under the leadership of Frank Bickerton, was to push as far west as possible along the coast. The team hoped to use the crippled air-tractor to propel it on its way. The Near Eastern Party, led by Frank Stillwell, a twenty-three-year-old engineer from Melbourne, was supposed to map the convoluted coastline east of the hut for some 100 miles. Leapfrogging past them to explore the coast farther east was the Eastern Coastal Party, whose leader was Cecil Madigan, the Rhodes scholar who had spent the first winter nursing his annoyance at Mawson. A Southern Party, led by Bob Bage, hoped to reach the south magnetic pole from the exact opposite direction of that followed by Mawson, Edgeworth David, and Alistair Mackay in 1908–09. Finally, the Far Eastern Party, led by Mawson himself, the only trio to use dogs to haul their sledges, would make the most ambitious thrust of all, trying to link the unknown land southeast of Cape Denison with the fugitive hills of Victoria Land glimpsed from shipboard by members of Scott's party two years before.

November 6 was fixed as the grand departure date. Inside the hut on the evening of the 5th, the men celebrated with a lavish farewell dinner. But the usual blizzard arrived the next day, delaying the departures. In the end, the various leave-takings were staggered over the following week.

Along with detailed instructions as to the kinds of research and mapping each team was supposed to accomplish, Mawson gave his parties a strict deadline: they were to be back at Winter Quarters by January 15 at the latest, so that the planned rendezvous with the *Aurora* might take place, ensuring that all eighteen men—as well as the eight operating under Wild out of the Western Base—would return to Australia before the end of the summer of 1913. Yet Mawson, in his thoroughness, imagined every possible outcome. In a scrawled note left in the hut, he penned an order to John King Davis, skipper of the *Aurora*, that sounds in hindsight a grim premonitory tone: "Should I or my party not have arrived back before the 1st Feb. you are to steam west and pick up Wild's party."

Of the four man-hauling trios, perhaps the strongest was the Southern Party. Bob Bage, its leader, was the quiet, confident twenty-three-year-old whom John Hunter, early on, had deemed "the most popular man of the party." His two colleagues were the effervescent photographer Frank Hurley and the dour magnetician Eric Webb. Except for Mawson's own Far Eastern Party, none of the teams streaming out from Winter Quarters would accomplish more that summer, and none, except Mawson's, would undergo a more perilous adventure on the ice.

The Southern Party's plan was simple: to haul sledges south, at first with the help of a supporting team, establish depots of food and fuel for the return journey twice along the way, and get as close to the south magnetic pole as possible before having to turn back. Once up on the polar plateau itself, however, the men were quickly intimidated by the barren hostility of endless snow and wind. Only 19 miles out from Winter Quarters, John Hunter, one of the supporting sledgers, wrote in his diary, "What a God forsaken country this plateau is." His comrade Charles Laseron concurred: "God damn this country. . . . Blowing a hurricane with drift as thick as peasoup."

Sixty-seven and a half miles out, the Southern Party said goodbye to their three supporters, who turned north to head back to the hut, after all six men had built a ten-foot-tall snow mound in which they cached food and fuel. Taking careful measurements of the place's latitude and longitude, Bage's team named the depot Southern Cross. Almost two months hence, finding it would be crucial to the men's safe return.

The daily fare for the sledging parties had been carefully worked out long before the *Aurora* had left Australia. Like nearly all the best-planned expeditions, the AAE relied on an inflexible menu, the same food for breakfast, lunch, and dinner every day. Even before reaching Cape Denison, the sledging rations were packed into bags that held either seven or fourteen days' meals for three men. The daily allotment of food, chosen for maximum calories and minimum weight, amounted to 34 ounces per man per day. To vary the regimen and entice the men with rewards, Mawson added 25 pounds of "perks" to the sledge load: special treats for celebratory occasions.

The staple main course for both breakfast and dinner was hoosh, a kind of porridge made up of pemmican (a fifty-fifty mélange of dried beef and animal fat), crumbled plasmon biscuit (whose crucial ingredient was powdered milk), and water, the whole cooked on the Primus stove. Each man had his own mug into which the hoosh was ladled. The second course was cocoa—one part cocoa powder to two parts sugar to four parts Glaxo (the brand name of an enriched powdered milk). The AAE's cocoa, one member reported, "sent the blood tingling into the fingers and toes." But that was all—hoosh and cocoa for breakfast and dinner.

Lunch was only a little more varied: plasmon biscuit, tea, chocolate, and butter. In polar sledging conditions, one's craving for fat becomes so intense that it is a delight to eat butter (or even lard) straight, without smearing it on bread or biscuit. The same aficionado who sang the praises of cocoa wrote, "if the weather was good it was pleasant to nibble alternately at a piece of frozen butter, chocolate and biscuit, and sip between whiles from a hot mug of tea." It was the brewing up of tea that necessitated pitching the tent for lunch when any substantial wind was blowing.

When the wind was strong, pitching the tent each afternoon or evening became a risky tribulation. Made of japara, a heavy cotton treated with wax to make it waterproof, the three-man tent combined with poles and ground cloth weighed an unwieldy 33 pounds. The tent was supported by a structure of five stout bamboo poles that were inserted into a hinged centerpiece at the apex. The shelter had been designed so that the cone of five poles was meant to be erected first, then the tent slung over it, but the men realized long before commencing their November jaunts that such a procedure invited disaster: in a strong wind, the tent itself was likely to be torn loose from the men's grasp as they struggled to hoist it over the pole pyramid. The AAE members had modified the design by sewing the poles inside sleeves of canvas loops on the inside of the tent. The whole apparatus thus resembled a giant umbrella. Tent pegs would have been useless to keep such a cumbersome shelter in place, but the tent itself came equipped with skirt-like flaps that, laid flat on the snow and covered with heavy objects, served to anchor it.

The men had practiced pitching the tents in gale-force winds for weeks before their November departure from Winter Quarters, for to lose the tent in a storm on the Antarctic plateau might well have spelled death. Charles Laseron left a vivid description of the extraor-

dinary sequence of tasks required to get the tent safely pitched in a
wind:

> First, enough large blocks of ice or hard snow were cut and
> placed handy; then the tent was laid down with the apex upwind
> and the entrance on top, so that it would be in the lee when the
> tent was raised; next, one man crawled inside and, with the other
> two hanging on, the tent was lifted and the man inside spread the
> three windward legs, one directly upwind, the others far enough
> apart to keep the material taut and at the same time give suffi-
> cient room for the leeward legs to fall into position. This required
> a considerable knack as the whole time the wind would be tearing
> at the structure, and it took the united strength of all hands to
> prevent it being blown away. . . . Once up it was found difficult to
> readjust the position of the legs, and if this was unsatisfactory the
> only thing was to do the whole job over again. The ballast was
> now placed on the outside flaps, and a canvas tent floor . . . was
> laid down, and all was ready for occupancy.

The door was a tunnel sleeve that could be tied shut from the inside.
In a bad wind, it could take three men more than an hour to pitch
the tent.

Day after day, Bage, Hurley, and Webb crossed a featureless plain
of snow. But on December 1, they suddenly confronted "an amazing
field of huge crevasses." Hurley took the lead as, roped to his partners, he tested each snow bridge by stomping forcefully on it. He was
halfway across the crevasse field when "suddenly I dropped through
a deep fissure. There was a sickening sensation of falling followed
by a violent jerk. As before, I shouted to my mates, 'Right-O! Haul
away!' " But as Bage and Webb slowly pulled their companion back
to the surface, the rope holding him sawed its way deep into the snow
of the near lip of the crevasse. Bage paused, then yelled to Hurley

that he would have to carve away the overhanging snow with his ax. Hurley called back anxiously, "Don't chip through the line."

In that moment of terror, the photographer in Hurley came to the fore. "I could not help noticing the unearthly beauty of the abyss into which I had fallen," he later recalled. The walls enclosing him were jade in color near the top, shading through sapphire to cobalt and, in the depths below, black. "The sheer faces were covered with exquisite crystals that scintillated as I moved." Still, as Hurley clambered at last out of the crevasse, "I emerged with the thought that there were worse places even than the plateau surface."

On December 12, at a spot the trio measured as 200 miles out, they left another cache of supplies—ten days' worth of food and a gallon of kerosene. They called it the Lucky Depot. Just as Mawson's team had discovered in early 1909, however, the closer Bage's party got to the magnetic pole, the harder it was to get accurate readings on the dip compass. Finally, on December 21, the men knew they had to turn around. By their own reckoning, they were 301 miles from Winter Quarters. The dip reading showed 89° 43.5'. They stood, they guessed, within 50 miles of the magnetic pole.

"What a temptation to go on and raise the needle to the vertical!" Hurley later wrote. "What lay beyond?" Instead, Webb made his final observations, the men ate lunch, then raised the flag of the Commonwealth and gave three cheers for the king—"they sounded very strange in the vast solitude." That night the temperature was minus 25 degrees Fahrenheit, the coldest yet recorded on the journey. "It was . . . Midsummer Day," Bage dryly noted, "so we concluded that the spot would be a very chilly one in winter."

The return journey would test the three men to the limits of their endurance. On December 27, they regained the Lucky Depot, where they celebrated Christmas two days late. Hurley prepared a formal menu, mocking the spartan paucity of the cuisine, with an hors d'oeuvre of "Angels on gliders. Made by placing a raisin on the top of a bar of chocolate previously fried" and, for entrée, "Biscuit fried in sledging suet."

On the way back, superbly fit, the three men pushed the pace, covering a total of 41½ miles in one continuous push of twenty-two hours. It was, Mawson later noted, "a record for man-hauling sledging between camp and camp." But slowly the men's optimism crumbled, as the weather grew steadily overcast, snow fell day after day, the wind was incessant, and the omnipresent sastrugi overturned the sledge again and again. Removing their goggles to try to get their bearings in the gray miasma of the plateau, all three men at different times suffered from snow blindness. And to make navigation all the more difficult, their sledgemeter broke down.

On January 4, the men reached what they thought should be the vicinity of the Southern Cross depot, but they could not find it. They searched for it for the next three days, crisscrossing the featureless plain as the snow fell thicker than ever, but found no trace of the vital cache. By now, they were almost out of food.

Something was clearly wrong. If they were looking in the wrong place for the depot, the men could not be sure they knew how to find their way back to the hut. With the diminution of their food, they felt their fitness ebbing away by the hour. By January 8, all the men had left to eat was half a hoosh, six lumps of sugar, and nine raisins. And snow blindness continued to wreak its ravages.

In his diary that day, Webb wrote, "Matter of life and death." And the next day: "Sitting in the tent tonight we have high hopes that we may get thro but it seems but a chance. We don't know where we are and can only trust to pure luck."

In a fit of morbid humor, Hurley started composing doggerel verses about the finest meals he could remember. A sample:

I've dined in many places, but never such as these—
It's like the Gates of Heaven, when you've found you've lost the
keys. . . .
I've feasted with Iguanas on a lonely desert isle;
Once in the shade of a wattle, and a maiden's winsome smile. . . .
In short, I've dined from Horn to Cape and up Alaska way,
But the finest, funniest dinner of all was that on Christmas Day!

When he read the verses aloud to his tentmates, Hurley later recalled, Bage commented "Pretty rotten," while Webb chimed in with the trio's motto for all the trip's vicissitudes, "Might be much worse." But in the privacy of his diary, Hurley added, "To hell with it all, let us die cheerfully."

"There was only one thing for it now," Bage concluded, "and that was to make a break for the coast." The men packed their tent, got back in their harnesses, and started hauling their sledge north. But January 8 was "the worst day's march of our journey," with 60 mph winds and drifting snow.

Two days later, guessing they were still 27 miles from the hut, the trio was on the verge of giving up. But Bage, in the lead, came over a slight rise and suddenly recognized the offshore islets in the distance, ones they had come to know well during the winter months at Cape Denison. January 10, Webb told his diary, was "The most memorable day of our lives so far!"

It took one more camp and another day's march to stagger down the final slope to the hut. "Never had I seen the Antarctic appear so serene and beautiful," Hurley later claimed. With Bage so snowblind he had to ride the sledge, the trio limped the last few hundred yards, as their teammates at the hut rushed out to greet them. "We three had never thought the Hut quite such a fine place, nor have we ever since," Bage concluded.

It was January 11, only four days before the rigid deadline Mawson had imposed on all the teams. Stillwell's Near Eastern Party, with Close and Laseron, had arrived six days earlier from their relatively modest exploration of the coast immediately east of the hut. But three other teams—nine men, including Mawson himself—were still out there somewhere on the ice.

What, exactly, had the Southern Party accomplished in its journey of 600 miles? The data minutely recorded in logbooks each day would find light only years later, in the AAE scientific reports. But in *The Home of the Blizzard*, Mawson succinctly hailed the team's achievement: "The information brought back proved that Adelie Land is continuous with South Victoria Land and part of the great Antarctic continent."

That may not sound like much to justify two months of intense hardship and danger. Yet by trudging across the polar plateau to reach an altitude of 5,900 feet, Bage's party had fulfilled the most ancient and cherished of exploratory goals—to go where no one else had ever been, to fill in a blank on the map. By the end of 1913, most of Antarctica would remain a blank, but no expedition ever discovered more land on the southern continent than the AAE.

The adventures of the other three man-hauling trios out of Cape Denison were not unlike those of the Southern Party. All the teams suffered greatly from wind and snow and cold, from storms that kept them tent-bound for days on end, from sastrugi overturning sledges, from the constant threat of hidden crevasses into which men plunged only to be saved by rope or harness. It will suffice here simply to summarize the deeds of the two more ambitious of those man-hauling units—Madigan's Eastern Coastal Party and Bickerton's Western Party.

Since there was only one feasible route onto the polar plateau from Winter Quarters—the snow ramp that backed Cape Denison to the south—all the sledging parties followed the same track for the first five, 10, or even 15 miles, before branching off on their separate itineraries. In August, at the 5-mile Depot site first explored by Mawson the previous February, the men spent two days digging a substantial snow cave. Aladdin's Cave, as the grotto was named, would play a pivotal role in the doings of the following summer.

"A refuge from the hurricane," as Mawson called it, Aladdin's Cave comprised a vertical entry shaft whose opening could be closed with a specially designed canvas flap, giving onto a cubicle in which several men could rest or sleep in horizontal comfort. Mawson would wax poetic about this "truly magical world of glassy facets and scintillating crystals," where "it was a great relief to be in a strong room,

with solid walls of ice, in place of the cramped tent flapping violently in the wind. Inside the silence was profound, the blizzard was
banished."

> Shelves for primus stove, spirit bottle, matches, kerosene and
> other oddments were chipped out at a moment's notice. In one
> wall a small hole was cut to communicate with a narrow crevasse
> fissure which provided ventilation without allowing the entrance
> of drifting snow. Another fissure crossing the floor at one corner
> was a natural receptacle for rubbish [including human excre-
> tions]. Whatever daylight there was filtered through the roof
> and walls without hindrance. The purest ice for cooking could
> be immediately hacked out from the walls without the incon-
> venience of having to don one's burberrys and go outside for
> it. Finally one neatly disposed of spare clothes by moistening
> the corner of each garment and pressing it against the wall for a
> few seconds, where it would freeze on and remain hanging until
> required.

In polar regions, as on high mountains, snow caves have often served
as welcome and even lifesaving alternatives to pitched tents. That the
AAE did not dig more of them was dictated simply by the time and
labor it took to construct them.

On November 17, 25 miles out from Winter Quarters, Madigan's
Eastern Coastal Party, with Archibald McLean and Percy Correll
(the youngest member of the AAE), bade farewell to Mawson, Ninnis, and Mertz as they bent their course north to follow the coast.
During the subsequent weeks, instead of the featureless plain across
which Bage's Southern Party had trudged, Madigan's trio wove an
intricate path among crevasse fields, rocky outcrops, and chaotic
jumbles of sea ice. Instead of the barren, lifeless plateau that had
chilled the souls of Bage's team, the Coastal Party found itself daily
visited by all kinds of birds, and in close proximity to strutting penguins and lolling seals.

On November 21, the trio roped up to make the AAE's only significant ascent, of a handsome 1,750-foot-tall tower of gneiss the team named Aurora Peak, after the ship that was their lifeline to Australia. The summit "was quite a knife-edge, with barely space for standing."

The next day, the team survived its worst crevasse fall, when Madigan broke through a snow bridge and plunged 25 feet. "I cannot say," he later wrote, "that 'my life flashed before me.' I just had time to think 'Now for the jerk—will my harness hold?' when there was a wrench, and I was hanging breathless over the blue depth." With the hauling line, McLean and Correll pulled a chastened but uninjured Madigan back to the surface.

In late November, the trio crossed the snout of a major glacier, subsequently named after Xavier Mertz. Then, on December 2, the trio ran into the even more gigantic snout of the ice-flow the team would later name the Ninnis Glacier, which sprawled far north into the sea. Here they left a small depot of food and fuel, 152 miles out from Winter Quarters. It took the men four days to cross the dangerously crevassed surface of the glacier. Once on the far side, they had no choice but to abandon land and cross the broken, frozen sea—"a plain of floe-ice, thickly studded with bergs and intersected by black leads of open water." The next six days, recalled Madigan with Edwardian understatement, "were full of incident." At one point, the trio gauged that they were a good 45 miles north of the coast. The sledge ran smoothly enough, but the men had to be on constant guard against open holes in the ice, through which they might suddenly plunge into the sea itself.

Back on land on December 17, the Coastal Party explored the prominent cape that they had named after Sir Douglas Freshfield. Here, in the midst of a steep talus pile—a rare expanse of rock laid bare to the sky—they discovered a substantial seam of coal. In *The Home of the Blizzard*, Mawson hailed this find as "a notable discovery," for he was still hopeful that Antarctica might eventually be mined for its mineral resources.

On December 21, the same day that the Southern Party had turned around, the Eastern Coastal Party started home, having traveled some 270 miles out from Winter Quarters. The return, though less perilous than the one Bage's trio had faced, imposed its trying ordeals. The worst of them was recrossing the Mertz Glacier, where now the men hauled the sledge on "a narrow ridge of hard snow, surrounded by blue, gaping pits in a pallid eternity of white." Time and again all three men fell up to their waists into small crevasses. Wrote Madigan, "I had never felt more nervous than I did in that ghostly light in the tense silence, surrounded by the hidden horror of fathomless depths."

Like Bage's party, Madigan's almost ran out of food, though penguin meat supplemented their larder. Only the recovery of their first depot of food, which Madigan accomplished on a bold solo jaunt, finding the original eight-foot mound of snow reduced by drifts to a barely discernible two-foot lump, gave the men the sustenance they needed to cover the rest of the journey back.

On January 16, one day after the deadline, the weary trio stumbled back to the hut. There they learned that both Bickerton's and Mawson's teams were still out. But Winter Quarters was abuzz with animation. Three days earlier, the *Aurora* had arrived.

John King Davis considered the passage from Australia that he had just completed "normal"—"by this I mean that we had experienced our fair share of gales and heavy seas while crossing the Southern Ocean." On January 13, he brought the *Aurora* to anchor in Commonwealth Bay, though out of sight of the hut. It was only ten hours later, when the ship's motor launch puttered toward shore, that Walter Hannam, stepping outside after lunch, spotted this proof of the blessed arrival of the relief vessel.

As Davis recalled the rendezvous decades later:

We were laden with mail and fresh provisions and the delight of these lonely men, who had lived for so long completely severed from their families and from the world, may be better imagined than described. To us they had the appearance almost of strangers, a band of wild, hairy veterans whose looks bore little resemblance to the hopeful young men we had landed here a year ago.

The *Aurora* also brought the men the first news from the outside world that they had had for twelve months. Of the keenest interest to them was the announcement that Amundsen's team had reached the South Pole successfully in December 1911, and that in January 1912 Scott had parted from his support teams 150 miles short of the pole, but that nothing of his subsequent fate was known. Laseron later summed up the impact of this flood of news: "Australia had lost the cricket Tests; the *Titanic* had been sunk with great loss of life; the Balkan War had been waged; Scott was spending another year in the Antarctic."

Although only nine men were in the hut when Davis greeted them on January 13, the captain was not unduly worried about "the parties out at present." Three days later, Madigan, McLean, and Correll came in. As early as January 15, Davis had written in his diary, "Dr Mawson is out 66 days today and is expected tonight. Bickerton ought to be in now, as he is out 43 days with only 40 days food."

The Western Party had started later than the others, because of Bickerton's endless tinkering with the air-tractor—the wingless fuselage of the Vickers monoplane that had crashed on its test flight near Adelaide. The canny engineer had converted the machine into a kind of motorized sledge. It was not until December 3, with Leslie Whetter and Alfred Hodgeman as his teammates, that Bickerton set out from Winter Quarters. Hauling a chain of three loaded sledges, the tractor chugged uphill the five miles to Aladdin's Cave in the remarkable time of one hour. There the trio added more cargo and a fourth sledge and started on, headed for a second campsite known as Cathedral Grotto.

All at once, a cylinder that had misfired repeatedly in tests failed again. It was only the harbinger of a more general mechanical breakdown. In Mawson's summary:

Very soon the engine developed an internal disorder which Bickerton was at a loss to diagnose or remedy. . . . Bickerton was
on the point of deciding to take the engine to pieces, when his
thoughts were brought to a sudden close by the engine, without
any warning, pulling up with such a jerk that the propeller was
smashed. A moment's examination showed that even more irre-
mediable damage had occurred inside the engine, so there was
nothing left but to abandon the air-tractor and continue on their
journey man-hauling the sledge.

Weeks later, after lugging the air-tractor back to Winter Quarters
and taking it apart, Bickerton discovered that a number of pistons
had seized and broken.

"We were very sorry to leave the machine," Bickerton later wrote.
"We had never dared expect a great deal from it, and it had not surprised us in an alarming matter. But the present situation was disappointing and it is not pleasant to have to admit this at the very outset
of a journey." So ended another chapter in the tragicomic history
of early attempts to adapt motorized travel to the Antarctic: Shackleton's motorcar in 1908, Scott's heavy tractors in 1911, and now
Bickerton's air-tractor.

The men consolidated their baggage on a single sledge and
donned their harnesses as they pushed on toward Cathedral Grotto.
Now, however, Bickerton found himself the weakest member of the
team: Whetter and Hodgeman had spent previous weeks learning to
man-haul, while their leader had devoted all his time to the contraption housed in the "hangar." The next day, Bickerton confessed, "by
lunch time I felt I could do no more."

It could hardly have been a more inauspicious beginning for the
Western Party, but the very next day, December 5, the three men
made one of the most electrifying discoveries of the whole AAE. Six
miles out from Cathedral Grotto, the men paused for lunch, then
sledged onward. Only 240 yards from their lunch spot, they sighted
an anomalous black object lying in the snow. They picked it up. It

was a black lump of stone, five inches by three by three and a half. Bickerton at once guessed that it was a meteorite.

The stone lay about two and a half inches below the surrounding surface of the snow. It "did not appear to have been there long," Bickerton speculated, "probably only a month or so." The leader's first guess was right: subsequent analysis of the Adélie Land Meteorite (the first ever found in Antarctica) classed it as a chondrite, one of the most common forms of meteorite. But the second guess was dead wrong. Specialists have since concluded that the lump of rock from outer space had hit the earth some 70,000 years ago. Rather than plunking down in the snow where Bickerton's team found it, it had probably been carried hundreds of miles over the millennia by the movement of the polar plateau.

Forty-nine years would elapse before a second meteorite was found in Antarctica, when Russian geologists prowling in the Humboldt Mountains in 1961, on almost the opposite side of the vast continent, discovered another one. Since then, Antarctica has become the most fertile ground on earth for meteorite sleuths. Since 1969, more than 30,000 specimens of stone from outer space that have survived their headlong plunge through the earth's atmosphere have been recovered from the southern continent. One of them, retrieved in 2003, has been proven, thanks to a remarkable analysis by spectrograph, to have once been part of the planet Mars.

During the next week, the weather was consistently bad. The men struggled westward as their spirits drooped. "This is a dismal rotten country," wrote Bickerton in his diary on December 11. "If I had not been through a winter in Adelie Land I would say 'But the weather must change this can't go on for ever.' " During their first week on the outward trail, the men had covered a wretched 31 miles. Bickerton calculated that at that rate, even if they postponed their return to Winter Quarters until as late as January 20, they would accomplish a trek of only 107 miles, as opposed to the minimum of 150 he had hoped for.

Then, on December 12, a mishap occurred that threatened to wreck the whole effort. The men had mounted a canvas sail to take advantage of the wind to propel the sledge. Around midnight, Bickerton slipped and fell on the ice, and the sledge slammed violently into a hard ridge of sastrugi. The bow of the sledge was shattered. Later that day, Bickerton, ever the tinkerer, managed to jury-rig a substitute bow out of pieces of a bamboo pole lashed in place with rawhide.

To compensate for their poor progress, Bickerton was willing to push his team beyond the turnaround date of December 21 that both the Southern Party and the Eastern Coastal Party had observed. On five successive days, they made excellent marches, covering 100 miles. But then, beginning on the 21st, a violent blizzard with winds up to 80 mph kept them tent-bound for four days. They celebrated Christmas by drawing a festive tree in the frost on the side of the tent, and by inventing imaginary presents for all the members of the AAE: these included a tin trumpet for Hannam, since he had never been able to get the radio working, and an "aeroplane" for Mawson.

The team's last outward march gained 13 miles on December 26, through a dangerously crevassed ice field. At last Bickerton surrendered to the inevitable. In his diary that night, he wrote, "I have decided this shall be our farthest west camp. . . . I had been thinking while coming along what a waste of time this all is."

The men started back on December 28. Having cut their rations for the last several days, all three now felt weak, with various kinds of ailments and possible illnesses. Feeling a metallic taste in their mouths, Whetter and Bickerton wondered if it signaled an attack of dysentery.

The three men had cut their margin of safety to an absolute minimum. Whetter later referred to their adventure as "a narrow squeal." During the next three weeks, the fickle weather tormented the trio. A glorious, sunny day that allowed fine sledging would alternate with whiteout so total the men could see nothing in front of them except the toes of their boots. One storm marooned them in their tent for thirty-six hours. Bickerton had been having trouble taking celestial observations, so the men began to wonder whether they were lost. And he had forgotten to wind his chronometer, so for a while the men even lost track of the date.

During this increasingly anxious retreat, Bickerton's veering moods reached new extremes. As his biographer, Stephen Haddelsey, writes, "His diary becomes a dialogue in which optimism and doubt vie for supremacy, one moment confidently asserting that their remaining week's rations would see them through the 50 or so miles to the hut, the next recollecting that it had sometimes taken as much as twelve days to cover that distance."

On January 15, the men came in sight of the ocean, but could not be sure if what they saw was part of Commonwealth Bay. The next morning, they trudged on in uncertainty. Suddenly Hodgeman stopped and pawed through the boxes on the sledge, retrieving the team's binoculars. He had seen a faint black mark in the snow ahead. Now, peering through the glasses, he let out a cry, "Yes it is, it's the aeroplane!" Attributing his colleague's sighting to a wishful hallucination, Bickerton took the glasses himself. Through them he saw the unmistakable carcass of the air-tractor, left where the men had abandoned it in the snow six weeks earlier. As Bickerton wrote that night, "I could have jumped for joy, there was the poor mouldy old thing as plain as anything, about 15 miles off. Let joy be unconfined, tonight we blow out the whisky from the medical outfit."

Despite this proof that they were on course, the men somehow managed to miss Cathedral Grotto altogether. On the 17th, just as navigational doubt was starting to fog their minds again, Bickerton spotted what looked to be a snow mound in the distance. Squinting through the binoculars, he recognized the marker that announced Aladdin's Cave. He and Hodgeman "felt inclined to drop the sledge and run," but restrained themselves. At 10 p.m. the men stood by a heap of stones reinforced with shovels and boxes to form a makeshift cairn. On top of this landmark, a pickax had been planted with a fresh orange impaled on one of its spikes—proof that the *Aurora* had arrived.

As Bickerton wrote:

We flung off our harnesses and dived at the cave. . . . In the centre of the floor was a food bag, the top covered with oranges and pineapples artistically arranged, on the shelf was a hurricane lamp covered with notes from earlier arrivals. . . . When I saw all this I let out a shout and the others soon came on top of me. We then set out to make more noise than one would imagine the little place capable of containing.

It was 1:30 a.m. on January 18 when the trio approached the hut:

All was very quiet and we sneaked in and all three stood in the doorway of the large hut unnoticed, some were asleep and some reading in bed, we shouted "Rise and shine!" at the top of our voices, and each man was out of his bunk like a Jack-in-the-Box. I still have only a confused idea of what followed. I remember eating strawberries and cream, drinking tea, smoking cigars and talking at a breakneck speed all the time.

Despite Bickerton's conviction that his ill-starred Western Party had accomplished far less than he had hoped, Mawson eventually saluted its achievements in *The Home of the Blizzard*. Noting that the team's retreat in "atrocious weather conditions remains a nightmare to the participants," Mawson added, "But the results were amply worth the sacrifice, for they have furnished concrete account of the hinterland of that stretch of coast which Dumont d'Urville sighted from sea and to which he gave the name of Adelie Land."

During the five days since the arrival of the *Aurora*, the men at Winter Quarters had been frantically packing boxes of gear and crates of scientific specimens before carrying them to the shore to load onto the ship. With the arrival of Bickerton's party, expectations reached a fever pitch. As soon as Mawson's Far Eastern Party came in, the *Aurora* could set sail westward, pick up Frank Wild's team, and head for Australia. So far, it seemed, the expedition had been an unqualified success.

On the 17th, someone in the hut reported that a party was coming in, apparently accompanied by dogs. "Then Thank God it is M[awson]," John King Davis wrote in his diary. "What a splendid thing. Only one more party now, and then we can away." The arrival instead of Bickerton's party came as "a great surprise. . . . The supposed dogs must have been a mirage."

On the 18th, Davis wrote, "There is still no news of the Doctor. I cannot help feeling a bit anxious. . . . We shall have to do something soon." The next day, he recorded, "There is no sign of the Doctor. I do not know what to think." The following day, January 20: "There is still no sign of Mawson. What has happened to him, I cannot think." Davis had found the papers ordering him, after a certain date, to leave Cape Denison to go to the relief of Frank Wild's party. But he could not quite bring himself to take that drastic course yet.

The vigil continued. Day after day, in his diary, Davis wrote some version of his mantra of mounting worry: "There is still no sign of Mawson." The men tried to keep dark thoughts out of their heads and free from their conversations, but they crowded in all the same. On January 24, Davis confessed, "There is still no sign of the Dr's party and I am therefore still feeling low and depressed." As Charles Laseron later recalled, "As day by day went by the sense deepened that something tragic had occurred."

Fifteen hundred miles to the west of Cape Denison, with no possible knowledge of what was transpiring among the Main Base parties, Frank Wild's eight-man team at Western Base was carrying out its own program of exploration. Reconnaissance forays during the spring months had given the men a good head start on their summer missions, as they had not only broken trails but laid depots of food, fuel, and even sledges to be picked up on the main thrusts.

Wild's scheme was similar to Mawson's, though simpler. Two three-man parties would follow the coastline east and west of the Shackleton Ice Shelf as far as they could before turning back. The other two men would remain at the hut—nicknamed the Grottoes, in homage to the snowpack covering its walls and the long snow tunnel that gave access to the door—as they kept the vital living quarters in good shape and made daily meteorological observations. Wild would lead the Eastern Coastal Party. The Western Party would be in the charge of Sydney Jones, twenty-four years old at the inception of the AAE. Raised in Queensland, Jones had studied medicine at the University of Sydney, where, according to one teammate, he was "considered the best surgeon the Sydney University has turned out in recent years."

Jones's teammates were Archibald Hoadley and George Dovers, twenty-four and twenty-one years old respectively when Mawson had signed them on. From Melbourne, Hoadley was a mining engineer; Dovers, from Sydney, worked for the government as a surveyor. Their mission was a comparatively straightforward one: to map the coastline west of the Shackleton Ice Shelf for some 200 miles. Thanks to the accidents of landscape, the journey of the Western Coastal Party would turn out to be the safest and the biologically richest of the six major journeys accomplished by the AAE.

Wild's two parties were burdened by no deadline such as the January 15 ultimatum Mawson had given the Main Base teams. The men at Western Base knew that the *Aurora* was due to arrive at Cape Denison by that date, but they had no idea when the ship would come to pick them up. Given that the year before, it had taken four weeks to explore west from Commonwealth Bay before finding a landing site 1,500 miles away, Wild's team knew only that, if all went well, the *Aurora* would arrive sometime—most likely weeks—after January 15. Wild had been ordered to be ready by January 30 for a pickup, but he was aware that that was an arbitrary date based on an educated guess on Mawson and Davis's parts. For all the men at Western Base knew, the *Aurora* (as "Gloomy" Davis had cautioned them the year before) might have been lost on its return to Australia in early 1912. If that were true, there was virtually no hope that the eight men could be rescued. All these uncertainties generated a psychological strain on the men at Western Base far crueler than anything the Main Base teams had to endure.

Unlike all five other major parties of the AAE, Jones's trio had a set, predetermined goal. The men knew that Gaussberg, an extinct

volcano that had been discovered and climbed by Erich von Drygalski's German team in 1902, lay about 200 miles west of the Grottoes.
There would be little point exploring beyond that peak, since the
terrain of Kaiser Wilhelm Land (as Drygalski had named the arena
of his exploration) was known. But it would be a handsome deed to
map the westernmost stretch of terra incognita along the coast of
Adélie Land and link up Australian discoveries with the decade-old
German ones.

The men set off on November 7. Two days later, they reached a
sizable depot the team had laid during the spring months. That cache
included a second sledge. Loading food for thirteen weeks and all the
requisite gear on both sledges, they found that their burden weighed
an ungainly 1,200 pounds. Although they tried to haul both sledges
in tandem, that feat proved impossible. Instead, the men reconciled
themselves to the demoralizing drudgery of relaying—pulling one
sledge ahead a few miles, leaving it there, hiking back, then pulling
the second sledge up to join the first.

The men suffered the minor crevasse plunges and the days of
tent-bound storm-waiting that all the AAE parties had to endure, but
still marched onward with clockwork efficiency—so much so that on
November 25, eighteen days out, they indulged in a weeklong detour.
That day, Dovers spotted what he thought was an ice-covered island
far to the northwest, towering out of the frozen sea. Haswell Island,
as the team named this apparition, seemed to be well worth investi-
gating. Leaving behind one sledge and most of their provisions, the
trio worked out a devious route to approach the anomalous outcrop-
ping of rock and ice.

There they stumbled upon a biological paradise. A floe attached
to the island was a rookery, so dense with emperor penguins that the
animals covered a tract of four or five acres. "The sound of their cries
coming across the ice," Jones reported, "reminded one of the noise
from a distant sports ground during a well-contested game. . . . We
estimated the numbers to be seven thousand five hundred, the great
majority being young birds."

Intending a visit of only twenty-four hours, the men were stuck on

Haswell by a five-day storm, during which they hiked out each day to explore their novel surroundings. The small, rocky island turned out to be the habitat of immense throngs of birds of all kinds. Here the men found the first nesting ground of the Antarctic petrel ever discovered. There were also hordes of skua gulls that swooped down to steal unguarded penguin eggs and chicks, cape pigeons, southern fulmars, and other species of petrel. The men marveled at the luxuriant green algae floating in meltwater pools, and at lush carpets of lichen furring the rocks. Out on the sea ice, near tide cracks, Weddell seals lounged in great numbers.

Unwilling simply to observe and photograph, Dovers gathered about a dozen eggs from Adélie penguins. Back in camp, the men fried them up. As Dovers wrote in his diary:

We had pepper & salt & Jones had with great forethought put in three tea tin lids to serve as plates. How shall I describe those eggs, fried in a little pemmican fat, we each ate three, & all voted them the best eggs we had ever tasted. Jones said there is a flavour about these that goes straight to the heart.

By December 3, the men had returned to their cached sledge and resumed their main trek. With them they brought all kinds of specimens from Haswell Island. Still relaying, they pushed onward, veering 20 miles inland to avoid gashing crevasse fields near the coast. On December 12, with a favorable wind filling their makeshift sails, for the first time the men were able to haul both sledges simultaneously. And on the 16th, they spotted Gaussberg in the distance. But the approach to the extinct volcano turned out to be even trickier than the route to Haswell Island. Another week passed before the men got to the peak and climbed the 1,200 feet to its summit.

On top, the men found two rock cairns and, lying beside them, bamboo poles that the Germans had mounted, but that had blown over during the intervening decade. Search as they might, however, they could find no note or written record from Drygalski's team. It was an eerie, tantalizing moment—the only occasion in the whole duration of the AAE that any of Mawson's men would behold human artifacts other than the ones they themselves had brought to the continent.

Jones calculated that, seven weeks out from The Grottoes, the men had marched some 300 miles (including relays) to gain a distance of 215. They could have pushed on for another week, but, as Jones later wrote, "from the summit of Gaussberg one could see almost as far as could be marched in a week." They turned homeward on December 26, having devoured a plum pudding on Christmas Day.

The return was essentially uneventful. On January 21, the men's seventy-sixth day on the trail, they reached The Grottoes, "concluding," as Mawson rather dryly wrote in *The Home of the Blizzard*, "an achievement of which Jones, Hoadley and Dovers should feel justly proud." There they found all five of their Western Base teammates in residence. The latter had quite a different tale to tell from that of the straightforward jaunt to Gaussberg, and a far more frightening one.

In late August, still under wintry conditions, Wild had led a party 84 miles east to lay a substantial depot for the upcoming summer's exploration. At a nunatak (an upthrust of bedrock poking through the surrounding ice) that the men named Hippo, they cached six weeks' food for three men, along with a sledge, which they buried in a three-foot-deep hole, then covered with a six-foot mound of snow with a bamboo pole mounted on top to serve as a landmark. The night before, the temperature had dropped to minus 47 degrees Fahrenheit.

Even that relatively modest journey was plagued with trials. On the return march, violent winds pinned the men down in an improvised bivouac hole. Wrote Wild later:

Many of the gusts must have been well over 100 miles an hour. One of them lifted Harrisson clean over my head and dropped him 20 feet away. . . . We remained in this hole five days, the

Frank Wild

Gathering ice outside the hut during a fierce blizzard

A winter evening around the gramophone

A petrel on its nest

An Adelie penguin with eggs

Blizzard, one of the husky pups born during the expedition

Two sledge dogs chained to a box

Two men standing in an ice hole

Mertz at the entrance of the hut

A "grotto of mysteries" in the ice

Keeping one's balance in a 100-mile-an-hour wind

The ice cliff coastline east of Winter Quarters

wind at hurricane force the whole time and horrible avalanches crashing down at frequent intervals, every one giving me pains in the stomach; I could not get over the dread of being flattened out like a squashed beetle.

For the summer's Eastern Coastal Party, Wild chose Alexander Kennedy and Andrew Watson as his companions. Yet another pair of young Aussie science graduates, they had attended the University of Sydney and the University of Adelaide respectively. To caretake the hut and make daily meteorological observations, Wild appointed the biologist Charles Harrisson and Morton Moyes, another of Mawson's students at Adelaide who was also a superb athlete, having starred in cricket matches and won the high jump championship of South Australia.

At the last minute, Harrisson begged to be allowed to accompany the Eastern Coastal Party as far as Hippo Depot. "As on the return he would have to travel nearly 100 miles alone," Wild admitted, "I did not like the idea, but he demonstrated that he could erect a tent by himself so I agreed that he should come."

Of the nine dogs Wild's team had brought to Western Base, only three were still alive, another having vanished in the winter. The survivors were named Amundsen, Zip, and Switzerland. Ever the dog-lover, Wild resolved to bring them on the journey, hoping they might aid in the sledge-hauling. In the end, the terrain proved too tough for the huskies, who had their annoying habits on the trail. "Zip broke loose one night," Wild reported, "and ate one of my socks which was hanging on the sledge to dry; it probably tasted of seal blubber from the boots. Switzerland, too, was rather a bother, eating his harness whenever he had a chance."

On October 30, the four men set out with two sledges, carrying food for fourteen weeks plus an additional four weeks' supplies for Harrisson and the dogs. The total weight was 970 pounds. The huskies and one man pulled one sledge, while three men hauled the other. It took them a week to reach Hippo Depot. There they received a rude shock. The cached food bags were scattered across the snow. But the sledge, buried three feet deep two months earlier, had disappeared. The men searched for it all the next day, probing the snow with shovels, but found no sign of it. Apparently the hurricane winds had lifted the heavy sledge out of its snow hole and blown it far away.

This unexpected setback forced a cruel decision on Wild. He would have to commandeer the sledge Harrisson had intended to pull back to The Grottoes to replace the one that had been carried away. And he would have to recruit Harrisson himself as a fourth member of the Eastern Coastal Party. As Harrisson wrote in his diary, "I cannot go back in any safety without a sledge." (Sledges, with sturdy harnesses leading from them to the sledgers, had served countless times on the AAE as a dead weight to check a man's crevasse fall. In addition, Harrisson could not possibly carry all the gear for the return journey on his back.) "The great trouble is poor Moyes. He will be left alone for the 12 weeks, thinking I have 'gone under' on the return journey. He will have a bad time, & I am concerned for him; but he is a sensible fellow, & should come thro this ordeal." Wild added, "I was extremely sorry for Moyes, but . . . it could not be helped."

Only two days beyond the Hippo nunatak, the men encountered crevasses and pressure ridges so thick the dogs had to be unharnessed, as the men lightened the loads and ferried the sledges delicately back and forth across the most treacherous passages. One snow bridge collapsed just after a sledge passed over it, leaving, Wild swore, "a hole 12 feet wide and hundreds of feet deep."

On November 14, the men left another depot of supplies for their return journey. Only three days later, they ran smack into the edge of a huge glacier. It would later be named by Mawson the Denman Glacier, after the governor-general of Australia, a patron of the expedition. The ice flow, between eight and 12 miles across and 80 miles from head to snout, stopped the team in its tracks. None of the four men, not even the vastly experienced Wild, had ever seen anything like it. Indeed, no one on the AAE would behold a more chaotic piece of topography anywhere in Adélie Land.

"Cascades of shattered ice, so broken that it stood out a great white scar on the icecap & not a single dark thread of unbroken ice through it!" wrote Harrisson later. Watson added, "To cross where

we were was impossible unless we had wings or aeroplanes." No matter what an obstacle the Denman Glacier presented to the party's
hopes, Wild later called it "the most wonderful sight I have ever
seen." It was impossible at the time to gauge the glacier's size, but
Wild understood the geologic torment it represented:

> The Denman Glacier moves much more rapidly than the Shack-
> leton Shelf and in tearing through the latter, breaks it up and also
> shatters its own sides. At the actual point of contact is an enormous
> cavern over 1,000 feet wide and 400 feet deep with crevasses at
> the bottom which appear to have no bottom. . . . Enormous blocks
> of solid ice forced high up into the air beyond. The whole was the
> wildest, maddest and yet the grandest thing imaginable.

The only hope for further progress was to skirt the glacier. Faced
with the choice of heading north out onto the sea ice to try to round
the glacier's snout or heading south inland to flank it at its head, Wild
chose the former course. The work of the next ten days was more
grueling, discouraging, and dangerous than anything the Eastern
Coastal Party had yet faced. On several days, storms and snowfall
kept the men tent-bound. There was no possibility of using the three
dogs to pull: instead, the men were reduced to "hauling up and lowering the sledges with an alpine rope and twisting and turning in
all directions, with waves and hills, monuments, statues, and fairy
castles in all directions, from a few feet to over 300 feet in height."
Visibility was usually limited to a few hundred yards, so the men had
to climb ice towers to scout the route ahead.

On November 26, a full day of brutal work gained the party only
1,050 yards. All four fell up to their waists in crevasses, Harrisson
15 feet into one. "I received rather a nasty squeeze," Wild recorded
that day, "through falling into a hole while going downhill, the sledge
running on to me before I could get clear. So far as we can see, the
same kind of country continues and one cannot help thinking about
having to return through this infernal mess."

On November 27, Wild made the inevitable decision. "We turn

back tomorrow," he wrote in his diary, "for the simple reason we cannot go any farther." He added, "We could push on further east from here, but it would be by lowering the gear piecemeal into chasms 50 to 100 feet deep, and hauling it up on the other side; each crevasse taking at least two hours to negotiate. For such slow progress, I don't feel justified in risking the lives of the party."

It was a bitter decision—Wild, after all, had hoped to sledge outward well into December—but a wise one. On the return to the Grottoes, the four-man Eastern Coastal Party would face all the tribulations it could handle.

Meanwhile, back at the Grottoes, Morton Moyes had settled in for a solitary vigil the likes of which no other AAE member would undergo. Even the other men's leave-takings at the end of October had had a certain ominous tone about them. "Wild gave me his Diaries in case of accident, & letter for Dr. Mawson," Moyes wrote in his diary on October 28. And a few days later, "George [Dovers] gave me a packet of letters to give to his father if he had an accident but I hope to return them to him in 3 months."

From in front of the hut, Moyes watched the men depart. "Seems strange to lose all these men for 3 months," he wrote, "& also to see them dying out as a faint speck on the white endless glacier." During the following weeks, he tried to fill his time cooking, recording meteorological data, and reading (appropriately, perhaps) Dante's *Inferno*. On November 11, he recorded, "Had a few ski runs on the slope after lunch, but no fun by one's self." Harrisson's imminent return would, he felt, make all the difference.

Moyes had been a member of the team that had laid Hippo Depot in early September. That trip had taken twelve days out (three of them tent-bound in a storm). Knowing the way, in warmer November with more hours of daylight, the Eastern Coastal Party ought to improve on that time, Moyes thought. Harrisson's job was only to drop his load of gear and food and return with the dogs to the Grottoes. When three weeks had passed, Moyes began to worry. "Harris-son out 26 days & no sign," he wrote on November 24. And the next day, "Harrisson must be short of grub. I'll have to move out after him if he is not back in 3 days." But five days later, Moyes was still in the hut. The anxiety was mounting. "Like to know where Harrisson is," he complained on November 30.

By the beginning of December, it was impossible to banish the fear that something terrible had happened to Harrisson, or even to the whole party. On the 3rd, the "sensible fellow" that Harrisson deemed his friend to be came to the fore as Moyes wrote out a memo to himself trying to solve the puzzle, almost in the terms of a Euclidean proof. The document was headed "Where is Harrisson?"

> I. May have gone with E party
> II. Came back homewards

>   I. a. With dog team would have been useful 1 month, then dogs had to be killed.
>   b. Extra man not needed after 4 weeks.
>   c. Reduce time from 14 to 11½ weeks.
>   d. More weight with tents & gear.
>   [Therefore] I. not probable.

>   II. 2a. Still out sketching [Harrisson was a gifted artist]
>   2b. Found a crevasse
>   2c. Snowed up
>   2a. (1) only grub for 4 weeks for self & dogs
>   (2) Not much to sketch
>   2b. (1) While on track of 1st journey, few crevasses & all visible, although may be hidden ones.
>   (2) Very careful & not likely to strike one.
>   2c. (1) No heavy snows for 2–3 weeks altho' bad light.
>   (2) Careful man in putting up tent.
>   (3) Could cut out as always has knife with him.
> *Answer*   by Echo???

Whatever Moyes meant by the cryptic last line of his memo, only he knew. But in his hyperlogical way, he had rejected as "not probable" the very explanation for Harrisson's absence that happened to be the true one.

Therefore, Moyes decided, Harrisson must be in serious trouble. On December 7, he set out pulling a spare sledge to look for his friend. He intended to search first in a badly crevassed area the August–September party had crossed. There, he speculated, "Harrisson with his dogs could be trapped in that honeycomb of death, waiting desperately for assistance." But three days later, when he arrived at the site, Moyes saw only a set of sledge tracks heading east.

Zigzagging to try to pick up a possible track laid by Harrisson on an alternative route home, Moyes felt himself starting to go snowblind. Tripping and stumbling in the snow, he realized that he had to head back at once himself, or else he might become the kind of victim he sought. He fell into one crevasse, but his sledge harness caught him.

Back at The Grottoes on December 17, Moyes felt his sanity starting to erode. "The silence is so painful now that I have a continual singing in my left ear," he wrote on December 20, "much like a barrel organ, only its the same tune all the time." The approach of Christmas brought only gloom: "Christmas Eve! . . . Dont think I'll hang up my stocking, looks like asking for presents."

As John King Davis would point out many years later, by not being able to cross the Denman Glacier, Wild's team missed a remarkable discovery that would not take place for another thirty-five years. Far to the east in the distance, Wild and his men had glimpsed patches of bare rock. These were but a hint of an anomalous ice-free cape, 300 square miles in extent, that lies on the 100th meridian east of Greenwich. The Bunger Hills, as they would subsequently be named, abound not only in bare bedrock but in meltwater lakes. They were first spotted from the air in 1947. A gutsy US Navy pilot, David Bunger, managed to land his plane on one of the lakes.

Bunger's effort was part of Operation Highjump, led by Admiral Richard E. Byrd, who called the place "one of the most remarkable regions on earth." Among the Bunger Hills, Byrd proclaimed, "An island suitable for life had been found in a universe of death."

To compensate for the disappointment of having to turn back early, Wild's team took its time returning to the Grottoes, making detours to explore isolated peaks and offshore islands. By now the three dogs had become mere companions, not sledge-haulers. On December 6, as Wild coldly recorded, "Switzerland had to be killed, as I cannot afford any more biscuit. Amundsen ate his flesh without hesitation, but Zip refused it." In disgust, Harrisson added that Amundsen "started whining and crying for the meat, almost before the poor wretch was dead, and when thrown the still hot liver, bolted it almost without a bite."

The return march was not without its perils. New snow had covered the men's outward tracks, so they had to probe the treacherous surface for crevasses all over again. One day Watson fell into a huge crevasse, stopped only by "a heavy jerk" on the alpine rope connecting him to Wild. It took the three men on the surface using two ropes twenty minutes to haul the frightened man out, "no worse," Wild laconically noted, "except for a bruised shin and the loss of a glove."

The men celebrated Christmas with "a little bottle—just a wee one—of whiskey which we made toddy," toasting friends far and near. Then Wild "formally took possession of the land in the name of the Expedition, for the Empire."

Back in the Grottoes, a dispirited Morton Moyes glumly rang in the New Year: "Another year gone, & no much [sic] but personal benefit to show for it." Five days later, during a Sunday snowstorm, Moyes read Macaulay and the Bible and tried not to worry about how "If this proportion of blizzards keeps up, the sledges will be overdue." He added, "These days inside seem very long, in fact it is strange what a difference a few hours on the floe makes."

Many years later, Moyes explained to his nephew the psychological toll his ten weeks alone in the hut had taken on him:

A man can be lonely in a crowd but not alone.

It was not loneliness, but a sense of acute aloneness that I felt most keenly . . .

Here in this type of desolation, surviving like the last leaf on a branch, a person becomes aware of his manhood but it is not enough.

He turns in upon himself. If he has never heard of God before, he is looking for him then, and instinctively searching for a spirit to whom he can reach out and draw near to for peace of mind, or so I found, otherwise I could have become mentally unbalanced.

On January 6, the day after the Sunday blizzard, Moyes sat reading in the hut when, at 12:30 p.m., he thought he heard a familiar ship's tune being sung. He told himself, "You are going dippy at last." But, as he wrote that day in his diary, "I rushed outside, & nearly crazy with delight saw a sledge party approaching with all flags set." Wild recorded Moyes's reaction: "When he saw there were four of us, he stood on his head for joy and was so overcome with emotion; it was some time before he could talk with us."

That evening, Moyes wrote, "Feel like a 2-year old tonight after my 10 weeks loneliness. Gave them a jolly fine feed all day."

Fifteen days later, the Western Coastal Party came in. Now there was little for the eight men to do but wait. They packed up most of their gear, their unused rations, and the scientific specimens and sledged them to the edge of the ice shelf, from which they might be loaded onto the *Aurora*. Harrisson went on happily biologizing, catching fish and crustaceans with cage traps and sounding the bay off the ice shelf for depth readings.

January 30, the date by which Wild had been told to be ready to depart, came and went. The next day, Moyes wrote, "The Aurora should have been in to-day, and great yarns about the mail being overdue." Ever the pragmatist, Wild decided to hunt seals to supplement the men's food, in the dire event that they had to spend a second winter on the ice. "The food supply would have been quite sufficient for a second year with the exception of meat," he later wrote. "There was a little more than two tons of coal out of the twelve landed, and by laying in a supply of blubber before the seals disappeared we should have done fairly well for fuel."

No Antarctic explorer ever faced tough situations with greater equanimity than Wild. But the unspoken corollary to the men's fate should the *Aurora*, for whatever reason, fail to arrive, was that whether or not the men survived a second winter, there was scant hope they would ever be found and rescued.

Adding to the men's anxiety was the fact that, despite the warming of two summer months, three miles of thin sea ice still lay beyond the edge of the towering Shackleton Shelf and open water. To aid potential searchers, Wild "had erected direction boards close to the cliff edge, one at two miles and the other five miles north of the hut, and also fitted a lamp and reflector at mast head which was lighted every night and would be visible at least eight miles."

The first two weeks of February passed, in almost continuously bad weather, with no sign of the ship. The men allowed themselves to speculate as to what might be causing the delay. "We surmise that one of the first base parties have been late returning—hence ship delayed at Adelie Land," Harrisson wrote in his diary on February 16; "there's time yet, and we hope for the best. But it makes me anxious when the thought of another year without seeing, without even a word from wife or children—and such thoughts will haunt me."

On February 20, Wild and Dovers carried a big signboard three and a half miles north to the edge of the sea cliff and erected it. They tied it to a bamboo pole, with a flag on top. In large letters, the sign read "3 MILES," with an arrow pointing toward the hut.

By now, however, hope was ebbing as despair crept in. "Started the [acetylene] gas again tonight," Moyes wrote on February 16, "but we hope it is not for another year." And six days later: "No ship yet. All our gear at floe edge ready for it." Exactly one year and one week had passed since the eight men had disembarked on the ice shelf to begin their Antarctic adventure.

6

DEAD EASY TO DIE

Back at Cape Denison, Captain John King Davis finally felt that he needed to take action. Nine days had passed since he had brought the *Aurora* into Commonwealth Bay, with no sign of Mawson's party—now a full week overdue after the deadline Mawson himself had imposed on all the teams before setting out the previous November.

Among the papers in the hut, Davis had found a more detailed note of instructions in Mawson's hand, addressed to him:

> Should I or my party not have arrived before the 1st Feb. you are to steam E scanning the coast—as far as lat 66° 45' South [by] 145° 50' [East]. If by that time no flag or other sign of the party appears you are to land 3 volunteers (Bage Madigan & Webb are the most capable leaders) capable of active sledging and navigation, and necessary equipment to winter at the hut—keep scientific records and in the summer of 1914 make a journey in our tracks to discover if possible our whereabouts. We shall have steered for the land seen by the Terra Nova in the summer of 1910–11.

It was a tall order, but not an impossible one. In fact, just the previous year, the members of Scott's *Terra Nova* expedition had faced a similar challenge and carried it out bravely. When the polar party of five had failed to return to base camp at Cape Evans by mid-February 1912, two parties set out one month apart to search for them. Finding no sign of Scott and his four partners, the men concluded that they were almost certainly dead. But those men wintered over for the second time, then launched a more ambitious search in October. On November 12, they found the tent with the bodies of Scott, Bowers, and Wilson (the last three to die) inside, only 11 miles south of a depot that would have saved their lives. By recovering Scott's diary, his teammates—and ultimately the world—learned the tragic story of the second party to reach the South Pole in day-by-day detail.

Had there been no Western Base party to pick up, Davis could have lingered in Commonwealth Bay well into February, departing only when new sea ice threatened to trap the ship. But if he tarried too long waiting for Mawson, Ninnis, and Mertz, Davis would risk dooming the eight men under Frank Wild, languishing 1,500 miles to the west.

On January 22, 1913, Davis—now officially in command of the AAE—announced the makeup of the party fated to winter over a second year. He appointed not three men to that thankless task, but six. They were Cecil Madigan, who was to be in charge, along with Bob Bage, Frank Bickerton, Archibald McLean, and Alfred Hodgeman. The sixth man, who had come down with the *Aurora*, was Sidney Jeffryes, an experienced radio operator who would relieve Walter Hannam. With the others' help, Jeffryes would try to get the masts up and the radio working, and thus finally establish contact via Macquarie Island with Australia.

A first draft of Davis's orders to the men survives. In it, Percy Correll was initially slated to be one of the six. At some point, Davis drew a line through Correll's name and wrote Hodgeman's directly above it. One wonders whether the youngest member of the expedition ever learned how close he came to spending another winter in the windiest place on earth.

Among the five men selected to winter over again, none was more distraught than Madigan. He had already postponed his Rhodes scholarship to Oxford for a year by agreeing to go on the AAE, and he had no idea whether the Rhodes committee would tolerate another year's deferment. On January 28, in an agonized letter to his fiancée, Madigan wrote, "My darling, this expedition, which has gone so happily so far, is, I fear, going to end in tragedy." He still held out hope for Mawson's party, but the three men were now thirteen days overdue.

Everything is being done to avoid a scare—they may have missed a depot and have gone down to the coast, and there be subsisting on seal and penguin—or they may have gone too far with the dogs, bitten off more than they can chew, so to speak, and cannot get back in time by man-hauling when the dogs are gone. . . .

I put this as it was put to me [by Davis]—I am the most efficient sledger . . . and Bage's eyes have gone, and he is the only man in that party who can navigate, I know the coast line for 300 m. East, where the Doctor went. . . .

I think I lose more by staying than anyone here. But there seemed nothing else for it—Captain Davis felt obliged to ask me to stay—and I could not go without a point blank refusal—I should have felt a coward and a deserter for the rest of my life, a miserable selfish being, if I had done so.

Frank Bickerton expressed his own dismay in more matter-of-fact language in a letter to his sister. After explaining the situation at Cape Denison, he concluded, "So the only thing to do is to leave a party in this breezy hole for another year. It is a rotten game & a rotten place but nevertheless has to be done by someone."

Percy Gray, second in command on the *Aurora*, who by now was thoroughly disenchanted with Davis's leadership, had a curious reaction to the wait for Mawson. As early as January 17, even before Bickerton's Western Party had come in, he anticipated the possibility of leaving men to winter over.

We clear out, as far as I can gather, on the 20th. whether the parties have turned up or not, so probably one or two will have to be
left behind. I don't expect many of the shore crowd will be particularly keen. I should very much like to stay the winter down
here myself, but I am afraid it is useless to suggest it to Gloomy
as he would never sanction anything he thinks anybody would
like to do. I should much prefer it to doing another dreadful year
in this ship under his command.

Gray also felt that Davis's deadline for departing from Commonwealth Bay was premature: "As a matter of fact, I think we could
hang on here quite well until the 27th., that would then leave us 24
days to get round to Wild and clear out north. . . . I wonder whether
Gloomy thinks about these things. I think he is in too much of a
panic to think about anything."

The ten AAE members not chosen to stay another winter kept
their feelings of relief to themselves. Yet as Laseron wrote decades
later, "We went about our tasks with heavy hearts at this time, and
those of us who were to depart had almost a guilty feeling at thus
leaving our comrades behind."

There was much to do to prepare the six men for a second winter.
The *Aurora* had come laden with provisions for just such a possibility, so that once all its cargo was offloaded, the men had enough food
and fuel. Penguins and seals were killed to supplement the larder.
And the radio masts were re-erected.

Now Davis revised his departure date. On January 22, the same
day that he deputized the six to winter over, he resolved to send a
search party out along the track of Mawson's Far Eastern Party, leaving on the 25th and returning no later than the 30th. Only if that
search proved fruitless would Davis steam out of Commonwealth
Bay toward the far-off Western Base.

The search party heading out on the 25th was made up of Hodgeman, McLean, and Frank Hurley. In four days of atrocious weather—
warm, wet, and windy, causing the surface to turn to slush—the men
sledged 25 miles east. "Our sleeping-bags and clothes became so

wet," Hurley recalled, "that in spite of fatigue, we preferred action in the open to the discomfort of resting and shivering in the shelter of the tent."

On the fourth day, with the team's turnaround imminent, the weather started to clear. The men built a big cairn of snow blocks on top of which they left a ration bag and directions back to Aladdin's Cave, from which refuge the hut lay only five and a half miles north. Wrote Hurley:

> Through the glasses I then swept the horizon—limited to a range of three miles owing to the mist—for signs of the missing men, but could see nothing of them. What could have happened? Had they passed us in the blizzard or had some terrible disaster befallen them? With these thoughts disturbing our minds we turned back.

On January 22, Davis had gone on shore to "stretch my legs" with a short hike inland. Two miles from the hut, he turned and gazed north. That view and the feelings it provoked stayed with him the rest of his life.

> Most of the ice around the winter quarters had melted and . . . the immediate surroundings of the hut looked like a handful of rubble that had been carelessly flung there by a giant. . . . With what nostalgic longing did I look upon that glorious expanse of open sea! Turning inland, the apparently level ice-cap met the sky line—a white, silent, frozen wilderness, dreary, but also lovely beyond all description. Somewhere beyond that sloping, dome-like horizon, somewhere beyond my limited vision, within that vast, unfeeling, sterile solitude, were Mawson and his companions, dead or alive.

On January 29, the day before the three-man search party returned, Davis steered the *Aurora* out of Commonwealth Bay to make a three-day scout along the eastern coast. If this search too proved fruitless, upon his return he would board the ten men not expected to winter over and head west to gather up Wild's Western Base. The men on the ship constantly swept the shore with binoculars, looking for a flag or a signal of any kind. Along the edge of the Mertz Glacier tongue they fired off rockets and flew a big kite, hoping that Mawson's party might spot these signals of rescue close at hand. An hour before midnight on January 30, Davis turned the ship around. "It is a terrible situation," he wrote in his diary. "We dare not delay much longer if we are to reach Wild this year."

But now, once again, the fiendish weather at Cape Denison thwarted the expedition's plans. The *Aurora* arrived back in Commonwealth Bay late on January 31, but the wind and waves were too strong to launch a motorboat toward the shore. Davis could not even communicate with the men anxiously awaiting his return and their escape. During the next seven days, the gales never moderated sufficiently for Davis to pick up the refugees. Instead, it was all he could do to steam in circles inside the bay, keeping the ship from ramming reefs or the surrounding cliffs. He was burning nine tons of coal a day. Davis's mood grew frantic. On February 6, the sixth straight day of hurricane winds, he wrote, "If we do not get these people off soon, I do not know what will happen. We shall have to leave them here I suppose."

Meanwhile, the men at Winter Quarters could see the ship, tantalizingly close, but could only wait for the weather to change. They began to fear that the *Aurora* itself might not survive the storm—an outcome that would doom them all. During that endless week's vigil, there was still no sign of Mawson's party.

Finally, on the morning of February 8, the gale died out. Davis brought the ship close to shore. Remembered Hurley, "From masthead to waterline she was sheathed with ice. . . . On the furrowed faces of Captain Davis and the crew was written an epic of struggle. Davis did not speak of the ordeal, but I afterwards learned that he had not left the bridge throughout the seven racking days and nights."

The parting between the men staying on for another winter and those freed to head back to Australia was hurried and deeply emotional. As soon as the latter were on board, Davis ordered "Full steam ahead." "As we drew away from the land," Hurley recalled, "six tiny specks were seen waving from a rocky summit—soon to be swallowed up in the vastness of the solitude."

For one of those specks—Archibald McLean, the AAE's doctor— the uncertainty had become intolerable. "We were all heartily glad," he wrote in his diary, "when [the *Aurora*] was out of sight."

Almost two months earlier, on December 14, 1912, Mawson, Mertz, and Ninnis had set out from their overnight camp on the polar plateau. In five weeks of sledging, they had reached a point more than 300 miles southeast of Winter Quarters. Thanks to the added pull provided by the huskies, the Far Eastern Party had covered more ground than any of the other three main exploratory missions that had left Cape Denison, and more than either of the Western Base's two coastal parties. They had not quite linked up the terra incognita of Adélie Land with the distant hills of Victoria Land seen from shipboard by Scott's men in 1911, but Mawson had every reason to hope that within the coming week, his trio could push on, attain a goal 350 miles out from the hut, and complete that cherished linkage.

Although Mawson could not know the other teams' turnaround dates, both Bage's Southern Party and Madigan's Eastern Coastal Party would head home only on December 21, while Bickerton's Western Party would not begin its voyage back to Winter Quarters until December 28. Another week of progress for Mawson's team seemed entirely reasonable, and by making faster times with lighter sledges on the return journey, the Far Eastern Party ought to be able to meet Mawson's own deadline of January 15 for its arrival at Cape Denison.

But then, utterly without warning, Ninnis had plunged with his sledge and the team's six best dogs into the gigantic crevasse that, as Mertz and Mawson had crossed it only minutes before, had seemed a harmless obstacle akin to scores of crevasses the team had sledged across without a serious incident during the previous five weeks. Having shouted for hours into the gaping abyss, unable to rig any kind of rope to descend into its dark depths, glimpsing only the broken body of a groaning dog, the dead body of another, and a few shattered pieces of gear that had fetched up on an ice shelf 150 feet below the surface, Mawson and Mertz had finally accepted the inevitable and started back on their homeward trek.

Among all the crevasse plunges suffered by all the three-man teams during the whole duration of the AAE, why, one wonders, had Ninnis's accident so far exceeded the others in its catastrophic result? Time and again, other men in other parts of Adélie Land had broken through snow bridges, only to be caught by ropes tied to teammates or by harnesses attached to their sledges, after falls that never left them dangling more than 25 feet below the surface and that never caused any of them a serious injury. Frank Wild's Eastern Coastal Party had been stopped cold by a chaotic labyrinth of crevasses that looked far more dangerous than the smooth, apparently innocuous plain of snow Mawson's trio traversed on December 14.

Nor can one find fault with Mawson's logistical plan. It seemed, in fact, a scheme ideally devised to maximize the team's safety— Mertz on skis scouting ahead, Mawson coming second with the least vital gear and food on his sledge, Ninnis taking up the rear and having to face hazards only after his teammates had successfully avoided them. No expedition exploring Antarctica, even today, has been able to figure out a way to reduce the danger to zero. Crevasses are a way of life on the southern continent, and for every one that lies open to the sky, announcing its treacheries, there are one or two whose wind-sculpted snow bridges hide them from sight, even to the keenest eyes of the most seasoned adventurers.

In the end, Ninnis's death, and the terrible survival ordeal into which it plunged his partners, must be attributed to sheer bad luck.

The two men now had food for themselves for only a week and a half, and no dog food whatsoever. Besides their tent, the team's shovel, its only ice ax, and such sundry items as their mugs and spoons had vanished into the crevasse with Ninnis. A more grievous loss than spoons was Mertz's burberry outer trousers. As a substitute to ward off the cold, he donned a pair of woolen under-trousers that had providentially been stored on Mawson's sledge. The first meal after the accident consisted, according to Mawson, of "a thin soup made by boiling up all the empty food bags preparatory to throwing them away." To feed the ravenous dogs, Mawson and Mertz "tossed them some worn out fur mitts, finnesko, and several spare raw hide straps."

Then, driven by the adrenaline of their despair, Mertz and Mawson sledged through the night of December 14–15, covering 24 miles in five and a half hours. That jaunt was a wild downhill dash, with Mertz calling upon all his alpine training to glide across the surface on skis, the dogs in mad pursuit behind him. It was all Mawson could do to hang onto the sledge, from which he was twice flung free. He guessed that the team crossed several crevasses without breaking through snow bridges only thanks to the pell-mell speed generated by the huskies.

At the end of that dash, the men regained the campsite they had occupied on December 12. There they found the remnants of the third sledge that they had scavenged for parts and abandoned three days before. With only a spare tent cover from which to improvise a shelter, Mertz contrived a frame made of his skis and two half-length sledge runners, the poles tied together at the apex, over which the men draped the japara cotton cover. This "unwieldy" edifice stood only four feet tall. "Inside there was just room for two one-man sleeping-bags on the floor," Mawson later wrote; "but, unfortunately, only one could move about at a time and neither of us could ever rise above a sitting posture."

Mawson's diary during these days is a telegraphic blueprint of exhaustion and grim pragmatism. "Up 10 am," he wrote on December 15. "Go on with packing, tent fixing, killing George, etc. Dogs very hungry. . . . We divide up stores and fry dog for breakfast at 5 pm. Cutting load down." The men had known at once that with the loss of the best dogs, all of the dog food, and most of their own food, the six remaining huskies would have to be killed and eaten on the return journey.

In his own diary, Mertz recorded, "On December 15th, we didn't sleep much. The events of December 14th were too fresh in our minds." Both men were still trying to puzzle out what had happened. "Now when I think about Ninnis," Mertz mused, "I am firmly persuaded that, walking beside his sledge, he was the first to crash through the crevasse. The dogs and the sledge must have fallen directly onto him." As for the larger, existential meaning of the tragedy, "Our only comfort was the thought that the death was a straight path from a happy life. The ways of God are often difficult to explain."

Later, in *The Home of the Blizzard*, Mawson would eloquently expand on the two survivors' dark thoughts as they began the homeward dash:

> Our companion, comrade, chum, in a woeful instant, buried in the bowels of the awful glacier. We tried to drive the nightmare from our thoughts; we strove to forget it in the necessity of work, but we knew that the truth would assuredly enter our souls even more poignantly in the dismal days to come. It was to be a fight with Death and the great Providence would decide the issue.

The two men now considered the expedient of heading straight north toward the coast, rather than retracing their outward track. If they could reach the edge of the sea, they might be able to kill seals for food. But the likelihood that that unknown stretch of plateau plunging toward the coast would be crisscrossed with even worse crevasses decided them against the detour.

For a while, the men settled into a routine of sleeping during the day and sledging through the night. On December 16, Mawson suffered from searing pain in his eyes. He thought it was conjunctivitis, but treated it as he would snow blindness, asking Mertz to place tablets of zinc and cocaine under his eyelids to dissolve and assuage the torment. He got almost no sleep.

That night's march was a dispirited one. The dogs were playing out. "Johnson gave in at 5 m & had to be carried," Mawson laconically recorded; "Mary gave in at 9 ½ m, so we had to camp. Pavlova also very much done." The next day: "The dogs now do nothing (except Ginger). I pulled most of the load all the time—we had to put Mary in sledge at 9 ½ miles. Mertz skinned her at camp. A wretched game. . . . Find the dog meat very stringy but nevertheless very welcome."

To make matters worse, it had started snowing, reducing visibility to close to nil. "As we could see nothing, going in the same direction was incredibly difficult," wrote Mertz in his diary. "Everything was in grey." Food longings preoccupied the men. "How lunch would have tasted good," Mertz complained, "with butter, hot chocolate and tea, like 4 days ago."

Mawson began to worry that he and Mertz had deviated from their outward track. "The course can be only approximate," he confessed on December 18. "We hope it is almost west." And the next day, "Surely we are south of our outcoming course."

Mawson's terse diary entries recording the deterioration of the dogs belie the real affection the men had developed for their huskies. Johnson was a particular favorite. In *The Home of the Blizzard*, Mawson remembered the dog's last day, as he had to be strapped atop the sledge: "Beyond the dismal whining of Johnson, into whose body the frost was swiftly penetrating, there was scarcely a sound; only the rustle of the thick, soft snow as we pushed on, weary but full of hope."

At the end of the day's march, Johnson was too weak to stand or even eat his "ration" of the meat of other dogs, so Mawson had to shoot him.

Johnson had always been a very faithful hard-working and willing beast, with rather droll ways of his own, and we were very sorry that his end should come so soon. He could never be accused of being a handsome dog, in fact he was generally disreputable and dirty, curiously enough these latter qualities seemed to be reflected even in the qualities of his meat, for it was permeated with a unique and unusually disagreeable flavour. This we subsequently referred to as "Johnsonian."

On December 18, another dog, Mary, who had completely collapsed, also had to be shot and eaten. The men were down to three dogs, and only one of them, the plucky Ginger, was capable of hauling. "To go forward," Mertz noted, "Mawson and I had to put on the harness and haul the sledge. The most uncomfortable thing was the bad light. Over the sastrugi, I often had the impression of walking like a drunkard, and more than once, each of us fell onto his face."

On December 19, the men tried traveling during the day and sleeping at night. It was a dubious tradeoff: sun sights might help them to calculate their latitude and longitude, but in the daytime warmth the snow turned soggy and made the sledging more onerous. That day, the character of the surface modulated from hard sastrugi to bare ice seamed with crevasses. Mawson deduced that they had reached the head of the Ninnis Glacier. "It was very satisfactory to know this," he wrote, "to have some tangible proof that we really were where we thought we were." Even so, they had wandered 20 miles south of their outward track. The only consolation was that the Ninnis Glacier might prove easier to traverse at its head than in mid-flow, where it had taken the three men a full week to negotiate the crevasses at the end of November.

That same day, Mawson and Mertz almost lost Haldane in a crevasse. The dogs had grown so skinny that their harnesses no longer fit tight. Just as the men hauled the husky back to the surface, he slipped loose. "Fortunately I was just able to grab a fold of his skin at the same instant," Mawson later wrote, "otherwise many days' rations would have been lost. Haldane took to the harness once more, but soon became uncertain in his footsteps, staggered along and then tottered and fell."

"Splendid weather," Mertz crowed on December 20. But:

After 8 miles "Haldane" collapsed. We crossed an infinite number of hard sastrugis. We stop only for 2 hours, so that the dogs could recover their strength. "Pavlova" also nearly fell down. The effort is too big for the animals, they haul no more. Mawson and I have to pull the sledge. We realise that it is a laborious work. We drank a light tea made with leaves, previously used. Because of the foggy days, we don't know if we are too far north, or too far south. Tomorrow at midday, we hope to determine our latitude.

Sledging in whiteout and falling snow amounted to slow, relentless torture. As Mawson later recaptured the ordeal:

In the snow-blind light of an overcast day, the strain on the eyes to delineate the trend of the sastrugi would have been trying enough, but with all the surface markings blanketed in a shroud of soft, newly fallen snow, the task was rendered still more difficult. . . . Under these conditions our progress degenerated into a sort of shuffling march; pushing one's finnesko-covered feet through the soft snow, sliding them along the old hard surface, ever alert to correct direction of march by hints from the irregularities underfoot. This was very exhausting work.

Hunger had become a constant aggravation. During these days, Mawson and Mertz ate only six ounces each of their prepackaged sledging food, supplemented with a little dog meat, chopped up into small pieces, mixed with a smidgen of pemmican, and boiled in water. The rest of the canine carcass was fed to the surviving dogs. "They crunched the bones and ate the skin until nothing remained," Mawson wrote. Even with such severely reduced rations, the men knew they would soon have even less to eat.

From the start of the return journey on December 14, the dogs had been at least as famished as the men. At each camp, they had to be tethered fast, for, as Mawson wrote, "they were seized with a morbid desire to gnaw everything within reach, including the straps and even the wood of the sledges. . . . The most repugnant refuse was greedily devoured and dog ate dog so completely that the wonder was how the sledge-load and the team came to diminish in bulk."

On December 21, Midsummer Day, the two men accomplished a march of 11 miles. " 'Haldane' collapsed after 5 miles," Mertz recorded. "We put her on the sledge, and shot her in the evening. . . . The dogs pull no more. We just make sure that they don't collapse, to have food during the whole return trip." (As this passage indicates, the gender of the dogs is uncertain. Mertz referred to Haldane as "she," Mawson as "he.") By now, the huskies still alive had been reduced to two, Pavlova and Ginger.

It was evident to both Mawson and Mertz that they were growing weaker by the day. Every ounce of baggage on the sledge added to the day's grim toil. On the 21st they reduced the load slightly by throwing away several pairs of socks, some rope, and their precious rifle. Two days later, when it came time to kill Pavlova, Mawson had to accomplish the execution not with a gun but with a knife—"a revolting and depressing operation."

On the 23rd, the men discarded more of their gear, including their hypsometer (with which they had measured altitudes throughout the trek), the sledge runners they had used as tent poles (to be replaced by the legs of the theodolite), and Mawson's camera, together with most of his film packs. This last was a particularly painful sacrifice, for he had gone to great efforts to document the journey in images of land no one had ever seen before. That day Mertz calculated that the two men had covered 115 miles from the crevasse that had swallowed Ninnis—leaving almost 200 still to traverse to reach Winter Quarters.

Despite their efforts to banish thoughts of food from their minds, hunger invaded the men's waking and sleeping hours. "Very hungry tonight—can't sleep for it," Mawson wrote on December 23. The next day, "Dog stew this afternoon best yet." And the next, which happened to be Christmas, "Dreamt of a huge fancy cake last evening amidst weird surroundings."

The men tried to make some kind of festive occasion out of Christmas. "I found two bits of biscuit in my bag, so we had piece each," noted Mawson. Mertz went into richer detail:

At 1 am, Mawson woke me up and wished me a merry Christmas. I slept well after having eaten the cooked [dog] legs, yesterday evening. Thinking of our current hunger, we arranged to have an excellent meal with the best courses, every future Christmas day. . . . In order to still have a Christmas party on snow and ice, we demolished some dog meat with a little butter. I hope to live to share many merry Christmases with my friend Mawson, but if possible, as a real festivity in the civilized world.

On Christmas Day, the men covered 11 miles, aided by wind at their backs. Taking new sun sights for latitude and longitude, Mawson made his own calculation of how far they still had to go to reach Winter Quarters. He judged the distance to be 160 miles as the crow flies. It was an encouraging revelation, for it meant that, despite their hunger and debilitation, the men had covered almost half of their journey back to salvation.

The next day, however, they were slowed by bitter cold and a wind that reached 40 mph. They tried to improvise a sail with their tent cover, but, as Mawson wrote, "the excessive amount of lashing and unlashing connected with this arrangement when starting and camping, all of which had to be done with bare fingers in a biting wind, was a great drawback. . . . Whenever a halt was called for a few minutes' spell the conversation invariably turned on the subject of food and we laid plans for a celebration on board the *Aurora*." In the high wind, it took the men a full four hours to pitch the tent, cook dinner, and get inside their sleeping bags.

Yet another tribulation was caused by the necessity of cooking inside the cramped tent. The heat of the Primus stove melted any snow that had drifted onto the outside walls, sending a steady drip through the cloth. Even worse, the stove thawed the snow surface upon which the sleeping bags had to be laid, with no ground cloth (that too having gone down the crevasse with Ninnis). Day by day the bags grew soggier and heavier. But as soon as the men turned the stove off, the tent cooled so rapidly that the moisture on the walls froze to solid ice.

The cold affected Mertz more seriously than it did Mawson, in large part because of the loss of his burberry trousers. On December

27, he complained to his diary, "The drift is uncomfortable, because everything gradually gets wet. Without wearing mountain pants, the snow can penetrate into my underpants. At night, when I lie in my wet sleeping-bag, I realise how slowly one piece of clothing after another thaws on my body. One can't say that such conditions are comfortable."

Mawson was starting to worry about his partner's condition. "I promised to do all I could for Xavier for him to see Australia and New Zealand," he wrote in his diary.

During these days, dog meat was the staple of the men's diet, "to which was added one or two ounces of chocolate or raisins, three or four ounces of a mixture of pemmican and biscuit, and, as a beverage, very dilute cocoa." Mawson estimated the total weight of a day's rations as 14 ounces per man—this, compared with more than two pounds per man per day on the outward run. It was no surprise that Mawson and Mertz were steadily weakening. And of course the dog meat would eventually give out.

Only Ginger was still alive. With a fortitude matching the men's, she continued to help pull the sledge through December 26 and 27, but after a march of three miles on December 28, she collapsed. The men pushed on another two miles, then camped. "Ginger slain, meat cooked," Mawson wrote bluntly in his diary. Later, he would recall the macabre transformation that turned a faithful husky into desperately needed food:

> As we worked on a system which aimed at using up the bony parts of the carcase first, it happened that Ginger's skull figured as the dish for the next meal. As there was no instrument capable of dividing it, the skull was boiled whole and a line drawn round it marking it into right and left halves. . . . Passing the skull from one to the other, we took turns in eating our respective shares. The brain was certainly the most appreciated and nutritious section, Mertz, I remember well, remarking specially upon it.

On the 29th, the men broke the sledging into two shifts. From 2:30 till 8:30 a.m., they managed to cover seven and a half miles.

They pitched the tent, ate "a great breakfast off Ginger's skull—thyroid and brains," then tried to sleep before setting off again at 11:15 p.m. Mertz's annoyance with the camping routine spilled into his diary: "The tent is too small. Only one of us can move, meanwhile the other one has to remain sitting in a corner. . . . One wonders how it is possible."

Yet during the second shift of sledging, lasting almost ten hours, the men broke clear of the relentless uphill grade and emerged onto a flat terrace of snow. "We strode along at a good pace," Mawson later wrote, "and by 9 a.m. had accomplished a splendid march of fifteen miles. . . .

"Our spirits rose and the prospects for the future had more promise than for many days past," he added. "Fortune was beginning to smile upon us at last, but, alas! trouble of a new order was brewing."

Mertz's diary entry for December 30 was his shortest in weeks—three curt sentences. In them he noted a march of 15 miles, "light wind," "increasing wind," then: "As I am tired, I write no more." Mawson's own diary entry recorded his first hint of alarm: "Xavier off colour. . . . He turned in—all his things very wet, chiefly on account of no burberry pants." Later Mawson would reflect that his first intimation that something was wrong with Mertz came "when I realized that my companion was not as cheerful as usual. As he had always been so bright and energetic it was clear that there was some good reason for this change, but he gave no hint upon the subject and I was loath to speak to him directly about it as it would likely pass off."

Late that evening, snow started to fall. The next day, the men did not get off until 10 a.m. After two days of splendid progress, on December 31 they hauled "under wretched conditions, for the light was atrocious and the surface slippery and ridged. The wind, tending to blow the sledge along sideways, only added to our troubles." After gaining a paltry two and a half miles, they stopped to camp.

Mertz started his diary entry with a hearty proclamation of "New Year's Eve!," but his words were leaden: "Now it's 2 o'clock in the afternoon, and we sit again in our sleeping-bags. Outside there are snowfalls and a diffuse light, therefore one can see little or nothing."

During the previous evening, the men had had a long discussion about food. Mertz confessed that "he had found the dog meat very disagreeable and felt that he was getting little nutriment from it. He suggested that we should abstain from eating any further of this meat and draw solely upon the ordinary food of which we still had some days' supply carefully husbanded." Mawson agreed.

When the sun briefly reappeared at 9:30 p.m., the men packed up camp and started on again. But clouds moved in, and soon a dense fog enveloped them. "Can't be sure exactly where going so camped after 5 miles," Mawson glumly recorded.

"1 January New Year!" Mertz crowed in his diary. But the short entry was even gloomier than Mawson's: "It's not good weather to travel. Incredibly bad light, cloudy sky, therefore we didn't go far. We wait for better weather. The dog meat looks indigestible for me, because yesterday I felt a little weak."

It was the first time that Mertz had admitted to his diary that he was having trouble eating the dog meat. And it was the last entry he would write. After January 1, 1913, the Swiss ski champion and all-around athlete, who had faithfully kept his diary for a year and a half, from his departure from England aboard the *Aurora* in July 1911 through its arrival in Australia and then at Cape Denison, through the long winter in the hut, and through the first seven and a half weeks of the grueling Far Eastern journey, no longer had the energy to lift his pen and document the day's doings.

The abstention from dog meat did nothing to improve Mertz's condition. On January 2, the men stayed in their tent the whole day. On the 3rd, they managed five miles before calling it quits. And on the 4th, they "rested" inert for another whole day. Mawson's diary records his partner's decline. On January 3, the only day in three that the men sledged at all, he wrote, "Mertz boiled a small cocoa and had biscuit, and I had a bit of [dog] liver. . . . Did 5 miles but cold wind frost-bit Mertz's fingers, and he is generally in a very bad condition. Skin coming off legs, etc." Mertz himself could not believe that he had frostbitten fingers, for he had never before experienced frozen digits. "To convince himself," Mawson later wrote, "he bit a considerable piece of the fleshy part off the end of one of [his fingers]."

On January 4, Mawson recorded, "Intended getting up 10 am and going on as day very good but Mertz in bad condition, so I doctored him part of day and rested." On the 5th, Mertz's state was even worse: "I tried to get Xavier to start but he practically refused, saying it was suicide and that it much best for him to have the day in bag and dry it and get better, then do more on sun-shining day. I strongly advocated doing 2 to 5 miles only for exercise even if we could not see properly. Eventually we decided to rest today."

What was wrong with Mertz? Mawson later elaborated on his analysis of the predicament during those first days of January:

> I found that, like myself, he had from time to time a dull painful gnawing sensation in the abdomen; it may well have been that his was more acute than in my case. I had discovered that the pain was greatly relieved by frequently changing position as one rested. My theory, at the time, was that the gastric secretions, especially under the influence of food dreams, were so active in search of food as actually to attack the wall of the stomach itself. By turning over at intervals the damage would be distributed and less severe.

Yet Mertz's torpor was deeply disturbing, and so unlike the hardy comrade Mawson had come to respect and revere. It was as if the man no longer realized that the survival of both depended on making some march, no matter how short, every day. "All will depend on providence now—," wrote Mawson on January 5, "it is an even race to the hut."

By now, Mertz could not even eat the pieces of biscuit Mawson offered him. He could stomach only Glaxo, the powdered milk manufactured as baby food, so Mawson turned over the whole supply to his companion while he continued to eat biscuit and dog meat.

On the 5th, after Mertz had refused to move, Mawson spent the day inside the tent "cooking more meat and making appetizing broths which, however, my companion did not appreciate as I had hoped, furnishing additional evidence of the weakness of his digestive arrangements." All day the snow fell, lashing against the tent in a gale-force wind. The two men spent "wretched hours lying in the wet sleeping-bags—how we longed to get them properly dry!"

The next day, with a wan sun shining through thin clouds, the men packed up and tried to sledge onward, starting at 10:30 a.m. "The grade was slightly downhill and the wind well behind," Mawson wrote, "but these advantages were offset by an extremely slippery surface and awkward sastrugi ridges. Falls were frequent and they soon told severely upon my companion in his weak condition." Mawson himself felt "quite dizzy from long stay in bags," and "weak from want of food."

The men had not gone far before Mawson realized that Mertz was incapable of hauling. Mawson suggested that his partner ride the sledge. Mertz demurred several times, then finally gave in. In their debilitated state, even a week earlier it had been all the men could do to pull the sledge, sometimes aided by their tent-cover sail, more than five miles in a continuous march. The effort now required of Mawson, to haul all by himself with Mertz's added weight atop the sledge, is unimaginable. With his characteristic stoicism, in neither his diary nor *The Home of the Blizzard* does Mawson make any fuss about this superhuman feat. Instead, "With a wind blowing from behind, it required no great exertion to bring the load along, though it would often pull up suddenly against sastrugi."

Even so, immobile atop the sledge, Mertz grew too cold to continue. After a pitiful gain of two and a half miles, the men stopped to camp.

Mertz was depressed and, after a little refreshment, sank back into his bag without saying much. He was troubled from time to time with recurrences of dysentery and had no power to hold in his stomach the broth which he was prevailed upon to swallow at intervals. Occasionally, during the day, I would ask him how he felt, or we would return to the old subject of food. Even then the conversation often led to the discussion of what we would do on arrival aboard the *Aurora*, though I doubt if either of us at that time really expected to get through. I recollect that it was agreed that once on board the ship Mertz was to spend the day making penguin-egg omelettes, for the excellence of those he had made just prior to leaving the Hut had not been forgotten.

In the privacy of his diary, Mawson faced the true enormity of the men's situation: "Things are in a most serious state for both of us—if he cannot go on 8 or 10 m[iles] a day, in a day or two we are doomed. I could pull through myself with the provisions at hand but I cannot leave him. His heart seems to have gone."

By the morning of January 7, the two men had only nine days left to meet the January 15 deadline Mawson had imposed on all the teams for their return to Winter Quarters. But the hut was still 100 miles away. Over the last six days, the men had advanced only seven and a half miles—an average of just a little more than a mile a day. At that rate, it would take them three months to reach Cape Denison. And there seemed little hope that Mertz, in his desperate condition, could even match the effort of the previous week.

With hindsight, Mawson later analyzed the men's physical plight:

Starvation combined with superficial frost-bite, alternating with the damp conditions in the sleeping-bags, had by this time resulted in a wholesale peeling of the skin all over our bodies; in its place only a very poor unnourished substitute appeared which readily rubbed raw in many places. As a result of this, the chafing of the march had already developed large raw patches in just those places where they were most troublesome. As we never took off our clothes, the peelings of hair and skin from our bodies worked down into our under-trousers and socks, and regular clearances were made from the latter.

The men resolved to sledge on January 7 "at all cost." But that morning's departure fizzled into an utter fiasco. Somehow Mawson summed up the energy to recount it in detail in his diary:

Just as I got out [of the tent] at 8 am I found Xavier in a terrible state having fouled his pants. He must be very weak now for I do up and undo most of his things now and put him into & take him out of the bag. I have a long job cleaning him up, then put him into the bag to warm up. I have to turn in again to kill time & keep warm—for I feel the cold very much now. At 10 am I get up to dress Xavier & prepare breakfast but I find him in a kind of a fit & wrap him up in the bag & leave him—obviously we can't go on today, and it is a good day though bad light, the sun just gleaming through the clouds. This is terrible. I don't mind for myself, but it is for Paquita and for all the others connected with the expedition that I feel so deeply and sinfully. I pray to God to help us.

Mawson cooked cocoa and beef broth for Mertz, but had to lift him bodily to sit up enough to drink. After noon, he seemed to improve a bit. But then in the afternoon, "he has several fits & is delirious, fills his trousers again and I clean out for him." Unable to speak coherently, Mertz now refused to eat or drink. The end came quickly, but not without agony. "At 8 pm he raves & breaks a tent pole," wrote Mawson in his diary. "Continues to rave & call 'Oh Yen, Oh Yen' for hours. I hold him down, then he becomes more peaceful & I put him quietly in the bag. He dies peacefully at about 2 am on morning of 8th."

Mawson spent the rest of the night lying beside his dead comrade. "All that remained was his mortal frame," he later wrote, "which, toggled up in his sleeping-bag, still offered some sense of companionship." Late on the evening of January 8, Mawson "took the body of Mertz, still toggled up in his bag, outside the tent, piled snow blocks around it and raised a rough cross made of the two discarded halves of the sledge runners." Beside the grave, he read the burial service from the *Book of Common Prayer.*

At the time, Mawson thought he could explain the cause of his teammate's demise. "Death due to exposure finally bringing on a fever," he wrote in his diary, "result of weather exposure & want of food."

Want of food, indeed. By January 8, twenty-six days had passed since Ninnis's fatal accident. Supplementing their intake with stringy, hard-to-chew dog meat, the men had stretched normal rations for a week and a half into almost four weeks' survival fare. But now there was almost no food of any kind left, with still 100 miles to go.

In his diary on January 8, Mawson coolly weighed his chances:

For many days now (since 1st quite), Xavier's condition has prevented us going on and now I am afraid it has cooked my chances altogether, even of a single attempt either to the Coast or to the Hut—lying in the damp bag for a week on extremely low rations has reduced my condition seriously. However, I shall spend today remodelling the gear to make an attempt. I shall do my utmost to the last.

Ever since 1913, students of exploration history have wondered why Mertz, who had been in superb condition throughout the expedition, should have succumbed so much more rapidly and disastrously than Mawson. And they have puzzled over the symptoms that attacked the health of both men, as reported in Mawson's diary.

In 1969, eleven years after Mawson's death, two Australian medical researchers published a paper in *The Medical Journal of Australia* titled "Hypervitaminosis A in the Antarctic in the Australasian Antarctic Expedition of 1911–1914." It was the hypothesis of John Cleland and R. V. Southcott that Mertz and Mawson had been poisoned by overdoses of vitamin A caused by eating the dogs' livers. The fact that the huskies were from Greenland had everything to do with these toxic doses. For centuries, the Greenland Inuit had refrained from eating the livers of polar bears, wolves, and seals—and, in extremis, dogs—because they had apparently learned from immemorial trial and error that such food could cause a fatal poisoning.

Cleland and Southcott argued that symptoms such as shedding of skin, muscular weakness, weight loss, damage to the central nervous system that manifested itself in fits like the ones Mawson reported Mertz undergoing, and others that Mawson suffered after Mertz's death, such as his hair falling out in clumps, were all consistent with vitamin A poisoning. Some but not all of those symptoms would be produced by scurvy or slow starvation alone.

Riffenburgh calls the Cleland and Southcott analysis "the most plausible cause for both Mertz's death and the terrible symptoms that plagued Mawson in the ensuing weeks." As for why Mertz suffered more intensely than Mawson, Riffenburgh cites a letter that Mawson wrote to Mertz's father after the expedition. In it, Mawson speculates that "the actual final cause of his death was that his digestive system, becoming weaker by living on poor food, could not cope with the indigestible and non-nutritious dogs' meat. He told me that he believed my greater capability to deal with that food was probably due to the fact that Swiss people are not used to a large meat diet, whereas English people and especially Australians eat a large proportion of meat."

Other experts, however, disagree. Phillip Law, an Australian scientist and expedition leader and a good friend of Mawson, told Mawson's biographer Philip Ayres that the hypervitaminosis A theory was "completely unproven. . . . The symptoms that were described are exactly the ones you get from cold exposure."

For that matter, other explorers, including Amundsen's South Pole party in 1911–12, had supplemented their rations with the meat of the huskies that had pulled their sledges without suffering from the ravages that afflicted Mertz and Mawson. To be sure, Amundsen's team never came close to starvation.

Mawson set about "remodelling the gear" for his desperate dash toward Winter Quarters at 9 a.m. on January 8, a mere seven hours after Mertz's death. With only a serrated pocket knife as a tool, in a bravura feat of carpentry he sawed the sledge in half, keeping only the forward portion on which to stow his diminished supplies. He cut up Mertz's burberry jacket and a waterproof cloth bag and sewed them together to make a lighter sail than the one he and Mertz had improvised with the tent cover. He made a mast out of a rail from the discarded rear part of the sledge, with a spar fashioned from another rail as a crosspiece. Finally he discarded every possible piece of gear that would not be essential to his survival. The most painful of those sacrifices was the last of the exposed film packs from the outward journey, containing the only photographs of Ninnis and Mertz on the final journey of their lives. Yet Mawson kept Mertz's diary, determined to bring it back to the man's family.

Bad weather—winds up to 50 mph, with heavy snow drift—stalled Mawson through January 9 and 10. By himself, he thought that there was a good chance that if he took the tent down, he couldn't get it pitched again in the fierce gale. A single night out without the tent would be fatal. "I have more to eat today," he wrote with grim satisfaction on the 9th, "in hope that it will give me strength for the future." On the 10th, he cooked the rest of the dog meat.

His body was continuing to deteriorate. "One annoying effect of want of food is that wherever the skin breaks it refused to heal," he noted, "the nose and lips break open also. My scrotum, like Xavier's, is also getting in a painfully raw condition due to reduced condition, dampness and friction in walking. It is well nigh impossible to treat."

On January 11, Mawson got underway: "Almost calm, sun shining—a beautiful day," with "surface good, slow downhill." Although he "did not expect to make a very long day of it," he was determined not to stop before he had covered ten miles.

Almost at the outset of his march, however, Mawson made an appalling discovery.

From the start my feet felt curiously lumpy and sore. They had become so painful after a mile of walking that I decided to examine them on the spot, sitting in the lee of the sledge in brilliant sunshine. I had not had my socks off for some days for, while lying in camp, it had not seemed necessary. On taking off the third and inner pair of socks the sight of my feet gave me quite a shock, for the thickened skin of the soles had separated in each case as a complete layer, and abundant watery fluid had escaped saturating the sock. The new skin beneath was very much abraded and raw.

In that despairing moment, Mawson wondered whether he could walk at all, let alone haul a sledge.

However, there was nothing to be done but make the best of it. I smeared the new skin and the raw surfaces with lanoline . . . and then with the aid of bandages bound the old skin casts back in place. . . . Over the bandages were slipped six pairs of thick woollen socks, then fur boots and finally crampon over-shoes.

"Treading like a cat" to try to minimize the pain, Mawson limped ahead. By 5:30 p.m., he had covered a creditable six and a half miles. He felt "quite worn-out—nerve worn. . . . Had it not been a delightful evening I should not have found strength to erect the tent."

Yet even in this latest agony, Mawson could taste joy as the sky cleared. "So glorious was it to feel the sun on one's skin after being without it for so long," he wrote, "that I next removed most of my clothing and bathed my body in the rays until my flesh fairly tingled—a wonderful sensation which spread throughout my whole person, and made me feel stronger and happier."

The good weather did not last. Mawson woke on January 12 to find falling snow and wind up to 45 mph. He spent the whole day trying to "give my feet a chance," while he itemized his remaining food. "I sincerely wish it were twice as much," he wrote in his diary.

"As it is I have been continually picking fragments from the different bags."

In the middle of the night, Mawson discovered that his watch had stopped because he had forgotten to wind it. This was a serious blow, for without an accurate reckoning of the time, it was difficult to calculate one's longitude, even with a perfect sun sight. In the morning he reset the watch, guessing at the time. Dinner the evening before had consisted of "1 bisc., less ½ pem[mican], little dog meat, cocoa."

Slowly the weather improved, allowing Mawson to pack up and start by 2 p.m. Pulling the half-sledge on descending terrain, he covered five and a half miles in six hours. Shortly after noon, he topped a rise and suddenly recognized the Mertz Glacier ahead of him. The familiar landscape compensated for forgetting to wind the watch. "My heart leapt with joy," Mawson later wrote, "for all was like a map before me and I knew that over the hazy blue ridge in the far distance lay the Hut." But back inside the tent, he discovered "feet worse than ever. Things look bad, but I shall persevere."

At 11 p.m. that night, camped near the glacier, Mawson was startled by "loud reports like heavy gun shots." Lasting half an hour, they seemed to begin in the south and travel in a percussive wave toward the far-off coast. "It was hard to believe it was not caused by some human agency, but I learnt that it was due to the cracking of the glacier ice." On December 13, the day before Ninnis had died in the huge crevasse, the men had heard similar gunshot reports from the creaking ice. If the memory of that earlier fusillade, possibly prefiguring the disaster of the 14th, gave Mawson new apprehensions a month later, he did not confess them to his diary.

The next day, during which Mawson "had all I could do to pull the sledge downhill in the slop," he covered five miles. He was also able to calculate an approximate latitude and longitude. But the desperation of his plight was never far from his mind. "If my feet do not improve," he wrote that evening, "I must turn down the glacier and endeavour to reach the sea." This remark is somewhat puzzling. The seacoast, of course, was closer than the hut, but travel down the Mertz Glacier, Mawson knew, would be more difficult than across the plateau on a path parallel to the men's outward trek in November. Without the rifle, on the coast Mawson would have little chance of killing seals; even penguins might scuttle away from his feeble grasp. Perhaps Mawson hoped against hope that on the coast he might run into a search party or even the *Aurora* out looking for him.

Mawson opened his diary entry the next day with the lament, "We should be at the Hut now." The "we" is poignant. It was January 15, the deadline Mawson himself had set for the return of all sledging parties to Winter Quarters. He was still, by his own reckoning, 87 miles in an airline distance away from the hut. Even if he could stagger five miles a day without a break, it would take him at least until February 2 to reach Cape Denison. By then, surely, the *Aurora* would have departed. Meanwhile, Mawson was growing very short on food, his feet were not getting better, and general debilitation closed its grip on him with each passing day.

On the 15th, Mawson managed only a single mile of sledging, thanks to a head wind and warmth that had softened the snow into a slush across which it was almost impossible to pull the sledge. During the day, inside the tent, "Try to sleep but cannot. . . . Am keeping food and mileage list at end of book now as checks on each other."

A day of such disheartening progress called for a redoubled effort on the morrow. Mawson was up at 2 a.m. on January 16. Even though heavy snow was falling, he got everything packed and was cinched into his sledge harness by 6:30. The wet snow made for miserable going. "It clung in lumps to the runners, which had to be scraped frequently," he later wrote. "Riven ice ridges as much as eighty feet in height passed on either hand." Without explaining why, Mawson had given up the idea of making a beeline for the coast. A grueling, daylong effort yielded only "an extremely heavy five miles." That evening, "I treated myself to an extra supper of jelly soup made from dog sinews. I thought at the time that the acute enjoyment of eating compensated in some measure for the sufferings of starvation." In his diary, he commented, "It takes quite a while dressing my feet each day now."

In the middle of his sledging push, Mawson had had a bad scare.

Having slogged up a steep snow slope in bad light, he suddenly found himself sliding almost out of control down the other side.

> A glance ahead, even in that uncertain light, flashed the truth upon me—I was on a snow cornice, rimming the brink of a great blue chasm like a quarry, the yawning mouth of an immense and partly filled crevasse. Already the sledge was gaining speed as it slid past me towards the gaping hole below. Mechanically, I bedded my feet firmly in the snow and, exerting every effort, was just able to take the weight and hold up the sledge as it reached the very brink of the abyss. There must have been an interval of quite a minute during which I held my ground without being able to make it budge. It seemed an interminable time; I found myself reckoning the odds as to who would win, the sledge or I. Then it slowly came my way, and the imminent danger was passed.

Had the sledge plunged into the crevasse, it would have pulled Mawson with it. He would have died a death very much like Ninnis's.

It was, Mawson knew, a close call. The next day would bring an even closer one.

On January 17, snow still fell under an overcast sky. Planning to take advantage of the nighttime hours and move over relatively frozen snow, Mawson overslept. He got off that morning only around 8 a.m. The light was terrible: "Everything from below one's feet to the sky above was one uniform ghostly glare." Mawson's progress had brought him into "a dangerous crevassed valley." It was so hard to discern even the little ridges and hollows in the snow surface, let alone the faint blue tint of bridged-over crevasses, that he would normally have rested on such a day, "but delay meant a reduction of the ration and that was out of the question."

In late morning, he crossed several hidden crevasses without even realizing it until he was past them. Then, on an uphill slope, he plowed through new snow so deep and soft that he sank in at times up to his thighs. Despite these annoyances, Mawson thought "the sledge was running fairly well."

Shortly before noon, on another uphill slope, he broke through a snow bridge. He fell in thigh-deep, but caught himself on the edges with his arms. Carefully he extricated himself from the hole. In the faint light, he could not detect the orientation of the crevasse, but, probing with a stick, he thought he could figure it out. He decided to try a second crossing about 50 yards to one side.

> Alas! It took an unexpected turn catching me unawares. This time I shot through the centre of the bridge in a flash, but the latter part of the fall was decelerated by the friction of the harness [rope] which, as the sledge ran up, sawed back into the thick compact snow forming the margin of the lid. Having seen my comrades perish in diverse ways and having lost hope of reaching the Hut, I had already many times speculated on what the end would be like. So it happened that as I fell through into the crevasse the thought "so this is the end" blazed up in my mind, for it was to be expected that the next moment the sledge would follow through, crash on my head and all go to the unseen bottom. But the unexpected happened and the sledge held, the deep snow acting as a brake.

The sledge sticking and acting as an anchor had prevented Mawson from duplicating the fatal plunge of Ninnis. But as his eyes adjusted to the semidarkness inside the crevasse, Mawson realized just how hopeless his situation looked. The reprieve, he sensed, was only temporary. The harness rope was 14 feet long. The crevasse walls were six feet apart, out of reach of even a wildly swinging boot. Mawson dangled free in space, 14 feet below the surface, which was visible only as a small hole directly above. The fall had filled his clothes with snow, which began to chill him at once.

In mid-plunge, Mawson had felt a "great regret" sweep through his mind: "that after having stinted myself so assiduously in order to save food, I should now pass on to eternity without the satisfaction of what remained—to such an extent does food take possession of one under such circumstances."

The only hope of salvation was to climb hand over hand up the harness rope. Even for a fit man in dry, warm conditions, such an athletic feat would have been barely possible. Only a chance precaution that Mawson had put into effect days before gave him the slightest edge: he had tied knots in the harness rope. Almost at once, Mawson began the "great effort." He seized one of the knots, hung from it for a rest, then pulled himself violently upward until he could grasp the next knot. Hauling with all his waning strength, his legs still flailing in air, he reached the lip of the crevasse and tried to wrench his body past it.

Suddenly, the lip broke loose, and Mawson fell back in all fourteen feet until the rope caught him again with an abrupt jerk. Once more, the sledge had held as an anchor. But Mawson felt only despair.

> There, exhausted, weak and chilled, hanging freely in space and slowly turning round as the rope twisted one way and the other, I felt that I had done my utmost and failed, that I had no more strength to try again and that all was over except the passing. It was to be a miserable and slow end and I reflected with disappointment that there was in my pocket no antidote to speed matters; but there always remained the alternative of slipping from the harness. There on the brink of the great Beyond I well remember how I looked forward to the peace of the great release—how almost excited I was at the prospect of the unknown to be unveiled.

By "antidote to speed matters," Mawson seems to mean some kind of suicide pill such as cyanide. In the expedition medical list, there was no such potion: the closest approximation is veiled in the ambiguous phrase "an assortment of 'tabloid' drugs for general treatment." Yet on their doomed return from the South Pole the year before, Scott and his four companions had carried opium tablets for just such a purpose, but never used them.

From his diary and from *The Home of the Blizzard* alone, only a vague sense of Mawson's religious beliefs can be divined. If in that moment, dangling from the harness rope, anticipating death, he looked forward to the discovery of an afterlife, that sentence is the only hint of such a faith in "the great Beyond." After Ninnis's death on December 14, Mawson had written in his diary, "May God Help us." Elsewhere, however, it is not God that Mawson invokes, but Providence. Whether by the word he meant God's plan for each human being, or only an impersonal fate, it was "remembering how Providence had miraculously brought me so far" that now kept him from giving up.

That, and a verse from his favorite poet, Robert Service, that suddenly came into his head:

> *Just have one more try—it's dead easy to die,*
> *It's the keeping-on-living that's hard.*

So Mawson girded himself for one more "supreme attempt":

Fired by the passion that burns the blood in the act of strife, new power seemed to come as I applied myself to one last tremendous effort. The struggle occupied some time, but I slowly worked upward to the surface. This time emerging feet first, still clinging to the rope, I pushed myself out at full length on the lid and then shuffled safely on to the solid ground at the side.

At once Mawson passed out. Waking after an hour or even two—he could not tell how long he had been unconscious—he was surprised to find his body covered with a dusting of new snow.

"Numb with cold," Mawson managed to pitch the tent and crawl inside, though it took him three hours to complete the job. Lying at last in his sleeping bag, "I ate a little food and thought matters over." And in that moment, it was not Robert Service's poetry that came into his head, but a verse from the atheistic *Rubáiyát* of Omar Khayyám:

> *Unborn To-morrow and dead Yesterday,*
> *Why fret about them if To-day be sweet?*

"Never have I come so near to an end," Mawson later wrote about his ordeal in the crevasse; "never has anyone more miraculously escaped." His diary entry on the evening of January 17, however, is less dramatic. "I thought of Providence again giving me a chance," he wrote of the effort to summon up a second hand-over-hand climb of the rope. And upon emerging, "Then I felt grateful to Providence."

The phrase from the account of his near-death in *The Home of the Blizzard*, "having lost hope of reaching the Hut," indicates that by the 17th Mawson was convinced he could not survive a return journey. Certainly at some point during his desperate solo march, he gave up hope of survival. The only incentive for continuing to push on was the wish that he might be able to cache his and Mertz's diaries somewhere where they might be found by searchers, so that the world might learn the story of the heroic tragedy of the Far Eastern Party. Robert Scott, dying in a very different part of Antarctica ten months before, had expressed a kindred determination to save the story of his polar party's demise for posterity, as he wrote in a last "Message to the Public": "Had we lived, I should have had a tale to tell of the hardihood, endurance, and courage of my companions which would have stirred the heart of every Englishman. These rough notes and our dead bodies must tell the tale."

Yet Mawson's diary entry on the 17th, after escaping from the crevasse, implies that he still had hopes of pulling through: "It is impossible to say what is ahead, for the light gives no chance, and I sincerely hope that something will happen to change the state of the weather—else how am I to keep up my average. I trust in Providence, however, who has so many times already helped me."

After his hellish experience, Mawson got no sleep on the night of January 17–18. Instead, he did a lot of thinking. Part of it was philosophical: "I was confronted with this problem: whether it was better to enjoy life for a few days, sleeping and eating my fill until the provisions gave out, or to 'plug on' again in hunger with the prospect of plunging at any moment into eternity without the supreme satisfaction and pleasure of the food." But in the midst of such ruminations, a very pragmatic idea came into Mawson's head. "It was to construct a ladder from a length of alpine rope that remained," he wrote; "one end was to be secured to the bow of the sledge and the other carried over my left shoulder and loosely attached to the sledge harness. Thus if I fell into a crevasse again, provided the sledge was not also engulfed, it would be easy for me, even though weakened by starvation, to scramble out by the ladder."

Mawson was off shortly after 10 a.m. on the 18th. He had not gone far when "I sank to knees in one crevasse and got out and . . . noted open ones all around, so decided to camp and consider matters." After his brush with death, the panic and dread that Mawson must have felt that day, threading his way through open and hidden crevasses, ladder or no ladder, can only be imagined. Inside the tent, he noted further ravages to his body: "Now ration is being reduced blood is going back and several festerings broken out again. If only I had [good] light I could make the Hut. . . . If only I could get out of this hole."

The menace of the crevasses continued unabated on January 19, as Mawson got underway at 8:30 a.m. Yet "zigzagging about I found that at intervals they were choked with snow. At any rate I chanced them." Zigzagging, however, meant that he traveled much farther than he gained in distance from the still far-off hut. "I stopped awhile and considered the question. Everything seemed hopeless—the serac seemed to be endless, the glacier cracked and boomed below."

Mawson had underestimated the crevasses. Twice that day he broke through snow bridges and plunged over his head into the void, "but the sledge held up and the ladder proved 'trumps.' " He was able to scramble out "without much exertion, though half-smothered with snow." (Curiously, Mawson neglected to mention these close escapes in his diary, recalling them only in *The Home of the Blizzard*.)

In four and a half hours of all-out effort ("felt very tired"), Mawson gained a pitiful three and a half miles. "I decided to turn in early," he wrote in his diary, "and go in early morning hoping for a good day." During the last five days, constantly surrounded by crevasses, coming as close to death as he could and still survive, Mawson had nonetheless performed the considerable feat of sledging across the head of the Mertz Glacier, on a path some 20 miles south of the track he had laid down with Mertz and Ninnis in November. "I had never expected to get so far," he later wrote, "and now that it was an accomplished fact I was intoxicated with joy."

Recognizing that he had left behind the worst of the crevasses, Mawson hoped for better mileage in the coming days on the smooth plateau that stretched ahead. On the 20th, however, "a wretched overcast day," he gained only two and a half miles, and the next day, under sun and wind, a mere three miles. Desperate to improve his marches, that evening Mawson threw away more gear: his crampons (the loss of which would have grave consequences), the alpine rope from which he had made his rescue ladder, and the stick with which he probed for crevasses. But on a "gloriously sunny" January 22, he covered six miles—his best march since January 11. Mawson's spirits were buoyed, as he came in sight of an "old friend"—Aurora Peak, which Mawson, Mertz, and Ninnis had discovered on November 18 and named after the expedition ship. At the end of that day's effort, "I felt very weak and weary. My feet were now much improved and the old skin-casts [i. e., the soles] after shrivelling up a good deal had been thrown away. However, prolonged starvation aided by the unwholesomeness of the dog meat was taking its toll in other ways. My nails still continued to fester and numerous boils on my face and body required daily attention."

Mawson realized full well that he was getting weaker by the day. And on the 23rd, bad weather returned, with low clouds and a rising wind:

Everything became blotted out in a swirl of drifting snow . . . I wandered through it for several hours, the sledge capsizing at times owing to the strength of the wind. It was not possible to keep an accurate course, for even the wind changed direction as the day wore on. Underfoot there was soft snow which I found comfortable for my sore feet, but which made the sledge drag heavily at times.

That day, Mawson's progress added up to a discouraging three and a half miles.

On the 24th, to his incredulous delight, he was able to ride the sledge for half a mile, as a favorable wind filled his makeshift sail. He gained another five miles before camping, fortifying himself that evening with "an extra stick of chocolate." But in the tent, he found more evidence of his physical deterioration: "Both my hands have shed the skin in large sheets, very tender and it is a great nuisance."

The fickle weather seemed to tease Mawson with promises of clear skies and good sledging, only to slam the door in his face. He woke on January 25 to a "violent blizzard" that prohibited any travel. Mawson spent the day in his sleeping bag, his mind tormented with some of his darkest thoughts yet.

> I cannot sleep, and keep thinking of all manner of things—how to improve the cooker, etc.—to while away the time. The end is always food, how to save [cooking] oil, and as experiment I am going to make dog pem & put the cocoa in it. Freezing feet as too little food, new skin and no action: have to wear burberries in bag. The tent is closing in by weight of snow and is about coffin size now.

Yet even in these doldrums, he still had faith in a dwindling chance of survival: "I am full of hope and reliance in the great Providence, which has pulled me through so far."

Despite a continuing blizzard, with wind up to 60 mph, Mawson packed up and moved out on the 26th. It was, he noted wryly, "a great experiment," for he was not sure that he would be able to pitch the tent at the end of the day. If he could not, he knew he would die before the morning. Somehow, Mawson managed to sledge nine miles in terrible conditions—under the circumstances, a heroic feat. He got the tent pitched after a prolonged struggle. Not until after midnight was he able to cook his dinner.

On the morning of January 27, Mawson calculated, he was 48 miles from the hut. The previous day's effort had taken too much out of him, so despite the blizzard's starting to moderate, he spent the whole day in the tent. "My clothes and bag and all gear wet with yesterday's business," he recorded. "For the last 2 days my hair has been falling out in handfuls and rivals the reindeer hair from the moulting bag for nuisance in all food preparations. My beard on one side has come out in patches."

On the 28th, although snow still fell under a leaden overcast sky, the wind had dropped considerably. But so much snow had drifted around the tent that Mawson had a hard time crawling out of it. When he emerged, he saw that all but the top several inches of the tent's peak had been drifted under. (Other explorers have suffocated when they slept through snowstorms that completely buried their tents.) The sledge was nowhere in sight. It took Mawson hours to dig out the tent and to "prospect" for the sledge before digging it free as well.

By late afternoon, as the sky cleared magnificently, Mawson had sledged onward for eight miles. "My spirits rose to a high pitch," he later wrote, "for I felt for the first time that there was a really good chance of making the Hut." Yet his body was in a deplorable state, with skin coming off everywhere, hair falling out, boils on his face and body, and raw, tender skin underfoot instead of the "shriveled" soles he had tossed out. He was down to about two pounds of food— one day's fare for a man on the outward journey—after weeks of slowly starving himself by eking out the rations. All that was left were "about twenty small chips of cooked dog meat in addition to half a pound of raisins and a few ounces of chocolate."

Mawson had been navigating by compass, by the occasional sun sight, by the direction of the sastrugi, and above all by dead reckoning, aided by glimpses of familiar landmarks—first Aurora Peak, then Madigan Nunatak. By the evening of the 28th, he estimated the distance to the hut as 35 to 36 miles. But he was so weak, so tired, and so hungry that he had no assurance that he could drag himself through that last stretch of barren terrain. And even if he did reach Winter Quarters, what would he find there?

Once again, Mawson crawled out of the tent and packed the sledge on the morning of January 29. Snow was falling, and the wind rose to 45 mph. He set a compass course of north 45° west, and doggedly followed it for five miles. At that point, a minor miracle occurred.

About 300 yards to the north of his course, Mawson caught sight of "something dark loom[ing] through the haze." He veered north, dragging his sledge toward the apparition. When he came close, he could see that it was a cairn of snow blocks covered by a black cloth. Removing the cloth, he seized upon a bag of food. Inside a tin in the bag, he found a note. The message revealed that the cairn and food cache had been laid by Archibald McLean, Alfred Hodgeman, and Frank Hurley, out searching for the overdue trio, "on the chance that it might be picked up by us."

As he sat in the lee of the cairn, Mawson tore open the food bag and scattered the contents in the snow. Though he neglected to specify exactly what food and how much of it the three men had left, Mawson at once gobbled down chunks of frozen pemmican, stuffed more in his pockets, and carefully lashed the bag with the rest of its contents onto the sledge. He marveled at his good fortune in finding the depot: "a few hundred yards to either side and it would have been lost to sight in the drift."

Now he renewed his march. "As I left the depot," he wrote, "there appeared to be nothing on earth that could prevent me reaching the Hut within a couple of days." The note had indicated that Aladdin's Cave, the underground grotto carved out of the snow the previous autumn, lay only 23 miles away, on a compass bearing of north 45° west. From Aladdin's Cave, it was only five and a half miles to the hut. The note also contained the stunning news that the *Aurora* had arrived, that Amundsen had reached the South Pole the year before, and that Scott was wintering over again in Antarctica.

Yet for all the joy and hope the cairn, the food, and the note brought Mawson, it contained a tantalizing "what if." McLean, Hodgeman, and Hurley had recorded the time and date when they had left the cache. The trio had camped there overnight before departing at 8 a.m. that very morning of January 29. Mawson had found the cairn at 2 p.m. He had missed running into the search party by a mere six hours. And he realized that "during the night of the 28th our camps had been only some five miles apart."

Fired with new energy, Mawson plunged onward, though he knew better than to hope that he might catch up to the three fit and healthy searchers. He covered another eight miles on the 29th before stopping to camp. The day's run all told had been thirteen miles, Mawson's best in weeks. "It is a great joy to have plenty of food," he wrote in his diary, "but must see that [I] don't overload or disaster may result."

Yet Mawson's wild hope that he might reach the hut within a couple of days was destined to be cruelly dashed, by yet another all-but-unforeseeable vicissitude. And once again, his life would hang by the thinnest of threads.

At the end of his long march on the 29th, Mawson had found himself on a surface unlike any that he had trudged across during the previous weeks. "Am now on ice and half ice and falling every few yards on account of heavy side wind," he wrote in his diary. If only he had kept his crampons, he could have trodden blithely across the slippery plateau, but the soft soles of his finnesko were useless for purchase on ice, especially with the sledge behind him catching every gust of wind and pulling him off the track he hoped to pursue. "Before giving up [on January 29]," he later recalled, "I even tried crawling on my hands and knees."

The next morning, before emerging from the tent, Mawson tried to manufacture substitute crampons. As ingenious a tinkerer as ever, he cut up the theodolite case, producing a pair of thin, flat pieces of wood. Then he scavenged all the screws and nails he could find, taking apart both the sledgemeter and the theodolite. These he thrust through the pieces of wood until they protruded like crampon spikes. Before starting out on January 30, he lashed these devices to the soles of his finnesko. It took only a few miles of marching to break them to pieces.

The destruction of the "crampons" forced Mawson to camp after a little more than five miles, "on first bit of half snow I could find." To add to the miseries of the 30th, Mawson's trek took him back into a region crisscrossed with crevasses—terrain he thought he had left behind for good. "Sledge breaking through dangerously in several places," he dryly recorded. Having thrown away the alpine rope, Mawson no longer had his rescue ladder to extricate himself should he fall into yet another fissure in the ice.

At the end of the day's march, however, he had seen a distant object that looked very much like the "beacon" that had been erected months earlier to mark the location of Aladdin's Cave. It seemed, however, too near to fit the distances indicated in the note left by McLean, Hodgeman, and Hurley.

On January 31, as the wind blasted the plateau, Mawson spent all day inside the tent trying to craft a second set of crampons, scavenging yet more materials from various pieces of his sledge and gear, including parts of the box that held the Primus stove. "This work took an interminable time," he later recalled, "for the tools and appliances available were almost all contained in a small pocket knife that had belonged to Mertz. Besides a blade it was furnished with a spike, a gimlet and a screw-driver."

It was not until past noon on February 1 that Mawson was satisfied with his new crampons. The weather had turned favorable. As Mawson pulled the sledge, his balance unsteady on the ice, the black dot that he had seen two days earlier grew closer and clearer. And then, after a march of only two and a half miles, he came to Aladdin's Cave. "Great joy and thanksgiving," he noted in his diary. In *The Home of the Blizzard*, he elaborated on the momentous arrival:

> At 7 p.m. that haven within the ice was attained. It took but a few moments to dig away the snow and throw back the canvas flap sealing the entrance. A moment later I slid down inside, arriving amidst familiar surroundings. Something unusual in one corner caught the eye—three oranges and a pineapple—circumstantial evidence of the arrival of the *Aurora*.

Of course Mawson had already learned of the ship's arrival from the note in the snow cairn that he had discovered on January 29. Perhaps it took something as tangible as a pineapple to convince him that the note told the truth.

That evening, sleeping in the blissful refuge of the grotto, Mawson was only five and a half miles from the hut. Surely his ordeal was finally over. He could not know that at that very moment the *Aurora* lay at anchor in Commonwealth Bay, waiting to pick up the ten men who had not been delegated to stay a second winter and search for traces of the Far Eastern Party. But he might have guessed as much, since only three days had passed since McLean, Hodgeman, and Hurley had started back from the snow cairn on top of which they had deposited the food bag with the note.

But Mawson also knew that the five-and-a-half-mile slope leading from Aladdin's Cave to Winter Quarters had most likely turned into a treacherous toboggan run of hard ice. Even if he abandoned his sledge and made a dash for it, without proper footgear he would surely slip and tumble, perhaps to his death. In his diary that first evening, he wrote, "My new crampons want improving as one is quite unsatisfactory and has strained my right leg, so I must camp for the night." On arriving at Aladdin's Cave, as ecstatic as he was to discover bags full of food, his great disappointment was not finding an extra set of crampons.

In the night, a fierce gale blew in. The storm continued without respite for a week. It was the same storm that kept the *Aurora* steaming in circles in Commonwealth Bay, unable to launch the motorboat to pick up the ten men who were going home, as Captain John King Davis kept up his sleepless vigil. On the morning of February 2, Mawson slithered out of the cave, ready to head for the hut, only to be lashed by 50 mph winds. The temptation to make the dash was strong, but he dismissed it "as a last resort." How terrible it would be, he thought, to have survived a desperate trek of almost 300 miles from Ninnis's crevasse, only to kill himself trying to force the last homeward leg.

Instead, Mawson crawled back into the "comfortable cave" and spent the day trying to improve his fragile crampons. He ransacked the grotto for anything—benzine cases, food bags, loose nails, parts of a dead dog's sledge harness—that might aid his improvisation. On February 3, he emerged again, hoping to head out, but in the blowing snow, he realized he would have to haul his sledge in case he got lost and missed the hut. And that was an impossibility without adequate crampons.

"This is most exasperating," he wrote in his diary. And, "I turned in at midnight, very tired. It almost appears as if scurvy or something of the kind were upon me—joints very sore. Blood keeps coming from the right nostril in thin watery description, also from outbursts on the fingers."

February 4 was no better: "Blowing quite as hard as ever, and thick drift. I wait in the bag and listen for cessation for greater part of day. . . . Oh for a clear spell! Will the ship wait?"

On the 5th, Mawson almost set out. But when he tried out his new crampons on the icy surface, he was "disappointed to find that they had not sufficient grip to face the wind, so had to abandon the idea of attempting the descent." In his diary he agonized over the uncertain gamble: "With good crampons it would be a pleasure to walk down to the Hut, but with what I have, and the taking of sledge down, it would be a toss-up." Instead, he tried to console himself with the new luxury of food: "I bring in the tin of S & A biscuits, find it a great change—now eating chunks of pem out of tins and S & A biscuits. Have got to like very much boiled Glaxo with biscuit in it."

On the 6th and the 7th, the wind blew furiously, interrupted only by brief lulls. Mawson's diary entries were growing shorter and shorter. "Perfected second pair of crampons by screws got out of sledgemeter," he boasted on the 6th. But the next day, he wrote only six words: "Wind continues too strong for crampons."

It was only on February 8 that the weeklong gale finally blew itself out. The wind fell quickly after 8 a.m., but Mawson waited until 1 p.m. to make sure it was not a false lull. At last, he started downhill on the final trek to the hut. Wearing one pair of rickety, unreliable crampons and carrying a backup pair, Mawson had also outfitted the sledge with safety modifications—what he called "a patent anti-crevasse bar," as well as ropes wrapped under the runners to slow the sledge's glide on the icy slope.

During that risky jaunt, Mawson tormented himself with primal questions:

(1) Had the ship gone?
(2) If so, had they left a party at the Hut?
(3) Or had they abandoned us altogether?

While Mawson had been preparing the final march of his 300-mile return from disaster, Davis had finally brought the *Aurora* close to shore. Taking advantage of the windless hours on the morning of February 8, he sent the motorboat to pick up the ten men. In a desperate hurry to steam westward to relieve Wild's Western Party, Davis and his crew performed the task with commendable efficiency. Just before noon—an hour before Mawson set off from Aladdin's Cave—the ship headed out of Commonwealth Bay, as the men onboard waved their goodbyes to the six left behind.

One mile down the slope, Mawson finally came in clear sight of the bay. There was no ship in view, though Mawson tried to temper his disappointment with the supposition that the *Aurora* might be drifting eastward along the coast, still searching for the missing party. Three miles farther on, Mawson caught sight of "a speck on the north-west horizon. . . . It looked like a distant ship—Was it the *Aurora*?" And if it was the *Aurora*, was she steaming away for good, or still circling and searching?

Only moments later, Mawson's heart surged with relief, as "the boat harbour burst into view and I saw 3 men working at something on one side of it." Mawson stopped in his tracks and waved for thirty seconds. At last one of the men looked up, saw the apparition far above, and waved in response. Suddenly five men were running as fast as they could up the icy slope, while Mawson resumed his cautious downhill plod, still pulling his sledge.

The first to reach him was Frank Bickerton. From 50 yards away,

Mawson recognized his teammate, the man who had nursed the air-tractor through its year of feckless service for the AAE. But from the startled look on Bickerton's face, as he beheld the ravaged countenance of the man limping down the slope above him, Mawson knew exactly what Bickerton was thinking: *Which one are you?*

7

WINTER MADNESS

Bickerton and the five other men who had rushed up the slope—all but the new radio operator, Sidney Jeffryes—took charge of Mawson's sledge and helped their leader hobble down the last stretch to the hut. "I briefly recited the disaster and cause of my late arrival from the sledge journey," Mawson wrote in his diary that night. "There were tears in several eyes as the story proceeded."

Had Mawson come into view only five or six hours earlier, the whole of the Main Base party could have boarded the *Aurora* and steamed west to pick up Wild's men. As it was, however, there was still the chance of such a salvation. During the idle days as the men had waited at Winter Quarters for the return of the Far Eastern Party, they had gotten the radio mast erected and the transmitter working. Before parting, Captain Davis had arranged for Jeffryes to send messages to the ship while she was still in radio range. Because the *Aurora* could receive but not send, Jeffryes had promised to broadcast at 8, 9, and 10 p.m., with Walter Hannam on the ship manning the wireless set.

That evening, Hannam transcribed the terse but stunning message: "Arrived safely at Hut. Mertz and Ninnis dead. Return and pick up all hands. Mawson." Davis immediately turned the ship around, and by 9 p.m. she was steaming back toward Commonwealth Bay. "Thank God Mawson is alive at any rate," Davis wrote in his diary.

By the morning of February 9, the ship lay offshore opposite the hut. As Davis recalled decades later:

> As we neared those too well-remembered ice-slopes we were greeted by the first shrill notes of the coastal blizzard piping in the rigging. By the time we had reached the anchorage it was blowing a full gale. A boat's crew of volunteers . . . stood eagerly by the surf boat, but the wind was too violent to send them away.

At the time, however, Davis's feelings were less charitable. "Why did they recall us," he wrote in his diary. "It simply means that we are going to loose [*sic*] Wild for the sake of taking off a party who are in perfect safety. I wish we have never received the message. . . . I am just worn out and a heap of nerves."

A heap of nerves could also have characterized the state of the seven refugees standing on the shore, staring at the gale-lashed ship, so close and yet so inaccessible. "We tried to be patient," wrote Bickerton. "We looked at the sea, the wind instruments and the barometer and the ship. Every lull brought hope and every gust might be the last. If only the wind would drop ever so little a boat could fetch us."

Mawson directed Jeffryes to send another wireless message to Hannam: "Anxious to get off, hope Capt Davis could wait a few days longer." Yet despite the tantalizing prospect of a quick motor launch ride to the *Aurora*, Mawson could put Davis's quandary in perspective. As he wrote in his diary on the 9th:

> Of course I did not like commanding him to remain as he was responsible for picking up Wild's party, which he had left in a difficult situation, and the probabilities were that as the season was now so far advanced he would either not get in to Wild's base or, having got in, would not get out.

At 6:30 p.m. on February 9, Davis met with the whole ship's crew to ask their advice. His own judgment was already firm in his mind: "This party are in perfect safety and have everything they want. Wild on the other hand, has not, and I feel that I am no longer justified in remaining here and risking losing the 2nd party." The crew concurred. "I am sorry for the party left behind," Davis added, "but have done what I believe to be right."

Mawson woke on February 10 to a sharp disappointment. "Well, next morning strong wind and no ship in view," he wrote. "The wind calmed off in afternoon, so that we could have got off if ship here." The men left behind at Cape Denison still held out the faint hope that the *Aurora* might be able to return to gather them up after recovering Wild's party.

Despite the calming of the wind in the afternoon, Davis had no second thoughts. "The strain of the last fortnight has been about as much as anyone could put up with I think, and still keep his senses," he wrote in his diary. "I got a bit of sleep last night for the first time for nearly a week." The men on the ship still had no clear idea of what had caused the deaths of Ninnis and Mertz. That evening, Hannam received a last, garbled wireless message. The only words he could make out were "crevasse, Ninnis and Mertz, broken" and "cable." Davis concluded, "From this it would appear as if the two of them had been lost in a crevasse."

The disheartened seven left behind at Cape Denison settled back into the hut to wait—whether for only a month or so, if the *Aurora* should manage to return, or for another year, until the ship could pick them up the following summer, they could only guess. The previous winter, Madigan, Bickerton, Mertz, and Ninnis had occupied the four double bunks that Ninnis had jocularly nicknamed Hyde Park Corner. Now Madigan wrote in his diary, "Of the four happy members of the Hyde Park Corner . . . only two remain. Bickerton and I sleep in the old corner—how desolate it seems—I have heard Bick sobbing under his blankets—and their terrible end, I cannot write of it."

Mawson was so debilitated by his ordeal that, as he later wrote,

"It was several weeks before normal sleep returned; during that time I did little else than potter about, eat and doze, with frequent interruptions from internal disorders." On February 12, only three days after the ship had left, he wrote in his diary, "I am invaliding yet. I have shaken to pieces somewhat, and I anticipate it will take some time to pull me up to anything like I was physically before that awful journey home." The rest of the men did their best to nurse their leader back to health. "For the first few weeks," Paquita Mawson was later told by those teammates, "he would follow them round, not so much to talk to them as just to be with them."

Mawson later told his friend and protégé Phillip Law "that he probably would have died had he gone on the ship."

Fifteen hundred miles to the west, the eight men at the Western Base had begun to despair of the *Aurora*'s arrival. They had killed seals to shore up their supplies of food and blubber against the grim possibility of having to endure a second winter on the Shackleton Ice Shelf, and they had carried signboards out to the edge of the sea cliff in hopes of directing the ship's crew toward their hut. But by February 20, they had lingered for almost three weeks beyond the January 30 date by which Frank Wild had been told to be ready for the pickup.

The men talked constantly about the *Aurora*, with George Dovers, the twenty-two-year-old surveyor, the most anxious of them all. According to Charles Harrisson, the biologist who was twice Dovers's age, "George . . . announces in his positive way each morning that the ship will be in that day. Each night that we 'will sleep on the ship tomorrow night!' How continually that stretch of open water is swept for the sight of her!" Two days later, Harrisson added, "Trust nothing has happened to [the ship]. Her name constantly heard this day & twice George gave false alarm this morning."

The *Aurora*'s all-out charge westward after leaving Commonwealth Bay, Davis later wrote, "remains in my memory as one long continuous battle with the elements. When it wasn't headwinds, fog, gales or pack-ice, it was blizzards or icebergs." By now, darkness was starting to fall at 9 p.m. "From then on until morning we had to grope our way as best we could, the blizzard wind flinging the snow into our faces with stinging force, while weaving through vast fields of pack-ice or twisting and turning to avoid being blown down upon the innumerable bergs that lay, silent and menacing, athwart our track."

Davis's diary during this trying voyage is a litany of complaints and maledictions. (Reading them, one understands how the young captain acquired the nickname Gloomy.) "We are too late in the season, that is the trouble," he wrote on February 11. The next day: "A very poor run to the Westward. . . . I hope that we shall get a change soon or things will look very bad." On the 15th, "A terrible day, running before an Easterly gale in thick snow, unable to see anything, barometer falling steadily. . . . I do not know how long a man would last out at this sort of thing. I know that it would not take a great deal more to wear me out."

On top of bad weather, icebergs, and fog, Davis had an unexpected obstacle to deal with. As the *Aurora* pushed on to the west, he noted that "The [pack] ice is nearly 60 miles further North than last year. Whether we shall ever get to the 2nd base seems doubtful, unless there is a decided change in the trend of this pack." But on February 21, Davis found a change. "It was much better than it looked," he noted in a rare expression of optimism, as the ship steamed southward through open leads under a bright moon.

Ensconced inside the Grottoes, their snow-smothered base camp hut, Wild's men waited out an 80 mph blizzard on February 22. The next day, however, the wind dwindled to a light breeze. Peering through binoculars, Wild saw to his delight that the pack ice stretching beyond the edge of the Shackleton Ice Shelf had broken up dramatically. That day, he and Sydney Jones hiked out to retrieve a sledge that had been used to make ocean soundings. "We had gone less than half a mile," wrote Wild, "when we saw what at first appeared to be a penguin standing on some heavy pack-ice in the distance, but which we soon made out to be the mast head of the 'Aurora.' "

Knowing it would take hours for the ship to come alongside, Wild and Jones dashed back to The Grottoes to share the joyous news with their teammates. By the time Davis had brought the *Aurora* to the edge of the shelf, the men had hauled two sledge loads of gear a mile and a half to the sea cliff "in record time."

"As the ship came alongside, we gave three hearty cheers for Captain Davis and were surprised at the subdued nature of the return cheers from the ship and an atmosphere of gloom over the whole ship's company," wrote Wild. On first hearing of the ship's arrival, Harrisson had cheered out loud with his teammates. "But instead of the elation I expected to feel," he wrote in his diary, "was an intense anxiety. The suspense of the last year was to end in an hour. What was the news she brought . . . good or bad?"

Harrisson continued: "Wild hailed & asked if Dr Mawson & First Party all well. But only an ominous silence."

Many years later Charles Laseron, on board the *Aurora*, recalled the ship's approach to Western Base:

> At the foot of the barrier was a narrow shelf of sea-ice some hundreds of yards wide. At its edge stood a number of figures, some of whom we could see waving their arms. We rubbed our eyes, and counted again. There should have been eight, but here were twenty or more. Then, as the distance lessened, the figures separated into two groups. Eight of them were men, the others emperor penguins.
>
> All, then, were safe. Our relief was more than great. The tragedy at the main base was so recent that subconsciously we had almost dreaded this moment, lest we learn that further calamity had overtaken us.

Wild's men were stunned by the news of Mertz's and Ninnis's deaths, especially because the men on board the *Aurora* could supply no details as to how those two well-loved teammates had met their end. But the Western Base party was so eager to escape the Shackleton Shelf that it took them only a matter of hours to load all their belongings onto the ship, lay in a supply of ice for drinking water, and start north.

For Davis, there was no possibility of returning to Cape Denison to pick up Mawson and his six companions. The supply of coal on board was barely adequate for the return to Australia, and to dodge further among the bergs and pack ice as February darkened into March would be to invite getting the ship frozen in—as had already happened to several Antarctic expedition vessels, and would happen again. As the ship steamed north, Davis summed up the recent trials in his diary: "It seems like a dream to think that the awful nightmare of the last fortnight is over, and that the party are safe on board. I wish we had the people from the other base, but they will have to remain there now until next year."

Among all the scientific specimens and personal belongings the men of the Western Base brought back with them, Wild was proudest (and fondest) of the two huskies that had survived the year in Antarctica. By late February, Zip and Amundsen were "woefully thin and weak, all their ribs showing and backbones sticking up like sharp wedges." But on board ship, the dogs ate so heartily that they arrived in Hobart "as fat as butter."

Later, in Sydney, Wild gave Zip to a lady friend "who kept him for several years." But upon first landing at Hobart, where a late-summer heat wave reigned, Amundsen suffered from a distress utterly different from anything he had undergone in Antarctica. Despite efforts to pack his kennel in ice, within days Amundsen had died of heat stroke.

On March 4, in the hut at Cape Denison, Archibald McLean wrote in his diary, "Hope for the Aurora's return is at a very low ebb." The only compensation for the seven men facing imprisonment in Antarctica for another year came from the fact that they had gotten the wireless apparatus working. Via the relay station on Macquarie Island, for the first time in fourteen months the remaining members of the AAE were in contact with Australia, and thus with the rest of the world. On March 9, McLean chortled, "Last night quite a budget of messages came through—seven in all.—It was quite like a morning paper to hear the contents at breakfast time."

Basking in his triumph in the race for the South Pole, Roald Amundsen sent Mawson a short message, "hop[ing] he would have 'a pleasant winter.' " On March 16, the radio sent news that the *Aurora* had arrived safely in Hobart. The men at Winter Quarters accepted the news stoically.

An unexpected corollary to the second overwintering was the necessity for the men on Macquarie Island to winter over again as well, simply to keep the radio link up and running. Life at 55° south was not nearly as onerous as existence in the "home of the blizzard," at 67° south, but Macquarie was bleak enough—a raw, storm-swept, treeless landscape of rugged hills covered with tussock grass, though the prevalence of seals and penguins year-round relieved the monotony. Upon learning via radio from Mawson about the need to keep the relay station going for another year, George Ainsworth, the leader of the five-man party, offered his teammates the chance to return to Australia in May aboard a relief vessel, returning only in November. But such was the loyalty of the men to Mawson and the AAE that all four volunteered to stick it out through the whole winter.

At Cape Denison, Mawson imposed a strict discipline on his men, limiting their personal use of the radio to a bare minimum. The precious wireless connection, he felt, should be saved for official scientific and business purposes. He did manage, however, to embed a brief telegraphic missive to Paquita in a longer message to the AAE secretary in Australia. It read,

DEEPLY REGRET DELAY ONLY JUST MANAGED
TO REACH HUT EFFECTS NOW GONE BUT LOST
MY HAIR YOU ARE FREE TO CONSIDER YOUR
CONTRACT BUT TRUST YOU WILL NOT ABANDON
YOUR SECOND HAND DOUGLAS

Paquita promptly replied:

DEEPLY THANKFUL YOU ARE SAFE WARMEST
WELCOME AWAITING YOUR HUNTERS RETURN
REGARDING CONTRACT SAME AS EVER ONLY
MORE SO THOUGHTS ALWAYS WITH YOU ALL WELL
HERE MONTHS SOON PASS TAKE THINGS EASIER
THIS WINTER SPEAK AS OFTEN AS POSSIBLE

During February and March, Mawson was too depleted to contribute much to the chores and duties of the hut. His diary entries are
more clipped and lethargic than during any previous period of the
AAE. Many are one-liners: "Covering Hut and fitting store," "Drifting and strong wind," "Macquarie Id heard but could not catch."

Yet as leader, Mawson thought it critical to the men's morale to
keep them busy. This was not a machiavellian ploy: Mawson sincerely believed that "there still remained useful work to be undertaken." Accordingly, he directed operations "to make the Hut,
if anything, safer and snugger." The principal remodeling effort
consisted of covering the roof with an old sail left behind by the
Aurora, which, Mawson was convinced, made the building more
windproof.

Bob Bage was put in charge of magnetic and astronomical observations, and he also served as storeman, arranging such delicacies as
penguin eggs and seal steaks in accessible cases on the windward side
of the overhanging veranda. Cecil Madigan kept up the meteorological records, and Mawson put him in charge of twenty-one huskies
that had served on Amundsen's South Pole expedition. A gift from
the Norwegian, the dogs had been carried south aboard the *Aurora*
on its relief expedition in 1913. Frank Bickerton was the mechanical
handyman, charged also with keeping the vital radio mast and wires
from breaking down. Archibald McLean, ever the biologist, took on
the odd jobs of gathering ice for drinking water and carrying coal
for the stove. He also launched bottles filled with messages into the
sea, "on the chance of their being picked up, thereby giving some
indication of the direction of the currents." Alfred Hodgeman, the
architect, assisted Madigan with the meteorological notes, and made

maps and plans to help document the expedition. And Jeffryes, the newcomer, reputed to be a more skillful operator than Walter Hannam, took charge of sending and receiving the all-important radio messages.

Yet it was impossible for the men not to feel that most of these chores were little better than make-work to fill the empty days of the second winter. Mawson tacitly acknowledged as much, setting the wake-up call later than the year before. Breakfast occupied the hour from 9 to 10 a.m., so that the chores themselves began as late as 11. As Bickerton later wrote:

> The hut was not so cold the second winter and we were not so crowded. . . . But the wind was unvarying as ever, the food we knew too well in every possible combination, and we felt badly the need of occasional entertainment with people not subject to our routine or monotonous climate. We came to accept our life as the normal and an effort of the imagination was needed to see oneself in a world supplied with grass and friendly weather and modern plumbing.

Mawson was determined to keep up some semblance of scientific research beyond making daily weather observations. A stray comment in McLean's diary records a bizarre experiment not mentioned in *The Home of the Blizzard*: "DM and AM [i. e., McLean himself] paint penguins black—like tagging—to see if they return to the same rookeries." The men knew the penguins would soon desert the continent for their breeding grounds farther north. McLean vigilantly observed their piecemeal departure. "Last penguins have gone north," he wrote on March 29, only to glimpse a few stragglers several days later. But by April 21, "No luck looking for last solitary penguins."

On February 22, via the radio, the men learned for the first time about the fate of Robert Scott and his four companions returning from the South Pole the year before. Wrote Mawson in his diary, "'Scott reached the Pole—died and 4 others.' I know what this means as I have been so near it myself recently." The wireless communication with Macquarie Island was spotty at best. Mawson's diary entries, still brief and telegraphic, record the team's frustration: "Wireless hears Macquarie talking but only for a short while"; "Jeffryes hears very little of Macquarie." Part of the problem was caused by atmospheric disturbances such as the aurora and St. Elmo's fire. "Jeffryes would sometimes spend the whole evening," Mawson wrote, "trying to transmit a single message, or conversely, trying to receive one."

On March 23, for the first time since reaching the hut, Mawson confessed his fragile psychological state to his diary:

> I find my nerves in a very serious state, and from the feeling I have in the base of my head I [have] suspicion that I may go off my rocker very soon. My nerves have evidently had a very great shock. Too much writing today brought this on. I shall take more exercise and less study, hoping for a beneficial turn.

Boredom was the ever-present enemy. "Reading is a great solace," McLean wrote on April 6, "and we fortunately have plenty of books." Mawson elaborated: "There was a fine supply of illustrated journals and periodicals which had arrived by the *Aurora* and with these we tried to make up the arrears of a year in exile. The 'Encyclopedia Britannica' was a great boon, being always the last word in the settlement of a debated point."

To leaven the monotony of the men's rations, each of the seven concocted some culinary specialty. Bage cooked steamed puddings, Madigan puff pastry, Jeffryes milk scones, and so on. In retrospect, Mawson could see humor in these efforts: "Bickerton once started out with the object of cooking a ginger pudding, and in an unguarded moment used mixed-spice instead of ginger. The result, though highly spiced, was rather appetizing, so 'mixed-spice pudding' was added to our list of discoveries."

What to do with the huskies Amundsen had donated to the expedition presented a curious dilemma. There was no longer any need for sledging journeys, so the dogs became in effect pets. But they had to be fed (mostly on rotting seal carcasses), quartered in the veranda, and kept from tearing into the food supplies. They also had an unpleasant penchant for fighting viciously with one another. As Mawson noted:

> On May 23 Lassie, one of the dogs, had his abdomen ripped open in a fight and had to be shot. Quarrels amongst the dogs had to be quelled immediately, otherwise they would probably mean the death of some unfortunate animal which happened to be thrown down amongst the pack. Whenever a dog was down, it was the way of these brutes to attack him irrespective of whether they were friends or foes.

Yet despite the best efforts of the seven men to keep up morale, tensions began to invade the hut. The most disaffected member was Cecil Madigan. He had, of course, been sorely disappointed at being chosen to spend a second winter in Antarctica, for it meant delaying his Rhodes scholarship yet another year—a hiatus he was not at all sure the committee would tolerate. The antagonism toward Mawson that had been latent through the first winter now flared into an intense resentment, even disgust.

Since Madigan's diary is not available to scholars, the only source for the man's feelings and judgments during the second winter is the secondhand paraphrase in *Vixere Fortes*, the family memoir written by his son David Madigan and privately published in 2000. As Riffenburgh argues about this chronicle, "the assessments of Mawson break down at points into little more than a litany of complaints or a vitriolic rant." Since the sentiments expressed in this book are so at odds with the diaries and later writings of the other team members, *Vixere Fortes* must be regarded as somewhat unreliable.

According to David Madigan, in March "Cecil's gloom deepened as he surveyed the narrow space of his confinement. He was in a strange and wonderful country, but one week of it was enough. . . .

Such was Adelie Land, which had become loathsome to him." In that gloom, Madigan turned his contempt on the man he had jeeringly nicknamed Dux Ipse.

> Not the least of his tribulations was Mawson, of whom his opinion changed greatly, becoming steadily worse, as did that of his colleagues, particularly Bickerton. By April everybody except Mawson was sick to death with everything, and chiefly with Mawson himself. They had made a great sacrifice in staying behind for Mertz and Ninnis, and lastly for Mawson, but they received no thanks, nor did Mawson give any sign that he felt the least gratitude, quite the reverse: it was Mawson first and the rest nowhere, and he even dropped hints that they might not be paid their salaries. He did nothing himself but eat and he seemed to think that everybody else was equally idle, since he was constantly suggesting things for them to do, yet the more one did for him the more he grumbled.

The imputation that Bickerton shared Madigan's extremely negative feelings toward Mawson is not borne out by Bickeron's biographer, Stephen Haddelsey, who categorically states that "there are no criticisms of Mawson, either real or implied, in Bickerton's writings." Another contraindication to *Vixere Fortes* lies in the fact that Mawson's diary contains very little criticism of Madigan during the second winter, or evidence of conflict between the men.

By April, however, the seven men marooned in the hut began to face a far graver crisis than any antagonism on the part of Madigan. It had to do with Sidney Jeffryes. The first hint of it emerges in a cryptic single line Mawson wrote in his diary sometime between April 1 and 6: "Jeffryes sat in the batter pudding."

By the beginning of April, the radio was working splendidly. "Wireless good—but too good, so that jammed out by Australian stations," wrote Mawson on the 21st. But on May 8, "Wireless last few days nil but very free from static." The problems continued during the following days. Mawson wondered whether atmospheric disturbances were interfering with transmitting or receiving.

The men had been dreading the onset of May, for along with increased darkness and cold, the winds had averaged their highest velocity of any month during the previous May. At first the winds in May 1913 did not match the blizzards of 1912, but just as much snow fell. Then on May 17 and 18, a shrieking gale set in: over the first twenty-four-hour period, the wind averaged 83 mph, and almost 94 mph on the 18th, with a peak gust of 103 mph.

The hut withstood these blasts, but all seven men were worried that the radio mast would collapse. But it was not the equipment that was the problem. Something was happening to Jeffryes. Mawson's first acknowledgment of trouble came in a long diary entry on May 26—by far the longest he had written since returning to the hut on February 8:

> On evening of 26th I dozed till near midnight, then on coming out, found Jeffryes asleep—had been practically all evening. . . . It was a great pity about the wireless as it was a good night. After waking up he got in only a little before Sawyer went to bed. [On Macquarie Island, Arthur Sawyer was one of the two radio operators, and the agreement was to exchange messages between 8 p.m. and midnight.] Jeffryes stops up all day—goes for tiring walks, etc, and then is not fit to keep an alert watch during the 8 to 12 hours. This is bad management.

Exacerbating the problem was the fact that only Jeffryes knew how to operate the wireless. Bickerton, in charge of keeping the mast up and the guy wires tight, had at best a very rudimentary understanding of how the radio worked.

On June 6, Mawson voiced another complaint: "Tonight Jeffryes goes to bed before midnight when the aurora had died out & calm, said there was some noise, inferring a kind of static in the telephone. I can't get him or Bickerton to take the subject up scientifically."

Jeffryes's sleepiness might at first have seemed only a case of depression, a state that all seven men in the hut had to struggle to avoid. But radio contact with the outside world was the most important antidote to the doldrums of another winter, with too much time on the men's hands and too little real work to do.

On June 8, what all the men feared came to pass. A whirly—one of the sudden, violent, cyclonic gusts that seemed so often to assail Cape Denison—blew away the top section of the radio mast, shattered the middle section, and brought the whole thing crashing to the ground. "Another Black Sunday," Mawson wrote, alluding to the kindred catastrophe of October 13, 1912, when a similar gust had flattened the north radio mast. "Hope something can be done." Only thirteen days before Midwinter's Day, the men had to reconcile themselves to the kind of isolation from the outside world that they had borne through the whole of the previous winter. Almost two months would pass before the mast could be repaired and erected, allowing radio contact to resume.

In the meantime, Jeffryes's mental state passed beyond the realm of simple depression. The first flare-up, recorded by Mawson on July 7, was deeply alarming:

Last night Jeffryes at the table suddenly asked Madigan to go into the next room (to fight) as he believed that something had been said against him—nothing whatever had. Madigan had mentioned the name of a novel he had read that day *The Hound of the Baskervilles* and Jeffryes appears to have taken it to be a reference to him. A ridiculous thing, for everybody has felt on the best of terms with him. I stopped the row and he talked it over with Madigan after, but was not very satisfactory. . . .

This morning after breakfast Madigan was filling his lamp with kerosene in the gangway and Jeffryes went out, pushing him. Asked him to fight again, danced round in a towering rage, struck Madigan, rough and tumble. Madigan got a clinch on him, then I had to speak to him and others.

Despite this evidence of extreme paranoia, McLean, the expedition doctor, and Mawson were inclined to minimize the significance of the outburst. "McLean thinks [Jeffryes] is a bit off his head," Mawson added. "I think that his touchy temperament is being very hard tested with bad weather and indoor life. A case of polar depression. I trust it will go now."

Instead of going away, Jeffryes's dementia worsened during the following days. On July 9, Mawson tersely noted, "Jeffryes confides in Bage, makes Bage think he is not all there. Blizzard continues." The next day:

Jeffryes has been on night watch. He comes to me after breakfast and confides in me that he "went the pace" when he was younger and it left him with a venereal trouble. This trouble has caused him to make seminal emissions of late, he says. Asks me to get McLean to give him poison. This makes me think he surely must be going off his base.

And the day after that, July 11:

Last night Jeffryes spoke to McLean and it seems that most of what he told me re venereal disease was a hallucination. McLean gave him a sleeping draught but could not get him to go to bed. . . .

McLean gave him another sleeping draught this morning and he slept most of the day. Just before dinner he came into my room and said that he "wished we would state clearly all the accusations imputed against him." This showed him to be still at sea in his mind. I tried to get from him what he supposed we had against him, assuring him that there was nothing but good feeling toward him. At last he ventured that "he could not understand what we meant in referring to the *Aurora*'s Log." Later on he "could not see what Capt Davis had to do with the wireless."

At last Mawson had to acknowledge that Jeffryes's mental insta-
bility went far beyond "polar depression." On the 12th, the paranoia
reached a new depth:

> Jeffryes came to me in the anteroom and talked at length. He
> believes that every word we utter is an imputation against him,
> and keeps referring to a "judge and jury business". . . .
>
> He said once that the whole trouble arose through McLean
> analysing his urine and deducing from that things against his
> past. McLean never of course had anything to do with his urine.

On the same day, Madigan discovered that Jeffryes had been collecting his own urine in jars that he placed on the shelf above his
bunk.

Jeffryes was not the first Antarctic explorer to be stricken with
insanity during an overwintering. As mentioned in chapter four, on
the *Belgica* expedition of 1897–99, the two team leaders, Adrien de
Gerlache and Georges Lecointe, gave up on life and took more or
less permanently to their beds. But theirs was a passive craziness,
threatening the rest of the team only because they abdicated their
leadership. Jeffryes's madness was more ominous, for in his paranoia
he promised to become an active menace to the six men marooned
in the hut with him.

On July 17, Mawson wrote, "Jeffryes continues to be a trouble. . . .
Says we will all be put in gaol on arrival in Australia for contemplat-
ing murdering him. Looks bad at times and might become violent,
so always have somebody watching him." The strain of enduring the
darkest, coldest part of the winter without radio contact with Australia, exacerbated by Jeffryes's madness, took its toll on Mawson, still
weak both physically and psychologically. That same day, he confessed, "Last night I felt almost at my limit, my brain felt to be on the
point of bursting."

The men's enforced leisure, however, found a stimulating outlet
in a new project. Chiefly the brainchild of Mawson and McLean, *The
Adelie Blizzard* was to become an in-house newspaper (though effec-

tively a magazine), written by the various members and typed up by McLean, who would serve as editor. The precedents were obvious: Scott's first expedition from 1901–04 had produced the *South Polar Times*, and Shackleton's BAE from 1907–09 had manufactured a veritable book, called *Aurora Australis*. Mawson had contributed a bizarre science fiction fantasy, "Bathybia," to the latter work. In fact, expeditions producing periodicals during polar overwinterings can be traced back to the *New Georgia Gazette*, a weekly printed on shipboard in the winter of 1819–20 as a team led by William Edward Parry, attempting the Northwest Passage, lay ice-bound in the Arctic north of Canada.

The Adelie Blizzard had two purposes. First and foremost, it was to occupy the time of the men waiting out the winter, and to entertain them with all kinds of inside jokes and parodic whimsies about their hut-bound life. But Mawson also hoped to publish the collected issues upon the men's return to Australia, just as Scott had arranged the publication of the *South Polar Times* in London. Between April and October five issues of *The Adelie Blizzard* appeared, filling a total of 217 pages.

The deadline for articles for the first issue was April 23. With handwritten copies on his tabletop, McLean laboriously typed up the pieces on the expedition's battered Smith Premier typewriter. He had a small supply of ribbons, some in different colors. The paper had been supplied by a pair of stationers, one in England, one in Australia. Alfred Hodgeman, the architect, designed the intricate title headings.

Since the articles were published without attribution, it is difficult to determine today who wrote what. Not all the men were equally keen to contribute. According to the editors of a modern facsimile edition published in 2010, "Madigan showed little enthusiasm, and Bickerton apparently had to be nagged to contribute."

The mock-formal tone of the newspaper (as Mawson insisted on calling it) was struck at once, in a line directly beneath the title: "Registered at the General Plateau Office for transmission by wind." The first issue contained seventeen pieces, ranging from relatively straight history ("Scott's British Antarctic Expedition") to fanciful poems and essays ("Ode to Tobacco," "The Evolution of Women"). For all the frivolity of the production, the April issue opened with an "In Memoriam" poem dedicated to Mertz and Ninnis. It closed:

> *"Could we but greet thee, comrades of our heart,*
> *What warmth of human kindness were our speech!"*
> *Were we happier, then? Better were Faith—*
> *Fragrant the knightly flower of beauteous youth—*
> *Then had we said:—"Nobler to have won the fight,*
> *Wresting the prize of thrice-hard duty, wrought*
> *Amid the chilling wastes of pathless snow!"*

With the first lines of the editorial on the facing page, however, the *Blizzard* strikes a humorous note. Under the heading "Marooned," the writer compares the seven men's situation to that of Robinson Crusoe: "This somewhat lugubrious title describes the present state of 'society,' so far as we are concerned." He goes on to minimize the tribulations of winter in the hut, declaring, "We are surrounded with most of the advantages of civilization, and even if there is none of the gay tinsel of the Comic Opera, we may discover, living in this misguided climate, the vein of humour which has always taught Britishers to laugh at misfortune."

Except for the opening "In Memoriam," the poetry in the *Blizzard* is unabashed doggerel. Thus a stanza from "Ode to Tobacco," about the condition of team members addicted to the weed:

> *How they go down at heels,*
> *Too tired to take their meals,*
> *Meager as Weddell seals,*
> *   Silly as rabbits.*
> *How their glances grow oblique,*
> *Matches they all learn to sneak,*
> *Hyde Park Corner!—What a reek!*
> *   Horrible habits.*

Or the opening of "Sledging Song":

> *An explorer's life is the life for me,*
> *O'er the ice to roam—a life so free.*
> *O'er snow-field wide and barrier wall*
> *With comrade true the sledge we haul.*

Some of the articles in the *Blizzard* were serious, and patently intended for the public audience Mawson and McLean hoped eventually to attract. Mawson's own four-part "The Commercial Resources of Antarctica" expounds at length, and with no irony, on the huge potential for whale-hunting, mining, oil exploration, and the like that formed a major part of the motivation for the AAE in the first place. "Mining in the vicinity of an accessible landing should not offer great difficulties," he wrote, gazing into his crystal ball. And despite the terrible ordeal he had recently survived, he added, as if writing advertising copy for the continent, "The climate is healthy. Food stuffs keep indefinitely anywhere in the great natural refrigerator."

Yet other entries were so arcane and in-joke-ish as to remain opaque to any reader not on the expedition. A notice in the June issue, under the rubric "Gleanings," purports to define "championship"—the cry that echoed through the hut whenever someone committed a foolish mistake or act of unintentional comedy:

A championship is a grave misdemeanour usually accompanied by an audible crash, though, in a subtler sense, it may be unwittingly and silently performed on the stillest of still nights. The defaulter may be a nervous person, or the most blatant and adamant of citizens. The definition is necessarily elastic enough to include anything from the dislodgement of a roof-garden to the destruction of an anemometer.

One of the most delightful pieces in the *Blizzard* is "An Adelian Alphabet," which begins:

> *A is Antarctic where I'm writing this rot,*
> *B is our Bay; a more definite spot.*
> *C is the Cold which tries to frost-bite you,*
> *D is the Drift which we find here "in situ."*

Yet even in this poem, it would have required an insider's knowledge to detect the dig at Mawson's strict budgeting of personal radio use in this couplet:

> *M are the Messages others must spurn,*
> *For N is the Nothing they send in return.*

Mawson and McLean had no illusions about the literary quality of *The Adelie Blizzard*. Yet read at the distance of a century from its composition, the newspaper opens an intimate window on daily life in the hut during the winter of 1913—at least, on the lighter side of that life. (But for the opening "In Memoriam," there is no allusion in the *Blizzard* to Ninnis and Mertz's deaths, and no comment whatsoever on Mawson's incredible survival story.) Likewise at the distance of a century, the five issues bespeak the high level of competence in writing that was taken for granted among university-educated men in Edwardian times, and that today's expeditions would be hard put to match. It takes considerable wit and skill, after all, to produce rhyming, metrical doggerel of any sort.

In the introduction to the 2010 facsimile edition of *The Adelie Blizzard*, Elizabeth Leane and Mark Pharaoh cogently analyze the functions the newspaper served for the men stuck in the hut through a second winter. "The most obvious was the alleviation of boredom," they write.

> But a newspaper was not only a good antidote for individual depression. It was also a way of dealing with group dynamics. Its production was a team activity, and the sharing of its contents encouraged group cohesion. . . . It could also act as a form

of debriefing, in which trying aspects of expedition life could be dealt with comically, and feelings that might otherwise have been interpreted as complaints or whining could be expressed and shared. . . . In addition, by allowing the men gentle digs at each other, the newspaper provided a release-valve for simmering tensions.

As winter modulated into spring, McLean found it more and more stressful to put out issues, and they slipped from monthly to bimonthly. As if trying to hurry the seasons through wishful thinking, he headlined the August issue "Spring," the October issue "Summer." In his own diary on October 25, 1913, having put to bed the last of the five issues, he reported that he was "glad there's no more to be done!"

After the expedition, to both men's disappointment, Mawson and McLean failed to find a publisher for *The Adelie Blizzard*. Today, the sole original copy is one of the most prized possessions of the Mawson Centre in the South Australian Museum in Adelaide.

Desperate for exercise and for temporary escape from the hut, the men devised various activities. A favorite pastime was racing down the snow slope west of the hut, with the men sitting on packing-case lids. "We had some really exciting slides down an almost sheer drop of thirty feet," wrote McLean, "ending in great drifts of snow out of which we could pick ourselves, only to climb up some steps cut with an ice-axe and start again. . . . It is quite the best sport I have had for a long time."

The men also played football (soccer) in the snow, and tried once more to master the art of skiing, this time without the tutelage of the expert, Xavier Mertz. When the weather allowed, the men took walks around the shores of Commonwealth Bay. Discovering a novel sight, Bickerton declared, was "like a new kind of drink when you are thirsty!"

The weather, however, did not often permit such larks. The "home of the blizzard" lived up to the ominous reputation it had earned the previous year. During the entire month of July, the wind averaged 63.6 mph, a new record, surpassing the 61 mph of May 1912. No amount of activities or distractions sufficed to cure the general anomie that pervaded the hut. Despite his tireless efforts to produce *The Adelie Blizzard*, McLean suffered deep funks. On June 4, he wrote in his diary, "I must say I felt very lonely today." And the next day, "It is very difficult to keep the diary going at times. It seems to one like the same old repetition."

Hovering over everything was Jeffryes's madness. It was exacerbated by his personal slovenliness, so that his body odor started to disturb the others. "I spoke to him sharply last evening," Mawson wrote on July 18, "telling him to keep himself and his bunk clean. Had the darkroom prepared for a private washing chamber for him. It seems to have sunk in, for today he has washed out some of his clothes." Two weeks later, however, "He seems to have no interest in life. Eats ravenously, lies in his bunk all day dirtying books. Never offers to help anyone. . . . Several times I have told him to have a bath. He washed more clothes but did not have a bath."

Jeffryes's hygiene issue came to a head in August, in a way that seemed almost grotesque. On the 12th, Mawson noted in his diary, "At ten to 1 pm Jeffryes appeared. It appears that when we all went out Jeffryes had a hurried bath—how much of his body nobody knows, but everybody is decided that the canvas bath will now want disinfecting."

On July 13, in his distress, Jeffryes had written Mawson a letter:

Sir,

You have been previously forewarned that you were almost on the eve of a dastardly murder. I have found it impossible to make you believe that I am in a perfectly normal state of mind.

What Jeffryes, in his delusional state, meant about "murder" is fleshed out in an even more bizarre letter that Jeffryes wrote the same day to his sister in Australia (though how he hoped to send it remains a mystery):

> I am to be done to death by a jury of six murderers who are try-ing to prove me insane originating from the jealousy of six of them. . . . They . . . have insinuated the most outrageous and dastardly things against me all on Dr. McLeans evidence & sur-mise. . . . My services to this expedition have found their reward in death. . . . Farewell to all. I am unable to prevent their folly and so must die a martyr to their bloody mindedness.

The day after being reprimanded about keeping himself and his bunk clean, Jeffryes wrote another letter to Mawson:

> I did not come down here to foment trouble. I have done my duty by the expedition . . . in the face of all obstacles led to the absurd jealousy of Madigan & others. . . .
>
> My constitution is absolutely unimpaired & McLean's charge of insanity is ridiculous. My vision is clearer than theirs inas-much as it is not warped by jealousy.

Mawson did not know what to make of this screed. "It is curiously logical and well-written," he remarked in his diary. "The only thing is that he starts off on the assumption that we are leagued against him." The "curiously logical" tone of Jeffryes's utterances led the other men to hope that he was cured. On July 20, McLean was "over-joyed to find that Jeffryes had almost recovered."

July 20 was also Jeffryes's twenty-eighth birthday. Normally, a man's birthday became the occasion for a special dinner with toasts and joke presents, an interlude all the more welcome in 1913 with only seven men in the hut. But with Jeffryes in such a terrible men-tal state, Mawson was at a loss to craft a celebration. The result, as recorded in Mawson's diary, sounds lugubrious:

I had intended to cook as I had taken over his work entirely. However, he got to work and McLean suggested leaving him at it, so we did. The pudding he made was a revelation in rotten egg and grease. He made a speech in which he spoke clearly and well, but the matter foolish cant like his letters.

During the last few weeks, the men had been struggling during the brief lulls in the nearly constant winds to get the mast reerected and the radio operating again. "Jeffryes helpless in this," Mawson noted. "Bickerton takes charge of the work."

On July 27, Jeffryes offered Mawson a written declaration: "I am now reluctantly obliged to tender my resignation as a member of this expedition as I am unable to carry on owing to the bellicose attitude shown to me by the other members. I have already stated that my health is perfect & my character irreproachable." This letter prompted Mawson to address the whole team about the radio operator's state. In the awkward meeting after dinner on the 28th, Mawson "pointed out the impossibility of resigning, as there was no accommodation, food, or Antarctic clothing that was not the property of the expedition." Speaking of Jeffryes in the third person, even though the man sat at the table with the others, Mawson added, "What I desire is that he shall recognise that he was ill for a time and to continue a full member of the expedition, then the matter will be forgotten."

The words seemed to strike home. Jeffryes "instantly got up and spoke for a long time, apologising for his actions and stating that he was ill and wished everything forgotten. I then stated that we accepted his explanation and things were to go on as they had 2 months previously."

Yet any hope that the group meeting might have ameliorated Jeffryes's condition was quickly dashed. The very next day, Mawson recorded, "Jeffryes makes no attempt to do anything." And the day after that, "Jeffryes writes me another letter. He interjected again at breakfast and is evidently 'bug' again. I have great difficulty getting him to go out in the sunshine for a few minutes. No attempt to help anybody." In that letter, Jeffryes wrote, "I deeply regret having made such calumnious remarks & statements," but in the next breath threatened to bring lawsuits against all his teammates once he returned to Australia.

The six men stranded in the hut with Jeffryes—even McLean, who had studied medicine at the University of Sydney and who served as the team's doctor—had virtually no comprehension of mental illness. They knew well the stories of insanity breaking out on the *Belgica* and other Antarctic expeditions, but attributed those breakdowns only to the vague condition they called "polar depression." Very little is known of Jeffryes's life before the AAE, and it is impossible to diagnose the poor man at the distance of a century. Yet the delusions, the extreme paranoia, the alternation of surrender and aggression, the terror of annihilation interspersed with grandiose pronouncements, even the periods of relative lucidity, all hint at some kind of psychosis. It is possible that a latent vulnerability came to the fore under the intense stress of wintering over in one of the most inhospitable places on earth. In view of Jeffryes's young age, however, and the subsequent course of his life after he returned to Australia, it may be that the psychotic break at Cape Denison heralded the onset of incurable schizophrenia.

As if dealing with Jeffryes were not trial enough, Mawson's own health was still fragile. Hardly a man to complain about his own ailments, he wrote, on July 30:

> I appear to be suffering from a mild irritation of the bladder, felt only when feet are cold. My health is very poor. Have been suffering for some days from a large deep-seated inflammation over practically the whole of the right side of my face. The day before yesterday it began to burst as a boil. Now appears to be on the mend. Some teeth want attending to.

Cecil Madigan was going through his own agonies. Although he had gotten word in March from the Rhodes committee, before the wireless ceased to function, that his scholarship would be renewed for the following year, he spent a good part of the winter in a dark funk. In the paraphrase of his son, David Madigan, "He went through many stages of depression, abject and thorough, and was eaten up by inaction and impatience. He felt utterly miserable to see time slipping by and all his hopes miscarrying; he had displeased his mother, who had not wanted him to join the expedition, and brought care and anxiety to Wynnis [his fiancée]." As for Dux Ipse, as far as Madigan was concerned, "Though he could never respect Mawson, for many reasons which he could not put down since one often regretted what was written, he would bear his authority."

It was Madigan against whom Jeffryes had turned his madness on July 7, demanding that the two go into a separate room to fight after Jeffryes had misinterpreted Madigan's innocent remark about *The Hound of the Baskervilles*. According to David Madigan—the anecdote was never reported by Bickerton or Mawson—the day after the "fight" (cut short by Mawson's intercession), "Jeffryes avoided Cecil but asked Bickerton to be his second in a shooting duel. Bickerton tried to pacify him but he continued talking about shooting so Cecil and Bickerton locked up the firearms and cartridges, which fortunately were in Cecil's care, since Mawson foolishly saw no need for such action."

Although there are no passages in Mawson's diary recording Jeffryes's threats to shoot his teammates, Cecil Madigan (if his son can be trusted) recalled an atmosphere of almost constant apprehension through the dark, windy days of July, with Jeffryes "walking up and down with a dreadful expression which every now and then he turned separately on each of them."

> He said that if he shot any of them the law would find him innocent, and he made such dreadful threats that they had always to be ready to spring on him. He asked McLean and Mawson for poison and told Cecil that he would sleep a last night in the hut, after which Cecil could shoot him in the morning. . . . He was convinced that they were going to kill him in the night and every now and then sat up to glare about, putting his head through

the string of clothes he had hung up in front of his bunk so that no one could see what he did. Someone had always to be awake through the night in case the watchman should call for assistance. Bage and Hodgeman found it difficult to sleep, and Bickerton was horribly nervous.

According to another secondhand source—a friend of Bickerton's, to whom he told the story after the expedition—one morning in July Jeffryes told his teammates that the night before he had seen Bickerton loading a gun in order to shoot him. Bickerton calmly denied the claim, only to provoke the following exchange:

> "Would you swear on the Bible that you did not and will not try to kill me." [Bickerton] of course said yes bring me a Bible. "Would you swear on your mother's bible." Yes if I had it. "Swear by all you ever held truest and dearest." Certainly I would. "Well even if you did all that I wouldn't believe you."

On August 5, after a hiatus of almost two months, the men got the mast up and the radio working. "To Bickerton is due all the credit, he has worked very well of late," wrote Mawson. That night messages were sent and received, the Macquarie relay forwarding the words to and from Australia. The men were overjoyed at the prospect of continuing contact with the outside world. The only problem was that Sidney Jeffryes was the sole member of the team who knew how to use the radio.

For the first two days, Jeffryes did his job. The news from Australia included the beguiling information that Frank Hurley and Frank Wild were already on the lecture circuit entertaining audiences with the story of the AAE, even though its last chapter had not yet been written. The men in the hut also learned that the name Wild had proposed for the territory explored by the Western Base party, Queen

Mary Land, had been accepted by King George V himself. Wild had
returned to his native England shortly after arriving in Australia. At
the Royal Geographical Society, he was told by three officers that
he had committed a "very grave breach of etiquette" in slapping the
queen's name on the territory without first asking for royal permission to do so. This led to an audience with the king, during which
a mortified Wild was reassured that both the king and his consort
were very pleased with the naming, and that so-called etiquette had
nothing to do with it.

Only weeks after returning from the AAE, with all the trials
and uncertainties the Western Base party had undergone, Wild was
asked by Sir Ernest Shackleton to join his upcoming expedition,
which intended to make a complete traverse of Antarctica from the
Weddell Sea to the Ross Sea. Shackleton offered his teammate from
two previous expeditions to the southern continent the post of second in command. Without hesitation, Wild accepted. On the *Endurance* expedition from 1914–17, he would play a pivotal role in the
adventure that today resonates as perhaps the most legendary of all
Antarctic voyages.

In August 1913 at Cape Denison, the newly reestablished radio
communication was so precious that Mawson at first forbade the
sending or receiving of any personal messages. But on the 8th, only
three days after getting the apparatus working again, Jeffryes started
to revert to his feckless, lethargic ways, going to bed long before the
short evening window for broadcasting had closed. On August 10,
when a vital cylinder tap blew out and was temporarily lost as Bickerton fired up the engine, "Jeffryes immediately undressed and went
to bed." The other six men pawed through the snow until Mawson
found the tap. By now, Mawson had reached the limit of his patience.
Of Jeffryes, he wrote:

> He does nothing now a day but cook once in 6 days; of that he
> makes a bad job. What can be done with him I can't imagine, for
> if I try to get him to keep up to scratch, his miserable tempera-
> ment is liable to cause trouble in sending [messages]. He takes

the crystal out of the setting each evening so that nobody else can use the instruments. I certainly feel like skinning him, but will wait another day and see how things go.

Without the crystal, the radio was inoperable. Removing it and hiding it from his teammates seem to indicate that Jeffryes had incorporated contact with the outside world in his paranoid delusions about persecution by the "others."

During the next week, Jeffryes made a half-hearted show of trying to send and receive, but he spent nearly all his time in his bunk. In the radio log, he jotted down short and unreliable notations of his efforts. "No sane man could surely act as he does," Mawson wrote on August 11. "I would certainly expel him from the expedition but for the fact that we could then no longer call upon him to operate the wireless. Nobody else is proficient in 'sending.' "

The radio log, which has been preserved, forms a blunt testament to Mawson's frustration. Even on a day when Jeffryes tried to work for four hours straight, his own annotations document nothing but futility:

8/am	Called Mq I. No response
9:15/am	Called Mq I. No response
9:20/am	Jambing [sic] & Static at McQ I
9:40/am	Called Mq I. No response

The notations continue for ten more lines, ending at 11:58 a.m. Every one reads either "Called Mq I. No response" or "No signals audible."

There are at least four ways to interpret these annotations. The most charitable, but the least likely, is that something was indeed interfering with transmission, and that Jeffryes accurately recorded signals sent without an answer from Macquarie. A second theory would suggest that in his madness, Jeffryes no longer knew how to send wireless messages. A third is that the communication was working fine, and Macquarie was sending back genuine responses, but that Jeffryes's paranoia prevented him from sharing their content with his teammates. A fourth explanation is the saddest of all—that the messages sent back from Macquarie, though perfectly coherent, were unintelligible to a man who had lost his mind.

All the while, Bickerton was attempting to master the craft, so that he could take over Jeffryes's job. But even for that master tinkerer, working the radio proved baffling.

Throughout the month of August, Mawson tried to nurse Jeffryes through the essential transmitting and receiving. He drew up a contract specifying duties and made the man sign it, only to have to tell him days later that he was failing to live up to it. No amount of haranguing seemed to jolt Jeffryes out of his passive uncooperativeness. Some evenings the radio could pick up stray messages from afar—ship's signals, even radio stations from Australia and New Zealand. But even these Jeffryes sabotaged. On August 27, "At midnight press was coming through well with short intervals of a minute or so breaks. He altered the gadgets so that nobody could listen, and jumped into bed."

On September 1, Jeffryes's madness seemed to take a new twist:

> Before dinner Jeffryes came to me when in work-room and said that he would have to send a message to Australia that the Hut was being made too hot for him. Complained in a dazed sort of way of banging on the wall. Rambled on. Quite bug again. During evening seemed quite at sea with the wireless. . . . What is it? Is Jeffryes fooling us?

And the next day:

> Jeffryes is quite off. Tells me that he and I are the only two not mad—though has some doubts about Hodgeman. He starts to put spikes in his boots, says that he is going sledging. Says he and I must start sledging. Says the others are making it too hot for us. Says he is sorry he could not get the message through last night apprising the world that we are all mad. Says he will try tonight.

September 1, nonetheless, was a red-letter day for the men. "A new month and 100 days to the coming of the *Aurora*!" McLean gloated in his diary. A pickup date of December 9 or 10 was of course only arbitrary; depending on the condition of the ice in Commonwealth Bay, it might prove too early in the summer to bring the ship close to shore. But the men needed a date to fix their hopes upon. Even Mawson could not resist marking the new month with a joyous prediction: "100 days to ship's arrival!"

Now more than ever, communication with Australia seemed vital to keep up the men's morale. But Jeffryes thwarted every attempt. On September 3, Mawson watched the radio man's behavior with a mixture of puzzlement and rage:

> This evening Jeffryes sending a lot of stuff at a high rate, not looking at message part of time. McLean detected several words not on the message he had before him. He was going hard for almost half an hour. I felt certain he was sending something of his own which he did not wish us to know of. He sent very fast so that we could not read it.

Unable to bear Jeffryes's impertinence, Mawson ordered him into his private room, where he bluffed him with the accusation that McLean, looking over his shoulder, had read everything he had sent. A "very contrite" Jeffryes admitted that he had been trying to get out a kind of SOS, warning the outside world that five of the men in the hut were insane. "Once more I exacted a verbal promise from him to send exactly what I gave him," Mawson wrote, "but I fear it will be of little use."

Sure enough, the next day Jeffryes came to Mawson and "wished all wireless to cease, as he said it only brought trouble." When Mawson threatened to replace Jeffryes with Bickerton, the man relented and promised to continue with his job. "Has been walking about and glaring all morning," Mawson noted.

Mawson vowed to relieve Jeffryes of his duties on September 8, but changed his mind, mainly out of exasperation, for Bickerton had learned only how to send the most basic of messages, and he could not be sure they got through to Macquarie Island. On the 9th, Jeffryes simply sat in front of the wireless, "eyes closed, head on hand. I rouse him twice to call up. He calls but does not try to receive. . . . It is madness to let a lunatic humbug us like this."

The radio log for early September reads once more as a record of utter futility: "Sept. 3: Nil," "Sept. 4: Nil." Some of the entries seem to be code words designed to verify contact with Macquarie: "Febrile. Ralph. Nine," "Festa. Rondo. Nine." On the 8th, Mawson suspected Jeffryes of sneaking in a personal message, and the log, in Jeffryes's handwriting, bears out the suspicion: "To Norma Jeffryes. . . . Wire at once how mother much love to all. Sid."

As the days grew longer, Mawson insisted on carrying out further scientific work. The men made forays from the hut to gather specimens of rock to be analyzed back in Australia. (Ever the geologist, Mawson filled his diary with notes such as "Red granites, some much more porphyritic than others; some show no evidence of metamorphism and may be younger than the red and grey granite gneisses so abundant.") The men scrupulously kept up their records of weather and magnetism. And when the ice in the bay began to break up, they went out on excursions to search for marine life.

On September 14, Mawson relieved Jeffryes of his radio duties. Bickerton tried to take over, but the result was a failure. Two days before, Mawson had typed out a formal letter to Jeffryes, castigating him for his "eccentric behavior" and warning him that "should any further breach of faith on your part be discovered you will be held responsible on arrival in Australia." He also threatened to withhold Jeffryes's expedition salary if any such "breach of faith" could be proved. And he raised the specter of having the man prosecuted in criminal court in Australia.

None of these threats penetrated Jeffryes's madness. His hygiene had once more become an uncomfortable issue, to the extent that "Does not even empty rears"—i.e., he apparently soiled himself regularly. On September 21, Jeffryes wrote another letter to Mawson, complaining indignantly about his treatment at the hands of McLean, Madigan, Bickerton, and Bage, who, he insisted, "for 3 months [have] diligently been endeavouring to send me insane by endeavouring to [?] my feelings by very subtle means & disturbing my sleep at every opportunity." In the letter, he accused Mawson of worse: "I have been continuing my duties for the past two weeks under the influence of a hypnotic spell under which you have found it incumbent upon you to place me to avert a calamity." Jeffryes offered once more to resign. And he threatened to "take provisions and take up my quarters in a tent apart from these four persons."

In his paranoia, Jeffryes planned a real physical escape from his tormentors. "He states that [he is] getting ready for sledging," Mawson noted on September 20. "Asks Bage for pemmican, spends part of afternoon looking around outside and digging for pemmican. Asks Hodge[man] how many dog harnesses there are, etc." There were moments, however, when Jeffryes seemed to rally. "He speaks moderately rationally at dinner," Mawson wrote on September 22. But only moments later, "Plays gramophone after dinner. McLean says to him when playing (gramophone) a weird thing: 'I never can understand that piece.' Jeffryes immediately packs his things, turns the sennegrass [boot insulation] out of its bag in next room, puts his clothes in, tells Dad [McLean] that he is moving." Calling his bluff, Mawson waited in his private chamber for Jeffryes "to come and say goodbye to me." But Jeffryes could not go through with it. Two hours passed after his threatened departure. "After standing at the verandah door for some time he returned and later went on with the wireless."

As spring gradually dawned on the southern continent, the men kept up a lookout for signs of animal life. On September 19, McLean made the startling discovery of a sea leopard lolling on an ice floe not far offshore. Mawson ordered all the men out of the hut to hunt the great prey, which Madigan dispatched with a rifle. The party loaded the sea leopard on a sledge and hauled it back to the hut. There they found Jeffryes, who had ignored the order to join the hunt, and whose duty it was to fix lunch, stuffing himself with food while making no effort to prepare a meal for his teammates.

The same day, Mawson "saw white worm-like creatures on the bottom of the bay"—a minor biological discovery, but one more sign of returning spring. The men started dredging the patches of open water for crustaceans and worms, and laid crab traps. McLean and Bickerton made a wager: "First one to bring a penguin to the hut gets 25 cigars back in Australia."

On September 24, Mawson wrote hopefully, "Jeffryes seems better today." But the very next day, matters again came to a head:

> Jeffryes calls up several times but does not bother to listen, sits without receiver on his head. . . . I look out 10 minutes after to find Jeffryes standing in front of fire having abandoned the wireless altogether believing me asleep. . . . I call him a something mongrel and have it out with him. He has no defence, says it is all due to the way four of the men treat him.

At that moment, Jeffryes handed Mawson the letter he had written on the 21st, with its "written statement of resignation. . . . I tell him he is in charge of the wireless no longer and that he has nevertheless to stand by in case he is wanted."

Through the next nine days, Jeffryes lent a hand on occasion when Bickerton, Bage, and Mawson could not make the radio work, but his efforts were as useless as before. It was not until October 4 that Mawson formally fired Jeffryes. In another typed letter, he warned Jeffryes against making any public accusations against his teammates when he returned to Australia. But he took a certain pity on the madman, promising to pay him "for time served."

By mid-October, Bickerton finally got the radio to work well enough to send and receive the occasional message. One of the first exchanges was with Charles Sandell, one of the two radio men on Macquarie. "This place is awful!" Bickerton sent. To which Sandell replied, "So is this—Hell!"

In October, the men started packing up the rocks and biological specimens. Out on a walk on the 17th, Madigan and Mawson discovered the first penguins, so Bickerton's bet with McLean was nullified. "They are 6 days late (allowing for Leap Year)," Mawson scolded the recalcitrant birds. Soon the men were eating scrambled penguin eggs.

The men's frenzy to leave Antarctica knew no bounds. Madigan, in particular, could barely stand the wait. In the paraphrase of his son, "As the end of the year approached Cecil became more and more impatient. He could scarcely contain himself and wondered how he had been able to live through the last nine months. . . . He cursed himself for having listened to Mawson's persuasion to join the Expedition."

On leaving Commonwealth Bay the previous February, Captain Davis had given Madigan a set of Thackeray's novels. Since "the only recreation was reading," Madigan was deeply grateful for the gift, but found himself unable to concentrate on the books. He picked up Xenophon's *Anabasis* instead, hoping to prep himself for his upcoming year at Oxford, but Greek grammar flummoxed him. He turned next to geology textbooks, with which Mawson offered to help him, but before long "Cecil was bored to extinction with it."

On October 31, the men were thrilled to receive a message relayed from Macquarie informing them that the *Aurora* would depart from Hobart around November 15. Mawson's diary for most of the month of November reverts to one- or two-line entries; sometimes he wrote only two words ("Dense drift," "Moderate weather"). Now that Jeffryes's work with the radio was no longer essential, the man seemed to recede into the background, though Mawson could not help recording his seesaw mental state. On the 15th, "Jeffryes appears to think he is going sledging, is preparing, mimics us in whatever we do." A week later: "Jeffryes is getting better. I spoke to him. He says he is helpless, that I have a spell on him. I tell him that I put a spell on him not to play monkey tricks when I am away."

On November 15, Bickerton picked up a fragmentary broadcast

from Macquarie: "Ship goes." The men unanimously agreed that "the word 'today' must have been lost in the ether." In actuality, the *Aurora* did not set out from Hobart until November 19. It took the ship ten days to reach Macquarie Island. On the morning of the 29th, the five men who had endured their own two-year vigil on that desolate island, all in the service of a radio link that almost never worked, gratefully boarded the *Aurora* and started lapping up news of the outside world from Captain Davis and his crew.

Mawson had decided to make one last sledging journey to recover the instruments that had been cached the year before by two of the exploring parties on their desperate homeward legs. He chose Madigan and Hodgeman to accompany him, leaving Bickerton, Bage, and McLean to maintain the hut. For the first time all year, Mawson put the huskies to work hauling the sledges. Before leaving, he wrote out "orders" to Bage about dealing with Jeffryes: "Do not hesitate to put him in irons if he becomes obstreperous. At all times keep a good watch on him. As he is wont to burn a light in a dangerous position it is not safe to leave him alone in the hut for long. He is told to do his share as cook."

One might think that after his terrible ordeal of the summer before, Mawson would have set off in November on a mission whose only aim was to salvage expensive instruments with a certain trepidation, or that the ever-present menace of unseen crevasses would still haunt him. But Mawson's diary during this journey records only annoyance at sastrugi ridges and crevasse fields, not fear. Intending to start on November 16, Mawson was delayed by bad weather until the 24th.

The men took along a small wireless receiving kit, in hopes that their teammates in the hut could send them regular messages. Like so much else to do with radio communication on the AAE, this effort failed. On only the second day out, Mawson wrote, "At 4:15 camped, as wished to hear wireless—but heard nothing."

With the dogs pulling well, the trio made good progress, covering as many as 21 miles in a single day. On November 28, five days out, they camped on the summit of a peak the team later named Mount

Murchison. There the previous summer Madigan's Eastern Coastal Party had planted a ten-foot flagpole. Now the men were shocked to find less than a foot of pole emerging from the drifts of winter. The pole ought to have guided the men to Madigan's cache, deposited in the nearby valley, but with nine feet of hard-packed snow overlying everything, the search for the instruments was fruitless.

Still unwilling to abandon the precious gear, Mawson started the men south toward the depot Bage's Southern Party had laid the summer before, 67 miles out from Winter Quarters. But on December 2, snow started falling, the wind rose to 40 mph, and visibility closed down almost to zero. The men stayed tent-bound for four days. Realizing that a search for Bage's cache would almost certainly be hopeless, Mawson decided to turn the team around.

Meanwhile, the men left at the hut found simply waiting for the *Aurora* a grueling psychological test. On November 28, McLean wrote, "Good weather. What a day for the ship to arrive. I'm afraid we think of nothing else but that ship. One becomes very impatient and distrustful." On December 2, Bickerton, the compulsive tinkerer, tried to use dynamite to blow up the ice that still clung to the shores at Cape Denison. The explosions made virtually no dent in the pack.

For the sledgers out on the plateau south of Winter Quarters, the return journey, in constant wind, with lashing snowstorms, brought back with a vengeance all the miseries they had endured on their journeys the previous summer. Tent-bound on December 11, Mawson at last gave vent to his feelings in his diary: "Nothing visible—no hope of travelling, direction nothing, the very ground invisible. Walking on, one slips and falls, stubs the toes and stumbles on sastrugi." And:

> The dreary outlook, the indefinite surroundings, the neverending seethe, rattle and ping of the drift. The flap of the tent; the uncertainty of clearance, the certainty of protracted abomination. The dwindling of food, the deterioration of tent, dogs, etc. The irksomeness, bone-wearying cramped quarters, the damp or the cold.

There was something glumly appropriate in the fact that the last of all the sledging missions of the most ambitious expedition yet launched in Antarctica should end up as a wild goose chase. Yet on the next day, the three sledgers were granted a soul-stirring benediction. As Mawson later remembered it:

> Descending the long blue slopes of the glacier just before midnight on December 12, from an outlook of a thousand feet above the Hut, I sighted a faint black bar on the seaward horizon; with the aid of glasses a black speck was discernible at the windward extremity of the bar—and it could be nothing but the smoke of the *Aurora*! The moment of which we had dreamt for months had assuredly come. The ship was in sight!

Dashing down the last thousand feet, the three men brought the good news to their teammates who, even as they gave vent to "wild cheers," scrambled with binoculars up to the nearest ridge behind the hut to verify the sighting themselves. Then, realizing that it would be some time before the *Aurora* could anchor close to shore, the men tried to catch a last few hours of sleep in the hut. As Mawson wrote:

> Just as most of us were dozing off an unusual sound floated in from without and the next moment in rushed Captain Davis, breezy, buoyant, brave and true. . . . His cheery familiar voice rang through the Hut as he pushed a way into the gloom of the living room. It was an indescribable moment, this meeting after two years.

For Davis, the rendezvous was every bit as emotional. As he recalled decades later, "As I shook [Mawson's] hand I was conscious of a sudden feeling of intense relief—relief that he was manifestly alive and well, relief that I had been able to do my duty. My life has given me few moments that have been more rewarding."

It took another ten days to load all the gear and specimens aboard the *Aurora*, but on December 23, the ship pulled out of Commonwealth Bay, bound for Australia. Over a lavish dinner in the ward-room, Mawson at last was free to ponder the meaning of what would prove to be the defining experience of his life:

> The two long years were over—for the moment they were to be effaced in the glorious present. We were to live in a land where drift and wind were unknown, where rain fell in mild refreshing showers, where the sky was blue for long weeks, and where the memories of the past were to fade into a dream—a nightmare?

Bickerton's last project on land before nailing the hut closed had been to construct a memorial cross for Ninnis and Mertz. He built it out of huge sections of the now irrelevant radio mast, bound with strips of brass. On November 30, he and McLean erected the cross on top of Azimuth Hill. Hodgeman had manufactured a plaque from a piece of the kitchen table, on which he stenciled an inscription: "Erected to commemorate the supreme sacrifice made by Lieut B. E. S. Ninnis, R. F. and Dr. X. Mertz in the cause of science."

Mawson hoped that the memorial cross was "solid enough to last for a hundred years even in that strenuous climate." Over the decades since 1913, the cross has been blown down several times, only to be reerected by subsequent expeditions. It stands today, a century after Bickerton and McLean first put it up, atop Azimuth Hill, looking down over the hut in which Mawson's men spent nearly two years—itself preserved, much as the AAE left it, as an Australian National Heritage Site.

EPILOGUE

One would expect that after an ordeal such as the forced second overwintering, Mawson would have been eager to head straight for Australia. Instead, so strong was the man's commitment to science that he directed Davis to steam east and west along the Antarctic shore for weeks so that he and the men on board could conduct further exploration, mapping, and collecting. Much of the time was spent trawling for marine life and dredging for ocean-bottom specimens, but at intervals, Mawson sent men on shore to examine islands and capes that had previously been all but unknown. Between December 23 and February 7, the *Aurora* coasted eastward as far as the Mertz Glacier, then west beyond the Shackleton Ice Shelf all the way to Drygalski Island, first discovered by the German expedition in 1902.

This extra voyaging was not without considerable risk. The day after the ship pulled out of Commonwealth Bay, a vicious storm struck. Davis had all he could do to keep the *Aurora*, dragging anchor, from wrecking. The motor launch, which was dangling off the side of the ship, started smashing into the vessel. "As it was being converted into a battering ram against the ship itself it had to be cut away," wrote Mawson, "and was soon swept astern and lost to sight." The next day, Davis confided to his diary, "We had a fortunate escape. I do not think a vessel has ever ridden out such a gale."

On December 25, Mawson wrote, "Blowing fresh all day. Everything wet. We have a very miserable Christmas." During the weeks of added exploring, Davis kept up a constant lookout for icebergs, and never stopped worrying about the ship getting stuck fast in pack ice. The strain took its toll on both men. Wrote Mawson on February 2, "This work is very trying on Capt Davis as he has to be on the alert so much. I wish he would take more rest when he may. . . . For myself—my nerves, damaged by the sledging adventure, are beginning to play up again."

By then, Davis was fed up with the extra work and danger. On February 7, he complained, "The party are all anxious to get back and this does not make it easier for M[awson] to decide whether to go on or go back. The consequence is that ever since we left [Commonwealth Bay], I have been in doubt as to what was really our programme. I can see that a relief voyage is, under present circumstance, best not extended into another expedition."

On February 6, Mawson finally ordered Davis to head north for Australia. It took twenty-one more days to cross the southern ocean. The first port of call was not to be Hobart but Adelaide, where Mawson lived and where a crowd was eager to greet him. Of that return, signaling the end of the AAE, Mawson wrote in the closing lines of *The Home of the Blizzard*, "The welcome home—the voice of the innumerable strangers—the hand-grips of many friends—it chokes one—it cannot be uttered."

The crowd wildly cheered the battered ship as she pulled into Port Adelaide on February 26. A small coterie of friends, including Edgeworth David, Mawson's former professor and comrade on the trek to the South Magnetic Pole in 1908–09, rode out in a motor launch to be the first to congratulate Mawson. Once on shore, however, he quickly escaped their company (not to mention the throng of citizens hailing his arrival) and made his way to the South Australia Hotel, where he was told Paquita and her mother, having traveled from Melbourne that same day, awaited him.

Decades later, Paquita recalled the reunion with her fiancé:

> It is hard to describe the feelings one has when meeting someone whose image has lived only in one's thoughts for so long. When he entered the room, I just had time to think: "Yes, of course, that's what he is like!" Douglas said, "You have had a long time to wait," and then everything was all right.
>
> We dined in our room at the hotel, just the four of us; Captain Davis and mother sat on the balcony, Douglas and I walked up and down. Mother said afterwards that Captain Davis said at least six times: "My word, I am glad to see them together."

Two public meetings were held in Adelaide during the next few days to celebrate Mawson and the AAE. One speaker claimed, "Douglas Mawson has returned from a journey that was absolutely unparalleled in the history of exploration." Of his survival feat, the speaker added, "It would have been easy to have died in such circumstances as Dr Mawson had then found himself; easy to have got into the bag and to have given in to the difficulties; but it was quite a different thing to go on and on, *alone* as Dr Mawson did for thirty solid days. That was the finest thing that had ever been done on such an expedition." At the first meeting, a messenger just arrived from Melbourne read a telegram of congratulations from King George V.

After dinner on February 26, the day of his arrival, Mawson and Paquita had walked to the telegraph office where "Douglas dictated a long message to be published in the London newspapers as soon as in the Australian." It was thus that for the first time the details of Mawson's desperate solo trek back to Winter Quarters reached a public audience. Remarkably, the very next day the London *Daily Mail* published a lengthy encomium on the man and the AAE, written by Sir Ernest Shackleton. "Mawson was born to be a leader of a

Man with iced-up mask

Penguins covered with ice after a blizzard

Sledging with a sail

Sledging across sastrugi

Opposite: Man traversing coastal slo

Man in cavern beneath ice cliffs

Man peering into open crevasse

Penguins at mid-summer midnight

Man in icefall chaos

Mawson's half-sledge, which saved his life

The Aurora *returns*

Frank Hurley at work (from later Endurance *expedition)*

Polar expedition," he declared, then summarized the deeds the man had performed on the BAE from 1907–09. Going on to praise the scientific achievements of Mawson's enterprise, Shackleton closed with a vivid evocation of "the tragic march in which two lives were lost." He imagined himself a member of the Far Eastern Party, setting out across the unknown plateau with such high hopes. "And then there comes the sudden change from relief to the shock of disaster." Shackleton went on:

> And I can picture that terrible march back through the area of crevasses, Mertz becoming weaker day by day, the food giving out, and at last Mawson, no thought of desertion in his mind, placing his sick comrade upon the sledge and dragging him painfully those weary miles—short distances in reality if you will, but age-long in effort and anxiety. Then came the death of Mertz; then the final struggle alone, utterly alone, day after day with no adequate shelter, no nourishing food. . . .
>
> What those thirty days must have meant to Mawson, he alone can tell.

Only five months later, on August 1, Shackleton himself set out on the *Endurance* at the head of his grandly titled Imperial Trans-Antarctic Expedition, intending to traverse the continent from the Weddell Sea to the Ross Sea. Although an utter failure, that adventure, lasting from 1914 into 1917, would become—thanks to Shackleton's heroism and the courage of all his crew, including Frank Wild and Frank Hurley—the most celebrated of all Antarctic expeditions.

A few days after the Adelaide receptions, Mawson and Paquita set off for Melbourne, where they were to be married on March 31. The evening before the wedding, Paquita's father gave Captain Davis a half-bottle of champagne, which he was to deliver to Mawson just before the event, as he "would probably need some extra strength to get him safely through the ceremony." As Davis came to pick up Mawson, he was shocked to see that he was wearing casual blue lounge suit trousers with his frock coat and waistcoat. "You can't possibly get married like that!" Davis expostulated. "Nonsense," said Mawson, "Paquita won't mind"—though he admitted he had probably misplaced his dress trousers in his in-laws' luggage.

Davis was adamant, so the two men commandeered a car to go search for the missing formal wear. There ensued a frantic comedy of errors, with Mawson gloomily predicting that he would be late for his own wedding. "Paquita won't mind that, either," he insisted. "People often have to wait at weddings."

"Not the bride," Davis rejoined.

It was then that Mawson noticed the champagne. "What is this bottle for?" he asked Davis, who relayed Paquita's father's fear that the groom might need "calming down or strengthening."

"Have it yourself," Mawson airily replied. "I'm all right." So Davis drank the half bottle—"and I needed it!" he later told Paquita.

Despite all the confusion, the wedding went off without a hitch. Mawson smiled so broadly throughout the ceremony that Paquita described the look on his face as "a real Cheshire cat grin." He later confessed, "The Reverend Masters told me brides were always nervous and I was to smile at you." Instead, it was Davis who was nervous—so nervous, in fact, that Paquita's mother noted that he "was so afraid of losing the ring that he kept passing it from one hand to another behind his back, and she was on tenterhooks lest he should drop it."

The next day, the newlyweds set sail for England. In Mawson's immediate future lay an important presentation before the Royal Geographical Society and an audience with the king—but also a grueling round of lectures that took him all the way to the United States, for the AAE was heavily in debt, and Mawson's fees had to go to paying off not only suppliers but the members of his team whose loyalty and endurance had won the expedition its triumphs.

And there was another doleful duty to be carried out. Mawson had resolved to visit the families of Belgrave Ninnis and Xavier Mertz, to pay homage to the men who had died "in the cause of science" and to console their loved ones in their grief.

From the harbor in Adelaide, the returning members of the AAE had dispersed to their separate jobs and families. The most poignant of aftermaths was the one that descended upon Sidney Jeffryes. Mawson put him on a train to Melbourne, with a link to his home town of Toowoomba, Queensland, where his sister Norma, alarmed by the madness evident in a letter she had received from her brother, was anxiously hoping to care for him. The bewildered Jeffryes, however, got off the train in the settlement of Ararat, Victoria, still 100 miles west of Melbourne. There he was reported to have wandered in the forest for six days before locals found him and took him to a nearby asylum.

A letter written from that asylum in July 1914 to a friend we know merely as Miss Eckford gives us a sustained insight into what Jeffryes really believed had happened to him in Antarctica, as well as offering details of the aftermath that no other sources supply. In that letter, Jeffryes asserts that "I left Sydney [in December 1912] anxious to succeed. . . . Once away from Australia I entered into the spirit of the thing with zest." When Captain Davis decided that he would have to appoint a party to winter over again at Cape Denison, Jeffryes "gladly accepted the offer." In his own account, Jeffryes insists that he almost single-handedly kept the mast up and the radio working for weeks, despite nearly constant hurricane winds. But:

> When it seemed apparent that the mast was going to weather the storms, a wave of jealousy swept over the other six members . . . . Evidences of something wrong first appeared in Madigan & McLean, who continually gave vent to cowardly insinuations . . . . I became the central point of attack by all except Mawson & Hodgeman. . . . In trying to finish the [radio] work on in [sic] accordance with Mawson's suggestion, I unhinged what remaining good was left in the others, and they used all the arts within their compass to drive me from the hut.

Soon, Jeffryes believed, Mawson and Hodgeman went over to the "enemy," while still pretending to be Jeffryes's ally.

They then made every effort to hypnotise me, although I could not make out what they were up to at that time, having no knowledge whatever of occult sciences. . . . I shortly after fell into a magnetic spell. . . . The fact is, that my will became suddenly magnetic and I am in a permanent state of mental thought transference, telepathy, or whatever you choose to call it. This is what people cannot bring themselves to believe, and consider it a delusion.

If Jeffryes believed he could read the minds of the other six men in the hut, that may help explain his paranoia during the darkest months of winter. Aboard the *Aurora* at last, en route to Australia, Jeffryes wrote, "I took an overdose of opium but although I took enough to dispose of any 2 men it never so much as made me feel drowsy." Once he boarded the train for Queensland, Jeffryes decided to take his own life by "more natural methods." Getting off the train at Ararat was not the act of a confused man, but of one determined "to starve to death. . . . Well, although I had twelve days without a bite, I felt little the worse for it, and was not roaming the bush, as people may imagine, but calmly awaiting the end, one which seemed so hard to reach." A meddlesome do-gooder, Jeffryes went on, alerted the authorities, which led to Jeffryes's commitment to the asylum. "I refused to give any information or explanation to the Law, except that I had been to the Antarctic & I blamed Dr Mawsons hypnotism as being the chief instrument in bringing about my mental condition."

Writing to Miss Eckford, Jeffryes is lucid enough to condemn the "bug-house" in which he was incarcerated, adding, "I don't altogether see how they can keep me locked up here." But he closed his eight-page letter by saying, "I long for the dissolution of mind & body. I have not the slightest fear of death, & would welcome it as my best friend."

Poor Jeffryes would spend the rest of his life in a series of mental hospitals, dying in 1942 in the Ararat facility to which he had first been committed. Through the middle of 1915, he corresponded occasionally with Mawson. By then, his insanity was full-blown. In March 1915, he wrote:

> It is now clear to me that we seven were chosen that scripture might be fulfilled. My mental condition has in no wise changed, but since my advent into asylums I have had God's truth made manifest to me in night visions. . . .
>
> I am come as Christ in the Spirit of Prophesy & the Wrath of God in the flesh.

Jeffryes promised to ask God to "help the other 5."

Three months later, in a letter that attempted to strike a conciliatory tone, Jeffryes foresaw his doom: "I have told you that I shall be arraigned before the court, & my death shall draw me nearer to God. Almighty God & myself alone know the whole secret of our second year."

By September 1915, after stays in several Melbourne hospitals, Jeffryes was back in the Ararat asylum. On the 17th, an official who signed himself "Master in Lunacy" tried to explain the man's state to Mawson:

> Mr. Jeffryes is very delusional. He denies making any charges against the expedition and members thereof. He says that he has nothing against them. He thought highly of Sir D. Mawson, but unfortunately Sir D. Mawson and all the others were quite insane, and insulted by his insinuations. He has numerous delusions.

Whether Mawson wrote back to Jeffryes is doubtful. After 1915, the former radio operator, still only twenty-nine years old, vanishes from the record. In *The Home of the Blizzard*, Mawson did his best to minimize and camouflage Jeffryes's madness and the havoc it wreaked during the second winter, and thereafter he never pub-

licly commented about the man. In 2010, the Australian Antarctic
Division named a small glacier on the coast of Adélie Land after
Jeffryes.

For all the panegyrics that were showered on the AAE, Mawson's
expedition was overshadowed, especially in England, by the tragedy
of Robert Scott's death with his four teammates on the return from
the South Pole in 1912. As *Scott's Last Expedition*, the leader's diary
had been published in 1913. The eloquence of that firsthand account,
culminating in the stoic resignation of its last pages, had seized the
attention of a whole nation. A century later, the book remains one of
the canonic texts of exploration literature.

Mawson had sent a letter of condolence to Kathleen Scott, the
explorer's widow, whom he had met in 1910 when Scott invited
him on the *Terra Nova* expedition. It had been Kathleen who had
arranged Mawson's purchase of the Vickers monoplane that, after
its crash on the test run near Adelaide, had been converted into the
all but useless air-tractor on the AAE. Now Mawson wrote, "Ah, but
is it not the height of being to accomplish great things against great
odds & to sacrifice oneself to a nobler cause. You cannot be the loser
though you may feel the loss."

In England, Mawson visited Kathleen, who promptly gave him
one thousand pounds—money earned from the royalties of *Scott's
Last Expedition*—to help defray the AAE debt. Kathleen insisted on
keeping the donation private, and even told Mawson not to thank
her for the gift. "Besides," she wittily appended, "it appears merely
stupid in the eyes of most people for a woman who is *known* (alas!) to
have an income of £700 a year to keep giving £1000's away." Kathleen knew that Paquita was trying to get pregnant, and that Mawson
hoped for a boy. In Scott's last letter to Kathleen, written as he lay
dying in his tent, he had conveyed tender advice as to how to raise
their own son, Peter, two years old when his father died. Now Kathleen mused to Mawson, "What fun it will be to have a little Master
Mawson—mind you feed him on fruit from the day he's born, and
make him as husky a fellow as Peter."

Over the years after 1914, on various trips to England, Mawson would visit Kathleen again. A letter she wrote to him in 1920 brims with intimacy:

> My dear Douglas. I am down at Sandwich which never fails to remind me of you. Do you remember your potato patch, & [the?] little tent on the beach which when the wind blew its canvas used to send you to sleep—No, of course you don't remember any of these trivialities—but I do.

The letter ends, "Goodbye my dear. I wish you were here. Don't get completely lost."

Some have speculated that Mawson and Kathleen Scott may have had an affair. She was a thoroughly bohemian woman and much attracted to men, and it is now known that even while Scott was on his fatal last expedition, she was conducting an affair with the great Norwegian explorer Fridtjof Nansen. Without citing his sources, Mawson biographer Philip Ayres states unequivocally that Paquita did not like Kathleen.

Kathleen's 1920 letter to Mawson also contains this prescient observation: "Shackleton has been lecturing to a *very* good film but he looks purple & bloated." Less than two years later, on South Georgia Island, at the outset of his fourth Antarctic expedition, Shackleton would collapse and die of a heart attack at the age of forty-seven.

On June 9, 1914, Mawson spoke to the Royal Geographical Society. The president, Douglas Freshfield, after whom the AAE had named a prominent cape in Adélie Land, introduced Mawson and several teammates in attendance with glowing words:

> We are here tonight to welcome the return to this country of the members of one of the most remarkable expeditions that has ever sailed into the polar regions. . . . All men of science will confirm what I say, that there has been no Antarctic expedition the results of which, geological, glaciological or in the way of throwing light on the past history of our planet, have been richer than that of which we are going to hear an account.

On May 13, Mawson had had an audience with King George V at Buckingham Palace. Then, on June 29, the king bestowed a knight-hood on the Australian explorer. The day before, in Sarajevo, the Archduke Franz Ferdinand had been assassinated—the event that would precipitate World War I.

Well before being knighted or lionized by the RGS, Mawson and Paquita had paid a visit to Belgrave Ninnis's family. While he was still in Antarctica, probably through one of the radio messages that reached Australia in 1913, Mawson had conveyed some of the details of his companion's death to the family. On August 29, 1913, appar-ently not realizing that Mawson was still marooned in Winter Quar-ters, Ninnis's father had written to him, thanking him for informing the family "of the dreadful tragedy of my sons death. The shock to my wife & to myself was dreadful."

From Australia in March 1914, Mawson had written to Ninnis *père*: "It was absolutely unexpected and your son must have been instantly killed practically before he realized that anything was happening."

In person, however, Mawson and Paquita found the family incon-solable. It was only a year later, after Ninnis's mother learned that the regiment to which her son had belonged, the Royal Fusiliers, "had early been cut to pieces in France," that she could make a gloomy sense of the notion that "somehow death in an icy crevasse seemed more fitting to his youth than slaughter in the mud of Flanders."

In July, Mawson and Paquita left England to make a short visit to Europe on the way back to Australia. Stopping first in the Nether-lands so that Mawson could meet his wife's relatives, the couple then made their way to Basel to spend a day with Mertz's family. Maw-son had previously mailed by registered post from Australia some of Mertz's belongings and his precious diary, secured in a soldered case. From England on July 8, he wrote to Mertz's father, trusting that he had received the diary:

You will note that the last entry was several days before his death. He appears to have lost interest in the diary before the end came. You will also note that the diary is without a back. The heavy back and a number of unused leaves I tore away to save weight in carrying it back.

Mertz's diary has since been copied in typescript and English translations prepared (though not yet published). Over the years, however, the original diary has somehow been lost.

The visit in Basel offered Mertz's family only scant consolation. As Paquita later recalled, "They were very kind to us but, naturally, the day was a sad one. It was a great grief to us to witness their sorrow. We sat for many hours answering their questions hoping in some way to make some response or to touch on an aspect that might lead their thoughts away from the actual tragic happening."

Once back in Australia, Mawson took up his teaching duties at the University of Adelaide again. He had been absent from his lecturer's post for two and a half years, during which time he had paid a replacement teacher out of his own salary. But the AAE debt was so onerous that Mawson completed only a single term before sailing for America, where he went on an exhausting lecture tour to raise funds.

Meanwhile, Australia had entered World War I in September 1914, with troops sent to New Guinea to attack German outposts. Several of the AAE men immediately enlisted. Bob Bage, the quiet, competent leader of the Southern Party, the man whom John Hunter had praised as the most popular teammate in the whole AAE, was killed at Gallipoli in May 1915. Cecil Madigan spent only one semester of his Rhodes scholarship at Oxford before signing up for the Royal Engineers. In action in France, he was shot in the thigh at the Battle of Loos. In 1914 and 1915, he wrote several friendly letters to Mawson, none of which hints at the antagonism that marks every page of his son's family memoir, *Vixere Fortes*, published fifty-three years after Madigan's death. In December 1915, invalided back to

England after being wounded, Madigan wrote to Mawson, "I had some close shaves in the trenches. . . . I can't walk far. I don't feel much like taking a load up to Aladdin's cave."

Archibald McLean, whose collaborative efforts with Mawson in preparing *The Home of the Blizzard* were so extensive that he might justly be regarded as co-author of that classic expedition narrative, served with both the Royal Army Medical Corps and the Australian Army Medical Corps. Late in the war in France, he was felled by poison gas. Though he survived the war, he died in 1922 from the aftereffects of the gas. John Hunter wrote to Mawson about the man's last days: "Poor old 'Dad' McLean passed away on 13th inst. He had a long spin, poor old chap, but was cheerful and optimistic to the last. Hannam & I saw him about a month before he died. Laseron, Correll, Jones, Hannam & myself went to the funeral."

Mawson himself tried to enlist in various branches of both the Australian and the British war efforts. In 1915 he wrote to Eric Webb, the AAE magnetician, "I have been itching to get to Gallipoli, but all the time am held up by expedition affairs." It is not clear why several Australian agencies turned down Mawson's offers to serve. Paquita had given birth to a daughter in April 1915, while Mawson was in the middle of his lecture tour of the United States, but many another young Australian father fought in the Great War. Mawson eventually found employment in England with the Commission Internationale de Ravitaillement, supervising the shipment of explosives to the front, but he never saw action in the war.

One other member of the AAE met an early death. Charles Harrisson, the even-keeled biologist and artist in Wild's Western Base Party, married with two children, had no sooner arrived in Australia after his year in Antarctica than he signed on as a member of a party sent from Hobart in the *Endeavour* to relieve the Macquarie Island crew that had replaced George Ainsworth's five-man team. The government fisheries research vessel reached Macquarie in early December 1914. Picking up the men on the island, the ship headed back to Australia. She was never heard from after December 3, and no trace of the vessel or the men aboard was ever found. The official verdict was that the *Endeavour* must have been caught in a violent gale and sunk.

Shackleton's *Endurance* expedition, lasting from 1914–17, is widely regarded as marking the close of the heroic age of Antarctic exploration. As the *Endurance* set off from Plymouth on August 1, 1914, Great Britain was on the verge of entering the war that was rapidly spreading across Europe. The nation's official declaration of war against Germany came only three days later. From shipboard, Shackleton telegraphed the Admiralty to offer the services of his men, but he was told to go ahead with the expedition. Two years later, when word of the ship's having been crushed in the ice in the Weddell Sea reached England, Winston Churchill—the man who had approved the *Endurance* expedition in the first place—wrote to his wife, "Fancy that ridiculous Shackleton & his South Pole—in the crash of the world."

After the war, when Shackleton lectured in London to recover the costs of the expedition, he often spoke in front of half-empty houses. As his biographer Roland Huntford writes, "London in the aftermath of the Great War was no place to talk about polar exploration." When he died in 1922 on South Georgia Island, at the head of yet another Antarctic expedition, one saddled with ill-defined objectives, Shackleton had become a quaint, anachronistic figure, far from the heroic survivalist and leader of men so celebrated today.

Likewise, as Mawson lectured about the AAE in England and the United States during the first months of the war, he was often discouraged by the lukewarm responses of his audiences. In a letter to Paquita in February 1915, for instance, he wrote, "The manager at Boston made a mess of it—nobody knew anything of my being there." The two-volume *The Home of the Blizzard*, published by William Heinemann in January 1915, was limited because of the war to a first edition of 3,500 copies. Three and a half years later, at the end of the war, combined sales in the United Kingdom and United States amounted to only 2,200 copies.

It would take nearly half a century for the great deeds of the heroic age to gain a broad, enthusiastic audience. The Shackleton cult, so vibrant today, got its start with the publication of Alfred Lansing's popular 1959 retelling of the story of the Imperial Trans-Antarctic Expedition, in *Endurance: Shackleton's Incredible Voyage*. Similarly, though Mawson remained lastingly famous in Australia, it took Lennard Bickel's popular (and vastly oversimplified) 1977 résumé of the AAE, *Mawson's Will: The Greatest Survival Story Ever Written*, to put Mawson on the radar screens of an international audience.

After the war, back in Australia, Mawson was promoted to a professorship in geology and mineralogy at the University of Adelaide. He would remain in that position for thirty-one years, until his retirement in 1952. During those years, he inspired generations of protégés in geology and exploration. Mawson's abiding passion, however, was to get the scientific results of the AAE published. Over decades, he met with one rebuff after another, ranging from team members who failed to produce the reports they had promised to university and government presses unwilling to finance the issuing of the costly volumes. Mawson firmly believed that the expedition itself had had little value unless those scientific reports could see the light of day.

Some of the reports were written by scientists not on the expedition, using notes recorded in the field and specimens curated at the university, such as Réné Koehler's esoterically titled *Echinodermata Ophiuroidea*, a 1922 treatise on starfish. As late as 1943, Mawson himself wrote up a report on the geography and geology of Macquarie Island, based on the thirty-year-old records of Leslie Blake, who, like Bob Bage, had been killed in World War I. Thanks to Mawson's doggedness, by 1947 twenty-two volumes comprising ninety-six separate scientific reports from the AAE had been published.

It would take some time for the value of those reports to be appreciated. As Riffenburgh notes, "The scientific goals of early Antarctic expeditions were not to make bold advances in theory, but to establish large databases and build up a corpus of information that would serve as a framework for future knowledge." In 2003, the scholar

Gordon E. Fogg, author of the definitive *A History of Antarctic Science*, told Riffenburgh that "the Australasian Expedition was easily the most productive scientific effort in the Antarctic before the International Geophysical Year of 1957–58."

The drama of the AAE may be forever overshadowed by the expeditions in search of the South Pole prosecuted by Scott, Shackleton, and Amundsen between 1901 and 1912. But in 1928, another expert on Antarctic history, J. Gordon Hayes, categorically stated:

> Sir Douglas Mawson's Expedition, judged by the magnitude both of its scale and of its achievements, was the greatest and most consummate expedition that ever sailed for Antarctica. The expeditions of Scott and Shackleton were great, and Amundsen's venture was the finest Polar reconnaissance ever made; but each of these must yield the premier position, when fairly compared with Mawson's magnificently conceived and executed scheme of exploration.

In 1929 and 1930, Mawson led two more expeditions to the Antarctic. The British, Australian and New Zealand Antarctic Research Expedition, or BANZARE, would produce its own slew of scientific reports, and would make further discoveries on the southern continent, but a principal motivation for the journeys was to forestall an aggressive thrust by the Norwegians to claim territory that the Australians felt belonged to them, or at least to the British Empire. Captain John King Davis was once again the pilot for the expedition ship on the 1929 voyage, during which he and Mawson fell out so angrily that they stopped speaking to each other, trading notes instead. The quarrel wrote a doleful finis to what ought to have been a lifelong friendship cemented by the two men's loyalty to each other on the AAE.

Though BANZARE made significant contributions to the further exploration of Antarctica, by 1930 the heroic age was over. Airplanes had started to reduce the remoteness of the southern continent, and the radio communication Mawson tried so futilely to establish in 1912 and 1913 had become a standard feature of voyages to Antarctica. As a saga of adventure, BANZARE cannot compare to the extraordinary story of the AAE.

For all the energy and drive that characterized Mawson's whole career, the desperate trek back to Winter Quarters after Mertz's death took a lasting toll. In 1976, Eric Webb, by then the last surviving member of the AAE, reminisced about his impressions of Mawson on first meeting with him in New Zealand after the expedition:

> He was still purposeful, but he was a noticeably chastened man—quieter, humble, and I think much closer to his God. . . . I saw he had aged, was worn, had lost much of his hair, and I fear he was never again the same iron man who started on that fateful journey. I am now convinced his terrible sufferings left scars on his physique and his constitution, and that he would have lived a lot longer than he did but for his awesome ordeal.

For the rest of his life, Mawson was regarded in his home country as the greatest explorer in Australian history. For decades, his face, wearing a balaclava in a Frank Hurley photo, graced the nation's one-hundred-dollar bill. Today, sadly, there are many young people in Australia who have never heard of Douglas Mawson.

Some of the AAE members went on to craft distinguished careers, many in academe. Frank Wild and Frank Hurley gained further fame as members of Shackleton's ill-starred *Endurance* expedition. Chosen to lead the refugee camp of twenty-one men on Elephant Island while Shackleton set off in an open boat for South Georgia Island, Wild kept the men alive and morale from crashing during their horrendous four-month vigil. On that journey, he became the first man in history to be the veteran of four major Antarctic expeditions. Hurley brought back photos and film footage from the *Endurance* expedition that were every bit as excellent as what he had shot on the AAE. The publication of scores of those photos in Caroline Alexander's 1998 retelling of the story, *The Endurance,* turned the book into a bestseller, and the riveting film footage of the ship breaking up and sinking in the ice anchored the accompanying traveling exhibition organized by the American Museum of Natural History.

Shackleton has come down to us as the exemplar of leadership and responsibility for his men. But Mawson deserves equal praise in this regard. The men of the AAE, with the exception of Cecil Madigan (and later, a disgruntled John King Davis), maintained a lifelong respect, bordering on awe, for Mawson's leadership through those two grueling years in one of the most inhospitable places on earth. Hurley closed his memoir *Argonauts of the South* with a tribute:

> No words of mine can do justice to Sir Douglas Mawson, to his judgement in choosing his men, his care for their welfare and the resourcefulness and courage with which he inspired them. Those who lived with him through the long tedious months in the blizzard-smitten South looked up to him not only as a leader but loved him as a comrade and a man.

Although only seven years Mawson's junior, Eric Webb wrote in 1976, "To me, when I was a young man in my early twenties, Mawson was already a hero." Growing up in Lyttleton, New Zealand, Webb as a boy had stood on the dock and watched Scott's expeditions depart for Antarctica in both 1902 and 1911. At the age of eighty-seven, he looked back and evaluated the three great Antarctic expedition leaders most admired by the English-speaking public:

> [Mawson] was not a Shackleton, nor a Scott—but he was no ordinary leader. Shackleton had a magnetic personality of the kind which is physical rather than intellectual, while Scott was, in the main, a naval martinet with scientific leanings. Mawson was, above everything, an intellectual leader with utter motivation and selfless dedication to his objective which he handed out to all of us in his party. . . . Mawson's dedication to scientific objectives infused a like spirit into us with the determination to emulate and excel the results of our peers.

In later years, the surviving Australian members of the AAE would gather annually in Sydney or Melbourne to renew their friendships and reminisce about the greatest adventure of their lives. On hearing that Mawson had suffered a heart attack in 1954, several of the AAE veterans sent him heartfelt testimonies to his role in shaping their lives. George Dovers, who had been the surveyor in Wild's Western Base party, wrote: "I consider that I was a most privileged person to have had the opportunity as a young man of serving under your leadership. . . . I do not think there is any doubt that the experience and example we had as young men under your command had a most tremendous effect for good on our characters."

The biologist John Hunter wrote, "The 1911–14 days will ever take pride of place in my memories, and the example you set in leadership has always inspired me over the years." And Charles Laseron testified, "The years 1911–13 are still the chief milestones in my life. . . . I think you would like to know that while writing my three books [including *South with Mawson*, published in 1947], it is your approbation as our old leader, that I have wanted more than anything else."

In September 1958, at the age of seventy-six, Mawson suffered a minor stroke that temporarily affected his speech. As Paquita recalled, "Knowing that he was not remembering words properly, he made himself write them down, copying them from books, carefully writing line after line to aid his slowly recovering memory. His mind was clear and active, and before long he was practically normal in speech."

It is not surprising that Mawson spent the last weekend of his life "worrying about some scientific work which he had not been able to finish." The end was sudden and relatively painless.

Sunday was a perfect October day and we sat out on the lawn with friends. But on Monday morning Douglas suffered a further stroke which rendered him unconscious and took him from us next day. He died peacefully, surrounded by his family, at 9 p. m. on 14 October 1958, in the house he had planned when he was in the Antarctic.

The prime minister of Australia arranged a state funeral for Mawson two days after his death. Hundreds of mourners stood outside the church, listening as the bell tolled seventy-six times, one for each year of the explorer's life.

Paquita spent six years writing the first biography of her husband. *Mawson of the Antarctic* was published in 1964. As a biography, it has since been superseded by the works of Philip Ayres and Beau Riffenburgh, but it remains the primary source for many anecdotes and insights into Mawson's character that only the person who knew him best could divulge.

In the South Australian Museum in Adelaide, a permanent exhibition celebrates the deeds of Mawson. For the visitor steeped in the story of the AAE, the relics preserved under glass have a powerful numen. Perhaps the artifact that most rivets one's attention is the half-sledge that Mawson hauled 100 miles back to Winter Quarters after burying Mertz, and that saved his life more than once when it served as an anchor arresting his crevasse falls. A hemp cord, apparently used to lash his belongings atop the sledge, is still tied to the framework. The fenders and runners bear the leather reinforcing strips Mawson improvised on the ice. And the short trunk of the mast across which he spread the sail made of Mertz's burberry jacket and a cloth bag stands in place. Nearby, the knife—labeled a "Bonsa tool kit"—with which he somehow cut the sledge in half rests on display.

Another case contains the homemade crampons Mawson jury-rigged out of the wooden pieces of the theodolite case, with the nails and screws he thrust through them still in place. As footgear, these crampons look woefully flimsy, but it is surprising to see how big they are—bigger than any man's boots, almost the size of mini-snowshoes. Inside the case, also, are the theodolite poles that held up the tent cover Mawson and Mertz slept under in lieu of the tent that had vanished with Ninnis.

The smallest items bespeak Mawson's desperate ingenuity: a

wooden spoon he carved out of something or other, shaped like a miniature spatula; a single ski pole that Ninnis used; a spade-like shovel made of a flat metal blade bound to a wooden handle with heavy twine.

The exhibition also recreates, in cutaway cross-section, part of the hut in which the men spent two long years. Mawson's bunk and office are immaculate, while a pair of other bunks—could they have been part of Hyde Park Corner?—are covered with a reindeer-skin sleeping bag, a pair of finnesko, a pair of fur mittens, a set of beige-colored burberry outerwear, and a crude-looking balaclava with a flap to close the front orifice to the size of a narrow tunnel.

There are stuffed penguins and petrels, penguin eggs, shelves bearing portraits of the men's sweethearts, smoking pipes mounted on the wall, old books in leather bindings, the sewing machine with which the men stitched their sledge harnesses, and even the "puff-ometer" Percy Correll rigged from a metal ball hanging on a chain affixed to a wooden packing case, the device the team used to measure the velocity of the peak gusts of wind. Perhaps the most beguiling of the objects in the exhibition is the doll that Anna Pavlova gave to Ninnis when she came on board the *Aurora* in London.

The whole exhibition has the eerie authority of a vanished age—the heroic age of Antarctic exploration. Compared to modern gear, all the objects look fragile, even inadequate. How could that sleeping bag, coated with ice from a night's exhalations, keep a man warm? How could burberry and finnesko have staved off frostbite? How could those books and pictures and pipes have kept the men occupied through an endless winter? How could the hut itself have withstood the blizzards?

Mark Pharaoh is the Senior Collection Manager of the Mawson Centre, housed in a separate building just behind the South Australian Museum itself. No one living, perhaps, has a deeper grasp of Mawson's character and career. In a thoughtful rumination in July 2011, Pharaoh summed up his judgment of Mawson as a man and as the leader of the AAE.

"Mawson had his faults, to be sure," said Pharaoh. "He was something of a control freak. He paid attention to every single detail, and was not always a very good at delegating chores and responsibilities. He hated waste. He worked too hard himself, and so overemphasized the importance of work for his men. He was not very flexible in this respect.

"Some have said that Mawson lacked a sense of humor, but I don't think that's entirely fair. It's true that he didn't handle being laughed at very well. On the AAE, he made some mistakes, just as Scott did on his own last expedition. Because he didn't know how to ski himself, he dismissed the value of skis altogether, so on the expedition only Mertz used them. Amundsen had proved how valuable skis are for travel in Antarctica.

"As a scientist, he believed that collecting was of prime importance. Theoretically, he wasn't very open-minded. All his life, he resisted Alfred Wegener's theory of continental drift, even after his mentor, Edgeworth David, took up the idea. Mawson tended to get locked into a priori paradigms.

"But look at what he accomplished. In only three years, he essentially went from being a passenger on board the *Nimrod* to playing a critical role on Shackleton's BAE, then to becoming the leader of the most ambitious Antarctic expedition of all. His very attention to detail was a virtue in its own right. He was really good at gleaning information by drawing on all the clues that he had at hand.

"His emphasis on work kept the team together during the terrible winters. By urging the men to go out of the hut in the strongest winds, he tried to keep them from succumbing to apathy and depression.

"I think he was personally quite modest. Paquita said that he was completely indifferent to fame. Whatever his faults, he cared deeply about the safety and well-being of his men, and he won the lifelong respect and loyalty of virtually all his teammates.

"And finally, you have to consider the feat of his survival after Ninnis and Mertz's deaths. There's nothing else like it in polar history."

In 2007, Australian Tim Jarvis decided to try to recreate Mawson's 300-mile trek from the crevasse in which Ninnis died on December 14, 1912, back to the hut at Winter Quarters, which Mawson finally reached on February 8, 1913. Jarvis was already one of the most accomplished Antarctic explorers of his generation, having set a record in 1999 by sledging solo to the South Pole in forty-seven days, two days faster than any other lone adventurer had performed such a trek unsupported. Jarvis was determined to undertake his 2007 march wearing the same clothing that Mawson and Mertz had worn, using the same equipment, and eating very much the same food.

The "recreation," however, was hedged about with loopholes that would make the 2007 journey crucially different from Mawson and Mertz's race against death. To play the role of Mertz, Jarvis recruited Evgeny Stoukalo, a very fit Russian who was an expert climber, competitive cross-country ski racer, and ex-military officer. Having grown up in Siberia, Stoukalo was accustomed to cold. He would not, of course, be asked to die as Mertz so agonizingly had. Instead, Stoukalo would share the man-hauling with Jarvis for 200 miles or twenty-five days, whichever came first. From that point, he would be "extracted" (Jarvis's word) by a helicopter that would whisk him off to a modern scientific research station on the coast. After that, Jarvis would go it alone.

Because, according to Jarvis, "the logistics of travelling over the same ground proved impossible to arrange," the two men chose to sledge across a part of Antarctica that was 1,600 miles west of Cape Denison as the crow flies. Instead of Adélie Land, Jarvis and Stoukalo would cross Princess Elizabeth Land. Standing in for the hut at Winter Quarters was Davis Station, the principal Australian research facility operating on the continent, manned in summer by a substantial corps of scientists. (The station, which first opened in 1957, had been named after John King Davis, the captain of the *Aurora*.)

Jarvis also decided that "To make the project viable, it had to be filmed." The insertion of a film crew changed the game profoundly. It meant that as Jarvis and Stoukalo sledged across the plateau, a caravan of motorized all-terrain vehicles would chug along on a parallel path, dropping by at regular intervals so that the cameramen could film and interview the recreators. Jarvis and Stoukalo were in radio contact with this armada, which was never far away. The filmmakers in turn received precision weather forecasts from Australia that they shared almost daily with the sledgers. And if any disaster befell the men impersonating Mawson and Mertz, the film crew would serve as an instant rescue service, with the capacity to summon a helicopter within hours.

As nearly as they could, Jarvis and Stoukalo reproduced the clothing and gear that their predecessors had relied on nearly a century before. The total amount of food that they carried was equal to the week and a half's worth of rations that Mawson and Mertz had been stranded with after Ninnis and his sledge disappeared into the crevasse. Like the AAE explorers, Jarvis and Stoukalo cooked up a hoosh made of pemmican, lard (instead of butter), and ground-up wheat biscuits. They drank tea, broth, and cocoa. Instead of dog meat—dogs have been banned altogether from Antarctica since 1994, out of concern that they might transmit canine distemper to the indigenous seals—the modern explorers ate kangaroo jerky, "as its leanness is very close to that of dog meat."

Jarvis was not oblivious to the differences between his reenactment and Mawson and Mertz's ordeal, but, curiously, he thought that all the logistical safety valves he built into his own journey threatened to pose a psychological disadvantage. As he later wrote, "Mawson and Mertz couldn't stop; we, assuming the weather was good, could have been reunited with the [film] crew inside a day—a fact I suspected would make it harder, in many respects, to keep going."

The change of location from Adélie Land to Princess Elizabeth Land, however, gave Jarvis and Stoukalo a huge advantage, one that Jarvis oddly fails to acknowledge in his expedition book. Not once on their long trek did the men even stick a foot into a bridged crevasse, let alone fall bodily into one. Nor did they have to steer clear of bad crevasse fields, as the Far Eastern Party had time and again both on the way out and the way back. The plateau across which they sledged happened to be one of those anomalously crevasse-free stretches on the southern continent.

Still, Jarvis and Stoukalo suffered extremely from cold and hunger. At the 200-mile mark, where the film crew awaited them, Stoukalo was "extracted" by helicopter. "Losing a Friend," Jarvis titles the chapter in his book covering this part of the journey, and the chapter following (with no apparent irony), "Alone on the Shores of the World." Of the days immediately succeeding Stoukalo's departure, he writes, "I was feeling extremely isolated and the occasional presence of the film crew offered suprisingly little solace. I expended a lot of mental energy in the tent just remaining calm and patient and reminding myself of what had been achieved already on the journey."

The comparison of Jarvis's made-for-television reenactment and Mawson's genuine ordeal serves not simply to undercut the gravity of the former. Jarvis was no dilettante of Antarctic travel, but one of its modern masters. What emerges from the recreation is a renewed appreciation of just how astounding a feat Mawson—and Mertz, before he weakened and died—pulled off. For through the first half of their journey, Jarvis and Stoukalo not only could not match the mileages the two men had covered in 1912–13, they fell far short of them. By the end of the journey, Jarvis had "caught up" with Mawson, and managed to finish his 300-mile trek two days faster than the man he was emulating. What is missing in Jarvis's narrative, however, is an acknowledgment of the fact that Mawson was twice badly stalled on his homeward dash—for nine days while Mertz was too weak to move, and for another eight in Aladdin's Cave as, without crampons, he dared not risk the final five-mile run to the hut. It was only because Jarvis suffered no such delays of his own that he was able to match and then barely exceed Mawson's pace through the fifty-six days of his trek back to Winter Quarters.

At Davis Station, Jarvis was fêted not only by the film crew but by the scientists in residence. Instead of missing by five hours the ship that would have taken him home and being condemned to spend another winter in Antarctica, Jarvis luxuriated in a hot shower, a bed with fresh sheets, lavish meals, phone calls to his girlfriend and parents, and, before long, a flight home to Australia.

Jarvis is too savvy an adventurer to ignore the central lesson of his reenactment. At the end of *Mawson: Life and Death in Antarctica*, he tips his cap to Mawson and Mertz:

> Despite pride at having completed my journey, I feel more than anything humbled by it. I have an even greater respect for what Mawson and Mertz achieved. Theirs was without doubt a terrible journey, and one that mine in the modern era could not claim to have replicated. I had done so as closely as I could and that was bad enough. By subjecting myself to a journey similar to that of Mawson and telling his story parallel with mine, I hope it will bring his ordeal to the attention of the larger audience I believe it deserves.

Before the hot shower and the clean sheets, the film crew imposed one last trial on Tim Jarvis. That was to recreate Mawson's escape from the crevasse on January 17, 1913. The team scouted out a photogenic crevasse near Davis Station. Jarvis donned a modern climbing harness, tied in to a perlon rope, and was lowered 14 feet into the blue abyss. The harness was also tied to a hemp rope knotted at 15-inch intervals, replicating the rope that had connected Mawson to his sledge. Still belayed on the perlon safety rope, Jarvis tried to climb up the hemp rope hand over hand, as the cameras rolled. The struggle became desperate, and Jarvis almost gave up six feet below the surface. But:

> I threw myself upward again with a mighty effort. . . . I thrust my left leg out and caught the hobnails on the toe of my boot on a small lip on the vertical wall. . . . With a frenzied push with my legs and a last weakening pull with my arms, I emerged on my stomach onto the snow. . . .

The camera rolled for another 30 seconds before the crew came forward and offered their heartfelt congratulations. I felt a great burden instantly lift. There was no more to do.

Unfortunately, the director now suggested that Jarvis perform the climb again, as Mawson had had to do after the lip of the crevasse broke on his first attempt, plunging him 14 feet back in to the length of his harness rope. Recognizing the justice of the historical analogy—"I owed it to Mawson"—Jarvis gamely volunteered. The team lowered him into the crevasse again. Still on belay, he grasped the knots in the hemp rope and pulled.

He got halfway out before collapsing and giving up. The second self-rescue was beyond his powers. In the end, the team hauled Jarvis out of his replicated death trap with the perlon rope.

Five years after making the first ascent of Mount Everest, in 1958 Sir Edmund Hillary led a team driving farm tractors adapted to polar terrain on a motorized journey from the Antarctic coast to the South Pole. His was the first party since Scott's in 1912 to reach the pole overland. Hillary's effort was a depot-laying mission in support of the first traverse of Antarctica, a massive effort organized by Sir Vivian Fuchs that finally accomplished the dream that Shackleton had tried to realize in 1914–17. By 1958, polar travel was still so daunting that driving tractors across the ice did not seem unsporting.

All his life, Hillary had a keen sense of the landmarks in the history of adventure. In 1976, he hailed Mawson's solo struggle back to Winter Quarters as "probably the greatest story of lone survival in Polar exploration." A few years later, Hillary outdid his own encomium. His final verdict on that journey deserves to stand as the enduring epigraph to Mawson's deed: "The greatest survival story in the history of exploration."

ACKNOWLEDGMENTS

I owe by far my greatest debt in the research for this book about Douglas Mawson and the Australasian Antarctic Expedition to Mark Pharaoh, the Senior Collection Manager of the Mawson Centre at the South Australian Museum in Adelaide. Mark knows more about Mawson than probably anyone alive, and during my week at the Mawson Centre he virtually turned himself over to me, offering again and again to help me hunt down whatever I needed or clear up my misconceptions. Thanks to his sage and comprehensive grasp of Antarctic history, I sidestepped many a foolish remark or outright error. Then, when I had finished the first draft of *Alone on the Ice*, Mark agreed to read it carefully, and in doing so he caught more infelicities and oversights on my part. In thirty years of museum and library research for various books and articles, I have seldom had as congenial a rapport with a scholar so gifted as Mark.

In Australia, I also received unfailing kindness and help from many staff members at the Mitchell Library in Sydney, the National Library of Australia in Canberra, the State Library of Victoria in Melbourne, and other curators at the South Australian Museum in Adelaide. Back home, I benefited greatly, as usual, from the incomparable collections at Harvard, particularly those of the Widener Library.

My friend from the Harvard Travellers Club, Rob Stephenson, whose "Antarctic Circle" is a splendid forum and resource about everything to do with the southern polar regions, gave me much advice and contact information. In two long visits to Rob's library in Jaffrey, New Hampshire, I gained a firsthand acquaintance with books and papers I hadn't known existed.

Other scholars who have written about Mawson and the AAE were unstinting in providing me with hints and help by e-mail. I'm especially grateful to Beau Riffenburgh, Stephen Haddelsey, Jonathan Chester, Heather Rossiter, the late Lincoln Hall, and Alasdair McGregor, not only for assistance but for the excellent books they've written, from the pages of which I gleaned many an insight. Alasdair and Margie McIntyre met me in Sydney for a fascinating lunch, during which they steered me in several proper directions. Margie also sent me a copy of *Two Below Zero*, cowritten with her husband Don McIntyre, an account of the joys and glooms of the first overwintering at Cape Denison since Mawson's, which the couple accomplished in 1995.

During my sojourn in Australia, the intensity of library research was leavened by a long, blissful weekend in the Blue Mountains with my climbing, hiking, and writing buddy Greg Child and his precocious daughter, Ariann. A native Aussie, Greg had known the Mawson story since he was a young boy, and his appreciation of the achievement of one of his lifelong heroes helped me see Mawson better. As for Ariann, only six years old during our walks under the cliffs that July, every day spent in her company is a gift of delight. Salley Oberlin kindly lent us her house in Blackheath to use as a base camp.

Other friends and scholars who performed valuable services for me at the drop of a hat include Greg Glade, owner of Top of the World Books, and Shannon O'Donoghue, former director of the Banff Mountain Film Festival. In Australia, Jemima Mowbray, whom I've never met, solved the potentially herculean task for me of obtaining permissions to quote from the unpublished diaries of AAE members. Kathryn Sall skillfully drew the maps that illustrate this book.

At W. W. Norton & Company, my editor, Starling Lawrence, saw the excitement of the Mawson story from the start and smoothly helped me steer it into port. His assistants, Melody Conroy and Ryan Harrington, handled most of the inevitably fussy details of converting a passion into a book. Allegra Huston did an excellent job of copyediting my manuscript.

My agent, Stuart Krichevsky, championed the Mawson project in his usual brilliant fashion. This is the twelfth book Stuart has helped me publish, and I count it one of the best turns of fortune in my career as a writer that back in 2001, he agreed to take me on, despite his loyal commitment to many another writer. Throughout those eleven years, Stuart has never let the slightest whimper from this often insecure scrivener go unanswered. Stuart's colleagues, Shana Cohen and Ross Harris, were enthusiastic and helpful at every stage of the game. (Thank God somebody like them understands the intricacies of the publishing business!)

Three close friends and my wife read *Alone on the Ice* in manuscript and gave me cogent reactions to the book. As always, I'm grateful to Jon Krakauer, Ed Ward, Matt Hale, and Sharon Roberts not only for faithfully reading what I wrote, but for telling me what they thought about it.

NOTES

The following abbreviations are used:
HOB: Douglas Mawson, *The Home of the Blizzard*, abridged edition (New York: St. Martin's Press, 1998). Unless otherwise indicated, all references to Mawson's *The Home of the Blizzard* are to this edition. *MAD*: Fred Jacka and Eleanor Jacka, eds., *Mawson's Antarctic Diaries* (North Sydney: Allen & Unwin, 1988).

Except where otherwise indicated, all references to Shackleton's *The Heart of the Antarctic* are to the abridged 1999 edition.

1. FORGOTTEN BY GOD

15 *After eight days*: Mertz, diary, November 17, 1912.

15 *Those eight days had been*: *HOB*, 137–44.

16 *"partly on account of"*: Laseron, "South with Mawson," 10.

16 *"From the creation"*: Ninnis, diary, January 22, 1912, quoted in http://www.mawsonshuts.aq/cape-denison/people.

16 *Xavier Mertz was nicknamed*: Laseron, "South with Mawson," 10.

16 *"a magnificent athlete"*: Ibid.

16 *his skill at making omelettes*: Riffenburgh, *Racing with Death*, 102.

17 *"from now our route goes"*: Mertz, diary, November 17, 1912.

17 *There is little or no evidence*: Mark Pharaoh, personal communication, July 2011.

17 *an outdoor dinner party*: Flannery, *This Everlasting Silence*, 2–4.

17 *In December 1910*: Ibid., 12.

18 *"this everlasting silence"*: Ibid., 102.

18 *"I have two good"*: Ibid., 47–48.

19 *Aboard the* Aurora: *HOB*, 9–10, 13–14, 142.

19 *Pavlova was an homage*: Bickel, *Mawson's Will*, 137–38.

19 *On November 10*: *HOB*, 140–42.

20 *"got badly damaged by dogs"*: *MAD*, 128.

20 *Weighing ten pounds each*: *HOB*, 141.

20 *"In the morning I had backache"*: Mertz, diary, November 12, 1912.

20 *Another nuisance derived*: *HOB*, 138.

20 *A 35 mph wind*: *MAD*, 129.

20 *There, during a spring foray*: Mertz, diary, November 13, 1912.

20 *"Strong blizzard threatened"*: *MAD*, 129.

20 *"Our Eskimo dogs"*: Mertz, diary, November 14, 1912.

20 *On the 15th, Pavlova*: Ibid., November 15, 1912.

21 *"A rather miserable animal,"*: *HOB*, 142.

21 *"We leave camp"*: *MAD*, 130.

21 *"They ate 'Gadget' meat"*: Mertz, diary, November 18, 1912.

21 *"Beautiful weather"*: Ibid.

21 *"This area seems"*: Ibid., November 15, 1912.

21 *"We found that they were glad"*: *HOB*, 143.

22 *"The sledges were now commencing"*: Ibid., 145.

22 *"I stopped, because I felt"*: Mertz, diary, November 19, 1912.

22 *On November 19, Ninnis*: Mertz, diary, November 20, 1912.

22 *Mawson ministered to his teammate*: *HOB*, 146.

22 *During the first week*: Ibid., 145, 147.

23 *By November 20, the men*: Ibid., 147.

23 *The huskies continued*: Mertz, diary, November 19, 1912.

23 *"Jappy killed"*: *MAD*, 133.

23 *One such cynosure*: *HOB*, 147.

25 *more than 99 percent*: http://www .coolantarctica.com/Antarctica.

25 *"Suddenly without any warning"*: *HOB*, 147–48.

25 *Not long after that debacle*: Ibid., 148.

25 *"gave birth to the first"*: *MAD*, 133.

25 *"Returning, we diverged"*: *HOB*, 148–49.

26 *"detours"*: Mertz, diary, November 21, 1912.

26 *Sure enough, between November*: *MAD*, 133–39.

26 *"Great difficulty in getting"*: Ibid., 137.

27 *"The dogs are in good shape"*: Mertz, diary, November 25 and 26, 1912.

27 *On November 27, the men unharnessed*: *MAD*, 137; Mertz, diary, November 27, 1912.

27 *The very next day, Mawson*: *HOB*, 153.

27 *On November 22, the day*: Ibid., 149–50.

27 *The next day, Ninnis's sledge*: Ibid., 150–51.

28 *"In front of us"*: Mertz, diary, November 27, 1912.

28 *"Just before lunch"*: *HOB*, 154.

29 *"Not less than 220"*: *MAD*, 139.

29 *"We have had a most aggravating"*: Ibid., 138–39.

29 *But on the 30th, they awoke*: Ibid., 139.

29 *"It's difficult to travel"*: Mertz, diary, November 30, 1912.

30 *On "rest days"*: Ibid.

30 *Unwilling to waste*: MAD, 139.

30 *"The snow became"*: HOB, 155.

30 *Despite a full day's*: MAD, 140.

30 *On December 2, a new obstacle*: HOB, 155.

30 *"The sledges flew round"*: Mertz, diary, December 2, 1912.

30 *During the next three days*: Ibid., December 3–5, 1912.

30 *"Ginger in last few hundred yards"*: MAD, 142.

31 *On December 6*: Ibid., 143.

31 *"Taunted by vivid dreams"*: Ibid.

31 *"This is an appalling state"*: Ibid.

31 *To make matters worse*: Ibid.

31 *"He had continued to do"*: HOB, 158.

31 *"Ninnis was not so badly"*: Ibid., 156.

31 *"The dogs and my comrades"*: Mertz, diary, December 9, 1912.

31 *During the next three days*: Ibid., December 10–12, 1912.

32 *By December 11, they had gained*: HOB, 158.

32 *On the 11th, Mertz calculated*: Mertz, diary, December 11, 1912.

32 *On December 10, Ninnis*: HOB, 157.

32 *On the 12th, the men*: MAD, 145.

32 *They abandoned the battered sledge*: Ibid., 147.

32 *Under Mawson's direction*: HOB, 158.

33 *The men did not start moving*: MAD, 147.

33 *"We are apparently coming"*: Ibid.

33 *"Booming sound heard today"*: Ibid.

33 *"Soon we reached a flat area"*: Mertz, diary, December 13, 1912.

34 *Ninnis's fingers were causing*: HOB, 158–59.

34 *"We were a happy party"*: Ibid., 159.

34 *The temperature at 9 a.m.*: MAD, 147.

34 *In the lead, Mertz sang*: HOB, 159.

34 *At noon, only a quarter mile*: MAD, 147.

34 *Shortly after noon, Mertz*: HOB, 159.

34 *"A moment later the faint"*: Ibid., 160.

35 *"I came to a gaping hole"*: Ibid.

35 *"I leaned over and shouted"*: Ibid., 160–61.

35 *By December 14, thanks*: Ibid., 161.

36 *"In such moments"*: Ibid., 161–62.

36 *"in case our companion might"*: Ibid., 162.

36 *In a stupor, the pair*: MAD, 148.

36 *So rigorously ingrained*: Ibid., 147.

37 *"At 4 am, we were on the way"*: Mertz, diary, December 14, 1912.

37 *With it were gone not only*: MAD, 148.

37 *"We could do nothing"*: Mertz, diary, December 14, 1912.

37 *In his own diary, after*: MAD, 148.

2. PROF DOGGO

38 *Mawson's family cherished*: P. Mawson, *Mawson of the Antarctic*, 15; Ayres, *Mawson*, 1.

38 *Douglas Mawson was born*: Ayres, *Mawson*, 2.

39 *In the village of Rooty Hill*: Ibid., 22–23.

39 *From Fort Street emerged*: Ibid., 23.

39 *Both William and Douglas entered*: Ibid.

39 *"in his forties"*: Ibid., 5.

39 *David had participated*: Branagan, *David*, 85–86, 104.

39 *In 1896, David had published*: Ibid., 141.

40 *Though Norwegian-born*: http://www.south-pole.com/p400087.htm.

40 *In 1901, David exhorted*: Branagan, *David*, 141–44.

40 *Several months earlier, David*: Ibid., 141.

40 *"sang his old student's"*: Ayres, *Mawson*, 12.

40 *After earning his bachelor's*: P. Mawson, *Mawson of the Antarctic*, 25.

41 *Mawson himself believed*: Ayres, *Mawson*, 7, 9.

41 *The boldest exploit*: Ibid., 7–8.

41 *"Stopped at 11 O'Clock"*: Douglas Mawson, New Hebrides diaries, June 13, 1903, quoted in Ayres, *Mawson*, 8.

42 *While he hammered away*: P. Mawson, *Mawson of the Antarctic*, 26–27.

42 *A fellow student later recalled*: H. G. Foxall, quoted ibid., 27.

42 *Mawson's own interest in glaciation*: http://adb.anu.edu.au/biography/howchin-walter-6744; Ayres, *Mawson*, 9.

43 *On March 1, 1905, Mawson*: P. Mawson, *Mawson of the Antarctic*, 29.

43 *During 1906 and 1907, Mawson*: Ayres, *Mawson*, 10–11.

43 *In December 1907, when Ernest Shackleton*: Ibid., 12.

43 *"My idea," Mawson later*: Mawson to Margery Fisher, quoted ibid.

43 *Shackleton rather brusquely*: Ibid.

43 *To his astonishment, one day*: Huntford, *Shackleton*, 188.

43 *In late December 1907*: Ayres, *Mawson*, 14.

44 *On January 1, 1908, hailed*: Riffenburgh, *Racing with Death*, 7.

44 *"a place that under ordinary"*: Raymond Priestley, diary, January 1–8, 1908, quoted in Riffenburgh, 8.

44 *"Mawson is useless & objectionable"*: Marshall, diary, January 9, 1908, quoted in Riffenburgh, 8.

44 *"As daylight came, I noticed"*: Davis, *High Latitude*, 71–73.

45 *But on learning of Shackleton's*: Huntford, *Shackleton*, 161.

45 *According to Scott's early*: Seaver, *Scott of the Antarctic*, quoted in Rosove, *Let Heroes Speak*, 95.

45 *One evening early in*: Huntford, *Shackleton*, 95.

46 *"Shackleton in his traces"*: Ibid., 96.

46 *"Wilson and Shackleton were packing up"*: A. B. Armitage memorandum, quoted ibid.

46 *Throughout the desperate return*: Ibid., 113.

46 *Back at Hut Point, the men*: Rosove, *Let Heroes Speak*, 99.

47 *"Of course all the officers"*: Scott, *Voyage of the Discovery*, quoted ibid.

47 *"Shackleton's enterprise was born"*: Huntford, *Shackleton*, 161.

47 *"Scott's assumption of prescriptive"*: Ibid., 162.

48 *"I am leaving the McMurdo"*: Shackleton to Scott, May 17, 1907, quoted in ibid., 177.

48 *The* Nimrod *first sighted*: ibid., 201–4.

48 *Even after embarking*: Ibid., 208–11.

49 *The essential structure*: Shackleton, *The Heart of the Antarctic*, 133–34.

49 *"Mawson, whose lair was a little"*: Ibid., 118–19.

49 *Shackleton was anxious to lay*: Ibid., 167.

50 *In 1904, three members of Scott's party*: Riffenburgh, *Nimrod*, 173.

50 *The idea, apparently*: Huntford, *Shackleton*, 221.

50 *"apart from scientific considerations"*: Shackleton, *Heart of the Antarctic*, 167–68.

50 *Given the men's lack*: Ibid., "The Ascent of Mount Erebus," *Aurora Australis, passim.*

51 *By the end of the first day*: Ibid.

51 *"Occasionally we came to blows"*: Ibid.

52 *That evening, snug*: Ibid.

52 *"Some of us . . . found"*: Ibid.

52 *"Some of us with our sleeping bags"*: Ibid.

53 *"It was a close call,"*: Ibid.

53 *"an even plain of névé"*: Ibid.

54 *"We were all surprised"*: Ibid.

54 *The next day, rather than head*: Ibid.

55 *On March 11, the men*: Ibid.

55 *"Many were the hand-shakings"*: Ibid.

55 *Modern scientists endorse*: Larson, *An Empire of Ice*, 128–31.

56 *"In a few minutes"*: Shackleton, *Heart of the Antarctic*, 189–90.

56 *Thus all kinds of entertainments*: Ibid., *passim.*

57 *By the end of October, Shackleton*: Riffenburgh, *Nimrod*, 189–96.

57 *Instead of dogs and skis*: Shackleton, *Heart of the Antarctic*, 21–22, 158–59.

57 *"a 12–15 horse-power"*: Ibid., 22.

57 *"It . . . went a few feet"*: Aeneas Mackintosh, diary, February 1, 1908, quoted in Riffenburgh, *Nimrod*, 159.

58 *The compass, invented in China*: Gurney, *Below the Convergence*, 23.

58 *In pursuit of the elusive*: http:// www.gsc.nrcan.gc.ca/geomag/ nmp/expeditions_e.php.

58 *Since 1831, the North Magnetic Pole*: http://www.athropolis.com/ arctic-facts/fact-nmp.htm.

59 *why do some planets*: http://www .astronomynotes.com/solarsys/ plantblb.htm.

59 *Ten years later, Ross*: http://www .south-pole.com/p0000081.htm.

59 *The written instructions*: Branagan, *David*, 181.

60 *"If you are not returned"*: Ibid., 178.

61 *"in the strange half-world"*: Huntford, *Shackleton*, 246.

61 *"The Professor dog tired"*: MAD, 9.

61 *"Prof broke attachment"*: Ibid.

62 *"He is so covered"*: Ibid.

62 *At the first promontory*: Riffenburgh, *Racing with Death*, 20.

63 *"His pockets are full"*: MAD, 12.

63 *On October 22, the three men*: Ibid., 13.

63 *On October 30, after twenty-five days*: Branagan, *David*, 185.

64 *The two younger men*: Ibid., 185–86.

64 *On October 31, the men dined*: MAD, 16–17.

64 *"On all occasions he has asked"*: Ibid., 15.

64 *"He is full of great words"*: Ibid.

64 *As the men trudged*: Riffenburgh, *Nimrod*, 239.

65 *"up at 10 p.m. very sleepy"*: Branagan, *David*, 188.

65 *"The Prof is certainly"*: *MAD*, 24–25.

65 *"a great billowy sea"*: Branagan, *David*, 189.

66 *"Country continued to grow worse"*: Mills, *Men of Ice*, 33.

66 *"twelve hours of continuous"*: Ibid., 34.

66 *"I had scarcely gone"*: Shackleton, *Heart of the Antarctic* (1909 edition), vol. 2, 145.

67 *On December 12, despairing*: Riffenburgh, *Nimrod*, 241; *MAD*, 29.

67 *"not less than 660 lbs"*: *MAD*, 30.

67 *"I fell into one"*: Ibid., 31.

67 *"It was a job"*: Mills, *Men of Ice*, 38.

67 *"Very coarse pegmatites"*: *MAD*, 31.

68 *"The Prof was doggo"*: Ibid., 32–33.

68 *"Had lunch, saving cheese"*: Ibid., 33.

68 *As a kind of joke*: Branagan, *David*, 191.

68 *On December 27, to lighten*: *MAD*, 33.

68 *"Dip reading very little less"*: Ibid., 35.

68 *On December 28, Mawson told*: Mills, *Men of Ice*, 41.

69 *"The Prof is dreadfully slow"*: *MAD*, 34.

69 *"We are now almost mad"*: Ibid., 36–37.

69 *"planned menus for dinner"*: Ibid., 39.

70 *"The Professor is very nearly"*: Mills, *Men of Ice*, 46.

70 *"The Professor seems most affected"*: *MAD*, 36.

70 *"I think now, that we have"*: Mills, *Men of Ice*, 46.

70 *In a blizzard, Mawson*: *MAD*, 38–39.

70 *"Last night," Mackay wrote*: Mills, *Men of Ice*, 46.

70 *The men had a strenuous debate*: *MAD*, 40.

71 *"Mac then protests"*: Ibid., 40.

71 *On January 15, Mawson got a dip*: Branagan, *David*, 193.

71 *The next day, they hauled*: Ibid.

71 *At 4:15 p.m., they hoisted*: Ibid.

71 *Mawson set up the expedition camera*: Ibid.

72 *"My feet and legs pain"*: *MAD*, 41–44.

72 *"I don't feel so horribly exhausted"*: Mills, *Men of Ice*, 50.

73 *"Prof crampy about left calf"*: *MAD*, 43.

73 *From January 16 to 27*: Mills, *Men of Ice*, 49–52.

73 *"an awful day of despair"*: *MAD*, 45.

73 *"Prof's burberry pants"*: Ibid.

73 *"Mac, it seems got on"*: Ibid.

73 *"Prof's boots were frozen on"*: Ibid., 46.

73 *"The Prof was now certainly"*: Ibid.

74 *"I have deposed the Professor"*: Mills, *Men of Ice*, 53.

74 *"I said I did not like it"*: *MAD*, 46.

74 *"I joined him a few minutes later"*: Shackleton, *Heart of the Antarctic* (1909 edition), vol. 2, 203–4.

75 *The relief ship*: Davis, *High Latitude*, 93–94.

75 *According to Davis, the instructions*: Ibid., 99.

75 *During the next several weeks*: Ibid., 93–102.

76 *"In order to carry out"*: Ibid., 103.

76 *Captain Evans was extremely agitated*: Ibid., 103–4.

76 *"There was nothing noteworthy"*: Ibid., 104.

76 *In their green, conical tent*: MAD, 46.

76 *"The Professor could not"*: Mills, *Men of Ice*, 55.

77 *On board the* Nimrod: Davis, *High Latitude*, 104–5.

77 *In the middle of the day*: MAD, 46–47.

77 *"Immediately on sighting"*: Davis, *High Latitude*, 106.

78 *"abnormally lean"*: Frederick Pryce Evans, narrative of BAE, quoted in Riffenburgh, *Nimrod*, 273.

78 *In Shackleton's absence*: Davis, *High Latitude*, 107–8.

3. CAPE DENISON

79 *"February 4.—Cannot write"*: Shackleton, *Heart of the Antarctic*, 353.

79 *By December 1, three of them*: Rosove, *Let Heroes Speak*, 152.

79 *But before the men could make*: Shackleton, *Heart of the Antarctic*, 310.

80 *"We have shot our bolt"*: Ibid., 343.

80 *Experts have wondered*: Huntford, *Shackleton*, 271–73.

80 *"Shackleton had set"*: Ibid., 273.

80 *Shackleton had left orders*: Ibid., 286.

81 *During the return journey*: Ibid.

81 *By February 25, Marshall*: Shackleton, *Heart of the Antarctic*, 362–63.

81 *"If the ship was gone"*: Ibid., 364.

82 *"Mackay fell"*: Mills, *Men of Ice*, 72.

82 *"Edwardian England knew how"*: Huntford, *Shackleton*, 294.

82 *"the greatest geographical event"*: Ibid., 298.

82 *In November, Shackleton was knighted*: Ibid., 315.

82 *Met at the railway station*: Ayres, *Mawson*, 29.

82 *"I say that Mawson"*: *Sydney Morning Herald*, March 31, 1909, quoted ibid., 29.

83 *During 122 days*: Ayres, *Mawson*, 28.

83 *Theirs would remain the longest*: http://en.wikipedia.org/wiki/Alistair_Mackay.

83 *On a visit to England in 1911*: Branagan, *David*, 223–25.

83 *According to Mawson's biographer*: Ayres, *Mawson*, 70.

83 *It seems likely that the true*: Branagan, *David*, 225.

84 *Barton's even gloomier assessment*: http://www.youtube.com/watch?v=u9jXbD5hZFI.

84 *As one of the experts who examined*: Branagan, *David*, 224–25.

84 *Upon regaining the* Nimrod: Ayres, *Mawson*, 28.

84 *Meanwhile, he dipped his toe*: Ibid., 37–41.

85 *He had made many visits*: Ibid., 29–30; P. Mawson, *Mawson of the Antarctic*, 47.

85 *"He had turned and smiled"*: P. Mawson, *Mawson of the Antarctic*, 47.

85 *"dark-haired, ivory-skinned"*: Ayres, *Mawson*, 29.

85 *Almost six feet tall*: McEwin, *An Antarctic Affair*, 27.

86 *"Who's that?"*: Flannery, *This Everlasting Silence*, 1, 16.

86 *"Her flashing black eyes"*: Ibid., 2.

86 *Once again taking a leave*: Ayres, *Mawson*, 31–32.

87 *"On no account see Scott"*: Ibid., 32.

87 *"a professed liar"*: Huntford, *Shackleton*, 304.

87 *Supported by his patrons*: Ibid., 308–9.

87 *"I have no connection"*: Ayres, *Mawson*, 32–33.

87 *Yet at the same time, Mawson*: Ibid., 39.

88 *"He offered me not less"*: MAD, 53.

88 *"I did not like Dr. Wilson"*: Ibid.

89 *"I have decided to go to the coast"*: Ibid., 54.

89 *"there was little hope"*: Ibid.

89 *The last straw came*: Ayres, *Mawson*, 45.

89 *"When it comes to the moral side"*: Douglas Mawson to H. R. Mill, July 18, 1922, quoted in Riffenburgh, *Aurora*, 58.

90 *"One day he telephoned me"*: P. Mawson, *Mawson of the Antarctic*, 47.

90 *"While the family were making music"*: Ibid.

90 *"My Dear Dr Delprat"*: Douglas Mawson to Guillaume Delprat, December 7, 1910, quoted in Flannery, *This Everlasting Silence*, 7–8.

90 *Mindful of the mining tycoon's*: Ibid., 8–9.

91 *"I fully approve of you"*: Guillaume Delprat to Douglas Mawson, December 8, 1910, quoted ibid., 10–11.

91 *They were formally engaged*: P. Mawson, *Mawson of the Antarctic*, 48.

93 *In his official account*: HOB, 2.

93 *After endless machinations*: Riffenburgh, *Aurora*, 62–63.

94 *"looked thinner"*: P. Mawson, *Mawson of the Antarctic*, 51.

94 *"I think we shall all be glad"*: Ibid.

94 *With Davis at the helm*: Riffenburgh, *Aurora*, 72.

94 *Ninnis, the young lieutenant*: Ibid., 52–53.

94 *Mertz, a lawyer from Basel*: Ibid., 67.

95 *"The only two idlers in the ship"*: Crossley, *Trial by Ice*, 11.

95 *The proximity of males and females*: Riffenburgh, *Aurora*, 77.

95 *Then several of the dogs*: Ibid., 81.

95 *"a mysterious hysterical disease"*: Ibid., 96, 453; Landy, "Pibloktoq (Hysteria) and Inuit Nutrition," 237–39.

95 *In any event, by the time*: Riffenburgh, *Aurora*, 102.

96 *"I remember feeling"*: Frank Wild to Maggie Wild, October 13, 1911, quoted ibid, 91.

97 *Discovered accidentally in 1810*: http://en.wikipedia.org/wiki/Macquarie_Island.

97 *On the afternoon of December 2*: Riffenburgh, *Aurora*, 102.

97 *Besides the thirty-eight huskies*: HOB, 14.

97 *Realizing that even an overloaded*: Riffenburgh, *Aurora*, 101–2.

97 *"If the skipper had a proper name"*: Laseron, "South with Mawson," 12.

98 *"The mate was deaf"*: Ibid.

98 *On the first day out of Hobart*: Davis, *High Latitude*, 163–64.

98 *"The crew are about the worst"*: Charles Laseron, diary, December 25, 1911.

98 *"The cook we have signed on"*:

Percy Gray, diary, December 3, 1911.

98 *"I shall be very sorry"*: Gray, diary, December 18, 1911.

99 *"The mate could navigate"*: Laseron, "South with Mawson," 12–13.

99 *"I have found this bloody island"*: Hunter, diary, December 13, 1911.

99 *On December 9, the worst*: Riffenburgh, *Aurora*, 103.

99 *"They were staggered by its beauty"*: Ibid., 106.

100 *"I felt that had I sufficient"*: Hurley, *Argonauts*, 24.

100 *"Fortunately we were not moving"*: Crossley, *Trial by Ice*, 13.

100 *"I received a verbal trouncing"*: Hurley, *Argonauts*, 25.

101 *His biographer, Alasdair McGregor*: McGregor, *Hurley*, 10–11.

101 *"I found a new toy"*: Hurley, *Argonauts*, 10.

101 *By 1911, Hurley was recognized*: McGregor, *Hurley*, 28–31.

102 *"I am certain that"*: Margaret Hurley to Douglas Mawson, October 6, 1911, quoted ibid., 32.

102 *Mawson was sufficiently alarmed*: McGregor, *Hurley*, 32–33.

102 *"evidently a recent victim"*: HOB, 21.

102 *"a human figure appeared"*: Ibid.

103 *After several aborted efforts*: Ibid., 22.

103 *In charge of the Macquarie party*: Riffenburgh, *Aurora*, 214–15.

103 *In Hasselborough Bay, the two*: Crossley, *Trial by Ice*, 14.

103 *Meanwhile, Frank Hurley set off*: Hurley, *Argonauts*, 25.

104 *"They slaughtered every flipper"*: Ibid., 28–30.

104 *The first night, the trio bivouacked*: Ibid., 31.

105 *On the second day, the men*: Ibid., 32–33.

105 *"peck[ing] viciously at our legs"*: Ibid., 34.

105 *It was not until the third afternoon*: Ibid., 35–38.

106 *During Hurley's absence*: HOB, 24–25.

106 *On top of Wireless Hill*: Riffenburgh, *Aurora*, 111.

106 *"The sheep allowed themselves"*: Frank Stillwell, general letter, January 6, 1912, quoted ibid., 112–13.

106 *"The last few days"*: Flannery, *This Everlasting Silence*, 24.

107 *"their cheers echoing to ours"*: HOB, 27.

107 *"It was difficult at first"*: Ibid., 28.

107 *"I jumped up on deck"*: Crossley, *Trial by Ice*, 15.

108 *Mawson and Davis's intention*: Ibid.

108 *But between Oates Land*: Rosove, *Let Heroes Speak*, 109–13.

108 *In January 1840, Wilkes thought*: Ibid., 35–37.

108 *At almost the same time in early 1840*: Ibid., 30–32.

109 *Astonishingly, on January 29*: Ibid., 32.

109 *Five days after leaving Macquarie*: HOB, 31.

109 *"The tranquility of the water"*: Ibid., 32.

109 *The icebergs soon gave way*: Crossley, *Trial by Ice*, 16–17.

110 *It would take another year*: HOB, 37.

110 *New Year's Day*: Crossley, *Trial by Ice*, 17.

110 *"We were all very much puzzled"*: Ibid., 18.

111 *"What an extraordinary thing"*: Ibid., 19.

111 *One of the chief objectives*: HOB, 40.

111 *"I feel that we must take chances"*: Crossley, *Trial by Ice*, 19.

111 *Privately, he began to reconfigure*: Riffenburgh, *Aurora*, 115–16.

111 *It was only on January 6*: Ibid., 116.

112 *"The coroners verdict"*: Kennedy, diary, January 6, 1912.

112 *At noon on January 8*: HOB, 40.

112 *"Advancing towards the mainland"*: Ibid., 41.

112 *"We had come to a fairyland"*: Hurley, *Argonauts*, 44–45.

113 *"Accidentally hit Bickerton in the eye"*: Kennedy, diary, January 8, 1912.

4. THE HOME OF THE BLIZZARD

114 *"By the time we had reached"*: HOB, 42.

115 *On one windy day*: Ibid., 43.

115 *Still the wind increased*: Ibid., 43–44.

115 *"I feel that I have not an officer"*: Crossley, *Trial by Ice*, 22.

115 *"It is his one hobby"*: Gray, diary, January 23, 1912.

116 *"They are beautiful birds"*: McLean, diary, January 14, 1912.

116 *"I shall be glad now"*: Gray, diary, January 5, 1912.

116 *The unloading proceeded*: HOB, 44.

116 *"We have been quite"*: Crossley, *Trial by Ice*, 23.

116 *"a great assortment of material"*: HOB, 44.

117 *the first crossing*: Rosove, *Let Heroes Speak*, 56.

117 *"long purple stockings"*: McLean, diary, January 19, 1912.

117 *The men sang "Auld Lang Syne"*: Riffenburgh, *Aurora*, 121.

117 *Last to leave was Mawson*: Davis, *High Latitude*, 170.

117 *"rather a pull"*: Laseron, diary, January 19, 1912.

117 *"we steamed away"*: Mills, *Wild*, 139.

117 *"The whole thing impressed me"*: Gray, diary, January 20, 1912.

117 *"I could have wept"*: Ninnis, diary, January 19, 1912, quoted in Riffenburgh, *Aurora*, 121.

118 *"They are a fine party"*: Crossley, *Trial by Ice*, 24.

118 *As the* Aurora *steamed away*: Wild, Memoirs, 123.

118 *Once again Davis fumed*: Crossley, *Trial by Ice*, 24.

118 *"I only wish that our observations"*: Ibid., 25.

119 *"We have still about 200 tons"*: Ibid., 26–29.

119 *"At 8. o'clock last night"*: Gray, diary, February 5, 1912.

120 *"We have just got enough"*: Ibid.

120 *"but there is such a crowd"*: Ibid.

120 *"I am feeling very low"*: Crossley, *Trial by Ice*, 30–31.

120 *"I do not know that"*: Ibid., 31.

121 *"I had hoped that"*: Ibid., 32–33.

121 *"Wild . . . reported that the land"*: Ibid., 32.

122 *The day after Wild*: Wild, Memoirs, 125–26.

122 *Knowing, however, that this desperate*: Ibid., 126.

122 *There followed a frenzy*: Ibid.

122 *"The party themselves do not seem to be"*: Crossley, *Trial by Ice*, 35.

123 *"I am a very poor hand"*: Mills, *Wild*, 142.

123 *"In the event of the* Aurora*"*: Davis, *High Latitude*, 223.

123 *"Wild's party is camped"*: Wild, Memoirs, 126.

124 *Back at Cape Denison*: Laseron, "South with Mawson," 37.

124 *"My first experience of a sleeping bag"*: Hunter, diary, January 16, 1912.

124 *"Come on, Joe"*: Laseron, "South with Mawson," 40.

125 *The prefabricated hut*: Riffenburgh, *Aurora*, 121–23.

125 *"Not a very big room," Laseron observed*: Laseron, "South with Mawson," 37.

125 *Since the* Aurora *had brought*: HOB, 55.

125 *"We, who were inexperienced"*: Hurley, *Argonauts*, 47.

127 *"Doctor Mertz was sitting"*: Ibid., 47–48.

127 *On January 30, for the first time*: HOB, 58.

127 *Frank Bickerton, the twenty-two-year-old*: Riffenburgh, *Aurora*, 125.

127 *"By the light of the ruby lamp"*: Hurley, *Argonauts*, 49.

128 *"Hannam is our 'Ring Snorer'"*: Hunter, diary, February 16, 1912.

128 *"The first day that the stove"*: Laseron, "South with Mawson," 43.

128 *As the months wore on*: Ibid., 45.

129 *"The rest [of the poems]"*: McLean, diary, February 18, 1912.

129 *Another of Mawson's favorite works*: Hunter, diary, May 14, 1912.

129 *The small library*: List of books, AAE.

129 *"I have always thought"*: Hunter, diary, January 30, 1912.

130 *Some were mere shorthand*: Laseron, "South with Mawson," 53.

130 *Other nicknames for the physician*: Hunter, diary, March 22, 1912.

130 *Hurley became Hoyle*: Laseron, "South with Mawson," 47.

130 *The architect Alfred Hodgeman*: Hunter, diary, March 22, 1912.

130 *Bob Bage, a twenty-three-year-old*: Ibid., April 17, 1912.

130 *The overweight Walter Hannam*: Ibid., April 24, 1912.

130 *Leslie Whetter, clumsy and inclined*: Laseron, "South with Mawson," 53.

130 *"Close was a great reader"*: Ibid., 52–53.

130 *Of the thirty-eight huskies*: HOB, 61.

131 *"Basilisk was the king"*: Laseron, "South with Mawson," 46.

131 *By early autumn*: Riffenburgh, *Aurora*, 126–27.

131 *Much closer to the huts*: Ibid., 158–59.

132 *"On the very first night"*: Laseron, "South with Mawson," 41.

132 *The stove inside the hut*: HOB, 71.

133 *"One evening, when we"*: Ibid., 65.

133 *"The Doctor says"*: Hannam, diary, March 15, 1912.

133 *"I had to go on all fours"*: MAD, 60–61.

133 *"To illustrate the pace"*: Hurley, *Argonauts*, 57.

134 *"Then with practice"*: Laseron, "South with Mawson," 55.

134 *"Day by day throughout March"*: Ibid.

134 *"for a sustained velocity"*: Ibid.

134 *"In such a position"*: HOB, 69.

135 *"No sooner would one"*: Ibid.

135 *During the first month and a half*: Ibid., 70.

135 *"Articles of value"*: Ibid., 80–81.

135 *"whirlwinds of a few yards"*: Ibid., 77–79.

136 *"On such occasions"*: Ibid., 77.

136 *On February 29, he took*: Riffenburgh, *Aurora*, 128.

136 *"Heavy pulling, drift"*: *MAD*, 60.

137 *"I have never met"*: Eric Webb to A. G. E. Jones, May 20, 1980, quoted in Riffenburgh, *Aurora*, 128.

137 *"I had just erected"*: Hurley, *Argonauts*, 58–59.

138 *"Leaving the door"*: *HOB*, 84–85.

138 *"Poor Hodgeman"*: Laseron, diary, April 5, 1912.

138 *"no doubt disgusted"*: *HOB*, 72.

139 *"We dwelt on the fringe"*: Ibid., 88.

139 *Eighty-five years later*: Wendler, et al., "On the Extraordinary Katabatic Winds of Adélie Land," 4473.

139 *Every morning precisely*: Mawson, "Report of Main Base."

140 *"The nightwatchman is to sift"*: Mawson, "Instructions to Night Watchman."

140 *"A final duty is that of emptying"*: Mawson, "Messman's Duties."

140 *"The 'pièce de résistance'"*: Mawson, "Cook's Notices."

140 *"No unnecessary refinements"*: *HOB*, 59.

141 *"To our sweethearts and wives"*: Harrisson, diary, n.d.

141 *"Dinner is ready"*: Laseron, "South with Mawson," 68–69.

141 *The monthly issue*: Hunter, diary, June 29, 1912.

141 *The most spirited wagers*: Ibid., May 1, 1912.

141 *"No one washes"*: Laseron, "South with Mawson," 65.

142 *"Three months without a bath"*: Hunter, diary, March 15, 1912.

142 *"Tonight I have had"*: Hannam, diary, February 14, 1912.

142 *John Hunter recorded*: Hunter, diary, July 14, 1912.

142 *"the life and soul"*: Laseron, diary, February 16, 1912.

142 *"Hurley caused some amusement"*: Hunter, diary, March 18, 1912.

142 *"On February 17, after dinner"*: Laseron, "South with Mawson," 47.

143 *"At dinner Hurley"*: Hunter, diary, March 10, 1912.

143 *Thirty-two years old, from an affluent*: Riffenburgh, *Aurora*, 89.

143 *What Mawson probably did not know*: Watson, *The Spy Who Loved Children*; Rossiter, *Lady Spy, Gentleman Explorer*.

143 *"Herbert fidgets"*: Laseron, "South with Mawson," 70.

144 *Along with the gramophone*: McLean, diary, June 6, 1912.

144 *"Today is best described"*: Ibid., March 27, 1912

144 *"Breakfast, 9 am"*: *MAD*, 94.

145 *"was a marvel"*: *HOB*, 111–12.

145 *" 'Championship' "*: Ibid., 100.

145 *"I don't know what we should do"*: Hunter, diary, April 9, 1912.

145 *Walter Hannam opened*: Hannam, diary, *passim*.

145 *Mawson himself began*: *MAD*, 77.

146 *"an exhilarating"*: Laseron, "South with Mawson," 57–58.

146 *"This adhered firmly"*: *HOB*, 86.

147 *The masts had been shipped*: Riffenburgh, *Aurora*, 158–59.

147 *"Given a few days"*: Hannam, diary, April 21, 1912.

147 *In the wind, the construction project*: Riffenburgh, *Aurora*, 159.

147 *"something over 17 stone"*: Hannam, diary, July 6, 1912.

147 *Instead it fell*: MAD, 102

147 *"Had a very bad turn"*: Hannam, diary, March 25, 1912.

147 *His most oft-repeated*: Ibid., passim.

147 *On May 15, Mawson told Hannam*: Ibid., May 15, 1912.

148 *But on February 14, they established*: HOB, 349.

148 *The linkage worked so well*: George Ainsworth, "A Land of Storm and Mist," in *HOB*, 381.

148 *It was not until September 12*: Ibid., 377.

148 *On October 13, dubbed*: MAD, 121–22.

148 *Between March and October*: Laseron, "South with Mawson," 60

149 *In May 1912, for thirty-one*: HOB, 94–95.

149 *"The day's tasks are ended"*: Laseron, "South with Mawson," 62.

149 *"The whole world is asleep"*: HOB, 104.

150 *"We have made a successful landing"*: Flannery, *This Everlasting Silence*, 29.

150 *"I have concluded"*: Ibid., 46.

151 *"It is one of the Doc's"*: Hunter, diary, September 30, 1912.

151 *"We now like"*: Laseron, diary, February 18, 1912.

151 *Madigan's decision to accept*: Riffenburgh, *Aurora*, 90.

151 *It was Madigan who coined*: Ninnis, diary, April 1, 1912, quoted in Riffenburgh, *Aurora*, 150.

152 *"Cecil had been 'Maddy' "*: D. Madigan, *Vixere Fortes*, 249.

152 *"with his usual clumsiness"*: Ibid., 263.

152 *"was as loyal as"*: Ibid., 265.

152 *"treated them like children"*: Ibid., 266.

152 *"His temperament was naturally equable"*: Ibid., 266.

152 *"irremediably prosaic"*: Ibid., 266–67.

153 *"Hurricane gusty"*: MAD, 60–61.

154 *"but I was sorry to see"*: Ibid., 78.

154 *"First are the accomplished"*: Ibid.

154 *"At breakfast Whetter"*: Ibid., 88.

154 *The next day, Mawson observed*: Ibid., 89.

155 *"Whetter was sick"*: Ibid., 90.

155 *"We then had a long talk"*: Ibid., 92.

155 *"Whetter has apparently drunk"*: Ibid., 97.

156 *On the* Belgica *expedition*: Cook, *Through the First Antarctic Night*, passim.

156 *"Whetter of course"*: Hunter, diary, March 22, 1912.

156 *"Whetter is a conundrum"*: Ibid., June 15, 1912.

156 *"Whetter was incurably lazy"*: D. Madigan, *Vixere Fortes*, 268.

157 *"He appears to have changed"*: Mawson, notes on Whetter.

157 *"At something to 4 pm"*: MAD, 115.

158 *"I gave quite a long address"*: Ibid., 116.

158 *According to historian Beau Riffenburgh*: Riffenburgh, *Aurora*, 415.

158 *"Whetter cooks but"*: MAD, 90.

158 *"Close has been laid up"*: Ibid., 97.

158 *"Close has put in much time"*: Ibid., 101.

159 *"He cannot yet read"*: Hunter, diary, April 7, 1912.

159 *"his deep breathing exercises"*: Ibid., May 3, 1912.

159 *"Poor old John Close"*: Ibid., May 17, 1912.

159 *"little acetylene bombs"*: Ibid., May 3, 1912.

159 *"There was one member"*: Laseron, "South with Mawson," 54–55.

160 *"rather vanished from sight"*: Riffenburgh, *Aurora*, 415.

5. THE PAINFUL SILENCE

163 *The prefabricated building*: Riffenburgh, *Aurora*, 140.

163 *"Mr. Wild"*: Mills, *Wild*, 143.

163 *"Mawson not only was driven"*: Riffenburgh, *Aurora*, 194.

163 *Wild had grown up*: Butler, *Quest*, 3.

163 *"As far back"*: Wild, Memoirs, quoted ibid., 136.

164 *At the age of sixteen, Wild*: Butler, *Quest*, 8.

164 *he would not marry*: Ibid., 22.

164 *He stood only*: Ibid., 3, 8–9.

164 *"It was more than affection"*: Laseron, "South with Mawson," 153–54.

165 *"refused to do any work"*: Wild, Memoirs, quoted in Butler, *Quest*, 136.

165 *But on March 13, just as a prolonged*: Ibid., 131–32.

165 *"This bad weather had its compensations"*: Ibid., 131.

165 *The one serious oversight*: Riffenburgh, *Aurora*, 141.

166 *"If we were to fall"*: Morton Moyes, "There Was No Ship," quoted in Riffenburgh, *Aurora*, 141.

166 *Instead of Mawson's day-long program*: Frank Wild, "Report on Operations," quoted in Riffenburgh, *Aurora*, 194.

166 *"Two medals were struck"*: Ibid., 197.

166 *"though diverting"*: Sydney Jones, loose notes, June 30, 1912, quoted in Riffenburgh, *Aurora*, 197.

166 *Instead, Wild devised golf balls*: Ibid.; Kennedy, diary, May 17, 1912.

166 *According to twenty-two-year-old*: Kennedy, diary, April 8, 1912.

166 *Eager to make the best use*: Wild, Memoirs, quoted in Butler, *Quest*, 132.

167 *"and we all had falls"*: Ibid.

167 *"We crossed one"*: Ibid.

167 *The weather was so fiendish*: Ibid., 135.

167 *"When it is understood"*: Ibid., 133.

167 *On the move again*: Ibid.

168 *On March 21, a seven-day storm*: Ibid.

168 *In the end, Wild's team*: Ibid., 134.

168 *"Unable to stand"*: Kennedy, diary, April 5, 1912.

169 *The most persistent source of conflict*: Riffenburgh, *Aurora*, 194–95.

169 *"Wondering when the buckets of kerosene"*: Moyes, diary, August 11, 1912.

171 *November 6 was fixed*: HOB, 136.

171 *"Should I or my party"*: Douglas Mawson to J. K. Davis, loose note, Mawson Collection.

171 *"the most popular man of the party"*: Hunter, diary, April 17, 1912.

172 *"What a God forsaken country"*: Hunter, diary, and Laseron, diary, November 14, 1912, quoted in Riffenburgh, *Aurora*, 254.

172 *Sixty-seven and a half miles*: Hurley, *Argonauts*, 71.

172 *Even before reaching Cape Denison*: Laseron, "South with Mawson," 87.

172 *To vary the regimen*: HOB, 142.

172 *The staple main course*: Laseron, "South with Mawson," 87.

173 *"if the weather was good"*: Ibid.

173 *Made of japara*: Ibid., 85.

173 *the three-man tent combined*: HOB, 140.

173 *The tent was supported*: Laseron, "South with Mawson," 85–86.

174 *"First, enough large blocks"*: Ibid., 86.

174 *"an amazing field of huge"*: Hurley, *Argonauts*, 77.

174 *"suddenly I dropped through"*: Ibid., 78–79.

175 *On December 12, at a spot*: Bage, narrative, quoted in HOB, 214.

175 *They called it the Lucky Depot*: Hurley, *Argonauts*, 81.

175 *Finally, on December 21, the men knew*: Bage, narrative, quoted in HOB, 216; Hurley, *Argonauts*, 80.

175 *"What a temptation to go on"*: Hurley, *Argonauts*, 80–81.

175 *"It was . . . Midsummer Day"*: Bage, narrative, quoted in HOB, 217.

175 *On December 27, they regained*: Hurley, *Argonauts*, 81–82.

176 *"a record for man-hauling"*: HOB, 219.

176 *But slowly the men's optimism*: Ibid., 219–20.

176 *On January 4, the men reached*: Ibid., 220.

176 *By January 8, all the men had left*: Bage, narrative, quoted in HOB, 220.

176 *"Matter of life and death"*: Webb, diary, January 8–9, 1912.

176 *"I've dined in many places"*: Hurley, *Argonauts*, 86–87.

177 *"There was only one thing"*: Bage, narrative, quoted in HOB, 220.

177 *"the worst day's march"*: Ibid., 221.

177 *Two days later, guessing*: Ibid., 222.

177 *"The most memorable day"*: Webb, diary, January 10, 1912.

177 *"Never had I seen the Antarctic appear"*: Hurley, *Argonauts*, 93.

177 *"We three had never thought"*: Bage, narrative, quoted in HOB, 223.

178 *"The information brought back"*: HOB, 223.

178 *"A refuge from the hurricane"*: Ibid., 120–21.

179 *On November 17, 25 miles out*: Ibid., 224.

180 *"was quite a knife-edge"*: Ibid., 226.

180 *"I cannot say"*: Madigan, narrative, quoted in HOB, 227.

180 *Then, on December 2, the trio*: Ibid., 229–31.

180 *Back on land on December 17*: Ibid., 231–32.

181 *some 270 miles*: Laseron, "South with Mawson," 143.

181 *"a narrow ridge of hard snow"*: Madigan, narrative, quoted in HOB, 235.

181 *Like Bage's party, Madigan's*: Ibid., 236–38.

181 *"by this I mean"*: Davis, *High Latitude*, 196.

181 *It was only ten hours later*: Laseron, "South with Mawson," 140.

181 *"We were laden with mail"*: Davis, *High Latitude*, 197.

182 *Of the keenest interest*: Riffenburgh, *Aurora*, 252.

182 *"Australia had lost"*: Laseron, "South with Mawson," 141.

182 *"Dr Mawson is out 66 days"*: Crossley, *Trial by Ice*, 51.

182 *It was not until December 3*: Haddelsey, *Born Adventurer*, 77.

183 *"Very soon the engine"*: HOB, 243–44.

183 *"We were very sorry"*: Frank Bickerton, "Western Sledging Journey," quoted in Haddelsey, *Born Adventurer*, 78–79.

183 *"by lunch time I felt"*: Bickerton, "A Log of the Western Journey," December 5, 1912, quoted in Haddelsey, *Born Adventurer*, 79.

183 *Six miles out from Cathedral Grotto*: Haddelsey, *Born Adventurer*, 79–80.

184 *"did not appear"*: Bickerton, "Log," December 5, 1912, quoted ibid., 80.

184 *The leader's first guess*: Ibid.

184 *Forty-nine years would elapse*: Haddesley, *Born Adventurer*, 80.

184 *Since then, Antarctica*: Riffenburgh, *Aurora*, 282.

184 *One of them, retrieved in 2003*: http://www1.nasa.gov/home/hqnews/2004/jul/HQ_04232_meteorite.html.

184 *"This is a dismal"*: Bickerton, "Log," quoted in Haddelsey, *Born Adventurer*, 86.

184 *During their first week*: Haddelsey, *Born Adventurer*, 83.

184 *Then, on December 12, a mishap*: Ibid., 86–87.

185 *On five successive days*: Ibid., 90–91.

185 *The team's last outward march*: Ibid., 91.

185 *"I have decided this"*: Bickerton, "Log," December 26, 1912, quoted ibid., 92.

185 *The men started back*: Haddelsey, *Born Adventurer*, 93–94.

185 *"a narrow squeal"*: Leslie Whetter to Robert Edgar Waite, March 3, 1913, quoted ibid., 105.

185 *During the next three weeks*: Haddelsey, *Born Adventurer*, 94–99.

186 *"His diary becomes a dialogue"*: Ibid., 99.

186 *On January 15, the men came*: Ibid., 99–100.

186 *"I could have jumped"*: Bickerton, "Log," January 16, 1913, quoted ibid., 100.

186 *On the 17th, just as navigational*: Haddelsey, *Born Adventurer*, 102.

186 *"We flung off our harnesses"*: Bickerton, "Log," January 17, 1913, quoted ibid., 102.

187 *"All was very quiet"*: Bickerton, "Log," n.d., quoted ibid., 103.

187 *"atrocious weather conditions"*: HOB, 247.

187 *"Then Thank God"*: Crossley, *Trial by Ice*, 52.

188 *"There is still no news"*: Ibid., 52–53.

188 *"There is still no sign"*: Ibid., 53–55.

188 *"As day by day"*: Laseron, "South with Mawson," 147.

189 *"considered the best surgeon"*: Kennedy, diary, January 21, 1912, quoted in Riffenburgh, *Aurora*, 314.

189 *Wild had been ordered*: Wild, Memoirs, quoted in Butler, *Quest*, 150.

190 *The men set off*: HOB, 301.

190 *weeklong detour*: Ibid., 304–5.

190 *"The sound of their cries"*: Sydney Jones, narrative, quoted in HOB, 305–6.

190 *Intending a visit*: Ibid., 305–7.

191 *"We had pepper"*: Dovers, diary,

November 27, 1912, quoted in Riffenburgh, *Aurora*, 312.

191 *By December 3, the men had returned*: HOB, 307–8.

191 *On top, the men found two*: Ibid., 310.

192 *Jones calculated that*: Jones, narrative, quoted in *HOB*, 310.

192 *"concluding," as Mawson*: HOB, 311.

192 *In late August, still under wintry*: Wild, Memoirs, quoted in Butler, *Quest*, 141.

192 *"Many of the gusts"*: Ibid., 142.

193 *Morton Moyes, another of Mawson's*: Riffenburgh, *Aurora*, 306–7.

193 *"As on the return"*: Wild, Memoirs, quoted in Butler, *Quest*, 144.

193 *"Zip broke loose"*: Wild, narrative, quoted in *HOB*, 289.

193 *On October 30, the four men*: Ibid., 286–87.

193 *There they received a rude shock*: Wild, Memoirs, quoted in Butler, *Quest*, 144–45.

194 *"I cannot go back"*: Harrisson, diary, n.d.

194 *"I was extremely sorry"*: Wild, Memoirs, quoted in Butler, *Quest*, 145.

194 *Only two days beyond the Hippo*: Ibid.

194 *It would later be named*: http://data.aad.gov.au/aadc/gaz/display_name.cfm?gaz_id=537.

194 *"Cascades of shattered ice"*: Charles Harrisson, report on an episode of the sledging journey, quoted in Riffenburgh, *Aurora*, 295.

194 *"To cross where we were"*: Watson, diary, November 17, 1912, quoted in Riffenburgh, *Aurora*, 295.

195 *"the most wonderful sight"*: Wild, Memoirs, quoted in Butler, *Quest*, 145.

195 *"The Denman Glacier moves"*: Ibid., 145–46.

195 *"hauling up and lowering"*: Ibid., 146.

195 *On November 26, a full day*: Ibid.

195 *"We turn back tomorrow"*: Ibid., 147.

196 *"Wild gave me his Diaries"*: Moyes, diary, October 28, 1912.

196 *"George [Dovers] gave me"*: Ibid., November 4, 1912.

196 *"Seems strange to lose"*: Ibid., October 30, 1912.

196 *"Had a few ski runs"*: Ibid., November 11, 1912.

197 *"Harrisson out 26 days"*: Ibid., November 24, 1912.

197 *"Harrisson must be short"*: Ibid., November 25, 1912.

197 *"Like to know where Harrisson is"*: Ibid., November 30, 1912.

197 *"I. May have gone"*: Ibid., December 3, 1912.

198 *"Harrisson with his dogs"*: Morton Moyes, "Season in Solitary," 21, quoted in Riffenburgh, *Aurora*, 307.

198 *Zigzagging to try*: Riffenburgh, *Aurora*, 307–8.

198 *"The silence is so painful"*: Moyes, diary, December 20, 1912.

198 *"Christmas Eve!"*: Ibid., December 24, 1912.

198 *As John King Davis would point out*: Davis, *High Latitude*, 225.

199 *"one of the most remarkable"*: Byrd, "Our Navy Explores Antarctica," 429–522.

199 *"Switzerland had to be killed"*: Wild, Memoirs, quoted in Butler, *Quest*, 148.

199 *"started whining and crying"*: Harrisson, diary, December 6, 1912,

quoted in Riffenburgh, *Aurora*, 299.

199 *One day Watson fell*: Wild, Memoirs, quoted in Butler, *Quest*, 147.

199 *"a little bottle"*: Watson, diary, December 25, 1912, quoted in Riffenburgh, *Aurora*, 302.

199 *"formally took possession"*: Wild, Memoirs, quoted in Butler, *Quest*, 149.

199 *"Another year gone"*: Moyes, diary, December 31, 1912.

199 *"If this proportion of blizzards"*: Ibid., January 5, 1913.

200 *"A man can be lonely"*: J. Moyes, *Exploring the Antarctic*, 52.

200 *"You are going dippy"*: Ibid., 53.

200 *"I rushed outside"*: Moyes, diary, January 6, 1913.

200 *"When he saw"*: Wild, Memoirs, quoted in Butler, *Quest*, 150.

200 *"Feel like a 2-year old"*: Moyes, diary, January 6, 1913.

200 *They packed up*: Riffenburgh, *Aurora*, 316.

200 *"The Aurora should have been in"*: Moyes, diary, January 31, 1913.

200 *"The food supply would have been"*: Wild, "Report on Operations," quoted in Riffenburgh, *Aurora*, 317.

201 *Adding to the men's anxiety*: Riffenburgh, *Aurora*, 318.

201 *"had erected direction boards"*: Wild, Memoirs, quoted in Butler, *Quest*, 152.

201 *"We surmise that one"*: Harrisson, diary, February 16, 1913.

201 *On February 20, Wild and Dovers*: Wild, "Report on Operations," quoted in Riffenburgh, *Aurora*, 318.

201 *"Started the [acetylene] gas"*:

Moyes, diary, February 16, 1913.

201 *"No ship yet."*: Ibid., February 22, 1913.

6. DEAD EASY TO DIE

202 *"Should I or my party"*: Douglas Mawson to J. K. Davis, n.d., Mawson Collection.

203 *In fact, just the previous year*: Cherry-Garrard, *The Worst Journey in the World, passim*.

203 *On January 22, 1913, Davis*: Crossley, *Trial by Ice*, 54.

203 *A first draft of Davis's orders*: Davis, draft note, January 22, 1913, Mawson Collection.

204 *"My darling, this expedition"*: Cecil Madigan to Wynnis Wollaston, January 25–28, 1913, quoted in Hoerr, *Clipped Wings*, 206.

204 *"So the only thing"*: Frank Bickerton to Dorothea Bussell, January 31, 1913, quoted in Haddelsey, *Born Adventurer*, 106.

205 *"We clear out"*: Gray, diary, January 17, 1913.

205 *"As a matter of fact"*: Ibid.

205 *"We went about our tasks"*: Laseron, "South with Mawson," 148.

205 *There was much to do*: Ibid.

205 *Now Davis revised*: Crossley, *Trial by Ice*, 54.

205 *"Our sleeping-bags"*: Hurley, *Argonauts*, 96.

206 *"Through the glasses"*: Ibid., 96–97.

206 *"Most of the ice"*: Davis, *High Latitude*, 207.

206 *On January 29, the day before*: Crossley, *Trial by Ice*, 57–58.

207 *But now, once again, the fiendish weather*: Ibid., 59–61.

207 *They began to fear that the* Aurora: Hurley, *Argonauts*, 98.

207 *"From masthead to waterline"*: Ibid., 99.

208 *"As we drew away"*: Ibid.

208 *"We were all heartily glad"*: McLean, diary, February 8, 1913, quoted in Haddelsey, *Born Adventurer*, 107.

209 *The two men now had food*: HOB, 164.

210 *That jaunt was a wild downhill*: Ibid., 165.

210 *With only a spare tent cover*: Ibid., 166.

210 *"Up 10 am"*: MAD, 150.

211 *"On December 15th, we didn't sleep"*: Mertz, diary, December 16, 1912.

211 *"Now when I think"*: Ibid.

211 *"Our only comfort"*: Ibid., December 14, 1912.

211 *"Our companion, comrade"*: HOB, 163.

211 *The two men now considered*: Ibid., 166.

211 *On December 16, Mawson suffered*: MAD, 151.

211 *"Johnson gave in"*: Ibid.,

212 *"The dogs now do nothing"*: Ibid.

212 *"As we could see nothing"*: Mertz, diary, December 17, 1912.

212 *"How lunch would have tasted"*: Ibid.

212 *"The course can be only"*: MAD, 152.

212 *"Beyond the dismal whining"*: HOB, 169–70.

213 *"To go forward"*: Mertz, diary, December 18, 1912.

213 *That day, the character*: HOB, 171.

213 *That same day, Mawson*: Ibid., 172.

213 *"Splendid weather"*: Mertz, diary, December 20, 1912.

214 *"In the snow-blind light"*: HOB, 169.

214 *Hunger had become*: Ibid., 170.

214 *"they were seized"*: Ibid., 172.

214 *"'Haldane' collapsed"*: Mertz, diary, December 21, 1912.

215 *On the 21st they reduced the load*: MAD, 153.

215 *"a revolting and depressing operation"*: HOB, 174.

215 *On the 23rd, the men discarded*: Ibid., 175.

215 *That day Mertz calculated*: Mertz, diary, December 23, 1912.

215 *"Very hungry tonight"*: MAD, 153.

215 *"I found two bits"*: Ibid., 154.

215 *"At 1 am, Mawson woke"*: Mertz, diary, December 25, 1912.

216 *On Christmas Day, the men covered*: HOB, 176–77.

216 *The next day, however, they were slowed*: Ibid., 177.

216 *In the high wind*: MAD, 154.

216 *Yet another tribulation*: Ibid., 178.

217 *"The drift is uncomfortable"*: Mertz, diary, December 27, 1912.

217 *"I promised to do all I could"*: MAD, 154.

217 *During these days, dog meat*: HOB, 178.

217 *Only Ginger was still alive*: MAD, 154–55.

217 *"As we worked"*: HOB, 178–79.

217 *On the 29th, the men broke*: MAD, 155.

218 *"The tent is too small"*: Mertz, diary, December 29, 1912.

218 *Yet during the second shift*: HOB, 179.

218 *Mertz's diary entry for December 30*: Mertz, diary, December 30, 1912.

218 *"Xavier off colour"*: MAD, 156.

218 *"when I realized that my companion"*: HOB, 179–80.

218 *"under wretched conditions"*: Ibid., 180.

219 *"Now it's 2 o'clock"*: Mertz, diary, December 31, 1912.

219 *"he had found the dog meat"*: HOB, 180.

219 *"Can't be sure exactly"*: MAD, 156.

219 *"It's not good weather"*: Mertz, diary, January 1, 1913.

219 *"Mertz boiled a small cocoa"*: MAD, 156.

220 *"To convince himself"*: HOB, 182.

220 *"Intended getting up"*: MAD, 156–57.

220 *"I found that, like myself"*: HOB, 181.

220 *"All will depend"*: MAD, 157.

220 *By now, Mertz could not even eat*: HOB, 181.

221 *"cooking more meat"*: Ibid., 182–83.

221 *"The grade was slightly downhill"*: Ibid., 183.

221 *"quite dizzy"*: MAD, 157.

221 *The men had not gone far*: HOB, 183.

221 *"Mertz was depressed"*: Ibid.

222 *"Things are in a most serious state"*: MAD, 157.

222 *"Starvation combined with superficial frost-bite"*: HOB, 183–84.

223 *"Just as I got out"*: MAD, 157–58.

223 *"he has several fits"*: Ibid., 158.

223 *"At 8 pm he raves"*: Ibid.

223 *"All that remained"*: HOB, 185.

223 *"took the body of Mertz"*: Ibid., 186.

224 *Beside the grave*: MAD, 158.

224 *"For many days now"*: Ibid.

224 *In 1969, eleven years after*: Cleland and Southcott, "Hypervitaminosis A."

225 *For centuries, the Greenland Inuit*: Riffenburgh, *Aurora*, 277.

225 *Cleland and Southcott argued*: Cleland and Southcott, "Hypervitaminosis A," *passim*.

225 *"the most plausible cause"*: Riffenburgh, *Aurora*, 276.

225 *"the actual final cause"*: Douglas Mawson to Emile Mertz, May 16, 1914, quoted in Riffenburgh, *Aurora*, 276.

225 *Phillip Law, an Australian scientist*: Ayres, *Mawson*, 80–81.

226 *"remodelling the gear"*: HOB, 186–87.

226 *Bad weather*: MAD, 158–59.

226 *"One annoying effect"*: Ibid., 158.

226 *"Almost calm"*: Ibid., 159.

227 *"From the start my feet"*: HOB, 187.

227 *"However, there was nothing"*: Ibid., 187–88.

227 *"Treading like a cat"*: Ibid., 188.

227 *"So glorious was it"*: Ibid.

227 *Mawson woke on January 12*: MAD, 159.

228 *In the middle of the night*: Ibid., 160.

228 *Slowly the weather improved*: Ibid.

228 *"My heart leapt"*: HOB, 188.

228 *"feet worse than ever"*: MAD, 160.

228 *At 11 p.m. that night*: HOB, 189.

228 *"If my feet do not improve"*: MAD, 160.

229 *"We should be at the Hut now"*: Ibid.

229 *On the 15th, Mawson managed*: Ibid., 160–61.

229 *Mawson was up at 2 a.m.*: Ibid., 161.

229 *"It clung in lumps"*: HOB, 190.

229 *"I treated myself"*: Ibid.

229 *"It takes quite a while"*: MAD, 161.

230 *"A glance ahead"*: HOB, 190.

230 *"Everything from below"*: Ibid., 190–91.

230 *In late morning, he crossed*: MAD, 161.

231 *Shortly before noon, on another uphill slope*: HOB, 191.

231 *In mid-plunge*: Ibid.

232 *"great effort"*: Ibid., 192.

232 *"an assortment of 'tabloid' drugs"*: Ibid., 141.

232 *Yet on their doomed return*: Huntford, *Scott and Amundsen*, 539.

233 *"remembering how Providence"*: HOB, 192.

233 *"Fired by the passion"*: Ibid., 192–93.

233 *"Numb with cold"*: Ibid., 193.

234 *"Never have I come so near"*: Ibid., 191.

234 *"I thought of Providence"*: MAD, 161–62.

234 *"Had we lived"*: Scott, *Scott's Last Expedition*, 417.

234 *"It is impossible to say"*: MAD, 162.

234 *After his hellish experience*: Ibid.

234 *"I was confronted"*: HOB, 193.

235 *"I sank to knees"*: MAD, 162.

235 *"Now ration is being reduced"*: Ibid.

235 *"zigzagging about I found"*: Ibid.

235 *"I stopped awhile"*: Ibid., 162–63.

235 *Twice that day he broke through*: HOB, 193–94.

235 *"I decided to turn in early"*: MAD, 163.

236 *"I had never expected"*: HOB, 194.

236 *"a wretched overcast day"*: Ibid., 195.

236 *Desperate to improve his marches*: MAD, 163.

236 *"Everything became blotted out"*: HOB, 195.

237 *On the 24th, to his incredulous delight*: MAD, 164–65.

237 *"violent blizzard"*: Ibid., 165.

237 *"I cannot sleep"*: Ibid.

237 *Despite a continuing blizzard*: Ibid.

237 *Somehow, Mawson managed to sledge*: HOB, 197.

237 *Not until after midnight*: MAD, 165.

238 *On the morning of January 27*: Ibid.

238 *On the 28th, although snow*: HOB, 197.

238 *"My spirits rose"*: Ibid.

238 *"about twenty small chips"*: Ibid., 197–98.

239 *Once again, Mawson crawled out*: MAD, 168.

239 *"something dark loom[ing]"*: HOB, 198.

239 *"As I left the depot"*: Ibid.

240 *He covered another eight miles*: MAD, 168.

240 *"Am now on ice"*: Ibid.

240 *"Before giving up"*: HOB, 199.

240 *The next morning, before emerging*: Ibid.

241 *"on first bit of half snow"*: MAD, 168.

241 *At the end of the day's march*: Ibid.

241 *"This work took an interminable time"*: HOB, 199–200.

241 *It was not until past noon*: MAD, 170.

241 *"At 7 p.m. that haven"*: HOB, 200.

242 *"My new crampons"*: MAD, 170.

242 *In the night, a fierce gale*: HOB, 200.

243 *He ransacked the grotto*: MAD, 170.

243 *On February 3, he emerged*: Ibid.

243 *"This is most exasperating"*: Ibid.

243 *"Blowing quite as hard"*: Ibid.
243 *"disappointed to find"*: HOB, 200–1.
243 *"With good crampons"*: MAD, 170–71.
243 *"Perfected second pair"*: Ibid., 171.
243 *The wind fell quickly*: Ibid.
244 *"(1) Had the ship gone?"*: Ibid.
244 *While Mawson had been preparing*: Crossley, *Trial by Ice*, 61.
244 *One mile down the slope*: MAD, 171.
244 *"a speck on the north-west horizon"*: HOB, 201.
244 *"the boat harbour burst into view"*: MAD, 171.
244 *The first to reach him*: Ibid.; Bickel, *Mawson's Will*, 211.

7. WINTER MADNESS

246 *"I briefly recited the disaster"*: MAD, 171.
246 *Before parting, Captain Davis*: HOB, 202.
246 *"Arrived safely at Hut"*: Crossley, *Trial by Ice*, 61.
247 *"Thank God Mawson"*: Ibid.
247 *"As we neared those"*: Davis, *High Latitude*, 215.
247 *"Why did they recall us"*: Crossley, *Trial by Ice*, 61.
247 *"We tried to be patient"*: Frank Bickerton, "Australian Antarctic Expedition," quoted in Haddelsey, *Born Adventurer*, 111.
247 *"Anxious to get off"*: MAD, 174.
247 *"Of course I did not like"*: Ibid.
248 *"This party are in perfect safety"*: Crossley, *Trial by Ice*, 61–62.
248 *"Well, next morning"*: MAD, 174.
248 *"The strain of the last fortnight"*: Crossley, *Trial by Ice*, 62.
248 *That evening, Hannam received*: Ibid.

248 *"Of the four happy members"*: Madigan, diary, February 13, 1913, quoted in Haddelsey, *Born Adventurer*, 112.
249 *"It was several weeks"*: HOB, 316.
249 *"I am invaliding yet"*: MAD, 174.
249 *"For the first few weeks"*: P. Mawson, *Mawson of the Antarctic*, 92.
249 *Mawson later told his friend*: Ayres, *Mawson*, 87.
249 *"George . . . announces in his positive way"*: Harrisson, diary, February 19, 1913.
249 *"Trust nothing has happened"*: Ibid., February 21, 1913.
249 *"remains in my memory"*: Davis, *High Latitude*, 219.
250 *"From then on until morning"*: Ibid.
250 *"We are too late in the season"*: Crossley, *Trial by Ice*, 62–63.
250 *"The [pack] ice is nearly"*: Ibid., 64.
250 *"It was much better"*: Ibid., 65.
250 *Ensconced inside the Grottoes*: Butler, *Quest*, 152.
251 *"As the ship came alongside"*: Ibid.
251 *"But instead of the elation"*: Harrisson, diary, February 23, 1913.
251 *"Wild hailed & asked"*: Ibid.
251 *"At the foot of the barrier"*: Laseron, "South with Mawson," 152–53.
251 *But the Western Base party*: Butler, *Quest*, 152.
252 *For Davis, there was no possibility*: Davis, *High Latitude*, 222.
252 *"It seems like a dream"*: Crossley, *Trial by Ice*, 66.
252 *Among all the scientific specimens*: Butler, *Quest*, 157.
252 *"Hope for the Aurora's return"*: McLean, diary, March 4, 1913.
253 *"Last night quite a budget"*: Ibid., March 9, 1913.

253 *Basking in his triumph*: Ibid., March 13 and 16, 1913.

253 *Upon learning via radio*: Ainsworth, narrative, quoted in *HOB*, 389–90.

253 *"DEEPLY REGRET DELAY"*: Flannery, *This Everlasting Silence*, 53–54.

254 *"Covering Hut and fitting store"*: *MAD*, 175, 183.

254 *"there still remained useful work"*: *HOB*, 315.

254 *Bob Bage was put in charge*: Ibid., 315–16.

255 *Mawson tacitly acknowledged*: Haddelsey, *Born Adventurer*, 113.

255 *"The hut was not so cold"*: Frank Bickerton, "Australian Antarctic Expedition," quoted ibid., 113.

255 *"DM and AM"*: McLean, diary, March 19, 1913.

255 *"Last penguins have gone north"*: Ibid., March 29 and April 21, 1913.

255 *"'Scott reached the Pole'"*: *MAD*, 183.

256 *"Wireless hears Macquarie"*: Ibid., 184.

256 *"Jeffryes would sometimes spend"*: *HOB*, 318.

256 *"I find my nerves"*: *MAD*, 185.

256 *"Reading is a great solace"*: Ibid., April 6, 1913.

256 *"There was a fine supply"*: *HOB*, 319–20.

256 *"Bickerton once started out"*: Ibid., 320.

257 *"On May 23 Lassie"*: Ibid., 322.

257 *"the assessments of Mawson"*: Riffenburgh, *Aurora*, 352–53.

257 *"Cecil's gloom deepened"*: D. Madigan, *Vixere Fortes*, 289.

258 *"there are no criticisms of Mawson"*: Haddelsey, *Born Adventurer*, 120.

258 *"Jeffryes sat in the batter pudding"*: *MAD*, 187.

259 *"Wireless good"*: Ibid., 188.

259 *"Wireless last few days"*: Ibid., 190.

259 *The men had been dreading*: *HOB*, 322.

259 *"On evening of 26th"*: *MAD*, 191.

259 *"Tonight Jeffryes goes to bed"*: Ibid., 192.

260 *On June 8, what all the men feared*: Ibid., 193.

260 *"Last night Jeffryes at the table"*: Ibid., 196.

261 *"Jeffryes confides in Bage"*: Ibid.

261 *"Jeffryes has been on night watch"*: Ibid.

261 *"Last night Jeffryes spoke"*: Ibid., 196–97.

262 *"Jeffryes came to me"*: Ibid., 197.

262 *On the same day, Madigan discovered*: Ibid.

262 *"Jeffryes continues to be a trouble"*: Ibid., 198.

262 *Chiefly the brainchild of Mawson and McLean*: Riffenburgh, *Aurora*, 354–55.

263 *expeditions producing periodicals*: Leane and Pharaoh, Introduction, *The Adelie Blizzard*, xi.

263 *The deadline for articles*: Ibid., xii–xiii.

263 *"Madigan showed little enthusiasm"*: Ibid., xiii.

263 *"Registered at the General Plateau"*: Ibid., n.p.

264 *"Could we but greet thee"*: Ibid., n.p.

264 *"This somewhat lugubrious title"*: Ibid., [1].

264 *"How they go down at heels"*: Ibid., 10.

265 *"An explorer's life is the life for me"*: Ibid., [2].

265 *"Mining in the vicinity"*: Ibid., 213.

265 *"A championship is"*: Ibid., 101.

266 *"A is Antarctic"*: Ibid., 75.

266 *"The most obvious was the alleviation"*: Ibid., xiv–xv.

267 *"glad there's no more to be done!"*: McLean, diary, October 25, 1913, quoted ibid., xiv.

267 *A favorite pastime was racing down*: McLean, diary, August 20, 1913, quoted in Haddesley, *Born Adventurer*, 120.

267 *The men also played football*: Haddesley, *Born Adventurer*, 120–21.

267 *"like a new kind of drink"*: McLean, diary, September 9, 1913, quoted ibid., 121.

268 *During the entire month of July*: *MAD*, 199.

268 *"I must say I felt very lonely"*: McLean, diary, June 4 and 5, 1913.

268 *"I spoke to him sharply"*: *MAD*, 198.

268 *"He seems to have no interest"*: Ibid., 199.

268 *"At ten to 1 pm Jeffryes appeared"*: Ibid., 201.

268 *"Sir, You have been"*: Sidney Jeffryes to Douglas Mawson, July 13, 1913.

269 *"I am to be done to death"*: Sidney Jeffryes to Norma Jeffryes, July 13, 1913.

269 *"I did not come down here to foment trouble"*: Sidney Jeffryes to Douglas Mawson, July 19, 1913.

269 *"It is curiously logical"*: *MAD*, 198.

269 *"overjoyed to find"*: McLean, diary, July 20, 1913.

270 *"I had intended to cook"*: *MAD*, 198.

270 *"Jeffryes helpless in this"*: Ibid.

270 *"I am now reluctantly obliged"*: Sidney Jeffryes to Douglas Mawson, July 27, 1913.

270 *"pointed out the impossibility"*: Riffenburgh, *Aurora*, 359.

270 *"What I desire is that"*: Douglas Mawson, handwritten speech, July 28, 1913, quoted ibid., 359.

270 *"instantly got up"*: *MAD*, 199.

270 *"Jeffryes makes no attempt"*: Ibid.

271 *"I deeply regret having made"*: Sidney Jeffryes to Douglas Mawson, July 30, 1913.

271 *Yet the delusions*: Sharon Roberts, personal communication, February 13, 2013.

271 *"I appear to be suffering"*: *MAD*, 199.

271 *Although he had gotten word*: D. Madigan, *Vixere Fortes*, 294.

272 *"He went through many stages"*: Ibid., 292.

272 *"Jeffryes avoided Cecil"*: Ibid., 296.

272 *"walking up and down"*: Ibid., 297.

273 *"'Would you swear on the Bible'"*: Stella Benson, diary, April 23, 1928, quoted in Haddesley, *Born Adventurer*, 117.

273 *"To Bickerton is due"*: *MAD*, 200.

273 *The news from Australia*: Ibid., 200.

274 *Wild had returned to his native England*: Butler, *Quest*, 159.

274 *Only weeks after returning*: Ibid., 160.

274 *In August 1913 at Cape Denison*: *MAD*, 200.

274 *"He does nothing now"*: Ibid., 200–1.

275 *"No sane man"*: Ibid., 201.

275 *"8/am Called Mq I"*: AAE wireless log, August 31, 1913.

276 *"At midnight press"*: *MAD*, 203.

276 *"Before dinner Jeffryes came"*: Ibid., 204.

276 *"Jeffryes is quite off"*: Ibid.

277 *"A new month"*: McLean, diary, September 1, 1913.

277 *"100 days to ship's arrival!"*: *MAD*, 204.

277 *"This evening Jeffryes sending"*: Ibid.

277 *Unable to bear Jeffryes's impertinence*: Ibid., 204–5.

277 *"wished all wireless to cease"*: Ibid., 205.

278 *On the 9th, Jeffryes simply sat*: Ibid.

278 *The radio log for early September*: AAE wireless log, September 1–8, 1913.

278 *"Red granites"*: *MAD*, 206.

278 *On September 14, Mawson relieved Jeffryes*: Ibid., 207.

278 *Two days before, Mawson had typed*: Douglas Mawson to Sidney Jeffryes, September 12, 1913.

278 *"Does not even empty rears"*: *MAD*, 207.

279 *"for 3 months [have] diligently"*: Sidney Jeffryes to Douglas Mawson, September 21, 1913.

279 *"He states that"*: *MAD*, 209.

279 *"He speaks moderately rationally"*: Ibid.

279 *On September 19, McLean made*: Ibid., 208.

280 *"First one to bring a penguin"*: McLean, diary, October 12, 1913.

280 *"Jeffryes seems better today"*: *MAD*, 210–11.

280 *It was not until October 4*: Douglas Mawson to Sidney Jeffryes, October 4. 1913.

280 *"This place is awful!"*: McLean, diary, November 20, 1913, quoted in Haddelsey, *Born Adventurer*, 121.

281 *Out on a walk on the 17th*: *MAD*, 214.

281 *"As the end of the year approached"*: D. Madigan, *Vixere Fortes*, 301, 303.

281 *On leaving Commonwealth Bay*: Ibid., 301–2.

281 *On October 31, the men were thrilled*: HOB, 330.

281 *Mawson's diary for most of the month*: *MAD*, 216–17.

281 *"Jeffryes appears to think"*: Ibid., 217.

281 *On November 15, Bickerton picked up*: Haddelsey, *Born Adventurer*, 121.

282 *In actuality, the* Aurora *did not*: Crossley, *Trial by Ice*, 70–72.

282 *Mawson had decided*: HOB, 331.

282 *"Do not hesitate to put him"*: Douglas Mawson to Bob Bage, November 19, 1913.

282 *Intending to start on November 16*: *MAD*, 217.

282 *"At 4:15 camped"*: Ibid., 219.

282 *With the dogs pulling well*: Ibid., 220.

282 *On November 28, five days out*: HOB, 331.

283 *But on December 2, snow started falling*: *MAD*, 222.

283 *"Good weather"*: McLean, diary, November 28, 1913.

283 *On December 2, Bickerton, the compulsive*: Haddelsey, *Born Adventurer*, 121.

283 *"Nothing visible"*: *MAD*, 225.

284 *"Descending the long blue slopes"*: HOB, 331–32.

284 *Dashing down the last thousand feet*: Ibid., 332.

284 *"Just as most of us were dozing"*: Ibid.

284 *"As I shook [Mawson's] hand"*: Davis, *High Latitude*, 229.

285 *"The two long years were over"*: HOB, 333.

285 *Bickerton's last project on land*: Haddelsey, *Born Adventurer*, 122.

285 *"Erected to commemorate"*: http://www.mawsonshuts.aq/national-heritage/physical-remains/memorial.html.

285 *"solid enough to last"*: HOB, 330.

285 *Over the decades since 1913*: http://www.mawsonshuts.aq/national-heritage/physical-remains/memorial.html.

EPILOGUE

286 *"As it was being converted"*: HOB, 404.

287 *"We had a fortunate escape"*: Crossley, *Trial by Ice*, 81.

287 *"Blowing fresh all day"*: MAD, 227.

287 *"This work is very trying"*: Ibid., 244.

287 *"The party are all anxious"*: Crossley, *Trial by Ice*, 95.

287 *"The welcome home"*: HOB, 416.

287 *A small coterie of friends*: Riffenburgh, *Aurora*, 384–85.

288 *"It is hard to describe"*: P. Mawson, *Mawson of the Antarctic*, 102–3.

288 *"Douglas Mawson has returned"*: Ibid., 103.

288 *At the first meeting, a messenger*: HOB, 417.

288 *"Douglas dictated a long message"*: P. Mawson, *Mawson of the Antarctic*, 103.

288 *"Mawson was born to be a leader"*: Ernest Shackleton, "The Man

and His Journey," quoted in MAD, 247–48.

289 *Only five months later, on August 1*: Huntford, *Shackleton*, 377.

289 *The evening before the wedding*: P. Mawson, *Mawson of the Antarctic*, 104–5.

291 *Mawson put him on a train*: Riffenburgh, *Aurora*, 388–89.

291 *"I left Sydney"*: Sidney Jeffryes to Miss Eckford, July 14, [1914].

292 *Poor Jeffryes would spend*: Riffenburgh, *Aurora*, 416.

293 *"It is now clear to me"*: Sidney Jeffryes to Douglas Mawson, March 13, 1915.

293 *"I have told you"*: Sidney Jeffryes to Douglas Mawson, June 6, 1915.

293 *"Mr. Jeffryes is very delusional"*: [signature illegible] to Douglas Mawson, September 17, 1915.

294 *In 2010, the Australian Antarctic Division*: http://www.antarctica.gov.au/media/news/2010/australian-antarctic-glaciers-named.

294 *"Ah, but is it not"*: Douglas Mawson to Kathleen Scott, n.d..

294 *"Besides," she wittily appended*: Kathleen Scott to Douglas Mawson, March 8, [1915].

295 *"My dear Douglas"*: Kathleen Scott to Douglas Mawson, April, 1920.

295 *Some have speculated*: Mark Pharaoh, personal communication, July 2011.

295 *she was conducting an affair*: Huntford, *Scott and Amundsen*, 545–46.

295 *Paquita did not like Kathleen*: Ayres, *Mawson*, 104.

295 *"Shackleton has been lecturing"*: Kathleen Scott to Douglas Mawson, April, 1920.

295 *Less than two years later, on South Georgia*: Huntford, *Shackleton*, 690.

295 *On June 9, 1914, Mawson spoke*: P. Mawson, *Mawson of the Antarctic*, 108.

296 *"of the dreadful tragedy"*: Belgrave Ninnis, senior, to Douglas Mawson, August 29, 1913.

296 *"It was absolutely unexpected"*: Douglas Mawson to Belgrave Ninnis, senior, March 17, 1914.

296 *"had early been cut to pieces"*: P. Mawson, *Mawson of the Antarctic*, 107.

297 *"You will note that"*: Douglas Mawson to Herr Mertz, July 8, 1914.

297 *the original diary has somehow been lost*: Mark Pharaoh, personal communication, July 2011.

297 *"They were very kind"*: P. Mawson, *Mawson of the Antarctic*, 117.

297 *He had been absent*: Ayres, *Mawson*, 104–5.

297 *Bob Bage, the quiet*: Riffenburgh, *Aurora*, 401–2.

297 *Cecil Madigan spent*: Ibid., 413; http://en.wikipedia.org/wiki/Cecil_Madigan.

298 *"I had some close shaves"*: Cecil Madigan to Douglas Mawson, December 18, 1915.

298 *Archibald McLean, whose collaborative*: Riffenburgh, *Aurora*, 406–7.

298 *"Poor old 'Dad' McLean"*: John Hunter to Douglas Mawson, n.d.

298 *"I have been itching"*: Douglas Mawson to Eric Webb, August 16, [1915].

298 *Mawson eventually found employment*: Ayres, *Mawson*, 115, 122.

298 *One other member of the AAE*: Rossiter, *Mawson's Forgotten Men*, xviii–xix.

299 *From shipboard, Shackleton telegraphed*: Huntford, *Shackleton*, 379.

299 *"Fancy that ridiculous Shackleton"*: Winston Churchill to Clementine Churchill, March 28, 1916, quoted ibid., 488.

299 *"London in the aftermath"*: Huntford, *Shackleton*, 673.

299 *"The manager at Boston"*: Douglas Mawson to Paquita Mawson, February 4, 1915, quoted in Ayres, *Mawson*, 107.

299 *The two-volume* The Home of the Blizzard: Ibid., 101.

300 *After the war, back in Australia*: Ibid., 250; Riffenburgh, *Aurora*, 407.

300 *Thanks to Mawson's doggedness*: Riffenburgh, *Aurora*, 408.

300 *"The scientific goals of early"*: Ibid., 421–22.

301 *"the Australasian Expedition was easily"*: Ibid., 421.

301 *"Sir Douglas Mawson's Expedition"*: Hayes, *Antarctica*, 210.

302 *"He was still purposeful"*: Eric Webb, "An Appreciation," in Bickel, *Mawson's Will*, 231.

303 *"No words of mine"*: Hurley, *Argonauts*, 120–21.

303 *"To me, when I was a young man"*: Eric Webb, "An Appreciation," in Bickel, *Mawson's Will*, 228–29.

304 *"I consider that I was"*: George Dovers to Douglas Mawson, July

20, 1954, quoted in Ayres, *Mawson*, 253.

304 *"The 1911–14 days will ever"*: John Hunter to Douglas Mawson, January 31, 1957, quoted in Ayres, *Mawson*, 254.

304 *"The years 1911–13 are still"*: Charles Laseron to Douglas Mawson, December 9, 1954.

304 *"Knowing that he was not"*: P. Mawson, *Mawson of the Antarctic*, 220.

304 *"Sunday was a perfect October day"*: Ibid.

305 *The prime minister of Australia*: Ibid., 221.

305 *Paquita spent six years*: McEwin, *An Antarctic Affair*, 216.

307 *"Mawson had his faults"*: Mark Pharaoh, personal communication, July 2011.

308 *Jarvis was already one*: Jarvis, *Mawson*, 12.

308 *To play the role of Mertz*: Ibid., 13–14.

308 *The station, which first opened*: http://www.antarcticconnection.com/antarctic/stations/davis.shtml.

308 *"To make the project viable"*: Jarvis, *Mawson*, 14.

309 *Like the AAE explorers, Jarvis*: Ibid., 58.

309 *dogs have been banned*: http://www.antarctica.ac.uk/about_antarctica/environment/wildlife/removal_of_sledge_dogs.php.

309 *"as its leanness"*: Jarvis, *Mawson*, 14.

309 *"Mawson and Mertz couldn't stop"*: Ibid., 15.

310 *"I was feeling extremely isolated"*: Ibid., 133.

310 *For through the first half*: Ibid., 71, 80, 225.

310 *At Davis Station, Jarvis*: Ibid., 217.

311 *"Despite pride at having completed"*: Ibid., 227.

311 *"I threw myself upward again"*: Ibid., 212.

312 *"probably the greatest story"*: Edmund Hillary, Foreword, in Bickel, *Mawson's Will*, 8.

312 *"The greatest survival story"*: Edmund Hillary, quoted in Riffenburgh, *Racing with Death*, front cover.

BIBLIOGRAPHY

UNPUBLISHED SOURCES

Key to Institutions:

MC Mawson Collection, South Australian Museum, Adelaide
ML Mitchell Library, State Library of New South Wales, Sydney
NLA National Library of Australia, Canberra
SLV State Library of Victoria, Melbourne

Blake, Leslie. Diary. SLV.
Davis, John King. Note appointing relief party for second overwintering. SLV.
Dovers, George. Diary. ML.
Gray, Percival. Diary (Letters). ML.
Hannam, Walter. Diary. ML.
Harrisson, Charles. Diary. ML.
Hunter, John. Diary. NLA.
———. Letter to Mawson. MC.
[Illegible signature—Ararat asylum warden]. Letter from Ararat asylum to Mawson. MC.
Jeffryes, Sidney. Letters to Mawson. MC.
———. Letter to Norma Jeffryes. MC.
———. Letter to Miss Eckford. MC.
Jones, Sydney. Diary. NLA.
Kennedy, Alexander. Sledging diary. MC.
Laseron, Charles. Diary. ML.

———. Letter to Mawson. MC.

Madigan, Cecil. Diary. Private possession.

———. Letters to Mawson. MC.

Mawson, Douglas. Cook's notices. MC.

———. "General instructions during my absence." MC.

———. Instructions to Davis, November 1912. SLV.

———. Instructions to nightwatchman. MC.

———. Letter to Bage ("Orders on leaving hut"). MC.

———. Letters to Davis. MC.

———. Letters to Jeffryes. MC.

———. Letters to Kathleen Scott. MC.

———. Letter to Belgrave Ninnis, senior. MC.

———. Letters to Mertz family. MC.

———. Letter to Webb. MC.

———. List of books at Winter Quarters. MC.

———. Loose notes. MC.

———. Messman's duties. MC.

———. Notes on Whetter. MC.

———. Report of Main Base. MC.

McLean, Archibald. Diary. ML.

Mertz, Xavier. Diary. Translated into English by Robyn Mundy. MC.

Moyes, Morton. Diary. ML.

Ninnis, Belgrave, senior. Letter to Mawson. MC.

Notes from Aladdin's Cave. MC.

Scott, Kathleen. Letters to Mawson. MC.

Watson, Andrew. Diary. ML.

———. Letter to Mawson. MC.

Webb, Eric. Sledging diary. ML.

———. Letter to Mawson. MC.

Wild, Frank. Memoirs. ML.

Wireless messages and log. MC.

PUBLISHED SOURCES

Ayres, Philip. *Mawson: A Life*. Melbourne: Miegunyah Press, 1999.

Bickel, Lennard. *Mawson's Will: The Greatest Survival Story Ever Written*. New York: Stein and Day, 1977.

Branagan, David. *T. W. Edgeworth David: A Life*. Canberra: National Library of Australia, 2005.

Butler, Angie. *The Quest for Frank Wild*. Warwick, UK: Jackleberry Press, 2011.

Byrd, Richard Evelyn. "Our Navy Explores Antarctica," *National Geographic*, October 1947.

Caesar, Adrian. *The White: Last Days in the Antarctic Journeys of Scott and Amundsen, 1911–1913.* Sydney: Pan Macmillan, 1999.

Cherry-Garrard, Apsley. *The Worst Journey in the World.* London: Chatto and Windus, 1922.

Chester, Jonathan. *Going to Extremes: Project Blizzard and Australia's Antarctic Heritage.* Sydney: Doubleday, 1986.

Cleland, Sir John, and R. V. Southcott. "Hypervitaminosis A in the Antarctic in the Australian Antarctic Expedition of 1911–1914." *The Medical Journal of Australia* 1 (26), 1969.

Cook, Frederick A. *Through the First Antarctic Night, 1898–1899.* New York: Doubleday & McLure, 1900.

Crossley, Louise, ed. *Trial by Ice: The Antarctic Journals of John King Davis.* Norwich, UK: Erskine Press, 1977.

Davis, J. K. *High Latitude.* Melbourne: Melbourne University Press, 1962.

Dixon, Robert, and Christopher Lee, eds. *The Diaries of Frank Hurley, 1912–1941.* London: Anthem Press, 2011.

Flannery, Nancy Robinson, ed. *This Everlasting Silence: The Love Letters of Paquita Delprat and Douglas Mawson, 1911–1914.* Melbourne: Melbourne University Press, 2000.

Gurney, Alan. *Below the Convergence: Voyages toward Antarctica, 1699–1839.* New York: Norton, 1997.

Haddelsey, Stephen. *Born Adventurer: The Life of Frank Bickerton, Antarctic Pioneer.* Stroud, UK: Sutton Publishing, 2005.

Hains, Brigid. *The Ice and the Inland: Mawson, Flynn, and the Myth of the Frontier.* Melbourne: Melbourne University Press, 2002.

Hayes, J. Gordon. *Antarctica: A Treatise on the Southern Continent.* London: Richards Press, 1928.

Hoerr, W. N. *Clipped Wings, or Memories of My Childhood and Youth.* Adelaide: privately published, n.d.

Huntford, Roland. *Scott and Amundsen.* New York: G. P. Putnam's Sons, 1980.

———. *Shackleton.* New York: Atheneum, 1986.

Hurley, Frank. *Argonauts of the South.* New York: G. P. Putnam's Sons, 1925.

Innes, Margaret, and Heather Duff. *Mawson's Papers: A Guide.* Adelaide: Mawson Institute for Antarctic Research, 1990.

Jacka, Fred, and Eleanor Jacka, eds. *Mawson's Antarctic Diaries.* North Sydney: Allen & Unwin, 1988.

Jarvis, Tim. *Mawson: Life and Death in Antarctica.* Melbourne: Miegunyah Press, 2008.

Landy, D. "Pibloktoq (Hysteria) and Inuit Nutrition: Possible Implication of Hypervitaminosis." *Social Science and Medicine* 21 (2), 1985.

Larson, Edward J. *An Empire of Ice: Scott, Shackleton, and the Heroic Age of Antarctic Science.* New Haven: Yale University Press, 2011.

Laseron, Charles F. "South with Mawson." In Tim Bowden, ed., *Antarctic Eyewitness*. Sydney: Angus & Robertson, 1999.

Leane, Elizabeth, and Mark Pharaoh, eds. *The Adelie Blizzard: Mawson's Forgotten Newspaper*. Facsimile edition. Adelaide: Friends of the State Library of South Australia, 2010.

Madigan, David. *Vixere Fortes: A Family Archive*. Kingston, Tasmania: privately published, 2000.

Mawson, Douglas. *The Home of the Blizzard*. Two volumes. London: Heinemann, 1914.

———. *The Home of the Blizzard*. Abridged one-volume edition. New York: St. Martin's Press, 1998.

Mawson, Paquita. *Mawson of the Antarctic: The Life of Sir Douglas Mawson*. London: Longmans, 1964.

McEwin, Emma. *An Antarctic Affair*. Bowden, Australia: East Street Publications, 2008.

McGregor, Alasdair. *Antarctica: That Sweep of Savage Splendour*. Camberwell, Australia: Viking, 2011.

———. *Frank Hurley: A Photographer's Life*. Camberwell, Australia: Viking, 2004.

———. *Mawson's Huts: An Antarctic Expedition Journal*. Alexandria, Australia: Hale & Iremonger, 1998.

McIntyre, Don and Margie. *Two Below Zero: A Year Alone in Antarctica*. Terrey Hills, Australia: Australian Geographic, 1996.

Mill, Hugh Robert. *The Siege of the South Pole: The Story of Antarctic Exploration*. London: A. Rivers, 1905.

Mills, Leif. *Frank Wild*. Whitby, UK: Caedmon of Whitby, 1999.

———. *Men of Ice*. Whitby, UK: Caedmon of Whitby, 2008.

Moyes, John L. *Exploring the Antarctic with Mawson and the Men of the 1911–1914 Expedition*. Adelaide: Openbook, n.d.

Riffenburgh, Beau. *Aurora: Douglas Mawson and the Australasian Antarctic Expedition, 1911–14*. Eccles, UK: Erskine Press, 2011.

———. *Nimrod: Ernest Shackleton and the Extraordinary Story of the 1907–09 British Antarctic Expedition*. London: Bloomsbury, 2004.

———. *Racing with Death: Douglas Mawson—Antarctic Explorer*. London: Bloomsbury, 2008.

Rosove, Michael H. *Let Heroes Speak: Antarctic Explorers, 1772–1922*. Annapolis, MD: Naval Institute Press, 2000.

Rossiter, Heather. *Lady Spy, Gentleman Explorer: The Life of Herbert Dyce Murphy*. Sydney: Random House Australia, 2001.

Rossiter, Heather, ed. *Mawson's Forgotten Men: The 1911–1913 Antarctic Diary of Charles Turnbull Harrisson*. Sydney: Pier 9, 2011.

Scott, Robert Falcon. *Scott's Last Expedition*. Two volumes. New York: Dodd, Mead, 1913.

Seaver, George. *Scott of the Antarctic: A Study in Character.* London: John Murray, 1940.

Shackleton, E. H. *The Heart of the Antarctic.* Two volumes. London: Heinemann, 1909.

———. *The Heart of the Antarctic.* Abridged edition. New York: Carroll & Graf, 1999.

Shackleton, E. H., et al. *Aurora Australis.* Facsimile edition. Auckland: Seto Publishing, 1988.

Watson, Moira. *The Spy Who Loved Children.* Melbourne: Melbourne University Press, 1997.

Wendler, Gerd, Charles Stearns, George Weidner, Guillaume Dargaud, and Thomas Parish. "On the Extraordinary Katabatic Winds of Adélie Land." *Journal of Geographical Research* 102 (D4), 1997.

INDEX